THE HITCHCOCK ROMANCE

LESLEY BRILL

The Hitchcock Romance

Love and Irony in Hitchcock's Films

PRINCETON UNIVERSITY PRESS

LIBRARY OF CONGRESS CATALOGING-IN-PUBLICATION DATA

Brill, Lesley, 1943-
The Hitchcock romance.
Includes index.
1. Hitchcock, Alfred, 1899- —Criticism and
interpretation. 2. Love in motion pictures.
3. Irony in motion pictures. I. Title.
PN1998.3.H58B7 1988   791.43'0233'0924   88-9819
ISBN 0-691-04055-9 (alk. paper)

Publication of this book has been aided by
the Eugene M. Kayden Fund, University of Colorado

This book has been composed in Linotron Sabon

Princeton University Press books are printed on acid-free paper,
and meet the guidelines for permanence and durability of the
Committee on Production Guidelines for Book Longevity of the
Council on Library Resources

Printed in the United States of America by Princeton Academic Press

10   9   8   7   6   5   4

This book is affectionately dedicated to the students in my film studies classes at the University of Colorado, my co-authors and severest critics.

CONTENTS

FRAME ENLARGEMENTS

Scratches and other optical defects result from the varying quality of the prints available.

ACKNOWLEDGMENTS

I AM grateful for suggestions and encouragement to the following friends and colleagues: Cathy Comstock, Marian Keane, James Palmer, Megan Parry, Harold Schechter, and the two impressively careful, erudite anonymous consultants for Princeton University Press. Joanna Hitchcock has been a supportive, intelligent editor, Cathie Brettschneider an attentive, sympathetic copy editor. I am especially grateful to James Kincaid, who commented with great tact upon the entire manuscript. The self-importance, fluff, and pedantry that remain are emphatically mine; a great deal of such pompousness has disappeared thanks to Jim. Bruce Kawin gave me valuable advice regarding preparation of the stills; and Marcia Johnston and Don Yannacito have kept me in prints, projectors, and hope for as long as I have been teaching film. To Virgil Grillo, Director of Film Studies at the University of Colorado, I owe an enormous debt not only for support with my teaching and scholarship, but for his tenacious, resourceful administration, without which neither the film studies program at Colorado nor this book would exist. For the shortcomings of the latter, of course, he bears no blame; its errors of fact and judgment are wholly my own.

THE discussion of *North by Northwest* appeared in a somewhat different version in *Film Criticism* and is reprinted by permission of the editor of that journal. The editors of *Literature/Film Criticism* have similarly granted permission to reprint a revised version of the essay on *The Lodger* first published there.

Frame enlargements are reproduced courtesy of the following companies. *Frenzy, Vertigo, Psycho, Marnie,* and *Topaz*: copyright by Universal Pictures, a Division of Universal City Studios, Inc. Courtesy of MCA Publishing Rights, a Division of MCA, Inc. *Shadow of a Doubt* and *I Confess*: Warner Bros., Inc. *To Catch a Thief*: Copyright © 1954 by Paramount Pictures Corporation; all rights reserved. *North by Northwest*: Turner Entertainment Company. *Spellbound*: ABC Distribution Company.

THIS study sets forth an understanding of Alfred Hitchcock's films, both individually and as a total body of work. Hitchcock's career may be seen as a complex but finally harmonious series of rotations of characteristic themes and aesthetic concerns. Loss and recovery and quests for innocence organize the plots of almost all his movies. In the majority of his works, the conventions of happy fairy tales, displaced into cinematic forms, lead to conclusions in which central lovers live more or less happily ever after. In the ironic movies, romantic expectations are raised only to be disappointed.

My discussion of Hitchcock's work does not come to any biographical conclusions, nor is it biographically based. If it were concerned with Hitchcock's personality, it would favor speculations that might surprise many viewers of his films and television shows. From my experience of his movies, I would guess that Hitchcock, far from being an exotic sadist, was deeply conventional, thoughtful, and rather softhearted. His dearest dreams were composed of nothing more remarkable than love and marriage, happy families, and a forgiving universe that allows such things. I have little idea what connection this sketch may have with Alfred Hitchcock as he existed in private life, but I am confident that it is a just representation of the artistic personality embodied in his films.

I am aware that this conception of Hitchcock reverses the one shared by most commentators. At the center of the greater part of his movies I find an affectionate, profoundly hopeful view of fallen human nature and the redemptive possibilities of love between women and men. Even when his movies are bitterly ironic, their sense of disappointment confirms the director's sentimental attraction to a happier view of human affairs. He is never, so far as I can tell, the cynical, macabre trifler with an audience's emotions that he liked to pretend to be.

At the same time, I am far from asserting that other commentators have been wildly "wrong" about Hitchcock. Rather, I feel that we need to adjust our view of his career as a whole. We have, I believe, allowed certain especially interesting but somewhat atypical films to distort our understanding of the larger shape of his work. We have taken the trunk and tail—to adapt the old parable—for the whole elephant and have tended to neglect the body. In giving equal emphasis to the less often

discussed romantic movies and their relation to the ironic ones, I hope
to provide a more comprehensive account of Hitchcock's work.

I have learned a great deal from my predecessors—Wood, Yacowar,
Spoto, Bellour, Rothman, and others. But the specificity of my argument leads me to examine Hitchcock's films from an angle of vision
that does not often require the citation of other critics. The paucity of
footnotes reflects not my rejection of their analyses but the particular-
ity of my own approach.

Recent revisions of "auteur theory" encourage me to make clear that
by "Hitchcock," I will normally refer not to the private individual but
to the director—always to some degree a corporate entity even for the
strongest "auteurs." Nor do I mean to denigrate the contributions of
such gifted collaborators as Saul Bass, Bernard Hermann, Robert
Burks, and a host of talented actors, technicians, and writers. It is the
task of this book to argue that Hitchcock's work, however we assess
its authorship, may be seen as unified in its totality. Whether we take
Hitchcock to have been a brilliant administrator, or writer, or graphic
artist, or editor, or businessman—and I am inclined to think that he
was all of these—he created a body of consistent, characteristic work.

As will be evident, my interest in politically oriented criticism of all
kinds is lukewarm. I hasten to add that this is a matter of taste, not
dogma. My limited concern with recent feminist attacks on Hitchcock
in particular may strike some readers as eccentric. Although I am sympathetic to the cultural commentary of feminism, my understanding of
the unifying principles of Hitchcock's movies is inimical to polemical
feminist critiques of his work. Since romance embodies a view of the
world in which women tend to be central agents of regeneration, and
since I regard Hitchcock as a creator of romance, I find his films to be
powerful criticisms of patriarchal assumptions rather than symptoms
of them. The culturally ingrained, unconscious sexual chauvinism for
which some commentators (and biographers) have reproached Hitchcock seems to me not only to be absent from his work, but to be actively opposed by it.

Although Hitchcock's artistic predilection for love and personal integrity attracts me as an alluring answer to the dilemmas of loneliness
and mortality, I have no strong opinion as to the effectiveness of these
remedies in what we vaguely call "the real world." I am not sure that
Hitchcock-the-person (as opposed to Hitchcock-the-director) did,
either. We will do well to remember that Hitchcock made movies—no
less meaningful for that, but not to be taken in quite the same way as
advice, let alone as a social program. Love that conquers all is as traditional in romantic narratives as death at the end of tragedy, or the

association of black and downwardness with evil and of lucent heavens with goodness and truth.

In general, I discuss films that seem especially well suited to illustrate particular aspects of Hitchcock's work, but alternative selections would often serve as well. In such cases, I have tried to favor less frequently analyzed movies over those that have received more attention. I have avoided detailed discussions of films that are not widely available. Hitchcock's last silent, *The Manxman*, is a wonderful movie and suits my argument very well; but it is virtually never shown and has not been available for rental for many years. I do not discuss Hitchcock's television shows either, because of similar problems of availability and great differences from movies in their circumstances of production.

Any critical approach, no matter how much it reveals, will also by its angle of view obscure or overlook some aspects of the movies to which it is applied. With films as astonishingly dense, varied, and multilayered as Hitchcock's, the omissions must be considerable. Furthermore, I have tried to avoid repeating every point for every film; so the reader who is looking at analyses of particular movies should be aware that some pertinent arguments may be omitted because they have already been made in an earlier discussion.

The conceptual framework that organizes my study is derived from the work of Northrop Frye—considerably simplified, I should add. I have adopted it because it illuminates Hitchcock's films both individually and as a body, and it makes comprehensible a wide range of details that are often seen as enigmatic or are simply ignored. My purpose is not to argue that this model should be generally applied in film studies, nor to maintain that it is uniquely suited to understanding Hitchcock. But Hitchcock's movies have a way of raising issues that encompass movies and directors generally. As Rohmer and Chabrol wrote, "The number of Hitchcockian stories in the world is certainly very great: a good third, if not a half, of all those that have been written until now."[1] Any ideas that structure our perception of Hitchcock's movies, then, are likely to be useful for thinking about the cinematic stories of other directors as well.

[1] Eric Rohmer and Claude Chabrol, *Hitchcock: The First Forty-Four Films*, trans. Stanley Hochman (New York: Frederick Ungar, 1979), p. 134. (*Hitchcock* was originally published in France in 1957.)

THE HITCHCOCK ROMANCE

CHAPTER ONE

North by Northwest and Romance

North by Northwest: Cary Grant and Eva Marie Saint. The maladies of being human are not beyond remedy. The cure is love, the most miraculous and unreasonable of the implausibilities of romance. And, of course, the most common.

WHEN Roger Thornhill (Cary Grant) arrives at "Prairie Stop" to face attempted assassination by crop-duster plane, the landscape turns a desiccated, lifeless brown. The camera surveys the desolate scene from a high panoramic viewpoint. The audience is unlikely to find anything notable about either of these facts; and, if it does notice them, it is unlikely to find them awkward. Yet for a viewer with realistic expectations, both the scorched countryside and the camera placement could be jarring. The foliage elsewhere—in New York, Long Island, and South Dakota—is lush and verdant; the elevation of the camera in the Prairie Stop scene provides a point of view that nobody in the film, including the men in the moving airplane, could possibly have. A viewer with realistic prejudices might feel other qualms as well. Why does the plane, so maneuverable throughout the rest of the scene, crash awkwardly into the gasoline truck at the end? Why does it first buzz Thornhill and begin firing at him only with its second pass? What sort of fool would lure someone to the country and try to run him over with an airplane, anyway? Surely a gun, rope, or knife would be more efficient, more plausible.

One can answer such questions only by pointing out that they are largely irrelevant. Phrased as logical objections, they have little to do with the sort of film *North by Northwest* is, and trying to explain them away obscures more than it clarifies. To ask why such questions miss the point, however, tells us a good deal, not only about *North by Northwest* but about Hitchcock's work in general. For the whole of Hitchcock's career, I believe, can be understood in terms of the themes, underlying assumptions, and techniques that shape the central meanings of *North by Northwest*. Along with *The Lady Vanishes*, it comes closest to compendiating its director's career.

Hitchcock's movies, much more varied than most people realize, nonetheless are knit together by a remarkable coherence within their variety. They may be seen as a series of rich rotations and recombinations of relatively few central themes and aesthetic preoccupations. The actions of loss, search, and recovery that provide a deep structure for *North by Northwest* underlie all Hitchcock's films, albeit sometimes chiefly as dreadfully disappointed and mocked possibilities. The outcomes of these actions provide the standard to measure human success and failure, as well as the temper of the universe itself.

Hitchcock's famous suspense is one of the techniques appropriate to the working out of many of the variations of his central story, but it is far from omnipresent or uniquely important. In the course of this study, I hope to elucidate the main features of Hitchcock's polymorphous cinematic landscape. I do not wish, however, to precede my ex-

amination of specific films with an abstract characterization of some
presumptive Hitchcockian world view. Such a unifying generalization
can usefully be distilled from the corpus of his movies for purposes of
understanding them in total, but we should never suppose that it precedes the creation of the films, or that we are somehow recovering it
from the artistic accretions in which it has been draped. The films
themselves, in their broadest shapes and smallest details, constitute
Hitchcock's artistic world. The unifying tendencies that we can extract
from them must arise from our experience as their audience. These
tendencies did not precede the making of the movies, nor can they precede our understanding. My own understanding of Hitchcock's career
will be presented as it arose, through a series of analyses of particular
films.

Nobody, so far as I know, has objected in print to the Prairie Stop
scene in *North by Northwest*, but complaints about implausibility
have been a general motif in Hitchcock criticism for half a century. The
obvious rear projection in *Marnie* and *Spellbound*, the painted backdrops and artificial sets of *Under Capricorn*, the trainwheels that whis-
per "save Ashenden" in *Secret Agent*, the comically speeded-up fireworks of *To Catch a Thief*, the anxious fantasy of Markham sinking
into impossibly plush carpet in *Murder!*—these and similar moments
in Hitchcock's work could be (and many have been) criticized as gross
disruptions of the realistic illusions of the films in which they appear.
The description is accurate, the complaint unjust. Though their importance varies from movie to movie, antirepresentational techniques in
Hitchcock's films express the basic assumptions of much of his work.
They signal a romanticism, a self-conscious sense of the fiction as a
story of a certain kind, that is the dominant mode of many Hitchcock
films and an important element in almost all of them.

I will often be using the word "romance" in a limited sense to talk
about the sort of story that forms the core of most of Hitchcock's movies, so a brief definition will be useful.[1] By romance I mean to indicate
the relatively fabulous kind of narrative that we associate with folklore
and fairy tale and their literary and cinematic offspring. In film, such
narratives may be as clearly related to their mythic and folkloric forebears as Cocteau's *Beauty and the Beast* or Murnau's *Nosferatu*; they
may be modernized fairy tales like *The Gold Rush* and *Star Wars*; or

[1] My conception of romance in this book relies heavily upon Northrop Frye, *Anatomy
of Criticism* (Princeton: Princeton University Press, 1957; rpnt. New York: Atheneum,
1967) and *The Secular Scripture* (Cambridge, Mass., and London: Harvard University
Press, 1976) by the same author.

they may underlie such rationalized and relatively distant relations as *Grand Illusion* or *She Done Him Wrong*.

In the world of romance, whether in film or in other narrative media, the ordinary constraints of natural law are loosened. As in dreams and nightmares, reality mixes with projections of desire and anxiety. This mixture produces an animism and a psychological transparency considerably greater than are found in more realistic fictions. As folk tales swarm with talking plants and animals and vindictive or grateful landscapes, the romantic world of more sophisticated fiction is peopled with extreme and relatively pure human traits. Heroes are brave, handsome, and unentangled by previous commitments; they seek and serve women who are lovely and pure of heart despite dreadfully compromising circumstances; and they oppose villains who reek of carrion and the smoky fires of hell. Characters fit epithets right off the rack: good old king, unjustly disinherited prince or princess, evil magician, wicked stepmother. But for all its sympathetic clarity, the characterization of romance is not drawn in the pitch blacks and unsullied whites of melodrama. Circumstances are frequently perplexed; and characterization, though uncomplicated by abundant detail or delicate shading, avoids simple uniformity. The hero or heroine does something equivocal. The villain attracts justifiable sympathy.

The plot of romance leads to adventure, with the killing of a hyperbolically evil figure the usual penultimate action and the winning of a mate the conclusion. In fairy tales, the destruction of a wicked king, dragon, or troll precedes a wedding to a prince or princess. In the more realistic but still romantic world of most of Hitchcock's films, the grouping of characters is analogous but the stratifications take modern symbolic forms—the upper class background of the hero in *Murder!*, for example, the beauty of Grace Kelly and Ingrid Bergman, or the association of villains with lower classes, foreigners, or sexual deviates. The plot normally revolves about a quest (often thrust upon the protagonist rather than chosen) and entails perilous journeys, violent struggles, mountaintop epiphanies, disappearances and apparent deaths, and triumphant returns. Rather than being rationalized or made plausible, such plots emphasize lucky coincidence and exhibit a high degree of conventionality and artificiality. Human wishes and their enemies and obstructions are anatomized and segregated more sharply in romance than in ironic fictions. Good and evil figures embody radically competing world views. Frye characterizes the conflict as a struggle to maintain "the integrity of the innocent world against the assault of experience."[2] This innocence is partly manifested by the

---

[2] Frye, *Anatomy of Criticism*, p. 201.

prominence of the miraculous, which, along with an accompanying emphasis on the fictionality of the narrative and an occasional anti-representationalism, clusters with other romantic elements.

Since the terms romantic and ironic are relative, one cannot speak of pure romance or pure irony. Hitchcock's most romantic works include *Young and Innocent*, *To Catch a Thief*, and *North by Northwest*; his films often become more ironic as the importance of their political content increases, as in *Secret Agent*, *Notorious*, and *Torn Curtain*. Yet the first three films all contain some politics and considerable ironic realism, whereas in the latter there remain elements of the miraculous quest with a bride or a husband to be claimed at its completion. Romantic and realistic elements mix in all Hitchcock's films, with one or the other usually providing a dominant modality. If we exaggerate either element, we distort our account of his work. Such distortion will be evident in parts of the argument of this chapter, which is devoted chiefly to defining the romantic core at the center of Hitchcock's cinematic vision. I will consequently give less emphasis to ironic tensions in the film than I would if my aim were simply to provide a comprehensive interpretation.

The story line of *North by Northwest* illustrates the sort of outlandish adventures that often make up the plots of romantic narratives. It coils and recoils intricately and exemplifies the exuberance of plot that characterizes many such stories. Like Sinbad the Sailor, Thornhill sails from adventure to adventure. In fact, a ship is practically the only common conveyance that he does not travel on. When things grow most desperate, he runs—away from his assassins in the elevator, out of the United Nations building, back and forth over the dusty fields of Prairie Stop, through the woods, and across the Mount Rushmore monument. Airplanes, which threaten both Eve (Eva Marie Saint) and Thornhill, play the role of modern Orc to Thornhill's Sinbad. (The creator can send his hero on such electrifying peregrinations, but he cannot accompany him, as the film suggests in the wry cameo appearance of Hitchcock with bus doors closing in his face.)

All Thornhill's rushing about emphasizes the centrality to the film of his quest. The "MacGuffin," a well-known idea in Hitchcock criticism, refers to the nominal goal of a film's characters. It is only partly relevant to the real concerns of the movie, but it provides an excuse for them.[3] In *North by Northwest* the MacGuffin is unspecified information, both that being smuggled out of the country by VanDamm and the knowledge of VanDamm's organization being sought by the Pro-

---

[3] Hitchcock's explanation is recorded in François Truffaut, *Hitchcock/Truffaut*, rev. ed. (New York: Simon and Schuster, 1984), pp. 138-39.

fessor. Like the Grail quests of medieval romances, the MacGuffins of Hitchcock's films give motive force to the characters—get them out having adventures, falling in love, slaying dragons. Although Hitchcock maintains interest in VanDamm and in his information through the end of the film, the fundamental object of the quest in *North by Northwest* lies elsewhere, in Roger Thornhill's search for identity and a proper mate—two aspects, it usually turns out, of a single goal.

Thornhill's continuous wayfaring epitomizes his personal rootlessness. With the exception of his last trip home as a newlywed, Thornhill crosses the country in a series of conveyances that are stolen, forced upon him, or associated with deceit. The taxi he takes from its rightful passenger in the first sequence, VanDamm's limousine, "Laura's Mercedes," the taxi he gets by brushing ahead of a waiting couple at the Plaza, his ticketless ride on the 20th Century Limited, the bus he is lured into taking to Prairie Stop, the truck he steals to get back to Chicago, the police car he "summons" to escape the auction, the ambulance that carries him away from the faked shooting in Rapid City, and the Ford sedan in which he effects his last-minute rescue of Eve—together all suggest the extent to which he is uprooted, dispossessed, and unable to establish his real identity. That VanDamm and his underlings insist on taking him for Kaplan further underscores the tenuousness of his existence as Thornhill.

As befalls innumerable folk-tale heroes who leave home to seek their fortunes, Thornhill ends up with a wife and something that looks suspiciously like a "happily ever after." The defects in his character and circumstances have been discussed by several other critics, so I will only sketch them here. Incipient alcoholism, frivolous and perhaps promiscuous relations with women, prolonged dependence upon his mother, and a readiness to lie to and impose upon other people are among his shortcomings hinted at in the opening scenes. In describing Thornhill's deficiencies, however, it is easy to misrepresent the tone of the film, which makes its hero a strongly sympathetic figure from the beginning. Indeed, he may be the more sympathetic for his venial sins. His marriage to Eve represents a maturing and a serious mating—the making of his fortune.

Eve shares Thornhill's personal defects and emotional voids. She, too, is deceitful and frivolous about sexual relations; but more than Thornhill, she seems conscious of the pathos in her life and of her anemic self-esteem. "I had nothing to do that weekend, so I decided to fall in love," she says by way of explaining her relationship to VanDamm, a man who seems more a father than a lover. Like Thornhill, she is too old to be unmated: "I'm twenty-six and unmarried. Now you know everything." When she marries Thornhill, she finds an identity and a legitimate place in the world. It is typical of Hitchcock, and of romantic fictions, that the concluding marriage should resolve the problems of both partners. There is a structural logic behind such plot configurations. Humans, injured and deficient by nature, can be healed and made whole only by the mundane miracle of love. It follows, since the love must be reciprocal and not adulterous, that both partners before their meeting are to some degree ill and in need and that their redemption must be mutual.

An odor of dragon-killing lingers in the deaths of VanDamm's knife-throwing gardener and Leonard, from whom Thornhill saves Eve with the providential aid of a sharpshooting state trooper. Leonard's death is of particular interest, in part because Hitchcock has spoken with satisfaction of dividing the villain's role among VanDamm and his associates.[4] By splitting the villain, Hitchcock presents evil as demonic and worthy of extirpation while at the same time he shows it as human and pathetic. With their dark suits and cold refinement, VanDamm and Leonard are strongly linked when they first appear in Townsend's library. Thereafter they are increasingly discriminated. Leonard, left behind in the library as VanDamm goes to join his guests, becomes an angel of death. He administers a gargantuan "libation" to Thornhill at Townsend's house, orchestrates attempts to kill him at Prairie Stop and the auction, and pushes Eve off the face of Mount Rushmore. He also commands the two thugs who seize Thornhill in the Plaza Hotel.

Leonard as dragon, moreover, shows traces of the deviant or equivocal sexuality that Hitchcock typically assigns to the thoroughly wicked figures who are killed or captured at the end of his films. Similarly sexually distorted antagonists include the androgynous Fane in *Murder!*, the hyperlibidinous General in *Secret Agent*, Squire Pengallan in *Jamaica Inn*, Uncle Charles in *Shadow of a Doubt*, Norman in *Psycho*, and the fruiterer-rapist in *Frenzy*. Suggestions of effeminacy arise with Leonard ("Call it my woman's intuition," he says at one point), and there are indications of homosexual feeling between him and VanDamm. When Thornhill, for example, is disguised as a redcap and walking with Eve from the train to the station in Chicago, he lightly remarks that she is "the smartest girl I ever spent the night on a train with." Eve looks away rather tensely because, no doubt, she is aware both of her growing affection for Thornhill and of her duplicitous role. At this moment the soundtrack reintroduces the "lover's theme," a motif associated with the tenderest moments of the couple's

[4] Truffaut, *Hitchcock/Truffaut*, p. 107.

unconventional courtship. Simultaneously, the camera pans from Eve's face to VanDamm and Leonard who are shadowing Eve and Thornhill. The "lover's theme" continues as the camera returns to Eve's face, then once more shows Eve and Thornhill together. The camera movement and cutting emphasize Eve's connection with VanDamm (which the audience learned of earlier); but the continuous playing of the "lover's theme" on the soundtrack during the shots first of Eve and Thornhill, then of VanDamm and Leonard, then of Eve and Thornhill again, obliquely suggests an amorous attraction between the two men as well as between the man and the woman. VanDamm and Leonard are shown similarly paired in parallel with Thornhill and Eve on the 20th Century Limited and at the Mount Rushmore cafeteria.

Leonard's uncertain sexuality, and that of other evil figures in Hitchcock's work, should not be dismissed as a reflection of the director's prudery. As I will argue later, true heterosexual love between well-matched partners approaches divine grace in many of Hitchcock's films. Deviance, therefore, is generally demonic; and it is artistically consistent that Hitchcock's villains often show signs of sexual perversity.

The love of VanDamm for Eve cannot accurately be called perverse (unless we emphasize its muted suggestion of father/daughter incest), but it is egotistical and possessive and thereby antithetical to the selflessness Hitchcock associates with true love and lovers. VanDamm nonetheless attracts considerable sympathy, for his wit and affection are genuine, if menacing, and his loyalty to Eve is deep. He does not even appear to consider Thornhill's proposal that he "turn over the girl," and he suffers intense anguish when he learns of his mistress's double agency. In his last appearance, standing beside the Professor as Leonard is shot, he preserves an urbanity under pressure that he shares with his chief adversary. "Not very sporting," he murmurs, "using real bullets." As Eve's lover, he opposes the murderous Leonard to the extent of slugging him when Leonard uncovers the truth of the sham shooting of Thornhill. But his rebellion against his evil side, expressive as it may be, is momentary. He remains of the devil's party, willing to murder Eve for political advantage and unredeemed by his love for her. Since the monstrous side of the villain has been partially split away from him and attached to his secretary, VanDamm gives rise to more pity than terror, even though we are never allowed to forget the ruthless intelligence that makes him, in the Professor's apt phrase, "rather a formidable gentleman."

The leader of the spies finds a surprising comrade in his adversary from the United States Government. For all the sympathy he attracts,

VanDamm remains identified with a world that is low and cynical when contrasted with that inhabited by Thornhill and Eve after they have fallen in love. The ideology and actions of the Professor link him with the world of cynical expediency inhabited by VanDamm and guarantee that the U.S. agency also will eventually become inimical to the lovers. Both VanDamm and the Professor, although they have considerable affection for Eve, are willing to sacrifice her. VanDamm decides to murder her after he learns of her treachery, and the Professor wants to send her off with VanDamm probably, as Thornhill says accusingly, "never to come back." "Much more than her life is at stake," the Professor exclaims after he has revealed to Thornhill that Eve "is one of our agents." For Thornhill, of course, nothing could count for "more than her life."

The Professor and VanDamm share vaguely academic identities, the Professor by virtue of his name and VanDamm because of the newspaper photo that shows him on what appear to be the steps of a university library. Both deal in information: VanDamm exports government secrets and the Professor refuses to have him arrested because "there's still too much we don't know about his organization." In contrast to the intelligence traded in by the Professor and VanDamm, Thornhill has the wisdom bestowed by love and a clear sense of the value of human life. "War is hell, Mr. Thornhill—even when it's a cold one," intones the Professor complacently. "Perhaps we'd better start learning to lose a few cold wars," Thornhill replies.

Thornhill does not dwell in this more gentle and innocent world at the beginning of the film; he attains it in the course of his adventures. Somewhat later, so does Eve. Their love lifts them above the soiled worlds of business and espionage. The crucial scenes en route to their final state of gratified desire take place, characteristically for both Hitchcock and romantic fictions, in elevated settings. In his quest for the truth, Thornhill ascends. He goes up to Kaplan's room at the Plaza and up to confront Townsend at the UN, but both of these unsuccessful attempts at clarification soon find him on ground level again. His most important encounters with Eve take place in elevated settings: her fourth-floor hotel room in Chicago, the mountainside pine forest after the fake shooting, her upstairs bedroom at VanDamm's, the top of the Mount Rushmore monument, and finally an upper berth on the 20th Century Limited. These climbs to illumination and love symbolize ascent to a higher plane of existence. Indeed, the vertical movement in the film may be more important than the horizontal northwesterly movement to which its title refers.

Though they are neither static nor uncomplicated, the central characters of *North by Northwest* have the moral and empathetic transparency and the oversized quality that we expect from figures in romance. Human in their failings, Thornhill and Eve are slightly greater than human in their virtues. For VanDamm, the reverse applies; he has attractive human qualities, along with vices magnified to the demonic.

Roger Thornhill is the sort of man who thinks of the perfectly aimed reply immediately, not later while brushing his teeth before bed. Although he has the defects of an ordinary man, he is handsomer, wittier, "better tailored," and more persistent than an ordinary man could be. His wit is partly that of a quick-thinking rogue, and its comic gaiety is important to his survival. A boyish playfulness inspires his escapes from the elevator at the Plaza and from the auction—where, even as the police lead him away, he insists on reiterating his absurd bid. His light touch seems partly to control a hazardous world. It keeps tragedy at bay and the fortuitous escape and happy ending in sight. Taller than anyone else in the film, he is capable of such feats of strength as surviving uninjured a collision with a truck and holding Eve above a precipice with one hand while hanging on to a cliff face with the other—while Leonard stamps on his fingers. His persistence, above all, raises him to heroic proportions. He never flags in his determination, never retreats in the face of fear, self-doubt, or exhaustion. This doggedness, as it has for romantic heroes since Odysseus, eventually rewards him with a wife and a return home.

"Where will I find you?" Thornhill asks Eve, a bit desperately, as they are parting in the train station at Chicago. Eve does not answer, but the movie eventually does, and just as one would expect of a fairy tale: in the dragon's lair, needing to be rescued. "The reward of the quest," writes Frye, "usually is or includes a bride . . . often to be found in a perilous, forbidden, or tabooed place . . . often rescued from the unwelcome embraces of another and generally older male or from giants or bandits or other usurpers."[5] VanDamm, an older male who is also a bandit and usurper (as his appropriation of Townsend's home suggests), offers Eve embraces that are not only unwelcome but about to become lethal at the end of the film. At the auction the close-up of VanDamm's hand threateningly encircling the back of Eve's neck suggests that even before he learns of her double role his affection may be dangerous.

Like most of Hitchcock's heroines, Eve retains hints of Persephone, the goddess of flowers and vegetative fertility kidnapped by the king

---

[5] Frye, *Anatomy of Criticism*, p. 193.

of Hades and finally rescued through the agency of Demeter and Zeus. She is shown with flowers on the dining car of the 20th Century Limited, on the bureau of her hotel room in Chicago and on the wallpaper there as well, and in the spectacular floral gown she wears to the auction. She resembles Persephone most, however, in her association with VanDamm who, along with Leonard and his thugs, persistently attracts demonic imagery. Shadow and dark colors are regularly associated with VanDamm, and we sometimes have a sense of him as a temple robber. Eve, his captive for all practical purposes, plays the part of Persephone in Hades or Scheherazade in her thousand and one nights, or any of a multitude of romantic heroines whose wits keep them alive in dens of danger until their true loves arrive to carry them away.

The names of its central characters illustrate the tendency of *North by Northwest* to evoke their archetypes. If my sense of the film is accurate, VanDamm, Eve, and Thornhill retain some qualities of the devil, the biblical Eve, and the savior who wore a crown of thorns and was crucified on a hill. To represent *North by Northwest* as a religious allegory would convince few of its viewers, but to argue that some of its resonance derives from its embodiment of a struggle between good and evil for the heart and life of a woman named Eve is not fundamentally antithetical. That Eve's rescuer "dies," disappears, and returns to save her enforces further an archetypal interpretation, as does the fact that Thornhill spends precisely three days and nights among the demons of international espionage in a kind of harrowing of hell.

Like its characters, the settings of *North by Northwest* are stratified and moralized. Counterpoising Thornhill's ascents to love and illumination are declivities in which he confronts confusion, evil, and danger. The first time we see him he is emerging from an elevator that has just descended to ground level; a little later he is hustled down the stairs of the Plaza and into his kidnappers' limousine; later still he is almost trapped by VanDamm's assassins in another descending elevator. The depth of the film's lower worlds is often established by an elevated camera looking conspicuously down on the action. After Townsend's murder, Thornhill flees the UN Building and we peer down the facade at a tiny speck far below, running for a cab. The scene in the conference room of the U.S. intelligence agency is photographed partly from an elevated camera position, a perspective that becomes emphatic at the end of the sequence, when we hear Thornhill rather pitilessly consigned to his fate: "Goodbye, Mr. Thornhill, wherever you are." Cut to Grand Central Station where more elevated camera placements give the scene a distinctly subterranean appearance. The high camera angles in the train station at Chicago warn us that Thornhill will neither find

Kaplan nor escape danger there. The startlingly elevated point of view at the opening of the Prairie Stop sequence confirms the foreshadowing in the station and establishes the landscape below as dangerous and infernal. When Thornhill looks down from the second floor of Van-Damm's home at Eve far below in the living room, we are presented with a particularly clear image of her entrapment in a lower world that threatens to destroy her.

The fact that airplanes are uniformly associated with danger may be one of the reversals of this intermittently ironic film; or, since we never see anyone in an airplane, their association with mortal hazards may serve to reflect the menace conveyed by elevated camera angles. In either event, the main pattern is not seriously disrupted; heights are associated with truth and love, depths with deceit and hostility. Two of the most desperate conflicts in the film, Thornhill's struggle not to succumb to his enforced drunkenness and the whole of the sequence on the face of Mount Rushmore, center on Thornhill's (and later Eve's) attempts to avoid being thrown off high places. Cinematographically and geographically, *North by Northwest* sets Thornhill and Eve the task of climbing above a corrupt world and resisting the people and circumstances that would pull them back down.

Within the romantic contexts of *North by Northwest*, the apparent anomalies of the Prairie Stop episode appear as consistent developments of emblematic patterns. The bizarre assassination attempt, Thornhill's journey to meet Kaplan and learn the truth of his inexplicable circumstances, the downward-looking camera, and the nightmare quality of the whole incident echo and anticipate similar events and settings throughout the film. The sere vegetation that contrasts with other verdant landscapes may perhaps be explainable as an early maturing corn crop, but it functions more importantly to emphasize the infernal world to which Thornhill has been sent. Dusty and desolate, Prairie Stop is hot as hell and as dangerous. It is a wasteland of the sort familiar to modern readers from T. S. Eliot's poem or the stretch between West Egg and New York City in *The Great Gatsby*. Hunted for murder by the police and for counterespionage by Van-Damm's spies, abandoned by the Professor and his agency, deceived by the woman he is in love with, isolated and exposed, Thornhill sinks to the nadir of his journey at Prairie Stop. After he returns to Chicago, his isolation begins to decrease and his ignorance is gradually replaced by understanding. But for the moment he can fall no lower, and the desolation of the place reflects the desolation of his fortunes.

Characteristic of romantic narratives, of Hitchcock's romantic films generally, and of *North by Northwest* in particular is an intermittent antirealism that takes three main forms: (1) explicit references within the work to its own fictionality and to ideas of fiction generally, (2) the frequent use of marvelous plot elements, and (3) conspicuous artificiality. The first of these forms of antirealism, often called "self-consciousness," is less specific to romance than the other two but seems to be associated with them in romantic narratives. In *North by Northwest* it takes the form of a pervasive concern with acting and assuming false identities.

The unfolding of the plot is determined largely by the conflicting and mutually misunderstood roles and the concealed aims of its main characters. His abduction having prevented him from going to the "Winter Garden Theater," Thornhill is told by VanDamm that his "expert playacting make[s] this very room a theater." As it happens, VanDamm is wrong in this particular case, but the accusation nonetheless rings broadly true for all the major and many of the minor characters in the film. VanDamm, by taking over Lester Townsend's estate, plays the role of the true owner. He also plays the role of art collector and, after he has discovered Eve's real identity, the continuing but no longer sincere part of devoted lover. Those about him act supporting roles: his sister as Mrs. Townsend, the knife-throwing assassin as a gardener, the thug's wife as a housekeeper, Leonard as private secretary. Eve plays VanDamm's mistress while spying for the American intelligence agency; she also adopts the role, for VanDamm, of a *femme fatale* on the 20th Century Limited. The Professor appears as an onlooker at the auction in Chicago and as a passing doctor in Rapid City.

Most versatile as an actor is Thornhill, the majority of whose parts are thrust upon him. For much of the film he plays, however unwillingly, George Kaplan. But he is also, as VanDamm says, "the outraged Madison Avenue man," "a fugitive from justice," and "the peevish lover, stung by jealousy and betrayal." In Chicago he plays a redcap, an expected visitor to Eve Kendall's hotel room, and the drunk and disorderly disrupter of a genteel auction; in Rapid City he dies in the cafeteria and is reborn in the hospital, where he manages to convince the Professor that "I'm a cooperator" in order to escape.

That this role-playing is at least partly to be taken as theatrical is made evident by the frequent allusions to acting and the theater that permeate the dialogue. "What a performance!" says Thornhill of VanDamm's sister at the Townsend mansion. "You fellows could stand a little less training from the FBI and a little more from the Actor's Studio," remarks VanDamm at the auction; but he later congratulates Thornhill on his "colorful exit" from that scene. Eve offers a critique of Thornhill's performance as shooting victim in the Mount

Rushmore cafeteria. *North by Northwest* is rich in allusions to other
kinds of fictionality and artifice as well. As Marian Keane points out,
its title alludes to the entrance of the traveling players in *Hamlet*. She
further shows that shot composition often depends on frames within
the larger frame of the screen and that the film exhibits a persistent
concern with "its very nature as a film."[6] The housekeeper at Van-
Damm's Rapid City home discovers the lurking Thornhill when she
sees his reflection in a television screen. Finally, the government secrets
that VanDamm is smuggling out of the country are recorded, appropriately, on a strip of film concealed inside a work of art.

The plot of *North by Northwest* progresses through a series of playlets scripted and staged by its characters but never wholly controlled
by them. The first consists of the death-by-drunk-driving arranged for
George Kaplan / Roger Thornhill; the second is the performance that
VanDamm's sister mounts to reassure the police the next day. Thornhill then bribes his mother to "put on that innocent look you do so
well" in order to get the key to Kaplan's hotel room. The sequence on
the 20th Century Limited, another play-within-the-play that takes an
unforeseen turn (its cast falls in love for real), is followed by the elaborate scenario of Prairie Stop and by further charades at the auction
that evening. There the main players congregate to perform and to mis-
interpret each other's performances. Thornhill plays a rejected lover
and a fugitive from justice—both parts he wrongly believes to be truly
his—then consciously adopts the role of "drunk and disorderly." The
Professor plays a member of the crowd. Eve is attempting to play
VanDamm's mistress and Thornhill's antagonist, the latter a role that
she is fast becoming unable to maintain with conviction for anybody
but Thornhill, who mistakes her entirely. VanDamm plays an art collector and joins Thornhill as a peevish lover. The collision of these
mutually deceived and deceiving figures leads to a complex confusion
that, like many of Hitchcock's plots, has a touch of the intricacy of
Restoration comedy. The next day at Rapid City, the Professor casts
Thornhill and Eve as victim and murderess for the benefit of Van-

[6] Marian Keane, "The Designs of Authorship," *Wide Angle* 4, no. 1 (1980): 44-52.
Ms. Keane's argument is echoed by George Wilson in *Narration in Light* (Baltimore:
The Johns Hopkins University Press, 1986). Stanley Cavell, in "*North by Northwest*"
[*Critical Inquiry* 7 (1981): 761-76] takes Hitchcock's allusion to *Hamlet* considerably
further, seeing in it an important indication that Hitchcock thought of *North by Northwest* as central to his own career and embedded in it particularly revealing signals of
how he regarded himself as a director. See also William Rothman, "*North by Northwest*: Hitchcock's Monument to the Hitchcock Film," *North Dakota Quarterly* 51
(Spring 1984): 11-23.

Damm in the last of the major internal productions of the film. Only in the final sequences, for the first time in *North by Northwest*, is everyone both playing and being perceived as himself.

It ought to be added that in this film playacting and other feigning are not necessarily equated with falsehood. Role and reality melt indistinguishably together. Eve Kendall the real lover of VanDamm becomes Eve Kendall the agent pretending to be a lover; Eve Kendall the sham lover of Roger Thornhill becomes Eve Thornhill. VanDamm may really collect art, and his associates doubtless perform their domestic duties along with more violent and exotic ones. For much of the film Thornhill almost seems to become George Kaplan, a role so pure that it needs no actor. It is an "expedient exaggeration," but not a very wild one, to say that in the world of *North by Northwest*, like that of advertising, "there are no lies." The fact that characters are most likely to accuse each other of lying at precisely those times when they are being unequivocally truthful indicates the plasticity of the relation between truth and fiction.

Associated with its theatricality and more specifically typical of romantic fictions is the conspicuous artifice and artificiality of *North by Northwest*. The spectacular abstraction of intersecting lines on which the titles appear draws the viewer's attention, from the first frames, to the film's dazzling technique. The opening also serves to introduce the important compositional principle of strong vertical lines, a motif that will reappear throughout the film, most notably perhaps in the UN sequence and in the pine forest meeting of Thornhill and Eve. Like the intersecting rails at the start of *Strangers on a Train*, the intersecting lines during the titles of *North by Northwest* serve as an emblem of the coincidences by which separate human paths come together. What is finally most notable about the opening is also most obvious: the conspicuous virtuosity by which it shows the real world with its quotidian shapes and sounds emerging almost insensibly from graphic design and music. This blending of real world and artifice anticipates the theme of fictionality in plot and language and the persistent interpenetration of the made-up and the real. An introductory voice-over that was written for the screenplay but abandoned somewhere in production may have had a similar intent.[7]

North by Northwest flaunts its polish and deftness. It is the opposite of that art that modestly conceals itself from its audience. Rich interior sets, such astonishing exterior scenes as the (recreated) Mount Rushmore Monument, the florid wit of the dialogue, attention-getting cam-

[7] Ernest Lehman, *North by Northwest* (New York: The Viking Press, 1972), p. 1.

era angles and movements, laboratory razzle-dazzle like the subjective double images of the drunk-driving sequence, opulent technicolor crashes, explosions, and cliff-hangings: the continuous glittering parade gives the film an atmosphere of technical exuberance.

The cinematic *tour de force* of *North by Northwest* draws attention as much to the style of its presentation as to what it presents. Stylization and emotional intensity, furthermore, increase together. The most technically arresting scenes—the UN sequence, Prairie Stop, the final chase—are also the most emotionally gripping. Among the artistic effects that become more conspicuous as emotional intensity increases, we may include the sound track. The lovers' theme, for instance, from its introduction on the train to its resolution as the returning 20th Century Limited enters the notorious vaginal tunnel, recurs with increasing emphasis while the love between Thornhill and Eve grows.

Plot development proceeds mainly by way of marvelous coincidence and elaborate obliquity. The quality of the action is thus associated with the antirealism implicit in the film's conspicuous artificiality and its emphasis on themes of pretense and the theater. Once we, like Thornhill, are compelled to accept the initial improbability of his mistaken identity, we are unlikely to protest any of the implausibilities by which the rest of the plot develops—so long as they bear with superficial consistency some relation to preceding events. Thus the theft of "Laura's Mercedes" and the damage to several other vehicles are cleared up for "two dollars" and pursued no further by the Glen Cove Police Department. The errant knife meant for Thornhill skewers Townsend just as he looks at VanDamm's picture; a photographer flashes Thornhill holding the weapon in an action so contrived that audiences invariably forget the innocent Townsend's death to laugh at the impudence of a film that frames its hero so shamelessly. Eve manages a seductive meeting with Thornhill on the 20th Century Limited, another coincidence whose fortuitousness is emphasized by the frantic improvisation of the fugitive's flight through Grand Central Station. And so it goes: when Thornhill needs quick transportation back to Chicago, a pickup truck presents itself; Eve writes the address of the auction on a pad that retains the impression of her writing; Thornhill overhears Leonard disclose Eve's real connections to VanDamm; the gun the housekeeper levels at Thornhill is Eve's, loaded with blanks; another vehicle presents itself for the planeside rescue. The world of *North by Northwest* is one of miraculous coincidence, not always happy but finally beneficent. It is a world in which the maker not only disdains to conceal his hand but insists on showing it through improbable plot manipulations, breathtaking artifice, and continuous musings on the interpenetration of the fictional and the true.

To what does the romantic journey of *North by Northwest* lead? Generally speaking, critics of Hitchcock's films have answered, "entertainment"—"mere" entertainment if they are hostile, and "superior" entertainment if they are friendly. Arguing that romantic fictions are more amusing than ironic seems to be a dubious enterprise; some of Hitchcock's ironic films—*Blackmail*, *Psycho*, or *Frenzy*—have been as popularly successful as his most romantic ones. The romantic mode of *North by Northwest*, and of similar films, is crucial not for entertainment value but because it determines the sort of world and human nature the films represent, the moral ideas they embody, and the relation they imply between themselves and the rest of the universe.

To judge by the condition of all the characters at the beginning of *North by Northwest*, humans are personally fragmented, anomic in crowds, and ruled by laws that regulate their disorder but do not meliorate it. To judge by the condition of Thornhill and Eve at the end of the film, the maladies of being human are not beyond remedy. The cure is love, the most miraculous and unreasonable of the implausibilities of romance. And, of course, the most common. As in Shakespeare's *Tempest*, in which not only does Ferdinand find a wife, but also "all of us ourselves / When no man was his own," so in *North by Northwest* Thornhill and Eve find not only each other but also themselves and their place in the world.

Before they achieve their love, both Thornhill and Eve wander unmated and misplaced among crowds and confusion. We first see Thornhill as one of the rush-hour mob, and it quickly becomes evident that despite his two previous marriages he is still under the aging wing of a domineering mother. He will spend most of the film establishing, literally, his right to be himself. Eve is twenty-six and unmarried, the mistress of a man she no longer cares for, and the employee of an agency that cares nothing for her. The sex lives of both Thornhill and Eve are trivial and loveless, at best. Early in the film Thornhill instructs his secretary to send goldfoil-wrapped candy, like money, to an unnamed mistress: "For your sweet tooth and all your other sweet parts." In addition to her treacherous relationship with VanDamm, Eve uses her sex appeal for hustling Thornhill on the train. But true love is fated, and not even the worst motives of counterespionage and frivolous promiscuity can thwart it. Eve and Roger begin by playing at love on the 20th Century Limited and end as Mr. and Mrs. Thornhill, homeward bound on the same train.

For Aristotle, tragedy did not need to be true but plausible, probable, necessary. For Hitchcock's romantic narratives, the opposite spirit presides. His art is implausible, improbable, and true. In the world of his romantic fictions, human life achieves integrity and joy through the miraculous coincidences and irrational feelings that make people more than a series of premises and conclusions. The antagonists to the world of innocence—VanDamm, the Professor, and the crowds of workers following their enlightened self-interest—live in conditions as infernal as they are logical. It is significant that Hitchcock, who very rarely responded with public impatience to even the most provocative imbecilities about his films, regularly aimed sarcastic blasts at "the logicians" and "our friends the plausibilists." Such critics reject the deepest convictions of Hitchcock's art; they judge it, indeed, by the standards of his villains rather than by those of his heroes. Even in love and madness, Hitchcock's villains are logical. For all that he treasures Eve, VanDamm decides to assassinate her when he learns of her true status. Thornhill, who has been quite as badly injured by both Eve and the agency she works for, comes to her rescue when he learns the truth.

Love between men and women, the most illogical and most common of the miracles of romantic fictions, is the central subject of nearly all Hitchcock's films. Like divine grace, love cannot be earned or deserved; it must be "amazing." And like divine grace, it brings clarity and purpose to a desperately corrupt world. The strongest indications that a quality of grace attaches to love in *North by Northwest* come negatively, from the demonic egotism to which it is opposed. VanDamm and his henchmen, and to a considerable extent the Professor and his aides, wage their struggle in conditions of conflicting self-interest and cynicism that are opposed to the higher world of innocence attained by Eve and Thornhill. As heterosexual love in Hitchcock's films tends to be an analogue of divine grace, demonic figures like VanDamm collect tinges of perversion.

Even when it is "normal," the love of such figures is distorted by egotism and possessiveness. VanDamm cherishes Eve as one of the accouterments of his refinement, and he uses her as he uses Leonard and the other people around him. In the latter respect, his relationship to Eve resembles the Professor's callous use of her as his agent. Hitchcock's famous aversion to police, whatever the truth of the anecdote of his father's having had him briefly confined at age five, has more to do with the romantic mode of his fictions than with early childhood trauma. The police, like Hitchcock's villains, embrace the world of experience and judge people with logic rather than love. Like their associates the criminals, the police are fixtures of a world of law, necessity, and evil; and like the stony faces of the Mount Rushmore monument, they are the stuff of earth itself, passive and indifferent. Love, spontaneously given and accepted with wonder, has nothing to do with laws, or force, or logic. It redeems a world that law and reason abandon by accepting.

Love heals. In some of Hitchcock's films the central figures are literally ill before they are cured by love; in *North by Northwest* Eve and Thornhill are alienated, uncertain of their identities, and in need of mates. Each for the other fills voids and ends idleness. As they ride back at the conclusion of the movie, they go neither up nor down but straight through a mountainside. Unlike the shots of the 20th Century Limited on its journey west—shots that showed landscapes so similar as to seem unchanged and thereby suggested a voyage going nowhere—the eastbound train is making progress, going home. The startling dissolve from monument ledge to upper berth draws our attention to the artifice of the film at its moment of greatest tension and release. That dissolve and the comically exaggerated symbolism of the train clattering into the tunnel as "The End" appears on the screen reasserts the power of the jolly director to impose a happy outcome on his story.

In the last sequence we may notice a delicate detail: the fingers of Thornhill's right hand are neatly taped where Leonard stood on them. In *North by Northwest* (and in Hitchcock's films generally), hands are an emblem of intimacy, sometimes frustrated or only potential. On Mount Rushmore they link Thornhill and Eve and, in that linking, save her life. The ending retains a few dissonant undertones: the tunnel raises ironic suggestions, and we may pause to hope that the new Mrs. Thornhill will fare better than her predecessors. But romantic cadences dominate. Thornhill's proposal to Eve on the stone face of the monument comes at a moment in this comic romance that is as convincing as it is implausible. As the movie concludes, his abraded hand is bandaged and healing. Not only is he married, but he has learned to "believe in marriage"—a point to which the film has been conveying him, and us, from its beginning.

CHAPTER TWO

Young and Innocent: Comic Romances of False Accusation

To Catch a Thief: Grace Kelly. "You know as well as I do they're fake," says John about Francie's diamonds. The emotion is fake, too, "weird excitement," not love. (Courtesy of Paramount Pictures Corporation.)

HITCHCOCK'S career, long and eventful as it was, has a striking coherence. André Bazin felt that a single frame was sufficient to identify any of his films. His name has been turned into an adjective by reviewers eager to characterize—and usually to praise—a certain sort of complex and witty suspense. Although the medium of his art changed during his life from silent to sound, to color, to wide screen, and briefly to 3-D, the integrity of Hitchcock's writing and direction stitches together films across more than fifty years. He adapted successfully to the fashions that made stars of Ivor Novello in the 1920s, Cary Grant and Jimmy Stewart in the 1940s and 1950s, and Paul Newman in the 1960s and 1970s. The unity of Hitchcock's work may be found in such trivial consistencies as his cameo appearances or his fondness for showing the identifying plaque of Scotland Yard or some analogous rectangular sign. Its integrity resides as well in more significant qualities like his hoarding of technical resources for crucial moments and his use of a personal iconography.

More important than any single formal characteristic of Hitchcock's movies, and supporting them all, is the flexible structure of a romancer's conception of his art and of human life. Looking backward and forward from 1959, one may see *North by Northwest* as a particularly thorough, but otherwise typical, compendium of Hitchcock's preoccupations. The romantic complications and solutions on which it is based underlie most of his other films. Even his ironic movies are best understood as parodies or inversions of romantic formulas.

Adventures that lead to harmony and renewal are central to Hitchcock's comic romances. Hitchcock varied every aspect of his work with wonderful resourcefulness, but beneath the surface variety we may see clearly a conception of life as a struggle to achieve, regain, or preserve innocence. In his most romantic films that quest is most successful; it fails in the most ironic ones. But in all his works, the quest for innocence, however reluctantly undertaken or ineptly pursued, organizes the plot and defines the center of hope for both protagonists and audience.

Roughly half of Hitchcock's films involve an attempt to clear the besmirched name of a central figure. *The Lodger, Young and Innocent, Number Seventeen, Saboteur, Spellbound, Strangers on a Train, I Confess, To Catch a Thief, North by Northwest, The Wrong Man*, and *Frenzy* all have fugitive protagonists. Such heroes and heroines must clear themselves of taints acquired by accident or malice and are frequently forced to struggle within ludicrous constraints. Harried from the rear by those who are convinced of their guilt, they must pursue and defend themselves from the truly wicked figures whose apprehension will remove the shadow of accusation from their names. Legally, as well as morally and pyschologically, they struggle to establish their innocence. Their mistakes or bouts of bad luck often prove to be their ultimate good fortune. They center their lives and discover their integrity when they are forced to confront evil, and they reach a deeper understanding of who they are. In the process, most of the time, they also gain spouses.

In *Blackmail*, *Murder!*, *Dial M for Murder*, and *Marnie*, an unpursued but morally implicated hero attempts to clear his beloved, with the added complication in *Murder!* and *Marnie* that she resists his efforts to help her. The sexes are reversed in *Spellbound*, but the shape of the plot remains. In *Under Capricorn* a third figure comes to the aid of a married couple, each of whom is contending with what is essentially a bum rap. *The Paradine Case* and *Stage Fright* vary the pattern further, for the accused prove to be guilty. Interestingly, however, the figure attempting to clear the criminal's name recovers his or her own innocence in the revelation of true guilt.

Intricate displacements of the quest for innocence arise in *Secret Agent*, *The Lady Vanishes*, and *Foreign Correspondent*. *Easy Virtue* presents an essentially innocent woman failing to clear her name, as does, in a more complex way, *Psycho*. *Rich and Strange* is constructed partly as a parody of the quest for innocence, partly as the consummation of that quest in a married life that has passed beyond the first blushes of young love. *The Manxman*, one of Hitchcock's most undervalued films, presents action largely prefatory to the quest. Its protagonists begin in naive and unexamined guiltlessness, experience the agony of mortal realization and loss, and eventually achieve a melancholy honesty and self-comprehension.

The works mentioned in the previous paragraphs encompass an enormous range of tone, technique, and meaning. To lump them under a single rubric risks substituting simple-mindedness for clarification. The pervasiveness of the quest for innocence in Hitchcock's movies is hard to overstate, but it is a theme that he realized with great variety and complication. We must take into account both its persistence across Hitchcock's career and the breadth of its permutations. As I have already suggested, Hitchcock's ironic films—and ironic moments within predominantly romantic ones—are usually developed as parodies or reversals of romantic conventions. In addition to the fact that Hitchcock made a number of deeply ironic movies, another objection to the idea that romance dominates his work may occur to us. The "transference of guilt" that various critics have shown to recur in Hitchcock's films obviously depends on ironic structures and actively breaks down the clear separation between good and wicked characters normal for romantic fictions.

This objection is less formidable than it initially appears. However persuasively intellectual analysis may link some of his heroes and villains, Hitchcock usually keeps them firmly distinct in terms of the sympathy they receive. For all the connections established between Uncle Charlie and Young Charlie in *Shadow of a Doubt*, to take a standard example, few viewers will be unclear whom they wish to fall from the speeding train during the struggle near the end. Similarly, we may find the police detective's behavior toward Mrs. Verloc equivocal in *Sabotage*, but we are unlikely to confuse his love and generosity with the cold venality of Mr. Verloc. Hitchcock entangles his heroes and heroines with his villains morally, but he rarely does so emotionally.

The world of Hitchcock's films is postlapsarian. Inhabitants of a fallen world, his heroes and heroines are inevitably flawed. But they are accessible to grace and love, through which they can recover innocence despite their hereditary faults. The repair of such faults, indeed, is the point of most of Hitchcock's films. His heroines and heroes must be implicated by the sins of his villains; after The Fall, everyone is to some degree sick and wicked. For the heroines and heroes of the romances, this circumstance is a *felix culpa*, the purging of which is the chief glory of human life. But many of his villains, like Mrs. Danvers in *Rebecca*, are beyond redemption. Though the audience may pity them, they remain damned spirits who can only fall back into the underworld they embody.

The superficial similarities between Hitchcock's villains and heroes finally emphasize their deep differences. Those contrasts are, as it were, the irony of his ironies. As a negative negative is a positive, so to turn an irony ironically returns it to romance. It is to follow Hitchcock only half way to notice that the apparently opposed figures of Tony, Swann, and Mark in *Dial M for Murder* actually have a great deal in common. The second step reverses the first. The ironic convergences at last serve a further irony: the first two characters differ profoundly from Mark after all; their relationships with women are as possessive and ego-centered as his love is selfless. For all the elaborate interweavings of Hitchcock's good and evil figures, there usually remains a great gulf fixed between them. The transferences of guilt and the identifications of the innocent with the wicked occur not as final ironies but as ironic precursors of romantic confirmations.

Little in my working definition of romance attaches it preferentially to either comedy or tragedy. Romantic characterizations tend toward the sharply dialectic; time in romances moves in cycles; romances fa-

vor preternaturally strong or wise figures who attract miraculous coincidences and the adventures that follow; and such fictions usually
suspend some of the constraints of ordinary reality. All such tendencies
are reversed in ironic fictions. Characterization leans toward ambiguous shadings rather than clear oppositions; time moves in a linear way
that complicates issues rather than clarifying them; protagonists of ordinary stature find themselves trapped in what Wallace Stevens called
the malady of the quotidian. I take comedy to describe—very generally
indeed—plots that move characters toward social harmony in worlds
that either exclude or constructively transform suffering and destruction; and tragedy—equally generally—as works in which central characters grow progressively isolated in a relentlessly fatal world. Nothing
in theory strongly favors the association of romance with either comedy or tragedy. In practice, however, Hitchcock's movies cluster about
the complementary pairs of comic romance and tragic irony. But there
are notable exceptions to this general tendency. *Rich and Strange* and
Mr. and Mrs. Smith are ironic comedies, and even a film as bleak as
Psycho has some of the elements of sacrifice and promised renewal that
we associate with such tragic romances as *Romeo and Juliet*.

The rest of this chapter will consider four comic romances of false
accusation: *The 39 Steps* (1935), *Young and Innocent* (1937), *Saboteur* (1942), and *To Catch a Thief* (1955). Later chapters will examine
films in which the tone and plot structure turn toward tragedy and
irony, and in which a particular feature of the quest for innocence, the
recovery of the past, assumes central importance. It is worth repeating,
in the meantime, that at the center of the body of Hitchcock's work
beats the heart of romance, with its adventures, marvelous coincidences, archetypal villains, heroines reminiscent of Persephone, demonic descents, and reascents to a vernal world of gratified desire.

Familiar and venerable features mark *Young and Innocent*, *The 39
Steps*, *Saboteur*, and *To Catch a Thief* as comedies. Their plots are
resolved by the clearing up of multitudinous misunderstandings and
by the founding and/or social acceptance of a firm connection between
the leading man and woman. In *Young and Innocent*, Robert Tisdall
(Derrick de Marney), at last exonerated from the double suspicion of
adultery and murder, assumes the role of approved suitor. "Father,"
murmurs Erica (Nova Pilbeam) in the final words of the film, "don't
you think we ought to ask Mr. Tisdall to dinner?" A mute closing shot
follows; she beams alternately at her parent and at the man the film
clearly promises will become her husband. The MacGuffin disposed
of, the movie concludes on its true concerns: the coming together of
the young lovers and the legitimizing of their relationship. As Erica's

father and the County Constable, Col. Burgoyne's (Percy Marmont) approval validates the love of the hero and heroine both as a personal and as a social accomplishment. *Young and Innocent* has it all ways. The prior family structure of Erica, her Father, and her brothers has not been destroyed but, with the addition of Tisdall, enriched and extended.

The last shot of *Saboteur* has Barry (Robert Cummings) scrambling back up the Statue of Liberty to safety and to Pat's (Priscilla Lane) embrace. The lovers have erased their misunderstandings and made firm connections earlier with a pair of desperately ardent kisses on the dance floor at the charity ball of a Fifth Column society lady. ("I'm afraid we're not behaving very well," says Pat after the first embrace. "What's the difference? We weren't invited anyway," responds Barry, as he proceeds to the second.) The end not only recalls those kisses but affirms the lovers' right to them—and to an invitation. Like Erica's father, the man who boosts Barry to security and into Pat's arms is a policeman, the representative of a society changed at the end of the movie from vengeful pursuer to grateful friend.

The last shot of *The 39 Steps* also shows its lovers embracing in the presence of police who have been transformed from adversaries to allies. Their restrained embrace consists of a gentle clasping of hands, an eloquent gesture at once confirming the mutuality of the lovers' affection and reversing earlier actions in which, full of reciprocal suspicion, they were unwillingly joined by handcuffs. As their hands move together, the shackle from which Pamela (Madeleine Carroll) earlier withdrew her wrist dangles from Hannay's (Robert Donat) cuff. Maurice Yacowar has argued that some elements in this last shot destabilize the general reassurance of the conclusion, but the lovers' confusions have passed.[1] If the world as a whole is less than comfortable and civilized, the two chief characters of the movie have at least attained a personal security.

The police are absent from the final scene of *To Catch a Thief* only because they have been disposed of in the previous one. Still, it is a police car that carries Francie (Grace Kelly) up to John's (Cary Grant) house. There a closing kiss (preceded by a handshake) cements the connections between lovers who have held each other at bay throughout the film. The last lines promise the usual marital sequel: "So this is where you live," purrs Francie as she gazes contentedly over John's

[1] Maurice Yacowar, *Hitchcock's British Films* (Hamden, Conn.: Archon, 1977), p. 192.

shoulder. "Oh, Mother will love it up here!" Robie raises his head
warily. A bell sounds—of recognition, warning, wedding.

The presence of the police at the conclusion of these films emphasizes the importance of the movement from social rejection to social
authorization. The heroes go from hunted pariahs to social saviors.
They not only regain respectability but help to catch the criminals they
were mistaken for. The consequent sense of a revived social order co-
alescing around the figures of the vindicated lovers is strongest in
Young and Innocent, but it is to a lesser degree present in the other
films as well.

Comedy, said Aristotle, involves the ludicrous, "that sort of mistake
or ugliness which is painless and not destructive."[2] *The 39 Steps*,
Young and Innocent, and *To Catch a Thief* all turn repeatedly to the
sort of alarming humor an audience can enjoy only because genuine
pain and destructiveness are largely banished or shunted onto exaggeratedly unsympathetic characters. The politically haunted *Saboteur*
takes a less casual attitude toward its mayhem.

The 39 Steps, after several threatening or destructive episodes, rescues its hero from a bullet in the heart by putting a hymnal in his front
pocket. From that point its great comic scenes follow in a rush: Hannay bolting through the police station window; escaping pursuit by
marching in a salvation army parade; delivering himself of an overwhelmingly successful political speech without knowing either whom
he is addressing or on what subject; pursuing his increasingly tender,
improbable romance with Pamela; and being saved by the ministra-
tions of the sentimental old couple at the Inn. Benign fate has entered
the action in the *deus ex machina* of the hymnal, and we are free to
laugh without fear thereafter. There have been hints of a safely comic
universe earlier—the episode with the milkman, for example, and that
of the undergarment salesman and the priest on the train. But there has
also been the murder of the lady spy, and the enduring impression of
lethal possibilities from that pathetic event clouds the subsequent gaiety. Moreover, traditional comic settings and actions early in the
film—the theater, Hannay's hospitality, the birthday celebration—all
turn sour or threatening.

A murder also occurs early in *Young and Innocent*, but it does not
have the same power to qualify the world of the film as the early death
in *The 39 Steps*. In part, the manifest silliness of Tisdall's accusers, the
immediate beginning of his romance with Erica, the absurd fatuity of

---

[2] Kenneth A. Telford, trans., *Aristotle's Poetics: Translation and Analysis* (Chicago:
Henry Regnery Co., 1961), p. 10.

his lawyer, and the broad comedy of his escape from the court all conspire to help the sunny morning replace the gloom and storm of the previous night. ("Mustn't be downhearted on a morning like this, must we?" says Briggs, the idiotic advocate. Surprisingly, he is quite correct.)

More important is the conspicuously theatrical—and therefore, in a way, unreal—quality of the opening sequence. After the extravagant contrasts between the two musical themes that accompany the opening credits (themes that will be associated with the murderer and with the young lovers later), we hear a loud cry of "Christina!" Her head fills the screen and she shouts histrionically in response, "Don't shout, I tell you, don't shout!" Her husband enters the frame in an equally tight shot and yells, "I'll shout if I want to, who's to prevent me from shouting!" As he finishes speaking, a crash of thunder is heard in the background. "You're a liar and a cheat," he continues, and the quarrel rages on accompanied by sounds of the storm. It ends with slaps that send the husband out to glare at a sea of surging waves. A flash of lightning reveals his face, twitching with emotion.

There is a good deal going on in this seventy-second sequence, but the important point is, as usual, the obvious one. The sequence is so melodramatic—so overwritten, overdirected, overstaged—that we cannot take it seriously. It is almost a surprise when the camera fails to pull back and reveal the stage set that the exaggerated close shots seem designed to conceal. The body of the actress in the surf the next morning and a menacing intercut of crying gulls (*The Birds*, twenty-six years before) give the violence some reality; but we hardly know the victim—who is only an overacting actress at that—so the power of the opening to inspire our pity or alarm remains slight.

Young and Innocent proceeds via a series of comic episodes to tumble its youthful heroine and hero toward a resolution of their problems and into each other's arms. The melee at the roadside stop, the birthday party, two flights from the police, and the cliff-hanging episode in the old mine are all presented with such a light touch that their potential for real harm is suppressed. Even the closing sequence leading up to the discovery of the real murderer includes enough incidental slapstick to assure us that nothing finally serious can go wrong.

Like *Young and Innocent, To Catch a Thief* contains little real anxiety. As does the earlier movie, it establishes the essential benignity of its world in ways that allow the audience to respond to its comedy and indulge in its suspense without much concern about the ultimate safety of its hero. It emphasizes its own artificiality throughout; like *Young and Innocent*, it is especially histrionic at the beginning. After the credits have run against the background of a travel agent's window, the camera dollies in to a tight shot of a travel poster of the French Riviera: "If you love life, you'll love France." Cut to a big head of a woman in a dressing gown screaming extravagantly. Cut to an empty jewel case. Still screaming, the woman hurries out onto her balcony and absurdly calls down to the boulevard ten stories below for the police. We recognize the hotel-lined bay behind her as the one portrayed on the travel poster we just saw. Cut to a night shot of a black cat trotting across a tiled roof. This sequence is immediately repeated twice with slight variations: a gloved hand in a jewelry box / the same night-prowling cat retracing its steps / the facade of the hotel while we hear a scream, "My diamonds! My diamonds!" / cat approaching again / hand under pillow / cat retreating again / facade and more screams for "la police." We are then taken to a meeting in the police commissar's office, after which the camera precedes the police to the hilltop chateau of John Robie. There we find a black cat reclining on an Art Buchwald column called *Europe's Lighter Side* and titled, for that day, "The Cat Prowls Again?"

This self-consciously amused beginning opens a film that ends with its masculine and feminine leads happily in each other's arms, all problems—amusements for the nonce—solved. There are a few gunshots en route, and one especially stylized villain is actually killed by an inept accomplice, but the two hours' commerce of this stage consists fundamentally of a series of comic anecdotes: how Robie escapes from the police via faked suicide, boat, and rooftop; how he drops a 10,000-franc chip down a buxom lady's low-cut dress in order to meet Mrs. Stevens (Jessie Royce Landis); how he's caught in the flower market; the cattiness of Francie and Danielle at the beach; the hyperbolical eroticism of the seduction of Robie by Francie to the accompaniment of overcranked fireworks; and so on. *To Catch a Thief* reverses the reversal of its opening. It presents, after all, what the travel agency posters promise: a fairy-tale world, "a kind of travel-folder heaven," as Huston the insurance investigator says, in which work and play are indistinguishable and no innocent being—not even the proverbial chicken crossing the road—need fear harm.

As one might expect from its 1942 date and its subjects, *Saboteur* contains more real anxiety and less incidental humor than the other three films. Most of its lighter episodes occur between sympathetic characters at moments of relative safety: when the two lovers come together among the circus freaks, for example, or when they appear to have escaped into the crowd at the charity ball. As a rule, real suffering and destruction lands in the enemy camp. But not always. Barry Kane cannot bring his friend back to life by taking his last name as an alias when he is fleeing the police. Generally serious and even anxious in tone, but structurally comic, *Saboteur* resembles those domestic melodramas that Northrop Frye called "comedies without laughter."[3]

What laughter *Saboteur* does contain is apt to be dangerous. In the ninety-second sequence at the movie theater preceding the final chase, comedy erupts into gunshots; a laughing audience who assumes that it is safely outside the screen panics when real bullets escape the movie world and kill a man in the front row. This spectacular insertion not only undermines what comic security *Saboteur* still contains but serves as a guide for interpretation. Like the oddly hazardous mirth in the movie-within-the-movie, the nervous laughter of *Saboteur* arises in contexts neither so safe nor so far removed from real life as we might suppose. The comic movie in front of which Frye stages his escape careens toward real threat: its outraged and suddenly dangerous husband roars, "I'll kill the rat if it's the last thing I do." "He was only kidding, I swear," cries the distraught wife as her husband prepares to fire his pistol again.

The pressure of time winds the mainsprings of all four films. Henri Bergson proposed that mechanically inappropriate action and language is a central device of most comedy.[4] Mistiming, the collision of human irregularity with natural inflexibility, is related. It is the benign opposite of the inexorable operations of fate in tragedy. Comic time works capriciously, creating unexpected problems one moment and solving them unexpectedly the next. In neither comedy nor tragedy can we often forget that life is change, and that all things are worked out for better or worse as they change in time.

An ominous alarm clock ticks loudly through all these movies. The aeronautical secrets stolen by The 39 Steps are scheduled to leave England in "a matter of days." This fact establishes an effective deadline before which Hannay must trap and expose his adversaries. If he fails, not only will the spies and their secret information escape, but with them will go his only plausible chance to clear himself of the murder for which the police are pursuing him. The protagonists of *Young and Innocent* are similarly tormented by time. They suffer a painful delay at the birthday party of Erica's niece; they've got to find Robert's stolen raincoat before the police net closes and the faint trail disappears entirely; lucky circumstances uncover the real murderer just as

[3] Frye, *Anatomy of Criticism*, p. 40.
[4] Henri Bergson, "Laughter," in *Comedy*, ed. Wylie Sypher (Garden City, N.Y.: Doubleday Anchor, 1956), pp. 61-190.

Robert Tisdall is being led to jail. Like that of *The 39 Steps*, the action of *Saboteur* is keyed to a deadline marked by the launching of a battleship that is the saboteurs' next target. Not only must the villains be thwarted for patriotic reasons, but (as in *The 39 Steps*) they must be exposed in order to clear Barry. The statutory limitations on John Robie's freedom after his apprehension in the flower market put temporal constraints upon him early in *To Catch a Thief*; the threat of going to jail after the costume ball puts the pressure of time on him at the end.

That all four movies turn out happily stands as the most obvious signal of their status as comedies, but the very fact that comic plots "turn out" at all reminds us of the importance of their temporal framework. That fact suggests, also, one source of the affinity of comedy for romance, with its emphasis on a time that turns and turns until it cycles around to begin anew.[5] The release from anxiety "in the nick of time" at the end of comedy can easily join with the redemption of the past that characterizes romance. Deadlines of various kinds give urgency and pace to the action of all four of these Hitchcockian romances, while their comic mode guarantees that the moment of truth will be either met successfully or somehow outsmarted and evaded.

An alternative to the theory of comedy that I have been using considers jokes, laughter, and literary comedy as a socially acceptable way to raise and cast out threats that might otherwise appear coarse, horrible, or excessively sentimental. From this perspective, Hitchcock's comedies may be regarded as working out serious issues while partly concealing their seriousness. It is easy to suppose that Hitchcock, who appears to have been a profoundly private person working in an exhibitionistic occupation, would have felt some impulse to conceal himself even as he was making public his most intimate fantasies.

The comic threat of false accusation meshes smoothly with the central romantic issues of identity and the recovery of innocence. Other elements of romantic narrative, most of which appeared in *North by Northwest*, figure prominently in the films of this chapter. Their plots are shaped by descents to infernal places and by ascents to truth and love, by episodes that have heavy overtones of death and return, and by quests that carry their heroes through wonderful adventures. Characterization is typically romantic, with larger- and wittier-than-life heroes, demonic villains, and equivalents of fairy tales' helpful elves and fairies—the last a feature not present in *North by Northwest*. Equally

---

[5] When tragedy is not overwhelmingly ironic, it often expresses some sense of cyclic time as well, in gestures that evoke a sacrificial ritual leading to cleansing and renewal.

typical are their self-conscious artificiality, their emphasis on art and ritual, and their love of marvelous coincidence.

The heroes of all four films make some sort of a descent into a night-world or underworld where they face deadly threats. In *The 39 Steps* and *Saboteur*, the less uniformly comic pair, this sense of descent is particularly emphatic; and in all four it is associated with water, in such contexts a common symbol of dissolution. The heroes of *The 39 Steps* and *Saboteur* cross or leap into rivers, an image Hitchcock uses in *Shadow of a Doubt* and other films. In *Shadow of a Doubt* we meet Uncle Charlie after a brief opening sequence of riverside dumps, as if the camera were crossing the Styx. A similar metaphysical crossing is suggested by Bruno's boatride to the Enchanted Isle in *Strangers on a Train* and by the opening shots of *Frenzy*. *Young and Innocent* and *To Catch a Thief* also bring their heroes down to water early. In *Young and Innocent*, Tisdall descends from clifftop to beach, where he finds the dead actress and is mistaken for the murderer. In *To Catch a Thief*, Robie first goes down from his hilltop villa to the seaside restaurant of his old comrades, then further to the grotto beneath the restaurant to get into a boat with Danielle.

Once plunged into hazardous lower worlds, the protagonists of Hitchcock's films usually undergo further descents before they struggle up from their nightmare adventures. In *The 39 Steps*, Hannay flees across dreary atmospheric landscapes in Scotland, slides down cataracts, creeps under a culvert, disappears into a fog, and finally hides under a waterfall.

In *Young and Innocent*, there are at least two notable descents after the opening. The first occurs when Tisdall and Erica, searching for Tisdall's raincoat, park in the darkness by a sunken railroad yard. Erica stays there while Tisdall goes off to a flophouse, a further descent (socially if not literally). The second begins with Tisdall and Erica driving into an abandoned mine. The ground under the car collapses and the car falls into the depths while Tisdall pulls Erica to safety in an action that anticipates quite precisely the next to last sequence of *North by Northwest*.

Saboteur proceeds through a series of falls and captivities, from the desolation of the ghost town called "Soda City," to a Manhattan first seen through the cables of one of its bridges at night, to the ballroom dance floor, then to a basement pantry from which Kane escapes by setting off the fire alarm system with a match. The dialogue of *Saboteur* also suggests demonic descents. In the first sequence, for example, one of the workers calls the fire at the factory "all hell come up."

To Catch a Thief, too, has intermittent downward movements: a fall into a pile of flowers at the market, the marine conversation with Danielle during which she talks of having to "kill the cat," the night prowl at which Danielle's father (standing in, as it were, for Robie) is killed and thrown off the cliff into the sea. All four movies thus not only begin by thrusting their central characters into low and/or dark worlds of hazard and deceit, but they continually threaten to push them lower. The heroes and heroines resist by trying, not surprisingly, to climb up. The conflicts in these four films are much like those in *North by Northwest*, with protagonists struggling upward while their adversaries try to hold them down.

The central figures climb to clarification and identity, to truth and love. In *The 39 Steps* an important turning point comes when Pamela and Hannay go to their inn room after their escape from the false detectives. Upstairs, Pamela comes to trust Hannay before—an important point—she has any reason to do so beyond the illogical one that she is sharing a bed with him. But such reasons for Hitchcock are the only good ones. Pamela's intuition is confirmed later when she gazes down on their pursuers from the balcony and overhears their phone conversation with the wife of the chief spy, Professor Jordan. Such epiphanies invariably occur, in Hitchcock's romantic films, in elevated settings, even if the degree of elevation involves no more than a second-floor balcony and bedroom.

An instructive example of Hitchcock's instinct to elevate his characters for unveilings occurs in *Torn Curtain*. After Miss Sherman (Julie Andrews) has exploded in patriotic exasperation at Michael (Paul Newman), he takes her outside to tell her that he is really a self-employed double agent. They turn aside from their guards and walk up a small wooded hill in a park. There Michael tells her the truth; so we gather from her face, for we cannot hear what he is saying at that moment. If the rest of the film strikes many people as slow and pointless, that is so, perhaps, because the hilltop clearing of the air that Hitchcock usually holds until late in the movie has occurred with a third of *Torn Curtain* remaining. This timing leaves only the espionage MacGuffin to occupy the audience for the remaining thirty minutes. When the real interest of Hitchcock's films, the relationship between the central man and woman, is resolved, the nominal one may appear feeble. All the technical virtuosity Hitchcock expends on the escape from East Germany cannot conceal the absence of compelling suspense once Miss Sherman learns the truth about her fiancee's "defection."

As in *The 39 Steps*, a clear moment of love and understanding in *Young and Innocent* occurs in an upstairs bedroom. Hitchcock emphasizes the ascent by photographing Erica, who has been sent to her room by her father, going up the stairs. Moonlight and romantic violins accompany the arrival of Tisdall, who has climbed up the side of the house to awaken her and announce that he is going to give himself up to the police. (Tisdall and Erica take turns throughout the movie playing the Prince who awakens Sleeping Beauty.) In the course of their tender farewell, the crucial clue surfaces—a packet of matches revealing that the true murderer "has been, or still is, at the Grand Hotel." This recognition leads to the brilliant solution of the final sequence, with its famous 240-foot track-in to the twitching eyes of the drummer/murderer.

The scene in Erica's bedroom is the last of several ascents that have brought the young woman and man both closer together and closer to the truth. After first reviving Tisdall at the police station, Erica next encounters him when her car runs out of fuel on a high road overlooking the surrounding countryside. When she brings him food in the old mill, delicate woodwinds and violins accompany her up the ladder to the hayloft where she once again revives him, this time from sleep. The brief scene in which Tisdall pulls Erica from her sinking car also belongs to the imagery of ascent. That these upward movements should so often be associated with awakening or regaining consciousness cues an underlying subject of Hitchcock's romantic comedy: the self-discovery and knowledge that lead to renewal.

Two ascents mark crucial moments in *Saboteur*: the episode in which Kane and Pat join a circus caravan, and the closing sequence on the Statue of Liberty. (In elevated settings that are threatening rather than reassuring—upstairs at the mansion where Kane has a primitive ideological debate with Tobin, for example, or in the skyscraper where Pat is imprisoned—the audience is not allowed to see anyone going up. The sense of ascent is thereby suppressed.) The sequence with the circus freaks begins with a low camera shooting up and silhouetting Kane and Pat against moonlit clouds. In a close-up that keeps them framed against the sky, Kane pleads his innocence. Pat responds with skepticism, but she weakens slightly, deciding to prefer Kane's company to that of the desert snakes he threatens her with. (Just before this sequence, a passing woman, as comically wrong and as prescient as the Innkeeper's wife in *The 39 Steps*, remarks to her husband, "My, they must be terribly in love.") Conventional background violins promise an amorous turn of events as the dialogue reiterates the idea of ascent. "I'm coming up in the world," cracks Barry as Pat runs after the van. A little later the head of the circus counsels the Bearded Lady to "get your eyes out of the mud and look up at the stars." When the police come to search the van, Barry climbs up again to hide in an overhead baggage rack. Pat and Barry have bumpy roads left to travel, but by the end of this scene Pat can say "I believe you" and fall asleep on Barry's shoulder.

The last sequence of the film also involves struggling upward, and though its themes have as much to do with politics as with love, it and the film end with Barry clambering onto the observation deck of the Statue of Liberty and into Pat's arms. The background sky is again full of fluffy white clouds. As the movie ends, jubilant violins run down to a tonic and the heavens fill the screen. Emotionally, however, if not ideologically, this romantic exultation is diminished a bit by Kane's failure to rescue his suddenly pathetic adversary and by the ghastly image of Frye falling.

Early in the circus sequence, when the two lovers-to-be hop onto the last wagon, a small, telling clue alerts the inveterate watcher of Hitchcock's films to an impending reconciliation. On the platform at the rear of the van a roof arches over the couple's heads. As early as *The Lodger*, Hitchcock signaled the coming together of potential lovers with the fireplace arch that visually joins Daisy and the Lodger as they play chess. The span of a bridge in the background in *Secret Agent* provides a similar composition at a similar moment between the hero and heroine. Erica and Robert drive through an arch after the birthday party in *Young and Innocent*, Hannay and Pamela are framed by an arch of the Inn in which they will fall in love in *The 39 Steps*, and Mark and Marnie kiss beneath the arches of the horse barn in *Marnie*. The arches of San Juan Bautista in *Vertigo* represent an ironic inversion of this motif, as does the sanctuary more generally—a place of safety and rebirth turned into an arena of danger and death.

More examples of this significant arch arise in other Hitchcock movies. Such visual and symbolic consistency is one reason why our understanding of his films grows not only as we analyze each one individually but as we become aware of their total coherence—the symbolic complexes and associations that recur in each work singly and resonate among them all collectively. A viewer who has seen many of Hitchcock's movies will (perhaps not entirely consciously) feel a reassuring promise in the setting that puts an arched neon light behind Young Charlie and Jack in *Shadow of a Doubt* as they argue on a park bench during their first date. The last shot of *Topaz*, to take a more intriguing example, is of a pair of men photographed from the rear, walking arm in arm toward the Arc de Triomphe. In a film that has dealt in deceit and betrayal from the level of the family to that of international relations, this persistent symbol of heterosexual love in Hitchcock's movies becomes ironic as it frames two men walking toward a public monument to national stability—the very idea of which the whole movie renders problematic.

As one would expect of a film featuring a pair of cat burglars, *To Catch a Thief* has elevated settings and ascents in abundance. John Robie climbs for two reasons, often combined: first, to escape; second, to achieve knowledge and make connections with other people. At the beginning of the film, he goes to his upstairs bedroom and then to his roof to evade the police. He will escape them again on the hotel roof after Francie summons them because she thinks that John has stolen her mother's jewels. A clifftop picnic involves both flight and the coming together of hero and heroine. Following a hair-raising chase along a twisting road, the police are left with a wrecked car and a fortunate chicken; Francie and John stop on a turnoff overlooking the Mediterranean to share cold fried fowl of the same species and their first real embrace.

In a related sequence, Huston comes to lunch with Robie at his villa overlooking the valley. There the insurance agent gives him the list of his wealthy clients. The ascent of this sequence leads to trust and friendship as well as (indirectly) to love; it occasions a growing regard and affection between the two men. On the roof of the mansion after the costume ball, Robie both escapes the police and finds the real cat burglar. He also frees himself from the false accusations that have pursued him throughout the film. In the final sequence, Robie tries to escape alone back to his hilltop home, but Francie follows him there for an embrace that promises marriage.

The most illuminating —as well as the most amusing—of the scenes of ascent and elevation in *To Catch a Thief* takes place during the fireworks-accompanied seduction that follows the clifftop picnic. Like much of *To Catch a Thief*, its elaborate parody of Hollywood conventions defines Hitchcock's true subjects at the same time that it makes fun of particularly silly contemporary movie clichés. We join the dinner for two in Francie's suite as room service wheels out the table of dirty dishes. Francie stands at one window gazing into a night full of fireworks; John stands at an adjacent one. Francie moves toward the light switch (and toward John): "If you really want to see fireworks, it's better with the lights off. I have a feeling that tonight you're going to see one of the Riviera's most fascinating sights. (Pause) I was talking about the fireworks." The dialogue will maintain this level of obvious, jejune double entendre throughout the sequence. The camera, sound track, and montage exultantly join the prurient horseplay. Francie backs partly into a shadow against which her spectacular body glows in her strapless white gown. A moment later, in torso close-up on the divan, she leans slightly toward John, her breasts, profile, and platinum blond hair still glowing in the darkness. "Look, John, hold them . . . diamonds." Cut to fireworks. Extravagant violins. Return, in tighter close-up, to the two gorgeous lovers. Francie kisses John's fingers, places his hand under her diamond necklace, leans very close, and murmurs, "Ever had a better offer in your whole life? One with everything." Cut again to the fireworks, speeding up insistently as the violins continue. After more verbal sparring, John kisses her. Cut to bright, racing flashes. Still kissing, they lie back on the couch. The music grows hysterical. Cut to a whole evening of skyrockets and roman candles condensed into a half-dozen seconds, as the seduction—one of the most beautiful, erotic, and ridiculous in the history of the movies—achieves its consummation.

This foolishness charms us partly because its self-conscious excesses are impossible to take seriously. The most familiar aural and visual clichés of cinematic courtship—violins, fireworks, divinely glamorous protagonists—are sent up together in an *inflatio ad absurdum*. Behind the amorous folly, however, uninsistent but unconcealed, Hitchcock makes his straightforward point: this is all make-believe, as unreal as it is overstated. "You know as well as I do they're fake," says John about Francie's diamonds. The emotion is fake, too, "weird excitement," not love. As Lil is "queer for liars" in *Marnie*, Francie is queer for cat burglars at this point of *To Catch a Thief*. She will discover her real love for John Robie when she learns of his innocence, and her best offer, "Give up, John, admit who you are," will neither be truly made nor accepted until the last scene. At the same time, we have no reason to suppose that Francie's sexual appetite for John will slacken; her desire for him has deepened and matured, but it has not become platonic.

Rising to truth and love characterizes all Hitchcock's romantic movies. His ironic ones insistently raise the motif to parody it. Going up opposes the demonic descents that his heroes suffer or are threatened with; such movement symbolizes the triumph of a higher world of recovered innocence over the fallen world of experience. Ascents are usually part of an action crucial for Hitchcock's (and for all) romantic fictions: the story of the death, disappearance, and return of a heroine or hero.

Outside fairy tale, myth, and religion, one usually finds death and resurrection displaced—that is, turned into something reminiscent of such events, like Thornhill's faked shooting in *North by Northwest*. A literal return to life, as in Dreyer's *Ordet*, constitutes a notable cinematic exception to the rule. Because of the obvious affinity of death and tragedy, the degree of displacement is likely to be greater in comic romances than in more dangerous stories. Among Hitchcock's romantic narratives, a few like *Notorious* and *Marnie* contain near or false deaths that come very close to evoking the sense of waste and bereavement that accompanies tragedy. More comic in structure and tone, *The 39 Steps, Young and Innocent, Saboteur,* and *To Catch a Thief* displace and deemphasize gestures toward death and return. Yet the idea cannot entirely disappear, for it is central to all romance.

When Hannay is shot by the Professor midway through *The 39 Steps* he slumps to the floor. Hitchcock then cuts briefly back to the house of the farmer and his wife with whom Hannay stayed earlier. The cut explains the hymnbook that, we learn in the next sequence, has stopped the Professor's bullet short of Hannay's heart. It also provides an interlude, however short, during which Hannay is dead and gone from the point of view of the audience. Hitchcock lightly underlines the religious allusiveness of the episode both by his use of the hymnal itself and by Hannay's wry remark, "hymns that have helped me." As I noted earlier, this brief incident shifts the tone of the rest of the film in the direction of a less ambiguous comedy.

At the same time, however, the remarkable cut in the sound track from the Scottish farmer's blow and his wife's scream to the hearty masculine laughter of Hannay and the Sheriff also underlines a theme that runs through the film from the death of the woman spy in the opening movement to the kicking chorus line of the last shot: the equivocal status of many women and their intermittent brutalization by men. This secondary theme damps somewhat the glow of the comedy while it adds a kind of subterranean sketch of a world in which love and forgiveness between men and women do not exist.

Young and Innocent and *Saboteur* both have fainter vestiges of death and return. At the end of *Young and Innocent* Tisdall turns himself over to the police and an apparently certain murder conviction. Only then does the true murderer betray himself and thereby clear Tisdall. *Saboteur* evokes resurrection twice, neither time emphatically. It mildly suggests that the worker who died in the opening fire "returns" when Barry adopts his surname of Mason as an alias. Later, Barry is clubbed unconscious and locked in a basement pantry from which he inexplicably escapes after triggering the fire alarm.

Beyond a number of allusions to the nine lives of a cat, death/disappearance/reappearance is directly suggested by several episodes of *To Catch a Thief*. The most important episode occurs when John visits at night a villa where he knows his adversaries are waiting in ambush. In deep shadow, he is grabbed from behind, a wrench is raised, the sounds of heavy blows are heard. A body pitches off the cliff and into the sea, that nearly omnipresent Hitchcockian symbol of dissolution. Between the fall of the body and the revelation that it is Fousard, not Robie, the camera cuts away to follow a group of police scurrying down to the scene of the attack. This cut takes twenty seconds of film time and does not advance the plot. But like the intercut of the farmer and his wife in *The 39 Steps*, it provides a brief space of time during which the audience may suppose Robie dead.

The false alarm of Robie's death is sounded for Francie and her mother in the next sequence by newspaper headlines that read "Le Chat Est Mort." Both women first assume that this means John, then realize that he is still alive and that he must, therefore, be innocent. For *To Catch a Thief*, as for *The 39 Steps*, the main sequence of "death and resurrection" marks a turning point. As her mother tells her that she had better start practicing apologies, the camera cuts to a close-up of Francie's face. She is realizing her true feelings about the man she has previously chased as a titilatingly dangerous erotic toy. The next time she sees him, outside the cemetery in which the putative Cat's funeral is taking place, she will declare that she loves him. Her obvious concern for Robie's safety when he tells her of his plan to catch the real Cat, moreover, substantiates the truth of what Robie calls "a ridiculous thing to say" ("I love you"). Behind John, further validating Francie's confession, rises a range of hills and mountains, suggesting ascent and epiphany.

Demonic falls, heavenly risings, hints at death and rebirth—all these make up what we may call the vertical component of the adventurous quests that normally move romantic fictions. These up-and-down movements serve the symbologies of identity, love, and innocence. Horizontal movements, usually of flight and pursuit simultaneously, tend to trace the plot of Hitchcock's films and are consequently often associated with the MacGuffin. Nonetheless, the horizontal motion in Hitchcock's romantic narratives carries an important cargo of meaning. The quest for knowledge discovers innocence. A loss or mistaking of identity results in a finding of self, family, society, and the mate who makes possible and defines all three. The world of romantic seeking turns and returns. As falling in love becomes a rising to heaven, so seeking or fleeing ends in coming back to the renewed security of beginnings.

All four of the films discussed in this chapter give the sort of emphasis to movement and transport that we observed in *North by Northwest*. They teem with cars, trains, trucks, cabs, boats, ships. *Saboteur* summarizes everyday America in the travels of its hero from the Pacific to the Atlantic coast. *The 39 Steps* takes Hannay from London to the desert north of Scotland. *Young and Innocent* and *To Catch a Thief* do not take anyone very far, but they nonetheless keep their heroes in transit. Tisdall spends a good deal of time in Erica's car, and Robie whirls about the Riviera in a variety of cars, buses, and boats. The most celebrated shot in *Young and Innocent*, the long slow crane over the dance floor to the drummer's twitching eyes, reiterates the sense of movement and quest. It also reassures us about the outcome of Tisdall's attempt to clear his name by enlisting on his behalf the most powerful of allies, the camera itself. As in *North by Northwest*, these films have heroes who must leave their conveyances when things grow desperate. Hannay scrambles on foot across the Highlands; Tisdall runs from the police in the mine shaft; Barry escapes a patrol car by leaping from a bridge and walking through the woods to the home of Pat's uncle; and John Robie, on nimble cat feet, takes to the roofs.

The faring forth of the protagonists of Hitchcock's romantic movies generally leads to some sort of homecoming or returning to origins. Both the hero and what he comes back to are renovated by the trials of the journey. As Thornhill's northwesterly trail finally doubles back upon itself, so Hannay returns to the Palladium after his trek to Scotland, Tisdall returns to the point of his departure, and Robie ends where he began, on the veranda of his villa. Though Barry does not go back to the West Coast at the end of *Saboteur*, his journey ends with a similar sense of return. He has gone from coast to coast; from city to mountain, forest, desert, and finally back to the city. He has cleared himself of a charge of treason and regained the certification of loyalty that he needed in order to work in the airplane factory in the first place. At the end of the film, he is secure not only in Pat's embrace, but also in the emblematic embrace of his country on the Statue of Liberty. Like the Manhattan shop girl Pat pretends to be, he has seen the place that has always been his but that he has never really explored.

All this questing underscores the personal rootlessness that is the condition of the heroes at the beginnings of these four films. Without disturbing wife or child, parents, boss, or friends, they rush off to their flights and pursuits. Although John Robie has a home to which he remains close, his social and family connections have no more substance than Hannay's, Tisdall's, or Barry Kane's. Such an absence of personal ties and encumbrances typifies romantic heroes and heroines who set out to seek their fortunes, whether by choice or by compulsion. This anomie of the protagonists has important consequences for the plots and the thematic content of the movies, but for the moment I wish to pursue further the general question of the characterization of the main figures.

The principal characters in Hitchcock's romantic films combine sympathetic clarity and moral complexity. The audience will not confuse good figures with bad, but neither goodness nor badness is so morally unequivocal as to appear spotless on the one hand or to lack human appeal entirely on the other. When the moral status and sympathetic appeal of central figures grows confused, the work enters the realm of irony; when the protagonists and antagonists are entirely separate and morally uncomplicated, it moves into caricature and melodrama. Irony is a common mode in Hitchcock's career; melodrama exists largely in such self-parodies as occur at the end of *Strangers on a Train* and *North by Northwest*.

Hannay behaves gallantly, resourcefully, patriotically; but he is also promiscuous and willing to use women somewhat casually and unfeelingly. For all his love of Erica, Tisdall puts her at considerable risk, and he carries at least faint traces of an unsavory connection with Christine, the married actress murdered in the opening of the movie. Robie's charm and courage, like Hannay's, are mixed with suggestions of emotional shallowness and male chauvinism. His physical connection with Francie precedes the emotional one, and he shows no hesitation about using women when it serves his purposes. His past identities as a burglar and as a resistance commando who claims to have killed "seventy-two" people also constitute ambiguous character references.

Barry Kane constitutes something of an exception to the rule of mixed moral character. For reasons that may have to do with casting (Hitchcock complained that Robert Cummings "belongs to the light-comedy class of actors"), or with the cultural tendency toward polarization that accompanies wartime, Barry lacks most of the blemishes of the heroes of the other films. Insofar as he exhibits defects, they derive from weakness rather than willfulness. He is a bit of a sucker and a tool; his own credulousness finds its ironic balance in his lack of credibility and in his helplessness at convincing anyone of his innocence or of the imminent dangers from the Fifth Columnists. Even Mrs. Mason, who is a sort of foster mother to Barry, can say no more than "I didn't tell the police anything . . . oh, I don't know" when Barry asks her to express her faith in his innocence. "Don't you believe me?" he asks incredulously. Only Pat, emphatically not a mother figure, can later answer that question with the uncritical "yes" of loving faith.

To avoid confusion, it is worth repeating that such moral ripples do not for most viewers seriously disturb the sympathetic, attractive characterization of the heroes of Hitchcock's comic romances. Insofar as they humanize the central figures, such flaws, venial rather than mortal, may even increase their attractiveness.

What one viewer responds to as a winning eccentricity, however, may appear as a serious moral boil to another. For critics with strong political leanings, for example, sexual chauvinism or idleness are likely to seem worse than humanizing foibles. Such commentators may be expected to give more emphasis to the undertone of turpitude in the heroes' make-up, and to reach stronger conclusions about its seriousness. William Rothman, for example, finds Tisdall fundamentally unsympathetic: "He has no compunctions about manipulating the girl of the film's title so that she falls in love with him and makes herself an accessory in his flight from the police. In the circumstances, his refusal to take his predicament seriously is self-serving and callous. We are gratified when he is chastened in the course of the film."[6] One might object that Tisdall falls in love with Erica before she falls in love with him, and that the tone of the film does not encourage such moralizing; but we would not be denying the partial validity of Rothman's point. Though for most viewers he is overemphasizing a minority mood, such moods are manifestly present in Hitchcock's films and only need to be treated tactfully in discussion. Part of the definition of tact, of course, depends upon the critic's personal, critical, and political dispositions.

One reason for such minority moods as that which Rothman emphasizes may be found in the fact that Hitchcock's films, even the most lighthearted of them, chronicle the events of an imperfect world. The best characters show least of their original inheritance of sin and shortcoming, but they cannot be exempt from it. (As Mark admits to Marnie, "I never said I was perfect.") Because Hitchcock's fables of love and innocence take place after The Fall, his heroes must stray to find the right way, and his audience will discover something of itself both in his most genial protagonists and in his most debased villains. Nothing human is foreign to Hitchcock's movies.

Despite their defects, Hannay, Tisdall, Barry Kane, and John Robie appear a bit larger and better than ordinary people. While sharing our deficiencies they exaggerate our virtues. All act with a decisiveness untroubled by self-doubt or ambiguity of perception. All have extraordinary courage. Hannay and Kane immediately understand why they must expose the spies and set after them; Tisdall decides with little hesitation to escape because, as he tells Erica, he knows that he is innocent; the moment Robie sees approaching police, he arranges the props that will allow him to avoid them and to pursue the proof of his innocence.

[6] William Rothman, *Hitchcock—The Murderous Gaze* (Cambridge, Mass.: Harvard University Press, 1982), p. 128.

The straightforward self-confidence of these characters is linked to their refusal to take anything too seriously. This self-deprecating gaiety, their most engaging quality, holds pain and destruction at a distance—as if the world's nightmares can hurt us only when we grant them power. The heroes of Hitchcock's comic romances preserve a universe in which their adversaries are intruders who must eventually be expelled. (The Laurel and Hardy fairy-tale allegory called *The March of the Wooden Soldiers* serves as a pleasantly clear pattern for such action, with its army of life-sized Christmas toys repelling an invasion of demonic gremlins.)

The youthful high spirits of these figures joins with an inventive imagination that, appealing in itself, inspires their stratagems for escapes and pursuits while it expresses their irrepressible exuberance. Hitchcock's romantic heroes are the most successful and surprising of the "screenwriters within the movie" who propel his narratives to their happy conclusions. In the course of *The 39 Steps*, Hannay casts himself as an adulterer trying to escape a husband's vengeance, a motor mechanic looking for work in the Scottish countryside, a marcher in a salvation army parade, a political orator, and a lover. The last role fails him when he first tries to play it with Pamela, but retakes achieve more success. Making his escape into a passing crowd, Tisdall uses his lawyer's glasses for disguise. Later he plays Erica's "young man" and Old Will's mate in his continuing flight, and he calls himself, with an abundance of creative energy, both "Beechcroft Manningtree" and "Beechtree Manningcroft." Barry Kane takes the alias of Mason, manages one escape by playing lover to an emphatically unwilling Pat, improvises the auction of Mrs. Sutton's bracelet, and convinces his enemies that he is one of them—thanks to a thoroughly overcooked performance as "the-fugitive-saboteur-on-the-brink-of-hysteria." Robie reassumes his identity of The Cat, a role no longer true for him, in order to catch whoever has resurrected that criminal fiction at his expense. En route to clearing himself, he too stages a series of playlets: Robie the suicide, Robie the lumberman, Robie at the costume ball.

The status of his heroes as casual artists has a good deal to do with the meditations upon his own art that Hitchcock incorporated into most of his films. That theme constitutes a chief point of focus for Rothman's *Hitchcock—The Murderous Gaze*. It is also part of the thematic pattern, which I will return to, of conspicuous artificiality in Hitchcock's romances. But we forget one of its most important functions if we fail to observe its power to characterize his protagonists as resourceful, fertile in invention, and, most alluringly, playful.

The heroines share this playful inventiveness with the men who win them—especially after they are won. In *The 39 Steps*, Pamela's sense of humor, her responsiveness to Hannay's droll representations of himself as a bloody murderer, first signal her affection for him and the possibility that she might aid rather than impede him. Erica's sense of the comic shows itself at the beginning of *Young and Innocent* in her pointed suggestion—when Tisdall reacts too ardently to her first aid— that the police revive him with brandy the next time he faints. She collaborates with him in trying to deceive her aunt during the birthday party, and she plays leading roles at Tom's Hat and, with Old Will, at the Grand Hotel. Pat's profession as a model foreshadows, in *Saboteur*, her dramatic aptitude. Ironically, she first uses her acting ability in an attempt to turn Barry over to the police. Her great scene as Barry's ally, however, is staged in the torch of the Statue of Liberty, when she stalls Fryc by pretending to be a shop girl on vacation. Her inventiveness matches Barry's in his earlier performances. During the elaborate costume ball trap that ends *To Catch a Thief*, Francie collaborates in the deceptions that lead to Danielle's exposure.

In addition to resourcefulness and high spirits, the central lovers share a personal generosity that shows itself as a capability for self-sacrifice. These qualities unite the protagonists and distinguish them sharply from the selfish, possessive antagonists.

The altruism of good love and the violent egotism of wicked passion contrast most vividly in *Young and Innocent*. The histrionics of the opening scene show love transformed into a possession—in both senses of the word, ownership and dark obsession. The thunder, lightning, and crashing waves outside echo the shouting of the enraged man and woman. At issue are will ("I'll shout if I want to, who's to prevent me from shouting!"), domain ("You're not going to get rid of me with your silly Reno divorce; you're my wife"), and sexual jealousy ("I'm not going to have any *boys* hanging round"). This diseased love ends in death, with the woman strangled and Robert Tisdall mistakenly accused of her murder.

The rest of *Young and Innocent* will trace the gradually developing love and trust between Tisdall and Erica, and so unfolds as a rejoinder to the characterization of marriage with which the film opens. Devoid of the anguish and anger rending Christine and "The Drummer Man," the relationship of the two young lovers inspires in them mutual protectiveness. Their eccentric courtship begins when Erica (rather roughly, to be sure) revives Tisdall, who has fainted from the strain of interrogation and from the shock of learning that Christine's will provides him an incriminating 1,200 pounds. At their next meeting, Tisdall comes to Erica's aid by pushing her car to a petrol station. She

returns the favor by leaving him concealed at the mill and later returning to bring him food. So it goes. The crucial clue, which will solve the
murder and exonerate Tisdall, emerges at a moment of self-sacrifice,
when Robert announces to Erica that he plans to turn himself in and
asks her to "tell them that I forced you into it."

Only once, but then most revealingly, are the two kinds of love in
Young and Innocent set explicitly in opposition. This occasion arises
during the birthday party sequence when the little boy Harold starts
to read a "motto" that goes, "love calls but once though passion oft."
(He is cut off at that point by Erica's officiously prudish aunt.) Harold's motto, broadly understood, expresses the central thematic conflict not only of *Young and Innocent* but of most of Hitchcock's work.
From *The Pleasure Garden* and *The Lodger*, through the great films of
the next four decades, to *Frenzy* and *Family Plot*, the conflict between
true, ego-annihilating love (which retains a great deal of healthy eroticism) and the mistrustful sexual greed of "passion" unfolds at the center of almost every film.

Even a movie like *Rope*, whose thematic concerns appear overwhelmingly social, contrasts the love of Ken, Jennifer, and the dead
David with the mania for control that Brandon directs in the name of
affection toward Philip. The motive for the choice of David as "inconsequential victim," moreover, appears to lie in Brandon's past rejection
by Jennifer. Brandon's murder of David and his efforts to bring Ken
and Jennifer back together reassert his control over her life. Like Cain,
he is not—as he says—his brother's keeper. He is rather like his Biblical
counterpart, his envious appropriator. And his sister's as well. (His
name recalls the brand of, or on, Cain and so invokes his Biblical archetype also.) True love fuses the faith, hope, and charity of the New
Testament without removing the sexual voltage that gives it life and
exuberance. "Passion" is a distorted form of the same human energy,
but it corrupts and enslaves where love purifies and enlarges.

In both *The 39 Steps* and *Saboteur* loyalty and patriotism precede
love. Both Hannay and Kane begin their quests partly to redeem a
death otherwise spent in vain, partly in response to threats to their
countries, and partly because circumstances implicate them in murder
and they are forced to clear themselves. For both men, the true lovers
they later discover become crucial helpmates in clearing their names
and thwarting their countries' enemies. At the same time they find
mates, the heroes find in the heroines reflections of their own loyalty,
patriotism, and selflessness.

The enemies of love and adventurousness embody not so much their
opposites (hatred and prudence, say) as their perversions, lust, and de-

fensiveness. The antagonists in *The 39 Steps* and *Saboteur* reverse the selflessness of the protagonists. The spy in *The 39 Steps* who is trying to "convey some very vital information out of the country" frets that his "whole existence would be jeopardized" if he were exposed. He hesitates pointedly before the word "convey," the commercial overtones of which thereby get special emphasis. The Scottish farmer at whose house Hannay briefly shelters also behaves, like the spy, with violence and venality. His greed leads him first to take Hannay in and then to betray him. As chary of his goods as he is jealous of his spouse, the farmer furiously strikes his wife when he learns that she has given Hannay his overcoat. Contrasted with the covetous, brutal figure of the farmer are the loving and sentimental Innkeeper and his wife, who forgo the profit of selling a drink to the chief spy's henchmen in order to avoid the risk of betraying Hannay and Pamela.

"Perhaps I can get what I want," Tobin explains to Kane, in *Saboteur*, just before he has him clubbed senseless. The opposition between politics and love is underlined as he continues: "Power. Yes, I want that as much as you want your comfort or your job or [hesitates] that girl." Kane declares for love; Tobin seeks "a more profitable type of government." Hitchcock, characteristically, portrays the perversion of love as manifesting itself in greed, expressed in Tobin's case as lust for power, control, and material luxury.

It is worth reviewing a distinction that I raised in discussing *North by Northwest*: most of Hitchcock's villains retain the human impulse to love, but that impulse has reversed direction and no longer flows outward to the world and/or another person but inward. The world and other people thus become reduced to profits and possessions. The over-regulated birthday party that Erica's bossy aunt gives her niece, the lukewarm celebration that the chief spy is giving for his daughter when Hannay arrives at his house, and Tobin's superficial affection for his granddaughter all suggest public gesture rather than heartfelt devotion.

We see the morbid, diminished capability for love of Hitchcock's antagonists in *Saboteur*, when Barry, accompanied by three of Tobin's henchmen, is driven from Soda City to New York. The trip begins with a brief detour past the Boulder Dam, a target the Fifth Columnists have been forced to abandon. The leader of the three, Doc Freeman, explains that he's become "a little sentimental" about this "monument to man's unceasing industry and, ah, his stubborn faith in the future." He utters the last words with something of the contempt with which Tobin later invests his antidemocratic phrase, "the moron millions" (a phrase Hitchcock evidently used once himself, to describe the public after it had failed to appreciate *Rich and Strange*). Speaking of his boss, he goes on to remark that "one of the things I like about old Tobin [is] his love for that little girl, evidence of a good heart." The spy has children of his own, two boys of four and two, "nice little fellows." But the elder has a passion for breaking things and Doc wishes that the younger had been born a girl. He does not want his wife to cut the boy's hair. "When I was a child," he continues, "I had long, golden, curls." The car moves across the dam and the scene dissolves into a shot looking back into the car. The two sleazy toughs in the front seat are discordantly rendering "Tonight We Love" while Doc Freeman sleeps against Barry in the back seat. The camera dollies forward to a close-up of Barry's half-skeptical, half-disgusted face as he looks at the man slumbering on his shoulder. As the thugs croak "Tonight we glow in the glow, that glows so softly I know," Kane looks out of the window and sees a billboard with a picture of Pat holding a bunch of flowers. "Beautiful Funeral $49.95," it blandly announces.

This transitional sequence, bizarrely comic and seemingly irrelevant to the central concerns of *Saboteur*, puts in the foreground the parodic reversal of love in its villains. Doc, despite himself, makes it evident that he does not deeply care for his children, any more than Tobin deeply cares for his granddaughter. Not only does he wish that his younger son were a girl, but he seems to wish that he were a girl himself. The mock-romantic ride and the serenade by the thugs underscores the element of incongruous perversity. At the end of the song, the status of Kane/Doc as an ironic inversion of Kane/Pamela is made almost explicit when the camera pans out the car window to her image. She is associated on the billboard—as is so often the case for Hitchcock's revivifying heroines—with a bunch of flowers. But for Kane, trapped in the back seat of an auto with Doc Freeman's head on his shoulder, the funeral bouquet commemorates not new life but death. The "Doc" brings disease, not health; and he is neither a free man himself nor a friend of free men.

The relation between love and its perverse mirrors is complicated, in *To Catch a Thief*, by the fact that the enemies of love include, for much of the movie, the hero and heroine as well as their adversaries. Danielle Fousard, the real jewel thief, is a thoroughly possessive, jealous, sexually greedy would-be lover of John Robie. Her father and his gang supply an ample component of sometimes lethal violence. When Danielle resentfully asks Robie, "What has she got more than me, except money," we may suspect that her desire and her motives for thievery are entangled. But though Danielle and her father's accomplices provide *To Catch a Thief* with the usual Hitchcockian opponents of true love, John and Francie are also enemies to themselves.

Until the sophisticated toying with each other of the hero and heroine becomes irrelevant after the funeral sequence, the chemistry between them is compounded of equal parts of sex and money. Robie is interested in Mrs. Stevens as "the American woman with the diamonds and the daughter." The first time he draws their attention to himself, Francie's mother remarks to her daughter, "I wouldn't mind buying that for you." The second time he is admiring imitation jewelry, and the third occurs when he drops a 10,000-franc plaque down the décolletage of a woman at the roulette table. The last ploy succeeds in producing a meeting, and shortly thereafter Mrs. Stevens is telling "Mr. Burns" (Robie) of her twenty million barrels of oil and asking him if he makes "much money at lumber." The imagery of the film generally, and that surrounding the lovers in particular, fills the screen with symbols of conspicuous consumption: fancy hotels and restaurants, expensive clothes, jewelry, fast cars, palatial villas.

An appetite for sex, violence, and possession governs Francie's first responses to Robie. She shows her jealousy toward Danielle at the diving float and again when she and John are touring the grounds of the villa he wishes to case. The language of seduction and the language of commerce fuse as she undertakes her courtship of the supposed Cat, to whom she offers herself as a "new kitten." In order to attach herself to John when he sets out to look at the villa, she proposes herself as guide and chauffeur for "a wholesale rate, and no tipping." When he calls her proposal "too generous to refuse," she replies complacently, "My terms usually are." As they drive along the Riviera, she recounts a life story that is mostly economic and offers the bald opinion that "money handles most people." She denies that she is in Europe "to buy a husband," but there seems little reason to believe the disclaimer. She does not wear jewels because, she tells him suggestively, "I'd rather spend my money on more tangible excitement." This libidinal coin is disbursed most extravagantly in the fireworks seduction scene. There Francie's excitement appears to be kindled equally by Robie's attractiveness and by his criminality, and she assumes that his responses are directed indistinguishably at her person and her jewels.

The tone of all this licentiousness, of course, remains comic, and we can be sure that no lasting harm will come of it. Indeed, Francie is no more dangerous than the "pampered, insecure young woman" Robie perceives her to be, and Robie himself is far from being the "lone wolf" that he supposes. About their frivolity and bad faith there is nothing vicious because there is nothing genuinely destructive. The unequivocally comic mode of the film excludes real pain or isolation. But it does change the identity of love's enemies: greed, idle lust, jealousy, egotism.

Among love's friends in these four films is a class of figures common to most romances: the beneficent stranger. He or she is perhaps most familiar as the helpful elf, fay, godmother, or dwarf of many fairy tales. This figure typically emerges as a spirit of grace at especially desperate moments. Both as an expediter of the action and as a sort of benign place-spirit, the old china-mender Will symbolizes something like an indwelling spirit of goodness in the world. Only he can identify the true murderer. His appearance in dark, mysterious lodging houses, in the old mine, and on moonlit evenings associates him with a world of mysteries. He comes from the realm of benevolent but often cantankerous sprites like those that Hitchcock and most of his viewers would have been familiar with from any collection of English or American fairy lore, to say nothing of innumerable other films. From the depths of the demimonde of Nobby's Lodging House, Tisdall emerges with Old Will, his eventual vindicator and the only character besides Erica who

Young and Innocent: As a benign place-spirit, the old china-mender symbolizes an indwelling goodness in the world. His appearance in strange lodging houses and on moonlit evenings associates him with mysteries.

will come to believe on faith in his innocence. At the opposite end of the social ladder from Erica's father, Old Will serves as the trusting and supportive father that social position and his profession rule out for Col. Burgoyne. He thus prefigures both the social acceptance and the familial healing that accompany the happy conclusion. The Crofter's wife and the old couple who keep the Inn in *The 39 Steps* bring similar help to Hannay when he most urgently needs it.

Because of the importance of an animistic Spirit of America in *Saboteur*, benign, preternaturally insightful figures are especially prolific. Most conspicuous among them is Pat's blind uncle, a modern wood sprite who can "see" both Barry's handcuffs and the certainty of his innocence. The truck driver who gives Kane a ride and helps him to escape the police, the circus freaks who conceal him and whose trust serves to open Pat's eyes, the cabbie who is providentially present to take him to the naval yard, and the other cabbies who respond to Pat's signal for help occupy similar places in the film. Like Old Will, they are all from outside, and generally beneath, the middle-class mainstream of society. But also like Will, they are neither bums nor parasites; they are the productive, anonymous human foundations of society. Their opposites, the indifferent rich of *Saboteur* and the distrustful middle class of *Young and Innocent*, represent not Hitchcock's hostility to people of means but to those who have drifted away from or rejected the fundamental assumptions of trust and fellowship on which society must be based.

Mrs. Stevens, whose lower-class origins receive almost as much emphasis as her advocacy of Robie's innocence in *To Catch a Thief*, has a similar role. It amounts to something more significant than a touch of local color when she tells of her swindler husband and their ranch with "no plumbing, a little thing out back." Such details certify her as both a human being and a fairy godmother. Francie, who benefits from the wealth that falls into her parents' laps, plays a role analogous to the poor and beautiful young men and women of the fairy tales who are translated by good fortune into princes and princesses despite the humble origins of their forebears.

The other helper in *To Catch a Thief*, the insurance agent Huston, has similar credentials. Despite his dark suits and unexceptionable accent, he clearly originates in a class lower than the one occupied by his clients. He is astonished at Robie's villa and much taken with the lunch he has there of quiche Lorraine, which he has only heard of before. His role as Robie's substitute in the costume ball confirms him as the sort of paternal helper that Old Will becomes for Erica and Robert in *Young and Innocent*. The family group formed by him and Mrs. Stevens and Robie and Francie is unified, complete, and harmonious. The "parents" have moved into the monied classes but cannot be of them, however much they may be with them. The children attain real membership in that social stratum without losing sight of, or affection for, their origins. Those origins, indeed, make them poetically superior to the upper-class station they have attained, as if they are at once more deserving of their rank by having partly earned it, and more fully human for being of mixed social blood.

Like *North by Northwest*, the four films discussed in this chapter persistently raise issues of theater and cinema, emphasize internal artifice and ritual, and draw our attention to their status as made-up things. In general, they insist on magnifying the unlikeliness of the tissues of coincidence that make up their plots. This emphasis on their own improbability is especially characteristic of romantic narratives and conditions the meanings of the other reflexive or self-conscious devices that are more broadly distributed in fictions of all kinds.

The second dominant metaphor of *The 39 Steps*, after that of falsely accused innocence, comes from its insistently theatrical imagery. It begins and ends in a theater, and every major character spends most of his or her time playing one role or another. (*Sabotage*, released a year later, gives a similar place in its structure to a movie house.) Rothman calls *The 39 Steps* an "allegory about the condition of spectatorship."[7] Hannay solves most of the threats he faces by discovering and performing roles.

Unexpectedly, a number of his fictions achieve a considerable measure of truth. By the end of the film, the man who pretends on the train to be Pamela's lover looks in reality to be an imminent newlywed. As the enemy of his country's enemy, he is both a politician and, metaphorically, a marcher in its salvation army. In fleeing from the house of the treacherous Scottish farmer, he escapes a jealous husband as he had pretended to do in fleeing his own flat after the murder of Annabella Smith.

Thus the relation between fiction and reality in *The 39 Steps* turns fluid. The roles that its figures adopt or have forced upon them define both themselves and their relationships with other characters. While Mr. Memory unburdens himself of the airplane engine specifications that he has memorized, a line of chorus girls dances in the background. Among its many meanings, this evocative closing shot indicates the inseparability of public performances and private selves. When Mr. Memory dies, the camera dollies back and the police, along with Han-

[7] Rothman, *The Murderous Gaze*, p. 117.

nay and Pamela, serve visually as a curtain that blocks our view of both Mr. Memory and the chorus line. The performance ends, but the joined hands of Pamela and Hannay suggest a continuation of the story even while a visible handcuff reminds us of the episodes just concluded. The house lights will come up in a moment in the theater where a film called *The 39 Steps* has just been shown. Its audience will return to other roles. It may be, however, that they too will retain some reminder of the show they have witnessed and in which they have imaginatively taken part.

The motif of acting runs through *Young and Innocent* almost as pervasively as it does through *The 39 Steps*. Like the earlier film, *Young and Innocent* concludes with a public performance over which it rings down a curtain of humanity, hand-clasping, and the promise of a marriage. En route to his eventual vindication, Tisdall, like his counterparts in other films, improvises a series of serviceable roles: he disguises himself with his lawyer's glasses during his escape from court; he plays a family friend for Erica's aunt; he pretends to be a "mate" of Will at Nobby's Lodging House. The roles he plays, once more, become part of the truth of who he is. By working to vindicate himself, he takes the part that his lawyer is conspicuously unfitted to play; he becomes, in fact, the pal of Old Will; and he will become a friend and more to Erica's family.

Young and Innocent establishes itself as a comedy in part by the conspicuous artificiality of its overwrought opening. Its first sequence also introduces the motifs of theatricality and the equivocal relation between the made-up and the real. Contrary to our first suspicions, what we witness does not turn out to be theater but, as the cliché has it, deadly earnest. Later, at Felicity's seventh birthday celebration, the games are also partly in earnest—as the "motto" and the Aunt's inordinate interest in Tisdall suggest. But Felicity's name and her age promise a fortunate outcome. Boosted by a magician's tricks, party hats, pretenses about Tisdall's name, profession, and relation to Erica's family, the courtship of the two central figures moves toward fulfillment. As Yacowar has observed, *Young and Innocent* is in part about Erica's growing up.[8] Felicity's birthday party is also *her* birthday party.

Saboteur and *To Catch a Thief* depend equally heavily upon pretense. In both those films, as in the earlier ones, false roles modulate toward truth, at least for the sympathetic figures. In the western Amer-

---

[8] Yacowar, *Hitchcock's British Films*, p. 218. Rothman argues in *The Murderous Gaze* that "girls on the threshold of womanhood" are recurrent figures throughout Hitchcock's movies (p. 368).

ican desert, Hitchcock essentially repeats in *Saboteur* the inn sequence of *The 39 Steps*, even to the point of using handcuffs. When a passing couple convince themselves that Barry and the struggling Pat are having nothing more than a lover's quarrel, the sequence ends on a line lifted from *The 39 Steps*: "My, they must be terribly in love." As it did the first time that Hitchcock used it, the line proves to be more prescient than mistaken. The protagonists eventually become the devoted couple that they are taken for and that they later pretend to be in the circus wagon. Similarly Robie, who begins his social interaction with Francie and her mother by feigning interest in them when he is really attracted by their jewelry, eventually turns into their future husband and son-in-law.

The antagonists of comic romances also play roles. The English "Professor" of *The 39 Steps* is neither a professor nor an Englishman, but the agent of a foreign power. The true murderer of *Young and Innocent*, the Drummer, is literally unmasked when his blackface is wiped away. The chief villains of *Saboteur* masquerade as a prosperous rancher, a socially prominent patriot, and a broadcast engineer. The real cat burglar in *To Catch a Thief* rather overplays her part as a young woman smitten with John Robie. She, like all her analogues in the other films, is forced to show her true colors at the end of the movie.

In contrast to the heroes and heroines, the antagonists do not become what they pretend but are exposed for what they are. The fates of role-players for the most part vary systematically with the genres of Hitchcock's films. In comic romances the heroines and heroes achieve their identities by playing out and finally realizing their desires. Their opponents are exposed. Films like *Secret Agent*, *Rebecca*, *Foreign Correspondent*, and *The Paradine Case* obey roughly the same principles, though their comedy is considerably more muted or complicated by conflicting moods. Hitchcock's psychoanalytic melodramas, *Spellbound* and *Marnie*, and a closely related film, *Under Capricorn*, also exhibit this pattern and may be considered in a general way to be comic romances.

When the romantic narrative moves from relatively pure comedy toward a greater empowering of pain and threat, the pattern shifts and complicates. Villains continue to suffer at least a degree of unmasking, but the deceptive role-playing of the protagonists becomes less palatable and develops a more equivocal relation to the outcomes of the stories. Ted's disguise as a flirtatious greengrocer's assistant in *Sabotage*, for example, may strike many viewers as distasteful because his behavior threatens to lead to adultery and to destroy the family security of Sylvia and Stevie. By the end of the film, Verloc's callous egotism has been fully revealed and Ted has become the loving protector to Sylvia that he pretended to be at the beginning. But the cost in physical and emotional carnage has been enormous. The reverberations of earlier loss and pain compromise the sense of "happily ever after" that would, in a less painful movie, dominate the end. Stevie dies. He is ridiculously blown up, in fact, along with an equally cute and innocent puppy. As Sylvia stands in front of a milk company advertisement, her shiftings alternately change the message from "health" to "heal." We are assured that she will get better and are reminded that she has escaped the emotional rot of a life with Verloc. But she needs considerably more healing before achieving health, and her wounds will not close without leaving scars. In *Shadow of a Doubt* the swirls in the pattern go the other way, but they still run counter to the unequivocal satisfaction that ends comic plots. Jack has achieved the friendly relationship (and more) to Young Charlie and her family that he pretended to want earlier; but Uncle Charlie's unmasking has been only partial, and Young Charlie's relation to the memory of her uncle remains disturbing.

In Hitchcock's ironic films, the connections among the various figures and their pretenses tend toward complex reticulation rather than the clear dichotomies of the comic romances. Later I will discuss a number of Hitchcock's ironic films in detail, but for the moment consider the ways in which roles and their players are entangled in *Psycho*. The meeting of Marion and Sam at the beginning of the film involves several deceptions: she is supposed to be at lunch and Sam is pretending to be on a business trip. Marion aspires to a more respectable role than lunch-hour lover; she wants to be a wife or at least a publicly acknowledged girlfriend. With his abrasive suggestion that after the respectable family dinner, sister should be sent to the movie and mother's portrait turned to the wall, Sam imposes a disruptive reality on Marion's modest fantasy. Yet it is Sam who attempts to realize that fantasy later when he writes Marion, and Marion who sinks into a nether world more dangerous and hopeless than Sam's banal cynicism can begin to imagine. Marion eventually does achieve the self-acceptance she longs for, but only at the cost of her life. Norman is both exposed and becomes what he pretended to be—an uncommonly neat trick that may stand as an emblem for the paradoxes and ambiguities that are associated with role-playing and self-realization throughout the film.

This brief discussion should make clear not that *Psycho* is a better or profounder movie than Hitchcock's comic romances, but that it is a movie of a different kind, whose internal logic leads it to develop and resolve in quite different ways from films like *The 39 Steps* or *To Catch a Thief*. In those films, as we have seen, role-playing pervades the action as thoroughly as it does in *Psycho* but concludes very differently. Heroes and heroines pretend to be better or more straightforward than they are and eventually, through the agency of love, become what they feign. In an ironic mode, Hitchcock establishes masquerades that are equivocal from the beginning and become still more ambiguous by the end. He does not distinguish sharply between the pretenses of heroes and those of villains; on the contrary, his ironic films insistently draw attention to the similarities in character and situation of all the central figures. The very ideas of truth and feigning, for protagonists and antagonists alike, grow so confused as to become inseparable. While the romantic films sometimes approach such confusions, they invariably resolve them in their endings.

In *The 39 Steps*, the certified public arena for role-playing—the theater—functions as a controlling image. To appreciate fully the importance of internal make-believe and formal role-playing in *Young and Innocent*, *Saboteur*, and *To Catch a Thief*, we must broaden our conception of public ritual. Parties, music, and dance, all stylized and prescribed forms of human behavior, are central motifs for these movies. The climaxes of *Young and Innocent* and *To Catch a Thief* occur during or just after music and dancing—in the ballroom of the Grand Hotel for the one and after the costume ball for the other. The climax of the personal action in *Saboteur*, though not of its political plot, also occurs on a dance floor. At Mrs. Sutton's ball, Barry affirms, "This moment belongs to me. No matter what happens, they can never take it away from me."

Ritual role-playing in Hitchcock's romantic plots may be thought of as represented or internal artifice. Imposed or external artifice consists of conspicuous technique or other signs of artificiality in the work itself rather than in what it represents. A realistically and unobtrusively filmed scene of characters watching a ballet, for example, qualifies as a representation of internal artifice. A similar scene produced to draw attention to flashy camera work, exaggerated acting, or an intrusive asynchronous sound track—to imagine a contrary example—imposes external artifice as well. As a general tendency in Hitchcock's films, and especially in climactic scenes, imposed external artifice conjoins represented internal artifice. At such moments, a film draws attention not only to the rituals it represents but also to the ritual it constitutes.

During sequences of greatest emotional torsion in all four of these films, the maker's hand and eye draw attention to themselves most insistently. We often casually assume that profundity of audience response correlates with its degree of belief in the "reality" of the art it is witnessing. We might suppose, therefore, that Hitchcock works against himself by reminding his audience that what they are seeing is fictional at the very moments when he most desires to produce intense effects. That conclusion is inaccurate. The rhetoric of Hitchcock's conspicuous artificiality works as powerfully in the context of his romantic films as the rhetoric of a seamless realism works in other kinds of stories.

A film whose emotional pitch is high throughout, *The 39 Steps* has particularly suspenseful moments at the beginning, at the end, and during the shooting of Hannay. We are made conscious of its artistry by its first shots, an unusual left-to-right pan across the illuminated letters of a sign that says "MUSIC HALL," followed by an obtrusively slanted close-up of the box office across which falls the ominous shadow of a man. When Professor Jordan shoots Hannay, startling cutting and imagery—especially two close-ups of a coat hook and a hymnal—temporarily disorient us. Hitchcock's technique at the end of the film is no less remarkable with the striking composition of Mr. Memory in the foreground and the music and dancing girls in the aural and visual background.

The most remarkable technical achievement in *Young and Innocent* comes during its climax in the tracking crane shot across the ballroom and up to the Drummer's twitching eyes. Other moments of high emotion and conspicuous technical manipulation include the comic fight at Tom's Hat and the collapse of the mine shaft. In *Saboteur* there are similar congruences of technical flashiness and climaxes of plot in the striking shots of the fire in the beginning, the beautiful but obviously artificial forest scenes of Pat's uncle's cabin, the chase in the movie theater, and the plunge of Frye from the Statue of Liberty. In *To Catch a Thief*, both the outrageously overproduced seduction sequence and the opulence of the ball with its melodramatic roof-top hide-and-seek provide similar intersections of self-conscious technical dazzle with emotional peaks.

These sequences typify Hitchcock's fondness for representing artistic and ritual behavior and his tendency to foreground his own art at junctures of greatest emotional intensity. The most significant moments of human existence are bracketed and partly created by the frames of art and ritual. Weddings, funerals, theatrical performances, dancing and music, graduation exercises, movies—all weave together the scattered threads of meaning that run randomly through daily activity. To emphasize either represented or imposed artifice does not create a devaluing implausibility but rather signals a concentration of significance—life, as Hitchcock once said of movies, with "the dull bits cut out."

When Hitchcock draws attention to his own artfulness, the effect is not to remind us that what we are seeing is "unreal" and therefore of diminished meaning, but the opposite. We behold an artful condensation and revelation that is embodied in movies as well as in more ancient social rituals. Movies are not made-up reflections that are therefore false, but heightened and essentialized engagement with life. To push on a little further, Hitchcock's films perhaps hint that life itself, or at least our apprehension of it, is very like a movie, with a coherent narrative, constellations of images, and a star who is also the audience. Such conclusions chiefly apply in films dominated by romance. Hitchcock's predominantly ironic works show the opposite tendencies. Ritual and artifice in such movies tend to be hollow or deceptive—to be, as one would anticipate, ironic.

Within the elaborate obliquities and miraculous coincidences of the plots of Hitchcock's comic romances lies another way in which the films draw attention to their own artifice. All proceed by a kind of "and then, and then" structure in which succeeding twists and turns of the plot become progressively more astonishing and sensational. Gigantic improbabilities and radical deformation of realistic laws of plausibility arise regularly, like whales breaching. Such narratives are in no way chaotic or shapeless; they must be consistent with their own improbabilities and use their *dei ex machinae* with elegance—that is, to maximum effect.

As a general rule, Hitchcock's plots quickly establish unlikely but intriguing assumptions and then elaborate the consequences of such suppositions. Suppose that a man takes a woman home and she is murdered in his flat. She is a spy and he can clear himself of her murder only by completing her mission. Or consider absolutely plausible and ordinary behavior that all but convicts an innocent man of a murder he did not commit. Or imagine a man who must expose a ring of saboteurs before they can do any more harm, but who is being pursued as a traitor himself by his own government. Or assume a reformed criminal whose modus operandi had been highly idiosyncratic and whose reformation is suddenly cast into doubt by an imitator of his methods, an imitator too clever for the police to apprehend. Such are, of course, the situations with which the films discussed in this chapter begin, and they are entirely typical of Hitchcock's romantic fictions. Further examples: imagine a cunning madman who suggests to a stranger whom he meets on a train that they swap murders and then kills his new aquaintance's wife and expects the rest of the "bargain" to be kept; or a priest who hears a murderer's confession only to be suspected of the murder; or the birds of the world declaring war on the people.

Having begun on such preposterous notes, the plots unwind much as certain sorts of improvisatory music develop: they are as surprising as possible without ever quite losing the thread of the themes to which their beginnings commit them. Among the typical coincidences of *The 39 Steps* we may count Hannay's meeting with Pamela in the train to Scotland, the fortuitously placed hymnal, the passing salvation army parade, and the indiscreet telephone call that convinces an eavesdropping Pamela of Hannay's innocence. *Young and Innocent* proceeds by way of a similar series of providential congruences: the meetings of Tisdall and Erica, the loose-tongued patron at Tom's Hat, the book of matches in the overcoat, the clustering of all the main characters in the Grand Hotel at the crucial moment in the ending. *Saboteur*: more lucky meetings, first with a truck driver who is later encountered just when he is needed and then with another helpmate who will become a wife; a dropped envelope that proves to be a crucial clue; helpful strangers. And *To Catch a Thief*: a trusting insurance agent, another helper/ mate, a rooftop capture just before the police go home for the night.

Such plots have the audience appeal that kept Scheherazade's head on her shoulders. We want to see how they will come out; more urgently, we want to see what will happen next. The raising and satisfying of our desire for narrative ingenuity increase in another way our consciousness of the fact that we are witnessing a fabrication and emphasize the dexterity of its maker.

Providential coincidences also express the benign purposefulness of the world. They manifest the power for good of both the maker of that world (Hitchcock or his creative persona) and the informing spirit of a larger universe that at once includes and is represented by the films. The little god of the film is good; the larger God of the universe that the film imitates is also good.

Strictly speaking, none of this requires fantastic plot twists. Narratives can turn out alright without miracles. The overriding importance of Hitchcock's improbabilities lies precisely in their improbability. They reverse and refute the dreary conclusions of logic, cynicism, and necessity. As central features of romantic narratives, they oppose fundamentally the assumptions of ironic realism. They lead to clarity and completion whereas the multiple forces and perspectives of ironic fictions create a chaos of causes and reactions that only entropy can halt. Against an impassive matrix of natural laws, Hitchcock's benign improbabilities assert a triumphant protective purpose. Generally connected to the cycles of descent and return, winter and spring, frustration and satisfaction, this gracious universe comes into being through love and the magic that attends it.

The colloquial use of "romance" to designate the development of idealized sexual love between a man and a woman accurately reflects the centrality of the love stories in most romantic narratives. Not only are the majority of Hitchcock's movies finally about love between men and women, but he generally takes considerable pains to emphasize the *improbability* of its inception and development. He does so, typically, in two ways. First, his protagonists usually fall in love abruptly and incongruously. Second, their circumstances and the conditions of the action multiply the obstacles to their affection. Like Prospero overseeing Miranda and Ferdinand in *The Tempest*, Hitchcock takes pains that however abruptly attraction may commence, its consummation will not be so easy that it will be undervalued.

Love in *The 39 Steps* begins with Hannay concealing himself from his pursuers by forcing a kiss on a sedate, bespectacled woman who turns out to be Pamela. (This episode is preceded by some mildly

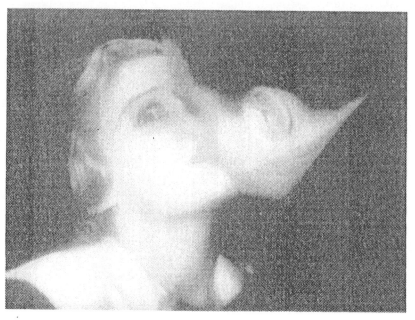

The 39 Steps: Madeleine Carroll and Robert Donat. Love in *The 39 Steps* begins with Hannay concealing himself from the police by forcing a kiss on a sedate stranger who turns out to be Pamela.

suggestive imagery of narrow corridor passages and the train entering the tunnel-like arch of a suspension bridge.) Though she resists his inexplicable embrace and subsequently betrays him to the police, two interpolated close-ups suggest Pamela's less sensible but deeper and finally more significant response. In the first, her initially terrified eyes close amorously and she turns her face slightly toward Hannay's kiss. The next shot is of her hand, gripped by Hannay's at the wrist, opening and dropping her glasses, symbol of her respectable spinsterhood. Her other hand moves langorously and uselessly to retrieve them.

The union of Pamela and Hannay is opposed by obstacles as convincing as the genesis of their conjunction is unlikely. Pamela knows that Hannay is a fugitive (and probably guilty) murder suspect. On his side, Hannay can hardly be captivated by Pamela's twice betraying him to the police. The most obstructive circumstance of all is so obvious that one almost overlooks it: the lovers are total strangers who collide only through wildly improbable coincidences.

The origin of the love between Tisdall and Erica in *Young and Innocent* also comes abruptly and incongruously, and the obstacles to its achievement appear equally great. They meet as Erica is twisting Tisdall's ears and slapping his face after he has passed out. She is the Chief Constable's daughter; he has been all but convicted of murder by massive circumstantial evidence. They are, again, strangers. Though the moment of falling in love is more obscure in *Saboteur*—probably it happens in the desert just before the circus caravan passes—its improbability and obstacles are much the same: strangers, one all but convicted by circumstances of a repellent crime, attempted betrayals.

The amorous situation, as we have already seen, has some complicated variations in *To Catch a Thief*, but it contains the same emphasis on the improbability of serious love. The lovers are more likely foes than mates. Again, they are strangers; again, there is an attempted betrayal when Francie calls the police on John after the disappearance of her mother's jewels. But love in *To Catch a Thief* lacks the prescience that it has in the other films. Francie discovers John's innocence very late, and then not through intuition but objective evidence. Her lack of faith in Robie may reflect his own lack of confidence in himself. Alone among the heroes of these comic romances, he does not seem to believe himself the likely object of the heroine's affection. When Francie announces that she loves him, Robie responds with incredulity. "That's a ridiculous thing to say."

From all perspectives but the final and most important one, Robie has it right. From that last point of view, however, the implausibility and logical superfluity of love refutes ridicule and restores the fallen world to innocence. Love injects its unifying plenty into the lean world of causes and effects. It joins the maker and his fiction in fertility and invention, and it unites the audience and the characters of the fiction in belief and affirmation.

Almost by definition, improbability implies superabundance, something that comes from nothing. For no reason other than that a need exists, a Salvation Army parade marches by or a flock of sheep blocks the road in *The 39 Steps*. The repair crew closes the right fork that leads back to rearrest for Tisdall in *Young and Innocent*. Erica, wavering, turns left. To emphasize the fragility of such good fortune, the crew removes the barricade before the pair are out of sight. From such turnings and narrow misses lives are saved, love created. A luckily obstructed bridge allows Barry to escape his captors after his first losing encounter with Tobin. *To Catch a Thief*, gay enough to parody its own conventions without irony, tangles Robie in snares of flowers for a capture that is no capture at all, as the succeeding shot of him at home makes clear.

Romantic plots and romantic love both announce the miracle of creation that underlies them. They spring into being *ex nihilo* and are finally inexplicable in terms of causes or components. They express the plenty of the universe. In the romantic artist's rich, improbable tales and in the conjunctions of their women and men, the teller imitates the creation of the universe and its continuous recreation of itself.

The idea of innocence combines the sense of creative and recreative energy that underlies Hitchcock's brightest films and is bitterly absent from his darkest ones. All the discussions of guilt and its transferences pertain to innocence in Hitchcock's films, but as a smaller subset of his thought than has been realized. The larger idea, innocence itself, has enormous complexity and pervades Hitchcock's work to the point that his movies may be categorized in relation to their treatments of that theme. Innocence unites the love, energy, and creative principles that are at issue in Hitchcock's films. It is tied to questions of belief and trust that pertain not only to human relationships within the films but to the relation between the film and its audience.

The audience of *Peter Pan* is called upon to save Tinkerbell's life by declaring its belief in fairies. The audience's relation to innocence in Hitchcock's films is not far different. We are called upon to lend our belief to a threatened innocence as simultaneously fragile and eternal as Tinkerbell and fairyland, and as conspicuously unrealistic. The adventures of the audience imitate crises within the works. The central issues of spectatorship in Hitchcock's romantic movies concern the self-acceptance and integrity of the audience as much as the integrity of the world of the film. Such acts of faith require incredibilities much as desire requires obstacles, reascents require falls, or love requires an ardent and inspired vision of the beloved that no one, however perfectly attractive, can ever deserve.

The issue of belief comes to a point, within the films themselves, in the relationship of the hero and heroine. Though Hitchcock sometimes reverses the sexual roles in other films, the comic romances studied in this chapter follow a single pattern. Their heroes all finally depend upon the heroines' belief in their innocence. When that belief comes—almost at once in *Young and Innocent*, less promptly in *Saboteur*, and very late in *The 39 Steps* and *To Catch a Thief*—it initiates an upward movement of the hero's fortunes and eventually the resolution of the plot. The audience is strongly encouraged to side with faith and love, which are on the side of the hero, and against appearance, prudence, and logic, all of which support his doubters and enemies.

The innocence that triumphs in Hitchcock's films—sometimes rather equivocally—is recovered, not discovered. Even at its most optimistic, Hitchcock's vision remains postlapsarian; his films, indeed, often positively embrace the human defectiveness that is the mythological legacy of The Fall. Innocence can know itself only through evil, as life can be aware of itself only through consciousness of death. What opposes innocence is not simply guilt—though that is part of it. The other side also includes a "present absence" of innocence. Such an active lacking may be conceived rather as Milton conceived "darkness visible" as the absence of light. To conclude this discussion of Hitchcockian comic romance, let us examine the crucial idea of innocence and the negations that oppose it.

Love and the achievement of selfhood accompany Hannay's recovery of innocence in *The 39 Steps*. Superficially sophisticated and self-assured, Hannay at the beginning of the movie gives the impression of being unlocated, or alienated. Has he a job? A family? A destination? We never find out. He has come to England from Canada, but the absence of any information about his motives emphasizes his status as an outsider. Why is he spending his evening at the Paladium watching vaudeville acts that seem beneath someone of his evident cultivation? Why does he so casually agree to take home Annabella "Smith," a woman who seems as out of place as he? Such questions receive no answers. Like most of Hitchcock's romantic heroes, Hannay at the start of the movie has begun a change. What he was no longer matters, and what he will become is not yet manifest. He has considerable personality, but for the moment no place or purpose.

As generations of busy moralists have claimed, empty hands and hours are the Devil's tools, and our first view of Hannay finds him getting into trouble. His difficulty begins, predictably, with sex. It is roughly true that Hitchcock's adult figures are either married, working toward marriage, or in danger. The capacity and need for sexual love that comes with adulthood impels either fall or redemption—often, in Hitchcock's movies, both. Lacking a wife or any other stable attachment, Hannay is easily compromised by the woman whose advances he idly accepts. When she is murdered in his flat, he loses, in the eyes of society, his innocence. What lawman would believe the excuses of a bachelor in whose flat late at night, alone, a single woman is murdered? About such sexual misadventures no aura of innocence is likely. The presumption that Hannay has proclivities toward irresponsible sexual behavior—a presumption to some degree justified by his actions—will threaten his safety twice more: first when Pamela decides to betray him on the train, and later because of the Crofter's jealousy about his young wife.

What appears to be promiscuity, however, may more charitably be regarded as evidence of Hannay's ripeness for a mate. The film finally supports this latter view, although Hannay himself is probably unaware of his own motives. He makes a permanent connection with the only suitable young woman he meets, and in winning her he at once regains his innocence in the eyes of society and satisfies the loneliness and sexual longing that are implied in his taking Annabella Smith home in the first sequence.

A good deal has been made of Hitchcock's alleged delight in the discomfiture of his two leading actors when, during the filming of *The 39 Steps*, he left them handcuffed together for an afternoon. Whether or not that anecdote has been accurately transmitted, the episode in the movie itself has a characteristic Hitchcockian point behind it: intimacy, even forced or faked, leads to the growth of affection in normal young men and women who need mates. Hitchcock's is a sanguine view of human affairs. Bluntly, making love makes love. The misfortunes that throw Hannay and Pamela together become blessings because it is the nature of men and women to love each other, especially when the need is most acute. Pamela's belief in Hannay and her affection for him arrive almost simultaneously, shortly after they have first been to bed together (chastely, to be sure). Social approbation follows. Hannay and Pamela, freed equally from their shackles and the dangerous liberty of single blessedness, stand up together at the end of the movie. The forces of evil, at least temporarily, sink down.

Like a great many of Hitchcock's protagonists, Erica and Robert have outgrown childish attachments and are ready to fall in love and establish a new family. Such a moment in life entails its own hazards, and at the beginning of *Young and Innocent* both the hero and heroine are associated with older members of the opposite sex who are inappropriate substitutes for mates. As Hannay is compromised by his casual association with Annabella Smith, Tisdall's friendship with the murdered actress puts him under suspicion. Erica has outgrown her role as child and is occupying the place of the absent mother at her father's table—a role that suits her, but a setting that does not. She is ready for her own table, with a husband, not a father, at its head. (*Suspicion*, *Shadow of a Doubt*, and *Stage Fright*, among a number of Hitchcock films with similar beginnings, present heroines whose personal development has outrun their situation. Their relationships to their parents, especially their fathers, have become slightly uncomfortable. An odd variation of this typical comic opening occurs in Hitchcock's screwball comedy, *Mr. and Mrs. Smith*. Though the heroine and hero of the film have been married for some years at its beginning, their behavior makes their immaturity perfectly clear. Mrs. Smith's officious mother and the staid parents of Mr. Smith's law partner play the stuffy, obstructive roles that we would expect of elders in any comedy of young love.)

Between Erica and her father there is no pathology, but we can see, even in this most benign of examples, outlines of the dangers of being an overaged child. In Hitchcock's movies these dangers have two axes: incest and egotism. *Young and Innocent* very gently hints at the first—in the shots of Erica occupying the mother's place at the family table, for example. Hitchcock signals her transition from late daughter to early wife when, after Erica has more or less openly announced her allegiance to Robert, we see a subdued family table with her father's space conspicuously empty. Tisdall cannot yet occupy the seat opposite Erica, and her father can occupy it no longer.

Tisdall experiences more direct threats as a result of being an unmated young adult. He is vulnerable to the Drummer's aspersion about his being one of the actress's "boys." Less threatening, but also falling into the general category of the hazard of being young, attractive, and single, is the curious awkwardness that arises near the end of the birthday party when Erica's aunt briefly intrudes herself between Tisdall and Erica like an amorous rival. When Erica and Robert escape her during a game of blind man's bluff, she makes a mistake that emphasizes the sexual undertones of her groping, eagerly misidentifying her husband's face for that of the younger man.

Innocuous as these incestual suggestions are in *Young and Innocent*, one easily recalls more anxious, ironic contexts in which they appear less benign. Mrs. Danvers in *Rebecca*, Alex Sebastian and his mother in *Notorious*, and Norman Bates in *Psycho* are darker representatives of what can become of parents (or parental surrogates) and children who do not properly let go of each other. In the band of thieves or usurpers from whom romantic heroes so frequently rescue their heroines, we may detect the sublimation of a clinging family and, in particular, of a potentially incestuous father.

Egotism, the other axis of error, also results from a failure to leave childhood ties for adult ones. This retardation occurs not because the character—physically or psychologically—stays or is kept home, but because he or she turns the capacity for love inward to self rather than outward to a mate. Egotism as psychic and moral deformation erupts in Hitchcock's movies as a prominent defect of many antagonists. The vanity and possessiveness, in *Young and Innocent*, of the jealous drummer combines self-absorption with a juvenile petulance. This combination of childishness and sexual greed may be seen most clearly among Hitchcockian antagonists in Alex Sebastian, the aging mother's boy of *Notorious*.

When Erica and Tisdall win the right to each other, they also rejuvenate their society. *Young and Innocent* is unequivocally a "New Comedy." A young man and woman overcome the ossified imbecilities of their elders and establish both their love and a new social order. Any society whose laws and lawyers see as poorly as those portrayed in the opening minutes of *Young and Innocent* needs youthful reformation. In addition, the lovers restore their world because *Young and Innocent* is a romance and shares with all romances patterns of descent and ascent, winter and spring, sacrifice and resurrection. In the coming together of the lovers and the founding of new families, society is reborn both biologically and culturally.

The curious business about "Beechcroft Manningtree" and "Beechtree Manningcroft" and the persistent visual emphasis on trees throughout the film evokes the flora of the central myths of romance. The most extreme example of such symbolism in Hitchcock's work appears in *The Trouble with Harry*, in which the gorgeous New England fall gives spectacular visual emphasis to vegetative death and rebirth. Though Hitchcock's characteristic comic tone is quite different from directors we usually think of as heavily symbolic, his imagery in films like *The Trouble with Harry*, *The Farmer's Wife*, or *The Manxman*, grows from the same visionary seed as movies like Dovzhenko's *Earth* or Bergman's films such as *Hour of the Wolf*, *Wild Strawberries*, and *The Virgin Spring*. All depend upon the natural symbolism of the seasons and of the plant world's cycle of germination, growth, harvest, death, and new life.

The dynamics of love and belief and the exculpation of the hero also power the action of *Saboteur*. At the center of its plot is the question of whether Barry can convince Pat of his innocence. Upon this, we feel, all else depends. The progress is gradual, and as her belief in his innocence grows, so does her love. She and Barry are, as usual, of marrying age but unmated. They need to establish a family: Pat has only a surrogate father in her blind uncle and Barry a surrogate parent in his dead friend's mother. The frequent theme of dangerous undirected sexual energy has been reduced to the barest hint in the early sequence in which his soon-to-die buddy trips and brings down Frye because he (the friend) is looking back at the flirtatious glances of a female coworker. Yet it *is* that glance, that fall, that leads to Barry's involvement with Tobin and his thugs.

More insistently than in most of Hitchcock's films, the worlds of innocence and corruption in *Saboteur* are clearly polarized. On one side are the faithful and true: Barry Kane, the truck driver, the blind seer, some of the circus freaks, and—eventually—Pat. All these figures in one way or another commit themselves to the unity and improvability of humankind. All act with generosity. Against them are aligned the Fifth Columnists whose views, articulated by Tobin, derive from contempt for "the moron millions" and a cynicism that reduces all issues to unenlightened self-interest.

Because the moral conflicts are delineated so sharply in *Saboteur*, certain Hitchcockian assumptions appear with unusual clarity. One of these is the idea of the family as the center of human solidarity and coherence. Parodies of familial love, Tobin and Doc Freeman cherish a proprietary affection for granddaughter and sons. Mrs. Sutton acts as a bad, fat mother to New York high society. On the other side, most obviously, stands the good father represented by Pat's uncle. He is joined by the affectionate, protective Circus Owner and the incongruously maternal Bearded Lady. The distinction between Hitchcock's true and selfless lovers and his false, egotistical ones extends, in *Saboteur*, to families and finally to the human community in its entirety. "Love and hate," snaps Barry, "the world's choosing up sides."

Surveying Hitchcock's career, one concludes that in general he portrays cynicism and corruption as practically congruent with the political world, regardless of ideological specifics. In most Hitchcock films, humans acting in concert very quickly begin to degenerate into mobs. Three or four seems to be an upper limit for morally coherent behavior. The opposing political sides in *Secret Agent*, *Notorious*, and *North by Northwest* are ethically indistinguishable. *Saboteur*, however, provides an exception. With its west to east sweep of the U.S.A., it suggests that humankind *en masse* may attain the selfless mutuality that is ordinarily reserved in Hitchcock's films for the central lovers. Only *Foreign Correspondent* approaches such a broadly charitable view of political behavior. (It was made, of course, under the same Nazi shadow as *Saboteur*.) Full as both films are of splendid scenes and moments, neither strikes many viewers as wholly successful or characteristic of Hitchcock. It is broadly true that Hitchcock shows humanity as fallen collectively and redeemable in pairs. (Or occasionally in small family groups like those on screen at the conclusions of both versions of *The Man Who Knew Too Much* and *The Birds*.)

Despite its full apparatus of false accusation and circumstantial evidence, *To Catch a Thief* shows that real innocence exists personally and internally, and that the opinions of society are significant chiefly as echoes of private convictions. Such an introspective quality is somewhat less emphatic in Hitchcock's comic films than it is in those with more tragic elements. In such psychoanalytic romances as *Spellbound*, *Under Capricorn*, and *Marnie*, we see most clearly the centrality of personal innocence and the relative unimportance of social certification. Private, personal self-acceptance is also a theme of great importance in *Rebecca* and *The Paradine Case*.

In *To Catch a Thief*, John's adversaries undermine society's faith in his innocence, but the chief obstacles to love between him and Francie are the doubts and psychological defenses of the lovers themselves. Francie has been turned out by the slickest finishing schools, but she remains unfinished for all her expensive education. She needs—as Robie remarks a trifle coarsely—"two weeks with a good man at Niagara Falls." Robie has been pardoned for his criminal career, but his social certification, like Francie's, appears neither secure nor reassuring. The fake suicide he stages for the police early in the film may be a ploy to gain time, but in its plausibility it emphasizes the fragility of both his social status and his personal resources. He too has his insecurities; and he too, as we become increasingly aware, could use a couple of weeks at Niagara Falls with a good woman.

Again Hitchcock presents a heroine and hero who are too old to be under the mothers' wings that at once shelter and constrict them. Francie traipses about Europe exclaiming with exasperation, "Oh, Mother!" but showing less interest in finding a husband than her parent does on her behalf. Robie has evidently lived under his housekeeper's maternal care since the end of the war. Like the protagonists of *The 39 Steps*, *Young and Innocent*, and *Saboteur*, neither Francie nor

Robie has a complete family. This circumstance underlines their readiness for establishing their own new family.

For our view of Francie, however, the absence of her father, the much-missed Jeremiah, presents some complications. Robie is almost old enough to court her mother; Francie is almost young enough to be his daughter. This submerged, incestual *ménage à trois* threatens to break the surface a few times and lends some equivocal resonance to Francie's "Oh, Mother will love it here" at the end of the film. Robie, it appears, will complete the lives of not one woman but two. Yet Mrs. Stevens's earthy good sense reassures us; nothing harmful or dangerous can come to pass through her agency. By his paternal presence, moreover, Huston siphons off much of this potential incestual energy. The completion of the family in the alliance of Francie and Robie reminds us again of the cultural and physical renewal that love achieves, not only for the lovers but for the people whose lives touch theirs.

With the promise of settling down to the trusty old routine of lawful wedded bliss and mother-in-law jokes, the sense of sophisticated aimlessness that has enveloped *To Catch a Thief* vanishes. The recovery of innocence is signaled by the sounding bell that accompanies the closing embrace; by Robie's reascent to his hilltop villa; by the morning after the nights of gaming, seductions, costume parties, and cat burglaries. We have had it both ways. First, the pleasures of Hollywood glossiness, continental decadence, and sexual frivolity; then the affirmation that all this opulent glitter can be revealed as an empty fashion show by the love that restores human reality and purpose to the beautiful pair that we suddenly recognize as poor little rich kids. In their final acceptance of each other, Francie and Robie can be both the humble Americans they were and the fashionable personages they have become.

This acceptance and integration of past and present, however comic and light *To Catch a Thief* has been, contain the point and energy of the film. We see it worked out in far more desperate ways in films like *Notorious* or *Marnie*; and in *Shadow of a Doubt* and *Psycho* we witness the catastrophes that ensue when past and present remain at odds and love and belief fail. In *The 39 Steps, Young and Innocent, Saboteur,* and *To Catch a Thief,* the comic conventions relax anxiety to titillation and longing to confident anticipation. The central issues in these films, nonetheless, reiterate those of all Hitchcock's films: the recreation through love of innocence and full human identity, and the deviations and obstacles that must be avoided and overcome en route to the achievement of gratified desire.

CHAPTER THREE

Mixed Romances

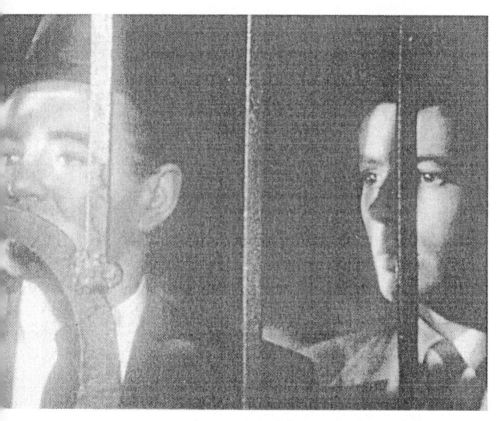

Strangers on a Train: Farley Granger and Robert Walker. Bruno assures Guy that he is "a free man, now." But the image of Guy behind jail-like bars tells us otherwise.

ALTHOUGH none of the films discussed in the previous chapter entirely excludes anxiety, pain, or death, such troubling material occurs relatively rarely and is, in various ways, deemphasized. This chapter considers five films that, taken sequentially, grow progressively darker and more painful. *Strangers on a Train* (1950), *The Lodger* (1926), *I Confess* (1952), *The Wrong Man* (1957), and *Frenzy* (1973) illustrate generic gradations, moving from the modes of comedy and romance toward those of tragedy and irony. With the exception of *The Lodger*, they move chronologically also, but that fact is of no significance; Hitchcock's view of life did not grow gloomier as he aged. *Family Plot* (1976), the last movie he directed, is a mellow, optimistic film. So are *The Trouble with Harry* (1956) and *Mr. and Mrs. Smith* (1941). A number of early films—*Easy Virtue* (1927) and *The Skin Game* (1931), for example—approach bitterness. The five films discussed here illustrate modal variations within Hitchcock's career and not a chronological development. The main point of this book is to explore the changes that Hitchcock rings upon the bells of his storytelling; the consistency and variety that result from modulations of reiterated situations, character types, images, and plots. In the films discussed in this chapter, he uses narrative conventions more skeptically than he does in the movies discussed thus far; but his materials and preoccupations remain remarkably similar.

We need more working definitions, this time for irony and tragedy. What follows is sketchy in the extreme, but enough—I hope—for present purposes. I have already roughed in general concepts of romance and comedy; irony and tragedy are their generic opposites. We may visualize what Frye calls the four proto-genres as defining the axes of Cartesian coordinates.

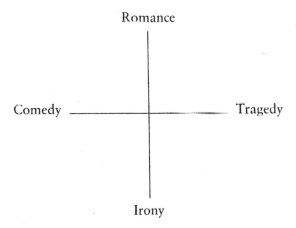

Tragedy opposes comedy as irony opposes romance. Comedies move their heroes toward social integration and the renewal promised by marriage; tragedies, on the contrary, progressively isolate their heroes, break up existing relationships between people, and end in death. Tragedy is driven by fate and necessity; comedy thrives on surprising coincidence. Tragic plots typically move by recognitions of one kind or another; comic stories frequently remain in motion thanks to the preposterous logical obtuseness of otherwise competent characters. The incidental, harmless, reassuring humor of comedy becomes scarcer and/or more threatening as works move toward tragedy. Most obviously, comedies end happily, tragedies in catastrophe.

As regards characterization, tragic heroes tend to be greater and more august than ordinary humans; they emanate a sense of high seriousness. Comic protagonists are characteristically "like us." They have ordinary capacities and express the wry truth that they are neither strong nor clever enough to control a complicated, powerful world. The more formidable heroes of tragedy present a sober version of the same theme: at its greatest, humankind can oppose but not overcome, glimpse but not understand, the overwhelming *logos* of the universe.

I need to recapitulate briefly the oppositions that define the tensions between irony and romance. Romance establishes a universe in which time cycles and rejuvenates: night comes around to day, winter to spring, age (often through progeny) to youth. Ironic time appears linear and unprogressive, entropic, neither returning to origins nor getting anywhere new. The adventures of Persephone and Demeter delineate a kernel myth for romance. The endlessly repeated bafflement and frustration of Sisyphus or Ixion may serve as pattern for ironic fictions.

Innocence is finally empowered in romance; irony succumbs to a cynicism in which corruption and the conqueror worm consume all that is good and fertile. The blacks and whites of romance turn to subtler grays in ironic characterization; opposed moral and intellectual issues, also, tend to run together. Structurally, ironic narratives do not so much conclude as simply stop or break off. Romance closes on roaring tonic chords, while ironic fictions dwindle away on subdominants. Knowledge leads to truth and clarity in romance; in ironic fictions, increasing information breeds increasing bewilderment. Romantic miracles are gracious; ironic coincidences mean.

As a little application of these general characteristics will make evident, most narratives contain elements of all four of the proto-genres. Two, one from each pair, usually dominate. They are experienced as complementary: comic romance, tragic irony, ironic comedy, and so on. The other elements will usually create tension within the work. In a comic romance, for example, tragic and ironic aspects will be felt as countermovements. Works may be poised near the balance point of either the vertical or the horizontal generic axis, or—more rarely— near the center of both. In any work that is relatively "undecided" between either tragedy and comedy or irony and romance, we may expect to encounter perfusive formal tension. About such works, predictably, we will often find deep and broad critical disagreement.

Rear Window, for example, unequivocally comic in its plot structure and only a little less so in characterization, hovers at the same time between irony and romance. Life's troubles, both for the main characters and for the echoic couples scattered about the other apartments, seem to be resolved by marriage. Yet marriage, in some cases, leads to new troubles. A woman and a man become one . . . but not entirely. As Jeffries dozes off, Lisa reads *Beyond the High Himalayas*. Then, perceiving herself unwatched, she puts it down for *Harper's Bazaar*. Jeffries snoozes peacefully, his insomnia cured, the temperature of the world returned to normal. But now he has two broken legs instead of one. The childless couple has a new dog, Miss Lonelyhearts and the composer have started a friendship, Miss Torso's Stanley has returned from the army. But the newlyweds have begun to quarrel, and Stanley seems more interested in Miss Torso's refrigerator than in her. The prospect of marriage between Lisa and Jeffries is shadowed by the memory of the man and woman who became Mr. and Mrs. Lars Thorwold.[1]

An image early in the movie anticipates the tension between the clarity of romance and the ambiguity of irony. After surveying the awakening block of apartments, the camera returns to Jeffries and pans over his broken leg, smashed camera, and the picture that resulted from his dangerous trackside photography. It then stops for a moment on a negative close-up, framed in a light-box, of a female model. From there it moves to the positive image of the same photograph on the cover of a fashion magazine. (Jeffries obviously can do the stay-at-home studio work that throughout the movie Lisa will try to persuade him to do.) These images, the picture and its negative, are at once identical and opposite to each other. Irreconcilably different, they reflect the same reality and are also, in a way, mutually defining. The experience of truth and falsehood, or of sympathy and repugnance, in *Rear Window* will be as clearly opposed and as closely related as the negative and its positive print. For Hitchcock's ironic films in general, this pair of im-

[1] David Bordwell, in *Narration in the Fiction Film* (Madison, Wis.: University of Wisconsin Press, 1985), p. 44, discusses the ambiguities of the ending in similar terms.

ages serves as a pattern for the way in which opposites refuse to stay in unequivocal opposition but implicate each other and complicate audience responses.

Strangers on a Train

Of the five films that constitute the main subject of this chapter, *Strangers on a Train* retains most fully the spirit of comic romance that presided over the movies discussed in Chapters One and Two. It ends with the exoneration of a falsely accused innocent and with his marriage. But that marriage comes at the cost of a murder, a grisly strangling that leaves considerable anxiety to dilute the joy of its conclusion. The sense of a reintegrated society arising around the newlyweds is also considerably diminished. The extended embrace of full comic resolution is prevented by the separation of Guy (Farley Granger) and Ann (Ruth Roman) at the moment of Guy's vindication.

There is, indeed, a nervous privatism about this movie that isolates Guy almost continuously. People in groups—at the carnival, the Senator's party, the tennis matches—appear indifferent to and thoroughly detached from the hero's struggles. Predatory and on the make, they do not promise sympathy or aid but threaten scandal and punishment. Guy spends most of *Strangers on a Train* hiding from society, sneaking around in the darkness of his dreadful knowledge.

He relates to individuals with only slightly more assurance. The sense of obliquity that imagery and cross-cutting establish in the opening movement of the film obtrudes into all Guy's friendships. Even with Ann, he remains curiously diffident. One critic has attributed his constraint to Ruth Roman's "dry and awkward nonacting," but that may be uncharitable.[2] Guy brings to most of his encounters with other people a defensive formality. The scenes with Ann have little more awkwardness than any others in which Guy is called upon to show some feeling. He does react to Bruno (Robert Walker) and Miriam, but only because they penetrate Guy's shell by assaulting him violently enough to shatter it.

Left to himself, Guy seems most comfortable with clearly defined, public, friendly but superficial relationships: on the tennis court, with the detectives assigned to keep him under surveillance, or with "the people" who are his future father-in-law's constituents: "When I'm through with tennis, I'm going into politics." The imposing, insistent

---

[2] Donald Spoto, *The Art of Alfred Hitchcock* (Garden City, N.Y.: Doubleday, 1979), p. 219.

background imagery of Washington's public edifices underscores Guy's rather distant, austere mien. Like the buildings, he has notable stature and solidity but little warmth. In the last sequence, when Guy and Ann leave the Capitol, we have the sense that the stony Guy may be softening into flesh. His rejection of an inquisitive clergyman may indicate a turning from public interactions with fans and other casual acquaintances to the intensity of the private relationship of love.

I do not wish to distort the movie in service of my point. Guy does move from a condition lonelier than being single to marriage and the establishing of a family. On the verge of arraignment for murder throughout most of the film, he is acknowledged as innocent at its end. But just as the prominence given to Guy's murderous desires shortens his mortal distance from the crime, his stiffness and reticence reduce our sense of his social reintegration. In contrast to the garrulous, lively heroes of the comic romances we have looked at so far, his reserve is striking. Such a restrained protagonist leaves the antic muse a bit subdued.

Other comic elements in *Strangers on a Train* are reduced or complicated also, mostly because its incidence of real suffering and anxiety excludes much of the humor that depends on the invulnerability of a hero who carries his friendly world with him. Its comic byplay leans toward the grotesque or the dangerously crazy: Bruno breaking a juvenile cowboy's balloon, his mother playing a loony hostess to Ann, the police idiotically firing at Guy and killing the merry-go-round operator. Yet the final impression of most viewers, I suspect, will be that the movie remains at bottom a comedy, however odd its sense of humor.

That final impression derives largely from its tall-tale exuberance, its artistic playfulness. Hitchcock's self-indulgent razzle-dazzle gives us the distance we need to laugh at what we might otherwise find painful or shocking. The world of *Strangers on a Train* may not be benign, but the universe that includes its maker and its enthralled audience is. The movie showcases an endlessly resourceful storyteller who lets us watch him slip out of one self-created impasse after another, beginning with the preposterous opening premise of the narrative. One need only suffer through the grinding claustrophobia of the novel on which the film is based to understand with what relative gaiety and relaxation Hitchcock treats the same materials.

The director flaunts his manipulativeness unapologetically near the end of the film in the sequence that cross-cuts between Guy's excruciatingly prolonged tennis match and Bruno's journey to plant Guy's incriminating monogrammed lighter at the amusement park. This scquence turns the movie into the sort of melodramatic cliffhanger that leaves us likelier to hiss the filmmaker than the villain. The outrageous contrivances with which Hitchcock pretends to generate suspense amuse us by their transparency, and in doing so they assure us that everything will turn out safely for the sympathetic characters. The foolishness, Hitchcock reminds us, is only a movie. Surely nobody squeezing such elaborate fun from a few sets of tennis and a dropped cigarette lighter could let his hero be hanged for a murder he did not commit.

Such inventive elongating of the story brings us to a point characteristic of romance, with its love of elaborately unrolling adventures. *Strangers on a Train* is amply stocked, as well, with the other apparatus of romantic narratives. In analyzing those aspects of the movie, however, we begin to see what will become more evident in darker, more ironic films. With the thinning of the comic broth comes a shift in the relative importance of various romantic elements. The power and prominence of the demonic increase. The more heartening conventions—ascents to truth and love, helpful elfin denizens, marvelously lucky coincidences—diminish in importance, disappear, or return as parodies. The assault upon innocence by experience intensifies. The power of faith to resist cynicism diminishes, while miracles of grace provided by the kindly spirit of a romantic world turn with increasing frequency into ironic reversals that suggest an environment indifferent to human pleasure or pain. *Frenzy* depends so heavily on such reversals that it is no longer accurate to call that film a romance at all. It is not a study in despair, but its romantic gestures occur largely to be mocked. Its innocence has been forced to retreat to eccentric pockets of order and calm in a world polluted by a craziness more sinister than comic.

Less tormented than *Frenzy*, *Strangers on a Train* nonetheless shifts its romantic conventions partly toward irony. Extremely low camera placements in the opening sequence prepare us for a film that will take place largely in a subterranean world of anxiety and nightmare. The credits run over a scene looking back from the inside of a cavernous train station to the brightness of the world outside. As they end, a cab turns into the entrance. It disgorges Bruno, or more accurately, Bruno's garish shoes and trouser legs. A second cab pulls up at the dark curb and unloads Guy's legs, feet, and tennis racquets. The film begins with a movement into darkness from which it will return only at the very end. The next to last sequence brings more dangerous feet, the plunging hooves of the carousel horses that run amok and threaten to trample Guy as he struggles with Bruno.

As the action of guilt and entrapment commences, images of descent and imprisonment proliferate. The camera stays at knee level for a minute and a half after the credits, until Bruno's foot and Guy's bump under a table in the lounge car. This opening sequence includes an expressive shot of the shadow of the train proceeding along the intersecting and diverging tracks of the railyard. Like the tracking crane shot after Joe Maloney's funeral in *Family Plot*, the image of the converging rails at the beginning of *Strangers on a Train* serves as an emblem of the plot, in which characters in a chaos of unconnected human lives coincidentally converge and collide, turn apart, and pursue crucial actions in parallel.

The railway tracks also establish the importance of the visual motif of strong parallel lines. The first shots of Bruno and Guy together are full of verticals and horizontals that will, as the film progresses, become increasingly associated with threats of entrapment and imprisonment—like the shadows of so many jail cell bars. Venetian blinds and long overhead fluorescent lights dominate the train cars. The vertical line of Bruno's tie is ornamented not only by his famous tieclip, emblem of his egotism and his rotten-ripe relationship with his mother, but by a stylized lobster with enormous claws, an appropriate logo for other, equally pathological, aspects of his personality. The tight close-up of his tie and tieclip includes also his index finger and the vertical stripes of his suit. It anticipates in one image much of what we will learn of him in the rest of the movie

Images of descent and stripes continue. Since the insane, satanic Bruno serves as the motive force for destruction in the film, he attracts much of the subterranean imagery. We twice view him from the feet up: first at the end of his lunch with Guy, and again at the climax of the story when Bruno is trying to kick loose Guy's hold on the merry-go-round. In the first shot, telephone poles flash by outside the train. The second is intercut with the bright, flashing stripes of the underside of the carousel as a carnival worker crawls beneath it.

After Guy has left his lighter behind, Bruno sinks almost out of sight behind the litter of dishes as he contemplates Guy's provocative "gift." (The notion that Guy forgot the lighter with subconscious intent seems to me ingenious but finally unsupported by the film.) Two overhead shots of Bruno later in the film further encourage our impression of him as a denizen of the underworld. In the first, he sits at a bus stop across from Miriam's house, waiting to stalk her. The second follows him into the carnival grounds when he returns to plant Guy's lighter at the murder scene. This shot differentiates Bruno from Guy, who enters by the same gate a few minutes later and is photographed entirely from eye level.

Whereas overhead camera angles and images of descent identify Bruno as a creature of the lower world, in Guy's case they have slightly different function. He attracts such imagery when he is put under duress by forces of evil—usually represented by Bruno. The high-angle establishing shot of Metcalf and the subsequent shots of its shadowy train station anticipate the vicious interview Guy will have with Miriam. The darkness of the telephone booth from which he calls Ann afterward confirms that he has been seized by the powers of blackness, both those attacking him from outside and those awakened within him. The same gloomy station, telephone booth, and overhead shot will frame Bruno when he arrives the next day to murder Guy's burdensome wife. As he unwraps the luger Bruno has sent him, Guy is visually pushed down by an extreme high-angle shot that recalls Bruno lurking at the bus stop. Guy is photographed from a similar angle as he sneaks down the fire escape of his apartment en route to the Anthony mansion.

Intensely slanted shots prefigure Guy's assault by demonic powers as he approaches his apartment just before Bruno tells him of Miriam's murder. As Bruno relates his killing of Guy's estranged wife, the symbolic significance of the stripe motif becomes nearly explicit. Guy is progressively implicated both by the dialogue ("You're the one who benefits, Guy") and by reverse shots from Bruno's side of an iron fence that make Guy, as well as Bruno, appear to be incarcerated. When a police car pulls up, Guy joins Bruno in the darkness. In three-quarters profile, they watch anxiously, side by side behind the fence. Bruno has assured Guy that he is "a free man, now." But the image of Guy through jail-like bars, his face cut in half vertically by a line of a black shadow, tells us otherwise.

A multitude of shots reiterates this prison bar symbolism. Among the more notable are the banister spindles and the striped shadow on the stairs in the Anthony house. A suggestive dissolve superimposes a police sergeant's stripes on a close-up of Guy and Ann. The vertical pillars of the Jefferson Memorial frame the tiny figure of Bruno as he gazes malignly down. Just after Guy shouts into the telephone that he could strangle his wife, Hitchcock cuts to four lethal vertical lines, an extreme close-up of Bruno's fingers while his mother gives him a manicure.[3]

[3] Rothman notes this compositional motif, which he labels "////," in all the films he discusses in *The Murderous Gaze* and asserts (accurately, in my view) that "it recurs at

Images of ascent or release rarely balance this emphasis on descent and the threat of confinement. The going up to truth and love of the comic romances happens infrequently in *Strangers on a Train*. An instance occurs when Ann, standing at the top of the steps of her father's home just after she has learned the truth about Miriam's murder, says, "Oh Guy, what are we going to do?" A crucially communal "we." But this moment of revelation and coming together has been considerably weakened by Ann's first reaction: "How did you get him to do it?" In a triad of chilly pronouns, an accusatory, isolating "you."

Otherwise, ascents that Guy and the audience might expect to lead to truth, love, or freedom instead produce deceit and the threat of entrapment. Guy climbs the steps to his building only to turn back down them in response to Bruno's whispered summons. He goes up to the grandstand after tennis practice to meet Ann, but he finds Bruno there with her. He ascends the stairs to the bedroom of Bruno's father to tell him of his son's madness and in hopes of finding an ally. He discovers instead, again, Bruno.

The episodes of disappearance and return that characterize Hitchcock's more comic romances also occur with decreased clarity and frequency in *Strangers on a Train*. At the end of the film, however, such a motif is emphatic. Guy finally thwarts Bruno and puts to rest the suspicions of the police during an action full of chaos and panic and plunging horses. In this climactic struggle, Guy defeats his demons. But as his wariness of the clergyman at the end of the film testifies, he has learned that darkness and disorder may surge up at any time to penetrate the realms of order and light.

Guy's vindication on the carnival grounds reverses the symbolic sense of Miriam's failure to return from her earlier journey to the same underworld. The imagery associated with Miriam's murder has remarkable mythological density. In a nocturnal scene celebrating physical appetite and license, passing with a scream through a watery tunnel of love in a boat named "Pluto," the pregnant Miriam wears a floral dress as she crosses to the deadly "Magic Isle." Persephone without a Demeter, she will never return. The famous shot of her strangling reflected in her glasses intersects a motif of seeing and blindness that

---

significant junctures in every one of his films. At one level, the //// serves as a Hitchcock signature: it is his mark on the frame, akin to his ritual cameo appearances. At another level, it signifies the confinement of the camera's subject within the frame and within the world of the film. Like the profile shot, it announces that we have arrived at the limit of our access to the camera's subject; we might say that it stands for the barrier of the screen itself. It is also associated with sexual fear and the specific threat of loss of control or breakdown" (p. 33).

runs through *Strangers on a Train*.[4] It also reflects the distortion of reality in the night world of the carnival and makes the audience watch Miriam's murder looking almost straight down, as if into depths where terrible things happen beyond the reach, or the aid, of the upper world.

Like such imagery, characterization in *Strangers on a Train* shifts toward evil and tends to weaken the good figures who resist it. A high-ranked amateur tennis player and the fiancé of a senator's daughter, Guy remains a larger-than-life figure. Once he realizes what Bruno is and joins battle with him, he resists his dangerous adversary with commendable tenacity. But he suffers more self-doubt than his counterparts in lighter films, and his opposite comes closer to overmatching him. At the same time, Bruno competes more successfully than the villains in the comic romances for the sympathy both of the audience and of the other characters.

Unquestionably insane, Bruno nonetheless has a preternatural energy and ambition that makes him both formidable and oddly admirable. His pain and his desire are not simply lunatic, they are also human, however much exaggerated. He wants to be liked, to be important. He believes that "you should do everything before you die." At the fair, he twice shows surprising physical strength, first in ringing the bell with the sledge, and then when he throttles Miriam. During the Senator's reception he talks of being able to see millions of miles and of "smelling a flower . . . on the planet Mars." He persists in his schemes with a doggedness that would be heroic were it not unbalanced. Dying in the wreckage of the merry-go-round, he plays his role to the very end. Only death can open his hand to reveal Guy's cigarette lighter.

But murderousness is not finally attractive and insanity does not qualify as heroism. Bruno's father's vow to have his son put under restraint has only the defect that it is not enforced. Although Bruno attracts the interest and sympathy both of other characters and of the audience, his lunatic egotism removes him from the human community. Like most of Hitchcock's villains, his psychological and sexual maladjustments get considerable play. An overaged mama's boy whose behavior with his female parent has more than a little grotesque sensuality about it, he seethes with a predictable hatred of his father. For all his arrogance, he is convinced of his own worthlessness: "All right, so I'm a bum."

Within his world of delusions and retarded development, however,

---

[4] See Robin Wood, *Hitchcock's Films*, 2d ed. (New York: Castle Books, 1969), pp. 49-50.

Bruno carries himself with indefatigable élan. Guy responds, however grudgingly, to his homosexual adulation. After punching him in the Senator's study, he straightens Bruno's clothing and takes him to his car with the solicitude of an apologetic lover. The last thing he has to say of him, for all its obvious irony, conveys some reluctant admiration. "Who was he, bud?" asks the boat-tender. "Bruno. Bruno Anthony. A very clever fellow."

The strong homosexual overtones in Bruno's behavior toward Guy have been widely remarked, but his sexual enticement of his mother, though more flagrant, has received less notice. Both are consistent with the streak of perversity that is present in nearly all Hitchcock's antagonists. Although Bruno seems to have a relatively healthy interest in Ann and her sister Barbara (Patricia Hitchcock), both his normal drives and his homosexual or incestuous ones are persistently associated with his hostilities. On the train, he alternates obsequiousness with aggressive intrusions into Guy's private life: "Who would like to marry whom, when his wife gets her divorce?" When Guy takes umbrage at such presumption, Bruno's response is composed of the mixture of deference and manipulativeness that characterizes all his social and sexual behavior: "Oh, there I go again—too friendly." The impulse to attack blends poisonously in Bruno with the ordinary human desire to love. There is also present in his wish for instant intimacy something sad, a suggestion of the pathetic desperation of a person without friends or the social graces to make them.

His murder of Miriam concludes an evening of oblique sexual foreplay that begins when Bruno postures for her like some amorous fowl. He displays his manly strength with the sledge hammer, sings along with her group on the carousel, follows her through the tunnel of love, and finally approaches her with a voice full of invitation. "Is your name Miriam?" "Why, yes. . . ." Miriam's "yes" confirms both her identity and the success of Bruno's courtship. Among the giggling of the other lovers on the "Magic Isle" he consummates his seduction of Guy's wife by murdering her.

His subsequent pursuit of the terrified Guy has much of the same loving/threatening quality. He alternately woos his mother and subjects her to his petulance. After warming up Mrs. Cunningham, a woman of his mother's age, he loses control of his flirtation and half chokes her as he stares transfixed at Barbara, whom his conscience has turned into Miriam's double. This episode particularly clarifies the mixture of hostility and attraction in his relations with women and the importance of his mother in his deformed sexuality. Bruno again pulls Guy into his weird lovelife a few moments later when, in the Senator's study, he responds to Guy's rage with, "But Guy, I like you." Like the embrace of the bear that his name suggests, Bruno's amorousness will crush the objects of his desire who are unlucky enough to experience it.

The other main antagonist of *Strangers on a Train*, Miriam, has transformed her capacity for love into possessiveness. Her sexuality has turned to promiscuity and material greed. She represents womanhood as whoredom, and Barbara explicitly calls her "a tramp." In the listening booth at the record store, she first entices Guy, then takes his money, before revealing to him that she plans to refuse him a divorce. She views Guy as a commodity to be exploited, and she looks at herself in the same way. Unable to understand that her deserted husband's love for Ann Morton may be less self-serving than her own calculating attachment to him, she responds to his threat to leave her by declaring, "You can't throw me away like an old shoe." (Bruno is similarly unable to perceive any but venal motives in Guy's relationship with Ann. "Marrying the boss's daughter," he says, "that makes a nice shortcut to a career, doesn't it?") Miriam goes to the carnival with a pair of dates to whom she adds, she thinks, a third conquest, the pursuing Bruno. He kills her among "the smoochers"—a pathetic, appropriate death.

Strangers on a Train shares with the films discussed in the last chapter villains who turn their amorous energies downward toward possessiveness and destruction. To a greater extent than the heroes of those films, however, Guy is implicated in the failings of his enemies. The resulting "transference of guilt," that phenomenon so appreciated by Hitchcock's commentators, has an important place in *Strangers on a Train*. Durgnat has provided sensible balance to interpretations that conclude that Guy shares the burden of crime equally with Bruno, but the insistent association of the hero and his antagonist is undeniable. They are young, equivocally attached men who look alike, sometimes dress alike, and share age and physical stature. The fact remains, moreover, that Guy benefits from the murder of his wife. Though his degree of culpability does not approach Bruno's, Guy is not innocent in the uncomplicated way of Tisdall or Barry Kane. The blurred line between hero and villain signals a movement toward irony. When villains and heroes become almost morally indistinguishable—which is not the case in *Strangers on a Train*—the fiction leaves the territory of romance altogether.

We may note another indication of a drift toward irony: the beneficent minor figures who confirm the fundamental goodness of the human spirit have largely disappeared from *Strangers on a Train*. Barbara Morton recalls them, perhaps, as does the boatkeeper at the amusement park; but they have little of the archetypal resonance of the innkeepers in *The 39 Steps* or Pat's blind uncle in *Saboteur*.

The framework that supports Hitchcock's romantic narratives consists of an often eccentric quest for fortunes, spouse, identity, and innocence. As its title promises, *Strangers on a Train* is also full of journeys. But its journeys frequently end in frustration or worse; romantic progress is parodied as often as it is realized. When Guy goes into the station, he has already slipped into a world of shadows. He will meet his nemesis on the train; and the same train carries him to his infuriating encounter with his estranged wife. He hails a taxi in order to flee Bruno, but his cab ride proves as futile as his train trip. As if to emphasize the hopelessness of Guy's attempt to escape, the cabbie, when he is told where to go, moans, "Oh no, not there. I always get lost." Guy does not shake off his pursuer. The next shot shows him opening a letter that Bruno has slid under his door.

The parodies of traveling that constitute the main entertainments of the carnival amplify the theme of futile journeys. The merry-go-round, the ferris wheel, and other rotating rides that stock the amusement park all contribute to the carnival's demonic caricature of the romantic quest. These mock conveyances go nowhere; and although they do cycle, they come around not to rejuvenation but to destruction and death. The plunging hooves of the horses on the carousel during the last struggle between Bruno and Guy show the amusement park ride at its most infernal. (Hitchcock had used the closely related image of an immobile plywood carriage near the end of *Stage Fright*, a film released a year earlier, to suggest the same frustration of an attempt to escape.) The one carnival ride that goes somewhere, the boat named "Pluto," takes Miriam across her Styx to death.

Only Guy's last trip back to Metcalf leads to success; but toward that success the shape of the entire film finally points. In the end, Guy gets where he needs to go. His second desperate trip back to Metcalf wins him his freedom, a wife, and a future. The earlier images of failed or perverted journeys do not reverse the significance of the ending, but they complicate its sense of triumph. We remember that most movement in *Strangers on a Train* either leads nowhere or angles downward. In the last sequence, on the train again, Guy also remembers.

Like the motif of the journey, the themes of faith, trust, and love begin to show the strains of ironic tension. Ann accepts Guy's innocence, but first she convicts him in her mind of conspiracy to commit murder. The contrast between her and her more trusting, starry-eyed sister emphasizes her lack of confidence in her lover. Of course, her lover is a married man—a fact that generates the central conflicts and some moral ambiguities in the plot. However rationally justifiable Guy's behavior is, his marital status must weaken the security of his relationship with his technically premature fiancée. Can the faithless husband's lover ever entirely trust the man who has deserted his wife, even for the best reasons? Moreover, he seems unable to arrange a divorce. Can she be sure that he is really trying?

Guy's complicated situation leads to some blurring of the lines between innocence and guilt. Hitchcock insists upon his hero's psychological involvement, if not his complicity, in the killing of his wife. Yet the audience is not likely to grow confused in its sympathies, and any analysis of the film must take into account the rhetorically dominant textures that keep light and mercy distinct from ruthless darkness. For all that they share of unsavory desire and physical similarity, Bruno and Guy remain distinct. Ann, Barbara, the police, Judge Cunningham, and others also have some of the human frailties of Bruno and Miriam; but they nonetheless exist on a different moral plane. Bruno and Miriam belong in the night world of the carnival, a place of desires neither gratified nor restrained. That other characters share some of their impulses should not lead us to conclude that all humans are as tarnished as the worst. All women and men may be potentially promiscuous, but not all follow Miriam's sexual lead. As Bruno points out, we have all wished someone dead, but Mr. Anthony's deranged son actually kills.

Innocent optimism and self-serving cynicism represent alternate responses to common human circumstances and possibilities. Mottos for the opposing ethical perspectives of *Strangers on a Train* may be found first in Bruno's "Some people are better off dead," and second in the Senator's Jeffersonian assessment of Miriam: "She was a human being. Let me remind you that even the most unworthy of us has a right to life and the pursuit of happiness."

The undisguised playfulness of the film's maker helps to keep *Strangers on a Train* mostly within the general area of comic romance. The improbability of the assumptions of the story, Hitchcock's ingenious fertility in complicating and solving them, and the implied assurances that everything will work out in the end constitute the principal guarantees of a fortunate and purposeful world. Hitchcock intrudes ostentatiously in the brazen artificiality of the runaway carousel sequence at the crisis, with all its obvious manipulations of image and audience reaction. The controlling presence is not finally Bruno but the filmmaker. We are all—the real audience of the film, its characters, the images of its world—in the power of an artist whose purposes are visibly benign. He is too clever to let us relax and too kind to let our anxieties go unrewarded by a happy ending. The astonishing and characteristically Hitchcockian climax of comedy, suspense, and extravagant special effects reminds us that everything we watch is made up, guaranteed harmless. But no less meaningful for being feigned. Rather the more so, for art does not stand apart from life but distills it to its essences. It reconstructs reality, to repeat Hitchcock's remark, with the dull bits cut out. It is pure significance. Exuberant about its own contrivances, the artistic high spirits of *Strangers on a Train* tip the balance in favor of a vision that is as wisely innocent as the pleasures of its maker.

That it contains the images of less innocent pleasures tempers, without discrediting, its concluding optimism. Yet that tempering contributes more to our final sense of the film than it does in less complexly textured comic romances. Hitchcock finally suggests that the world and most of its creatures are of the angels' party, but that suggestion sometimes feels a bit tentative. The control of the good party seems precarious, the effective power of its majority a delicate question. When we look back at the movie in its entirety, we are aware that its threats of pain and destruction often demand to be taken seriously. Compared with the films discussed in the last chapter, *Strangers on a Train* has increased its suspense and the multiplicity of responses it encourages. Its understanding of life is a little richer, a little less secure.

The Lodger

The Lodger confirms that the differences between the comic romances and a movie like *Strangers on a Train*, with its ironic and tragic overtones, derive not from the cynicism of an aging director but from the way in which Hitchcock treated his staple materials of falsely accused innocence. Most critics identify *The Lodger* as the "first Hitchcockian" film.[5] That assertion, even though Hitchcock echoed it, will not really bear inspection: *The Pleasure Garden* (1925), Hitchcock's first finished movie, is full of the themes that were to preoccupy its director for the next fifty-one years. It is true, however, that in his third feature-length movie, Hitchcock ventures into the genre of the suspense thriller, a kind of film that he would make over in his own image during the next fifty years.

The mythic subfoundation of *The Lodger*, as of many of Hitch-

---

[5] In Truffaut, *Hitchcock/Truffaut*, Hitchcock himself calls *The Lodger* "the first true 'Hitchcock movie' " (p. 43).

cock's films, is composed of a modern version of the Persephone myth. Its presence, however fragmented and reformulated, testifies to the underlying romantic structure of the movie. The story of Persephone constitutes one of the core myths of romance, and its centrality in Hitchcock's third work foreshadows five decades of variations on its central themes and motives.

Since Hitchcock has reworked the Persephone story according to the conventions of a commercial film of 1926, it may be useful to review the original briefly before examining its Hitchcockian metamorphosis. The daughter of Zeus and Demeter, Persephone is seized and carried down to Hades by Pluto while she is gathering flowers with her handmaidens. Demeter seeks her vainly until Zeus convinces Pluto to release her. But because she ate part of a pomegranate while in the underworld, Persephone is doomed to spend a portion of each year in Hades. She is thus associated mythologically with the appearance and growth of vegetation, especially flowers, in the spring and summer, and with its dying and disappearance in fall and winter. It may be relevant to *The Lodger* that Persephone's abductor is invisible and not able to be propitiated by sacrifice. It is certainly relevant, to *The Lodger* and to other Hitchcock films that evoke the Persephone myth, that one of Demeter's roles is guardian of marriage.

The Lodger changes the actors from gods into humans and locates the action entirely upon earth. The plot is partly obscured by the circumstance that the film starts in the midst of a story that it returns to complete only in a late flashback. The echoes of the Persephone myth are thus a bit confused but remain suggestive. Like Demeter's daughter, the Lodger's golden-haired sister is assaulted, while in the company of an attendant crowd, by an assailant who seems to rise up from the underworld and disappear as abruptly as he came. (This is more or less what happens to Miriam Haines on the Magic Isle.) The Lodger (Ivor Novello) descends into the strange dark world of London—the film is subtitled "A Tale of the London Fog"—and rescues another golden-haired girl with whom he returns to the bright and (socially) higher world of his home. The Demeter figure, The Lodger's mother, has transferred her authority as searcher to her son, and the Persephone figure is abducted in the person of his sister and recovered in the person of his new wife; but despite these and other alterations of the original myth, the outlines remain.

The imagery that dresses the plot is evocative of its mythic antecedent. The ball at which The Lodger's sister is murdered is brilliantly lit and shot from predominantly low camera angles that make it appear to be a brighter, higher world than the dark, foggy London into which

The Lodger descends on his quest. Darkness, as a mysterious hand that turns off the lights just before the murder of The Lodger's sister, erupts to seize the first Persephone figure; the second is carried up from the persistently shadowy world of her parents' flat to the brilliant mansion in which she clearly belongs. The insatiability of The Avenger associates him with the unpropitiable king of the underworld. He commits in the darkness of Tuesday nights his crimes against golden-haired girls, emblems of the light (the flashing sign advertising "Golden Curls" is literally embodied in light).

Daisy, in keeping with this imagery, is generally shot in bright light and shown full of gaity. Her name emphasizes her relationship to Persephone. In this very sparely titled silent, Hitchcock insists upon its significance with a pair of titles that say only "Daisy." At least one of these is entirely superfluous from a narrative standpoint.

"All stories have an end," reads the title that introduces the last sequence. Such an announcement emphasizes the self-consciously formulaic quality of Hitchcock's film, the fact that it is a story like "all stories." As it concludes, the golden-haired Daisy is in her lofty brilliant palace, The Avenger is out of business, and "TONIGHT GOLDEN CURLS" is again flashing in the background, but this time promising an imminent marital embrace rather than murder on a dark bridge over a symbolic Styx. "The End" is superimposed, significantly, on a shot of luxuriant foliage tossing in the wind. Summer has returned.

The presence of Daisy's parents in the final sequence suggests that she, like Persephone, will have to return occasionally to a lower world—not a symbolic Hades but a place closer to the underworld than The Lodger's mansion. That Daisy cannot (and would probably not want to) escape her ties to the "lower world" of her parents is not an especially melancholy matter. Like the sadder facts of the murders of the young women and the death of the hero's mother, the traces of Daisy's origins remain and must be lived with. *The Lodger* retains a romantic core that supports both tragic and comic movements, with the latter becoming ascendant only at the end.

The comedy of the romances may be diminished or even removed without removing the romance. In Hitchcock's films, however, an increase in destructive or retributive elements seems to push the work in the direction of irony as well. *I Confess* and *The Wrong Man* have the heft and dignity of tragedy while they retain their romantic structure. But that structure, as we shall see, is powerfully challenged by an ironic countermovement that subsides only in the conclusions of both films. With *Frenzy*, the romantic and ironic impulses remain in unresolved tension.

It seems unlikely that Hitchcock set out to "redo Persephone" in *The Lodger*, but it is worth noting that the mythic elements of plot and imagery are not to be found in the novel by Marie Belloc Lowndes on which the movie is based; they are artifacts of the film only. At the least, one can say that Hitchcock's narrative instincts are constructed on outcroppings of such mythic bedrock, to which he would return for support throughout his career. In *The Lodger*, as in many of his other films, the mythic subtext adds resonance to certain details—Daisy's name and the foliage behind the final title, for example—and unifies the plot. The particular myth evokes a powerful romantic tradition, which Hitchcock will explore, develop, and sometimes parody for the rest of his career.

The schematic but complex treatment of characters in *The Lodger* hovers between romantic clarity and ironic complication. The contrast between The Lodger and Joe, his rival, organizes the characterization of all the important figures. Ordinary-looking, somewhat burly, and unmistakably middle-class, Joe carries himself with a rough cordiality against which The Lodger's dark, slim beauty and gentle reserve appear exotic. Though the camera is manipulated to give The Lodger an air of menace, most of his actions are intrinsically protective. The scene in which he is discovered with Daisy in his arms after she has been frightened by a mouse typifies his solicitousness, as does his expression of distaste when he rushes into the hall after hearing a scream and finds Joe jocularly handcuffing Daisy to the newel post.

With cheerful self-satisfaction, Joe declares, "After I put a rope around The Avenger's neck, I'll put a ring on Daisy's finger." As this remark and the handcuffing suggest, Joe extends his hunt-and-catch profession into his courtship. When he later puts handcuffs on The Lodger, he symbolically links Daisy and his rival as victims of his assaults. In contrast to Joe's roughness, Hitchcock sets a delicate symbol of the intimacy growing between The Lodger and Daisy. During the scene in which they play chess, the hero and heroine face each other over a small table. Behind the table the arched opening of a fireplace rainbows between the two players and expresses, in contrast to the opposition of the chess game, a joining, a coming together.

Evidently somewhat older than Daisy, Joe is associated as much with her parents as with her. The Lodger, on the other hand, is Daisy's age and has virtually no social contact with her parents, who are suspicious of him. Like Daisy's parents, Joe is solidly middle-class. The Lodger, for most of the film, has the air at once of a criminal and of a gentleman. He will prove to be the latter, of course, but it is his equivocal status as much as his gentility that contrasts with the social clarity of the representative of law and order who is his rival.

We generally see Joe coming down the outside steps that lead from street level to the ground-floor kitchen. There Joe visits Daisy and socializes with her parents. The Lodger's rooms are upstairs and, as a consequence, we usually see him ascending. Daisy's parents seem uneasy in that part of the house; Joe is there only twice, and both times his presence leads to episodes of sharp hostility. Only Daisy appears to be a comfortable and welcome visitor to the second floor.

The association of Joe with downstairs and Daisy's parents, and The Lodger with upstairs and Daisy, has both social and archetypal consistency. If Daisy recalls Persephone, she also reminds us of Cinderella with The Lodger as her prince. The dress that The Lodger buys her serves as a glass slipper, a token of her natural fitness for a more refined world. The Lodger realizes while watching Daisy in the fashion show that she belongs in mansions on hills rather than in unfashionable flats down along the Embankment.

Stories like "Cinderella" usually contain a female blocking figure— a stepmother, wicked witch, or jealous hag. Hitchcock mildly evokes such a figure in Daisy's mother, who distrusts and fears The Lodger and tries to quell the budding affection between him and Daisy. Until the very end of the movie she favors Joe's suit to the point of collaboration. Daisy's father, though he is partly under his wife's sway, seems more inclined to trust The Lodger, and in the last scene he nudges his wife clownishly in the ribs to draw her attention to the embracing lovers. His action pointedly parallels an early scene in which Daisy's mother had nudged him during some amorous play between Daisy and Joe.

Daisy's mother is only occasionally unsympathetic and she is never especially fierce. As Hitchcock moves toward irony, however, the "terrible mother" grows more prominent and ferocious. Mrs. Danvers of *Rebecca*, Millie of *Under Capricorn*, Alex Sebastian's Nazi mother in *Notorious*, and Mrs. Whittaker of *Easy Virtue* come to mind. Perhaps the most interesting "terrible mother" in Hitchcock's work is to be found embodied in the psychotic Norman Bates as his second personality—a terrible mother, indeed.

In general outline, the central figures of *The Lodger* anticipate many of the protagonists of Hitchcock's romantic films at the outset of their careers. Somewhat isolated and under unjust suspicion, the hero is also attractive, unmated, of marriageable age, and inappropriately tied in some manner to family members whom he ought to be leaving for a spouse. In The Lodger's case the ties consist of the memory of his dead

sister and the promise to his mother; but the late flashback to his dancing with his sister also suggests the mild retardation of development
that Hitchcock often gives his main characters at the beginnings of his
films. Daisy too needs to escape her somewhat protracted dependence
on her parents. Joe serves as an early example of a typical Hitchcockian Mr. Wrong—wrong age (a little too old), wrong class, wrong style,
wrong intuitions.

As in *North by Northwest*, most impulses toward irony in *The
Lodger*—generally a romantic if not a comic film—emerge when it
broadens its gaze from its central characters to the society in which it
takes place. The reaction of London at large to The Avenger's crimes
is the theme of the opening movement. In the first shot the head of a
light-haired young woman fills the frame; we see her scream. Immediately, a crowd gathers to gape at the victim, newspaper reporters
phone their central offices, presses roll, and distribution trucks rush
into the streets. "Tuesday's my lucky day," crows a paper seller. Radio
accounts are broadcast and eagerly consumed. A bystander at the
scene pulls his coat across his face and pretends to be the murderer.
(Later we will see a young man play the same joke on a chorus girl in
the show "Golden Curls." Ironically, she proves to be The Avenger's
next victim.) The sequence that conveys society's response to the murder runs surprisingly long.

Why this concern with social response? Part of the answer is the
obvious one: Hitchcock devotes the opening of the film to social reactions because the murders have great significance for the whole society;
they are not represented as an isolated aberration. Furthermore, the
opening sequence establishes the extremes of an isolated individual
and a unparticularized crowd between which the central concerns of
The Lodger lie. First we see the face of a single woman, screaming for
help that does not come; then we witness the social appropriation of
her tragedy by crowds of people whose identities flow together as
smoothly as the dissolves of the radio listeners' faces. Between the solitary victim and the crowds, and illuminated by both perspectives, are
the central figures of the film.

London responds to the murders by making them a source of titillation for the idly curious. Details both in the opening and in later
sequences indicate that the amusement the people of London find in
The Avenger's murders is related to the voyeurist pleasures they take
in fair-haired young women generally. The murders occupy an extreme
place on the scale of social behavior, but the important point is that
they are on the scale at all. The film does not portray them as socially
incongruous acts. "Golden Curls," with its blond chorines, represents
one aspect of the general fascination with fair young women. Daisy's

job as a model is another. The pictures in The Lodger's rooms suggest that golden curls are consumed even in middle-class houses, and their sexy (in one case sadistic) renditions relate them to The Avenger's monstrous obsession. Even The Lodger is implicated. "Beautiful golden hair," he says, stretching his hand toward Daisy's head. The most startling indication that The Avenger's criminal passion has ordinary analogues occurs when The Lodger first kisses Daisy: the camera is very tight on Daisy's face, which is framed obliquely and lighted like the faces of the young murdered women. The concluding embrace between two lovers is also composed to recall the first shot of The Avenger's victim.

Joe's attitude toward The Avenger is determined by both his public and his private interests. From the public viewpoint, as a police detective, Joe regards The Avenger with the amused interest of London at large. He bets Daisy's father that the criminal will be caught before the next Tuesday and is delighted to be assigned to such a well-publicized case. But he has private interests as well, interests foreshadowed more clearly than he can know when he makes his remark about putting a rope around The Avenger's neck and a ring on Daisy's finger. Like the rest of London's citizens, Joe finds The Avenger murders a source of entertainment; and like the newspaper people and the radio broadcasters, he also finds in the crimes furtherance of his private interests. No more than the populace of London at large does Joe qualify as a villain. But his equivocal relation to the crimes gives him the sort of multisided moral status typical of characters drawn with an ironic pen. In discussing him, and the society to which he belongs and represents, the viewer has continuous recourse to "on the one hand . . . on the other" formulations.

Unlike Joe, and London at large, The Lodger expects no personal profit or pleasure from his pursuit of the murderer. Already a victim of The Avenger through the deaths of his sister and mother, he will suffer again in his "crucifixion" by the tavern mob. From the social as well as the mythological perspective, the association of Christ with The Lodger is appropriate. The Lodger's sister is the first, and The Lodger himself is the last, to suffer from The Avenger's crimes. In his dedication to pursuing the criminal and in his near dismemberment by the mob, he may be seen as a redemptive figure, one who suffers not on his own behalf but in place of the truly guilty, the society that gave rise to The Avenger and that is implicated in his crimes. That The Avenger is apprehended at the same time The Lodger is arrested and attacked by the mob underscores the redemptive aspect of the hero's sacrifice. The explicatives in the detective's two titles during this sequence are more resonant than usual: "My God, he is innocent" and "Thank God I got here in time."

Joe, who incites the mob against The Lodger, also rescues him from them. As clearly as Hitchcock renders the contrasts between his central male characters, he does not make either one uniformly vicious or valiant. Not only does Joe in an act of personal and professional integrity save his rival, but he is allowed to attract some empathy throughout. When Daisy returns Joe's cookie-dough heart and, more clearly, when she rejects him after he has discovered her with The Lodger on the beach, we are likely to regret his disappointment even while finding it mildly comic. For all his rough edges, Joe behaves in a straightforward manner and has an unfeigned affection for the heroine of the film. The Lodger, on the other hand, carries a slight stain of the vigilante and outlaw, however just and gentle the main lines of Hitchcock's drawing show him.

The mildly ironic suggestions of tarnish on the hero of *The Lodger* must not be exaggerated, however, or the central themes of the film are rendered incoherent. It deforms the tone of his characterization to argue that "The Avenger is only doing on a larger scale what the hero, the avenger, would do."[6] One critic makes The Lodger even more culpable than The Avenger himself: "He intends to kill the killer, and his crime—not of passion or a deranged mind . . . is a carefully premeditated act of hatred."[7] Such interpretations turn the diffident figure portrayed by Ivor Novello into a revenge-obsessed monomaniac. We do not know, in fact, that The Lodger "intends to kill the killer"; he never says so, and his possession of a gun is hardly conclusive proof of such an intention. To equate The Avenger with the hero asks us to forget that the former is a madman who has killed innocent young women and the latter is the grieving brother of one of his victims. We never know who or what The Avenger is revenging, but we know that his murderousness attacks all people, just as its potential may be found in all people. The Lodger, on the contrary, devotes himself to trying to put a stop to the cycles of murder and vengeance that rose from the underworld to strike his sister and the victims that followed.

Although she appears to be the most clearly stereotyped figure in the film, Daisy's character includes some surprising complications. A golden girl living below her natural station, she nonetheless seems to welcome Joe's rather coarse attentions, especially early in the film. At the same time she often retreats from him for no apparent reason. Her

---

[6] Yacowar, *Hitchcock's British Films*, p. 40.
[7] Spoto, *The Art of Alfred Hitchcock*, p. 7.

readiness for love precedes the arrival of its proper object, and her on-and-off receptiveness to Joe comes on the one hand from her maturing desire and on the other from her intuition of the detective's unsuitability.

When The Lodger arrives, Daisy immediately feels the pull of his attraction. Her prior involvement with Joe and her confusion about her own feelings lead to some intricate choreography. Daisy's indecision about the two men lasts until nearly the end of the film. It is echoed by triangular composition within the film frame and by prominent details of the sets—repeated shots of the chandelier, for instance, with its three glass shades. Medium shots frequently include three figures. The triangles that decorate the titles and The Avenger's triangular logo underscore the broad implications of the love triangle as a motive for the action of the film.[8]

Daisy is both the likely prey of The Avenger and the protector of The Lodger. Thus she is potentially victim and savior; a young woman murdered, or a wife. Only at the end of the film can we be sure which possibility will be realized. She protects her protector and, a revitalizing figure herself, marries another redemptive figure. Fulfilled love in Hitchcock's work nearly always heals and transforms mutually. The gallant heroes who carry away the heroines need to be lifted up and carried themselves; without each other, both lovers are lost.

Without each other they are also endangered. The onscreen murders of the two fair-haired young women and the arrest of The Lodger dramatize the vulnerability of the single and unprotected. The second murder occurs, significantly, after the victim and her boyfriend have quarreled and separated in anger, leaving her exposed to the madman who stalks the London fog. The Lodger's sister is stabbed at her "coming-out ball." *The Lodger* is concerned both with right courtship and marriage and with the dangers of growing up and going out. In *Easy Virtue, Notorious, Psycho,* and *Frenzy* the theme recurs: men and women, especially women, face terrible dangers from the distorted erotic impulses of other people when they are away from or fail to find their proper mates. Daisy and The Lodger have good reason to look gratefully heavenward as they stand in each other's arms at the end of their adventures.

Hitchcock's acute sense of physical geography and equally acute sense of social geography, class consciousness, contribute heavily to the details and themes of *The Lodger.* His famously unenthusiastic

---

[8] Yacowar discusses "the contrast of circle and triangle shapes" in *Hitchcock's British Films,* p. 38.

view of the police appears clearly in this early film, as does his less well known but more consistent demophobia. In a Hitchcock film any group of people larger than roughly half a dozen members registers as a mob—conformist, unimaginative, inhumane. (A curious variant on this pattern occurs in *The Birds*, in which the peaceful intimacy of a pair of lovebirds is set against the mob frenzy of the flocks that attack Bodega Bay.) These themes do not appear very emphatically in *The Lodger*, but their presence does suggest, as it did in the comic romances, the counterpull of a corrupt social mode against which is set the love and struggle for innocence of the central pair.

Hitchcock treats the more conspicuous conventions of detective fiction with obvious playfulness in *The Lodger* and manipulates openly and systematically his audience's expectations. Such pervasive self-consciousness, like similar reassurances in the comic romances, relaxes somewhat the anxiety aroused by the portrayal of corrupt human nature. As the audience of *Strangers on a Train* could take comfort in the playful benignity of the intrusive director, that of *The Lodger* is likely to be at least somewhat aware of the filmmaker's control of his story and his sympathies for the good figures.

Nonetheless, for the first half of the movie Hitchcock relentlessly uses the conventions of the murder mystery to cast suspicion upon The Lodger. As a result, we may be uncertain about who "the good figures" are. Shrouded in fog and masked by his muffler, The Lodger makes his first appearance on the Bunting's doorstep just after the gaslights have abruptly gone off inside the house. His rooms are full of spooky shadows. He behaves eccentrically—sneaking outside in the middle of the night, carelessly leaving money lying about his room (an idea Hitchcock repeats to cast suspicion on Uncle Charlie in the opening of *Shadow of a Doubt*), and making oracular pronouncements about the concerns of Providence. Radical camera angles and suggestive cutting give innocent gestures an aura of menace, and when The Lodger reaches for a poker to stir the fire and when he tries the bathroom doorknob while Daisy is in the tub (another idea, the vulnerability of a bathing woman, that Hitchcock was to use effectively late in his career). The famous shot through the ceiling of the room below The Lodger's chambers casts further suspicion on him.

The conclusion that these details show the unreliability of appearances has been drawn often enough. Equally, however, they show the untrustworthiness of the conventions of the mystery genre. In doing so they emphasize in another way the self-consciousness of the film, its tendency to draw attention to its status as a work of art as well as a representation of life. *The Lodger* gives its audience the sort of image they can easily recognize as conventional at the same time that it brings into question the reliability of those conventions. Hitchcock did not invent this game, but no one ever played it more deftly.

The uses society makes of The Avenger's crimes within the film parallel those that the film itself offers as a work of art in a social context. It too makes of murder an entertainment; it too transforms anxieties into stylized, distanced, cathartic representations. "The technique of art and the technique of life," as Sir John calls this mingling of real and fictional events in *Murder!*, blur and twine in *The Lodger*.

Although the film, like the news media it portrays, exploits the sensational appeal of homicide, it also brings to its subject a personal and social understanding quite beyond media accounts. The voyeuristic eyes suggested by the rear windows of the newspaper van represent only too well the public perspective on violent crimes, then and now.[9] But Hitchcock's film adopts a more comprehensive and humane perspective. *The Lodger*, like many of Hitchcock's movies for the next half-century, is a love story in which suspense and loss occasion resolution and marriage. It is, additionally, a self-conscious narrative turning its scrutiny inward at itself as well as outward at its characters and action. In doing so it asks, in contrast to the blankly staring eyes of the newspaper van, what it is and who is watching.

Hitchcock has complained that the presence of Ivor Novello as leading man compelled an exonerating ending to the story.[10] The changes he made in adapting the novel to the screen bring the narrative into a shape so characteristic of his later work, however, that I think we can discount as superficial the influence of the matinee idol on *The Lodger* as a whole. What Hitchcock changed, and kept, in Marie Belloc Lowndes's novel shows clearly his characteristic romanticism, social concerns, and self-consciousness as a storyteller. The changes demonstrate, in fact, Hitchcock's conversion of a predominantly ironic narrative into one of mixed irony and romance.

The center of attention in the novel, and the source of most of its point of view, is the landlady, Mrs. Bunting. In the film the center of attention shifts to the three younger people; and the point of view, with a few interruptions, is objective. The film adds Daisy's job as a model, an alteration that emphasizes her natural nobility. It changes The Lodger from a sham to a real gentleman and from a murderer to the innocent pursuer of The Avenger. From a few mild hints in the Lowndes story, the movie develops the involvement of Daisy and The

---

[9] Hitchcock discusses this shot in Truffaut, *Hitchcock/Truffaut*, p. 45.
[10] Ibid., p. 43.

Lodger, and it adds entirely the rivalry between The Lodger and Joe. Hitchcock kept most of the details that in the novel eventually reveal The Lodger's true identity as the murderer, but in the movie they are used deceptively to suggest a spurious guilt.

Hitchcock preserves almost unchanged from the novel the gossipy interest of media and populace in The Avenger's crimes, but he pushes the implications of that interest harder. Where the movie remains most true to its course, not surprisingly, it maintains its ironic perspective most emphatically. On the other hand, the flashback to the sister's coming-out party exists only in the film, as does the associated imagery invoking the Persephone myth. Hitchcock's partial maintaining of Marie Belloc Lowndes's ironic perspective, however, and the absence of comedy from most of the movie, shift *The Lodger* away from the relatively uncomplicated comedy and romance of the films considered in the last chapter toward tenser, more equivocal artistic spaces.

At age twenty-seven, Hitchcock showed a remarkably secure grasp of what were to be his central artistic preoccupations for the next fifty years. His conceptions were clear and, more remarkably, richly complicated. He had the self-confidence to treat a popular novel by a well-known writer with extreme freedom. Twenty-four years later, in the middle of his career, he made changes of a very similar nature in the source novel he obtained from another mystery writer, Patricia Highsmith. In doing so, he changed *Strangers on a Train*, as he changed *The Lodger*, from a gloomy obsessive study of the *Crime and Punishment* kind into something very mainstream Hitchcock, a romantic thriller with enough irony for suspense and a mythic substructure that gives it the power to move deeply as well as to entertain.

I Confess

Not much humor remains in *I Confess* or *The Wrong Man*. On the generic axis that runs between the tragic and the comic, these two films rest near the middle, with little of either. At the same time, they are poised between the renewing resolutions and clarities of romance and the endless complications and qualifications of irony. With regard to irony and romance, however, they balance, not in rest, but in tension. Each is full both of romantic formulae and of the parodies of those formulae that power an ironic narrative. From this tension between opposed conventions or genres arises much of what we think of as Hitchcockian suspense.

I Confess gained small popular or critical acclaim when it was released in 1952. Since then it has slowly achieved more esteem, but even its advocates still tend to discuss it with a certain condescension. Hitchcock himself, rarely able to regard affectionately his economically unsuccessful productions (*Rich and Strange* and *The Trouble with Harry* standing as exceptions), has had little good to say about it. All of which is, as Inspector Larue (Karl Malden) says to Father Logan (Montgomery Clift), "A pity. A great pity." It is a matter of taste as to whether *I Confess* ranks among Hitchcock's greatest films, but it seems to me to qualify, at the least, as an extraordinarily significant one. It renders many of the central concerns of Hitchcock's work with remarkable clarity. Near the midpoint of its director's career chronologically, it occupies a thematic position of equal centrality.

The most explicitly religious of Hitchcock's films, *I Confess* develops as its central issue the relation between faith and personal integrity. Divine and human forgiveness, understanding, and grace are also among its deepest concerns. It is worth digressing for a moment to remember that the romantic myth of most importance for Western society over the past two millennia is to be found not in the story of Persephone or in the numberless folk tales of descent and return, but in the continuous celebration of the life of Christ. His redeeming descent from heaven, assumption of human weakness and guilt, death, harrowing of hell, resurrection, and return to heaven constitute the most fully elaborated and explicated romantic myth in our culture. We should not expect then, that by turning to a religious story Hitchcock will change the kind of film that he usually makes. We may never have a satisfying answer to the question of how much Hitchcock's Catholicism influenced his filmmaking, but *I Confess* at least clarifies the analogues between the secular films and Christian doctrine. For that reason, as well as for its intrinsic interest, *I Confess* can claim our particular attention.

The centrality of religious concerns occurs uniquely among Hitchcock's movies in *I Confess*, but at least half-a-dozen or so others develop such issues explicitly at critical moments. The climax of *The Lodger* evokes the crucifixion of Christ. The gloomy, Calvinist self-righteousness of Caesar looms large in *The Manxman*. Millie's sanctimonious hypocrisy in *Under Capricorn* resembles the self-serving religiousness of Mrs. Edgar in *Marnie*. *The Wrong Man* pivots on a turning point of intense religious experience. During the most horrific sequence in *Frenzy*, the rape and murder of Brenda Blaney, the victim recites the 91st Psalm. Explorations of intricate connections among religion, art, magic, and fraud make up an essential thematic layer of *Family Plot*, Hitchcock's last film. Another dozen films, at least, use religious images more casually. Church scenes in both versions of *The*

Man Who Knew Too Much, Secret Agent, and *Shadow of a Doubt* come to mind. *Rich and Strange* has a sequence that ends with a comic bedtime prayer, and it shares with *The 39 Steps* a Salvation Army parade. *Vertigo*—nothing casual in that film—ends in the belltower of the Mission of San Juan Bautista.

From its first shots, *I Confess* invokes religious contexts with images of churches and religious ceremony, art, and emblems. The dialogue returns continually to questions of the inviolability of confession, the sacredness of a priest's vows, and the boundaries of civil and ecclesiastical powers. At the same time, it retains romantic conventions of plot, image, and character. The romantic elements remain recognizable but undergo some changes as a result of their religious context. The extent and quality of the differences, and of the similarities, between *I Confess* and more typical Hitchcock works illuminates both the one film and his work as a whole.

The plot centers, as it does in the majority of Hitchcock's films, on the false accusation of an innocent person, upon whom great suspicion is cast both by unlucky circumstances and by human antagonists. Because the hero of the film is a priest, the issue of faith is not so closely tied to romantic love as in other of Hitchcock's movies; and because he has heard the confession of the real murderer, he has the opportunity to clear himself at the expense of betraying his vows. His hearing of Otto Keller's confession is not necessary to the plot of false accusation, but it constitutes an essential part of his temptation. *I Confess* makes explicit what remains implicit in most of Hitchcock's other films: the quest for innocence has at its center the protagonist's struggle to achieve or retain his identity. Father Logan's trials create and confirm him. Before his ordeal begins, Logan is a priest; but as the nets of circumstantial evidence and Keller's plotting draw tight about him, he reaches a more profound understanding of what being a priest means. Stripped of the assumption of righteousness that his station ordinarily confers, and unable to do anything to establish his innocence in the eyes of society, he is forcibly reminded of his human vulnerability. Logan struggles to maintain his integrity against awful corrosives from both within and outside himself: his own despair, and the contemptuous outrage of his accusers.

Like *Strangers on a Train, I Confess* begins with a descent from which a full return will be managed only at the very end of the film. As the opening titles run, the camera very slowly crosses a river—that frequent boundary in Hitchcock's films between the ordinary and the chimerical world. With a sharply tilted close view of a statue in front of the Quebec House of Parliament, the musical sound track switches

I Confess: Montgomery Clift. Father Logan's trials create and confirm him. He struggles to maintain his integrity against awful corrosives from within and outside himself: his own despair, and the contemptuous outrage of his accusers.

from an extravagantly sentimental love song to heavy, ambiguous chords. The next shot contains what may be Hitchcock's most menacing cameo appearance. From a low position, the camera looks up a long, wide set of stairs. High above, silhouetted against a dark sky and bright clouds, the figure of Hitchcock strides across the screen. Businesslike, oblivious of the camera, gazing straight ahead, he walks into a shaft of light and disappears off the screen to the left. The filming of this unusually early and emphatic appearance of the director suggests that the audience, along with the characters whose lives it is about to enter, has been thrust into a dark and threatening world and left to its own resources.

That impression is partly wrong, but it will not be corrected until the end of the movie. As Father Logan's God, though he tempts him sorely, does not abandon him to the forces of darkness, so the god of the film audience, Hitchcock, will threaten us but not leave us in grief. We can see at the end of the film that Father Logan's ordeal has strengthened and instructed him. We may suppose that the mild reflection of his intense pain in us as we watch the movie may do something similar.

Following the opening credits comes a series of foreboding one-way arrows alternating with shots of Quebec City. The last of the "DIREC- TION" signs points the camera to an open window, into which it peeps to discover a body sprawled on the floor. The camera then passes through the still moving strings of a bead curtain to follow the appar- ent murderer as he walks downhill along a shadowy street. He stops to remove a priest's cassock at the bottom of another hill and continues to a church that Father Logan, from the rectory above, sees him enter. Although the plot of *I Confess* develops more slowly than usual for Hitchcock, the opening exposition has his normal economy. The first ninety seconds contain both the essentials of the crime and high and low shots, slanted angles, shadowy day-for-night sets, and ominous music—all of which firmly place the action and its audience in a world that is dark, hazardous, and depressed.

The descents to danger and ascents to release that we expect from a Hitchcock film occur repeatedly as the story unfolds, but movements downward and angled shots that visually lower the scenes dominate rising movements. An extremely low, harshly lighted shot shows Keller pinioning his wife's arms as he insists that Logan "cannot tell them what he heard in the confession." In the next sequence, Keller descends the rectory stairs on his way to work on Vilette's garden. The irony of the murderer tending his victim's garden is apparent, but the trip to Vilette's house has further expressive purposes. Walking toward the camera, Keller passes a white cross and pauses to look at the church. The shots of Keller in front of the cross and the church introduce an- other sort of demonic imagery that with images of descent and lower- ing camera angles will dominate the film. Ironically placed religious symbols, and similar ironic symbols of law and justice, enlist even the emblems of forgiveness and social order into the companies of venge- ance and tumult.

A few minutes later, Father Logan goes down the same rectory stairs to make his own visit to the house of the murdered man. There Larue begins to suspect him. Looking down on the street through Vilette's window, in an extraordinary shot that seems to give the detective only one eye, he sees Father Logan meet a woman. The silhouette of Larue observing the priest suggests, as do silhouettes generally in Hitchcock's work, an incompleteness of vision. He sees only half the truth. For the other half, he will require not a downward but an upward gaze.

At the rectory later, Keller begs Logan for advice. This strained meeting is largely shot from another high camera that puts Keller exaggeratedly below Logan, who is on a ladder painting a wall. That evening, as the police investigate the movements of Quebec City's priests on the night of the murder, Hitchcock intercuts four low, sharply angled shots of churches. The last and most radically slanted shows the church of Father Logan. As these images continue the visual representation of a skewed and submerged world, they also connect the danger to Father Logan personally with danger to his institution. For the clergyman's disgrace will tarnish the church and shake her faithful.

Significant descents also dominate the beginning of the flashback in which Madame Grandfort (Anne Baxter) recalls her youthful romance with Michael Logan before he began to study for the priesthood. In the subjective representation of her memory, while the extravagant love song first heard in the opening shots of the film plays again, she floats down a curving flight of stairs toward the uplifted face of young Michael. The scene is photographed from below and behind Logan, and the camera is again sharply tilted. Ruth descends in slow motion and the shot then cuts to a close-up of Michael's face, soon joined by Ruth's in an ecstatic kiss. Glowing highlights in the second shot make soft halos around the faces of the lovers.

Ruth's sentimental flashback with its overwrought romantic clichés may make us a bit wary. We may suspect that her memory is composed more of past and present projections of desire than of what we might call reality.[11] The flashback also suggests, with its powerful images of descent, that something dangerous lurks in Ruth's idealistic, emotional confession. She shows a not quite conscious eagerness to sacrifice her present life and reputation for her former love; only later does she seem to realize that she may also be injuring and endangering her husband. More directly destructive is the fact that without Ruth's attempt to clear Father Logan, the police could not arrest him. They lack detailed information and a plausible motive. After her testimony, the arrest warrant is issued. The low, slanted shot that begins Ruth's reminiscence thus leads to the most excruciating stage of Father Logan's ordeal.

This brief sequence exemplifies not only Hitchcock's technical resourcefulness and daring but also his restraint. The slow motion lasts ten seconds, the haloed embrace another ten.[12] Hitchcock uses neither effect again in I Confess, and he will use the haloing effect only once

[11] Robin Wood writes of Ruth's "self-indulgent clinging to romantic fantasy" in Hitchcock's Films, p. 40.
[12] The halo may have been achieved either by using film stock without antihalation backing or by using special filters on the camera lens.

again in his career, so far as I can remember, in *Vertigo*. He apparently
does not intend either to draw much attention to his technique at this
point or to insist heavily upon Ruth's distortion of the past. Obtrusive
technical effects, as we have seen, he normally reserves for climaxes of
emotion and action. As to the unreliability of Madame Grandfort's
memory, a brief hint suffices. More would risk destroying our sympathy for Father Logan's former lover who, misguided and self-deceiving
though she may be, is also loving and courageous.

When Father Logan knows he is to be charged, he leaves the rectory
to walk alone through the streets. The first part of his walk occasions
some gloomy humor; the priest looks at a movie poster of a man being
arrested and a few minutes later gazes at a headless display manikin in
a store window. In it he probably sees himself, convicted and executed.

This sequence turns on images of descent and, less conspicuously,
ascent. From a high camera position behind a statue of Christ, we look
down at the small, solitary figure of Logan. Hitchcock then cuts to a
medium close-up while the beleaguered priest covers his face and sags
against a massive stone doorframe. As he lowers his hands from his
face and regains his balance, the sound track modulates out of the dire
strains of a "Dies Irae" into something calmer and more hopeful. Simultaneously, Logan turns to go up the stairs that will take him into
the cathedral where he was ordained. The next time we see him, he has
arrived, tranquil and resolved, at Inspector Larue's office. His ordeal
has a painful way to go, but he has surmounted his temptation to avoid
it by putting down his cross, his identity as a priest. The moment at
which he nearly succumbs to his terror is photographed so that he is
placed in despair far below the camera. His recovery is initiated when
he turns to ascend the stairs into the cathedral.

With a few expressive exceptions, the camera work in the trial remains unobtrusive, characterized by middle distance shots at eyelevel.
The judge is photographed for a moment early in the trial with a low,
slightly tilted camera; Otto Keller receives one very low angle close-up
while he perjures himself on the witness stand; and the jury foreman
gets similar treatment as he damns Father Logan with his equivocal
verdict.

The dominant visual rhetoric of descent resumes after the trial, however, when the camera follows Logan's departure from the courtroom
down to face the hostile mob outside the Hall of Justice. A low slanted
shot shows us from the priest's point of view a spired and gabled
building that recalls the churches whose images have dominated the
film. But this structure has a sign under its eaves that reads HOTEL.
Logan's gaze proclaims his knowledge that he must seek refuge there

rather than in the church from which his scandalous trial has effectively barred him. A group of rough-looking young men hang like vultures over the roof of an automobile; a woman voraciously bites an apple (an evocative fruit in this context) as she devours with her eyes the spectacle of Father Logan's torment; the priest's arm is knocked through the window of the car while the young men on the roof peer down at him and at the low camera that records the action. From a public point of view, Father Logan has reached the nadir of his fortunes, and the intense imagery of descent emphasizes that fact.

The final shot repeats the opening view of the House of Parliament, but the camera movement is reversed. It retreats slowly from the building and therefore backs away from the river it crossed in the first shot. But this is a brief, extremely subtle gesture; only repeated viewings allow one to be certain that there is any camera movement at all. Similarly, the moment when Father Logan turns up the cathedral stairs is given but a few seconds of screen time. Besides those crucial but unobtrusive gestures, there is one emphatic ascent to truth and liberation. It takes place when Ruth and Pierre go upstairs and witness Keller's confession in the Hotel. There Madame Grandfort finds knowledge of the finality of Michael Logan's commitment to the priesthood; and, in that long overdue illumination, she also embraces at last her role as her husband's wife.

But that ascent has to do mainly with secondary characters and a subplot. In total, *I Confess*, more than *Strangers on a Train* or *The Lodger*, is plotted as a series of downward movements. Even the action of going up is occasionally shown with reversed connotation, as when Keller visits the attic to load his luger. Such reversals of more usual symbology provide significant clues that the film is moving in ironic directions. We may easily imagine that more peaceful days for Michael Logan precede and follow the time of the film, but they have as little to do with *I Confess* as Ophelia's possibly happy childhood or Fortinbras's presumed serene rule have to do with *Hamlet*. Imagistically, Hitchcock's religious drama remains a harrowing movie.

Characterization in *I Confess* incorporates the same tension between irony and romanticism that we found in the imagery of ascent and descent. Both the central hero and his antagonist are drawn somewhat larger than life, but the gaiety of the heroes of the comic romances has largely disappeared from the grave Michael Logan. None of the helpful figures who represent benevolent spirits of place or nature come forward. Wicked and equivocal characters proliferate: Otto Keller, Vilette, Alma Keller, the smug, superficial Crown Prosecutor, the antagonistic judge and jury, the mob that waits outside after the trial. Ruth and Pierre Grandfort and Inspector Larue, the most sympathetic figures, have little power to help the priest.

Serious, handsome, decorated in war, restrained when provoked, true to himself and his oath, Michael Logan represents that sort of figure we might characterize as like us but better. He is stronger, braver, better-looking than we, but he shares nonetheless some of our human weakness and self-doubt. He knows sexual desire and anger. He dreads shame and death. His human vulnerability is as central to his heroism as are his strengths; for great courage can exist only as an overcoming of terror, great virtue as an overcoming of passionate temptation. Father Logan's integrity sustains his courage and his goodness. He knows who he is, and he understands that self-betrayal to avoid death or disgrace would lead to personal dissolution worse than either.

Of all Hitchcock's heroes, he is most unequivocally a type of Christ. Searching out "Christ figures" has become, with some justification, a disreputable pastime among modern critics. But the identification of Father Logan with Christ is presented so insistently in *I Confess* that we will certainly misunderstand the movie if we ignore its typological structure. Most of Hitchcock's heroes, moreover, carry some hint of Christ about them, however secular the contexts in which they appear. The way in which Hitchcock identifies Christ and Father Logan in *I Confess* sheds considerable light on his other movies as well.

When Logan descends from the rectory to hear Keller's confession, he takes on himself (as the plot is managed) suspicion for the crime. His involvement does not constitute a transference of guilt, any more than Christ may be said to have shared the guilt of all human sins. It does involve, as did Christ's sacrifice, assuming the sin of another and being willing to stand and fall in his place. Thus the plot, considered from the Christian viewpoint that the film invites, imitates a portion of Christ's life, his sympathy for sin and misery and his descent to redeem humankind.

From early in the film, Father Logan is associated with the cross and with Christ. In the church, as he walks toward the camera looking for Keller, his image replaces that of the crucified Christ above the altar behind him. As Keller begins his confession, the shadow through the lattice of the confessional makes a cross on Father Logan's forehead. Keller, in a reverse shot through the lattice, appears confined. The next image of the priest shows him in a surplice with a large cross on the back. As if to emphasize the importance of the symbol and of Michael Logan's identification with it, Hitchcock first shows the cross and only reveals a little later that it is on the back of Father Logan. While he sits in the prisoner's box as Keller is testifying, Father Logan is photographed from an angle that gives a cruciform shape to the out-of-focus rail just to his left. Keller's testimony, of course, severely damages Logan; the slight suggestion of the cross is especially appropriate at that moment. Later in the trial, as the priest listens to the verdict, the door panels behind him again suggest crosses. The verdict of Not Guilty fails to end his ordeal, and a few minutes later his chief antagonist taunts him in terms that evoke Christ once more: "What has happened to your friends? They martyr you, they call at you!"

Two shots enforce most emphatically the identification of Logan with Christ. The first, the protracted long shot down on him through the sculptural Calvary scene, I have already discussed. At that point the priest, like Christ, suffers acutely under the weight of his cross; and, as Christ is flanked by Roman soldiers, Logan is being hunted by police, the soldiers of the temporal authority. The second shot comes during the trial while Logan is testifying. The Crown Prosecutor asks about the bloody cassock that Keller planted. "Have you any idea who might have put this cassock in your trunk?" As the question is asked, the camera shows Alma Keller, who starts slightly. Logan answers, "I can't say," by which the prosecutor no doubt understands "I don't know." We, however, know that the force of his utterance is more literal. The priest does have a very good idea who put the cassock in his trunk, but his adherence to his vows prevents him from revealing anything. As Logan evades this crucial question, and in doing so puts his life and reputation in terrible danger, the camera switches to a moderate low-angle close-up with Father Logan occupying the right half of the screen and an icon of Christ on the cross occupying the left. The indication of identity between the two figures could hardly be clearer. At the moment that Logan refuses to take the opportunity to clear himself of Keller's guilt, Hitchcock pointedly reminds us of his divine predecessor.

The same statue of Christ nailed to the cross appears once more. The jury foreman, who has earlier declared his certainty that Father Logan must have been involved in an affair of long duration with Madame Grandfort, delivers a damning little speech prior to announcing the verdict of Not Guilty. A very low, angled close-up records his self-satisfied face. Behind him, on the left side of the screen, hangs Christ on the cross. With its prefatory remarks ("While we attach grave suspicion to the accused") the jury has, as Larue angrily says a moment later, ruined Logan. The long hiss and derisory laughter that break out in the courtroom when Logan is discharged confirm Larue's point. Later, Keller sums up the disaster that the verdict, and the trial that preceded it, represents for Father Logan: "To kill you now would be a favor to you."

Soon after the trial, Father Logan performs a Christlike office (and a priestly one, of course) when he administers the last rites to his chief persecutors, Alma and Otto Keller. In asking God to have mercy on them, he intercedes on their behalf as Christ interceded on behalf of the suffering and sin-stained humanity that persecuted and martyred him.

That Logan is strongly and systematically identified with Christ can hardly be doubted. Of equal interest is the fact that this identification does not obscure the typical Hitchcockian story of falsely accused innocence. The heroine's faith in the victim-hero is still crucial to the story, but it has been transformed. Ruth Grandfort must discover not that she loves Michael, but that she loves Pierre and that her place is with her husband. Her acceptance of her former lover's innocence arrives simultaneously with her acceptance of his vocation. Michael Logan must win not her hand but her acknowledgment of what he has become—an achievement similar in its essential shape to that which Hitchcock's more conventional heroes manage when they win the love and acceptance of their future mates.

Indeed, Logan looks very much like most of Hitchcock's heroes: slightly larger, more steadfast, and more self-possessed than ordinary people; framed by enemies; trapped by a mountain of circumstantial evidence; forced to discover, or rediscover and confirm, his identity. In the harmony between his religious vocation and his identity as a romantic hero we may see clearly how Christian overtones attach to Hitchcock's more secular heroes as they face the same sorts of circumstances and antagonists, suffer the same kinds of descents, and make their glorious, redemptive returns.

Otto Keller—whose name, obviously, suggests both "killer" and "cellar"—contrasts with Michael Logan in complex and sometimes surprising ways. In many respects the diametrical reverse of the hero, he is presented nonetheless with considerable sympathy. By the end of the film, he has forfeited his claim to that sympathy, but by then the question of his mental competence, and therefore of his moral responsibility, has been raised sufficiently to prevent us from making a simple judgment about his villainy. His pathetic end, and Logan's apparent forgiveness of him, further complicates our response. Vicious as he unquestionably has been, he has also been human. He has loved and been loved; he has felt hope and terror and despair. Unlike Father Logan, he lacks the heroic faith to overcome his weakness. Wicked from the beginning of the film, he will never qualify as an innocent gone astray.

Yet Father Logan's administration of the last sacraments to him, and his insanity or acute disorientation, must soften our final assessment of his actions. He seems as much to be pitied, all things taken into account, as to be judged infernal.

A refugee, a "man without a country" and without any other social context besides that provided by his wife, Otto Keller occupies a place among other people that could hardly be more different from that of Michael Logan: war hero and member of the priesthood, with all the inherent social standing of the church behind him, and with connections to and the respect of the community in which he grew up. To the priest's kindness, Keller responds more with envy and resentment than with gratitude. This greed and egotism link him with Hitchcock's other villains, but they are feelings that Keller's situation makes understandable, if not attractive.

Toward Alma he displays a solicitude that we will eventually come to recognize as insincere. His concern for her amounts to another sort of self-absorption. Before making his confession to Father Logan, Keller introduces a lament that he will repeat throughout the film to justify his crime: "It was my wife, working so hard it breaks my heart." A little later he reveals his crime to Alma and appeals to the same rationale. "How could I watch you work so hard? I lie awake night after night and I think, 'All we need is two thousand dollars.'"

Keller's murder of his spouse when he thinks that she is about to reveal his guilt, even if we interpret it as evidence of his emotional disintegration, largely obviates the plausibility of his claims that he turned to crime on his wife's behalf. His love for Alma, such as it is, consists of the same possessiveness and egotism that characterize other "loving" villains like VanDamm, or the Drummer in *Young and Innocent*. When Keller shoots Alma, he dashes through a dark arch—a Hitchcockian image of love decayed—into the hotel. He will descend into the basement and shoot another person before he is stopped. The news that he has killed his wife affects him only because it increases his misery. "Then I am as alone," he says to Father Logan, "as you are." (This statement also reminds us of the extent to which he hates and envies his confessor; even upon receiving the news of his wife's death, he seems to find consolation in throwing Logan's misery in his face.)

Within the first sequence in which we see him, moreover, Keller shows enough slipperiness to undermine our trust in him. He tries to blame his crimes first on Father Logan, then on Alma. He neither admits his own guilt nor expresses the least regret for the murder, beyond its misfiring and his unhappiness that Father Logan has told him that he must return the money. He does not return it, despite his promise to do so; and thus he has yet another reason to hope for Logan's conviction. He appears more coldly and ruthlessly calculating as the film progresses, while at the same time his terror of being caught increasingly unbalances him. Yet these circumstances, for all that they may meliorate his guilt, do not explain away his evil. From the beginning of the movie, he behaves as an envious, self-absorbed man whose willingness to sacrifice his wife and his benefactor in order to conceal his crime confirms our sense of his insecurity and egocentricity. If Michael Logan embodies an extreme of the human capacity for idealistic self-sacrifice, Otto Keller exemplifies its absence.

The wickedness of the other chief antagonist, Vilette, is as simple and strange as Keller's is complex and familiar. Like the psychopathic murderer in *The Lodger* or the enemies of peace in *Foreign Correspondent*, he arises from nowhere, pure and archaic in his evil. "No one," muses Larue, "seems to have known this Vilette. . . . Not one of his clients have any information to give about the man." Vilette, unknown to either bride or groom, appears mysteriously in the reception line at Ruth's wedding to Pierre. Like other Hitchcock primitives of evil, he erupts from an underworld. The receiving line, ominously, flows toward the newlyweds from below them. Vilette appears in the frame just as the newly married Ruth Grandfort is trying to assign her unhappiness to a dead history: "I was happy. I was through with . . . I *thought* I was through with. . . ." Her sentence trails off; Vilette approaches. He will inflict himself on the bride like a vengeful and unresolved past.

His second appearance in her life, just after Michael returns from the war, also suggests the intrusion into present happiness of an evil from the past. Trapped by a late rainstorm, the pair spend the night in a gazebo on "the island." They awaken to sunlight and foliage and a stirring breeze. At the same time, the intensely romantic sound track resumes, its only decipherable words "every day's a lovely day." Vilette approaches, "as though he owned the garden." In fact, he does. He argues with Logan, who pushes him down. Then, lying on the ground, he recognizes and greets Ruth as *"Madame Grandfort"*— Ruth not having told Michael that she was married in his absence. The contextual signals have increased in urgency. Vilette in this sequence plays a very plausible stand-in for the snake in Eden. Ruth's cherished fantasy of recovering youthful love evaporates in the friction of reality in the fallen world, a world in which evil itself owns the garden from which fallen innocence was exiled and is here exiled again.

Five years later, Vilette reappears, this time at Michael Logan's ordination. Ruth, in fact, has not seen her former lover since the morning in Vilette's garden, but Vilette wrongly concludes from her presence in the church that she has been conducting an ongoing affair with him. In the months that follow, he tries to blackmail her into seeking her politically influential husband's intercession on his behalf.

The pattern of Vilette's appearances and his abrupt, unexplained arrival suggest that he functions both as an archetype of evil (his repellent name promises as much) and as the spirit of an unquiet past. He intrudes into the sanctuaries of Ruth and Pierre's wedding, the church-spired gazebo in the garden, the cathedral in which Michael Logan is ordained, and the House of Parliament. These incursions both suggest his ubiquity and give him the status of a sort of social cancer, undermining civilization's safe, sacred places. His invasions of church and government, garden and marriage, underline a central ideal of *I Confess*: institutions cannot protect men and women from evil; rather the contrary, persons must protect their institutions. "I never thought of the priesthood," replies Father Logan to the baiting of the Crown Prosecutor, "as offering a hiding place."

Vilette recalls Satan in *The Book of Job*, "walking to and fro in the earth and up and down in it," looking for a perfect, upright man to persecute. As a demonic figure he tests both persons and their governmental and ecclesiastical institutions. But mostly, of course, he tests Michael Logan. The priest triumphs as Job does, by retaining his faith and his integrity.

The division of the villain's role between two figures, one relatively complex and sympathetic and the other more purely evil, occurs fairly often in Hitchcock's films. *North by Northwest*, as we have seen, divides qualities of evil between VanDamm and Leonard. The weak husband and his vicious family in *Easy Virtue* and Alexander Sebastian and his mother in *Notorious* provide further examples of such division of spoilers, as do doubled or multiple villains in *The Manxman*, *Foreign Correspondent*, and *The Paradine Case*. Fragmented as the villain's role may be, the clear separation of the wicked from the good characters in *I Confess* marks its affinity with Hitchcock's comic romances and separates it from his more ironic works, with their moral and sympathetic ambiguity.

Compared with the comic romances examined in the previous two chapters, *I Confess* shows corruption larger and the power of innocence shrunken. In a parallel change, the marvelous, adventure-filled journeys that propelled the plots of the comic romances are constricted in *I Confess* into circular, restless little trips around Quebec City. These "journeys" emphasize not the hero's quest but the constraints that prevent him from gaining his freedom. Like many of Hitchcock's movies, *I Confess* is packed with images of conveyance. Cars, boats, bicycles, traffic signs, buses, and almost continuous walking give the film a quality of ceaseless motion. But the traffic signs point in one way only, and so are restrictive rather than liberating. None of the conveyances carry anyone away from pursuing threats or to justification. The ferry serves only as an ill-judged rendezvous for Ruth and Michael, where a police detective's surveillance brings Michael under increased suspicion. Even escape on foot, that last best resort of the Hitchcock hero, is thwarted. Walking through the maze of Quebec City streets leads first to Vilette's corpse and later to the police station.

Father Logan's attempt to establish his innocence is baffled by his obligation to respect the confidentiality of the confessional, and the imagery of restrained or fruitless motion reflects his powerlessness. In the last scene, when the priest's innocence finally becomes manifest, he is able to push aside the restraints on his movement. Ignoring Larue's command, he walks across the ballroom toward Keller, with a straightforwardness that he has been denied since the opening sequences.

Like its baffled journeys, the coincidences of *I Confess* parody the lucky improbabilities of comic romance (until the astonishing events of the last scene). The malign mischances of Father Logan's unsought relationships with Otto Keller and Ruth Grandfort, and the coincidental collisions of those characters with Vilette, bring the priest to the edge of catastrophe. But the wonderful good fortune of the last sequences reverses the earlier malignities. The unlikeliness of these episodes, as is usual for Hitchcock, is insisted upon. Starting with Otto's panic-stricken shooting of his wife, events dispose themselves with astonishing economy before just the right witnesses. Father Logan is fully, quickly, and publicly exonerated.

As is again usual for Hitchcock, the conspicuous improbability of miraculous coincidence and the conspicuous artificiality of a self-conscious artist are congruent. The contrivance of the plot increases our consciousness of watching a manufactured and manipulated situation. The setting, the ballroom/theater of the hotel, underscores the sense of artifice. A benign artist and a benign fate are associated. Job recovers his original prosperity and more after his ordeal, thanks to the intervention of an openhanded and gratified deity. So Father Logan, the truth of his innocence and heroism at last known, will recover his repute and more.

Until the closing revelation, however, ritual and fiction, turning downward along with other romantic motifs, largely express deceit and delusion. The maker of the film, as Hitchcock's cameo appearance suggests, takes us to a shadowy underworld and abandons us there. Keller dresses as a priest to commit his crime, then plays an increasingly deliberate and destructive role as he collaborates with circumstances to frame Father Logan. The ceremonies of Ruth's marriage and Michael's ordination are both polluted by Vilette's presence, and the elaborate social ceremony of justice, the trial, ruins Logan even though it does not formally convict him.

Most notable for its delusions is the memory of Ruth Grandfort, as Hitchcock renders it in her flashback. "As for the earthly paradise," writes Northrop Frye in what may serve as an apt summary here, "according to Christian doctrine it was, but it cannot now be; consequently in romance the paradisal is frequently a deceitful illusion that turns out to be demonic, or a destructive vision."[13] Ruth Grandfort's statement to the police damages Father Logan nearly as much as Keller's machinations. She intends, of course, the opposite. But deluded as she is by her dream of past perfection and its continuation into the present, she unwittingly joins the tempest of darkness swirling about Logan. "I was going to help Michael, was I?" she says. "I've destroyed him."

Her redemption begins at this moment, when she recognizes the destructive effects of her sentimental clinging to the past. Full acceptance of the present and of her love for her husband makes possible Madame Grandfort's escape from her self-created demons. At the beginning of the sequence in which she learns of the injury her statement has done Michael Logan, she opens her bedroom shutters and stands bathed in the light that streams in. That light will visually and metaphorically dominate the scene as her understanding grows. When she says, "I've destroyed him," she sits on her bed facing and framed by the light of the window. Then, significantly, she turns toward her husband. "And you, Pierre. What have I done to you?" Ruth's perception of the destructiveness of her fantasy about the past and—equally important—her concern for her husband's welfare lead eventually to self-discovery and self-acceptance. Her terse last speech summarizes her recovery: "Pierre, take me home." At the moment that Keller's deceits are fully revealed and their power to injure Michael Logan dispelled, Ruth's final rejection of her own delusions frees her and her husband.

The innocent and eternal world prevails. In the next-to-last shot of the film, Logan prays for Keller and closes the dead man's eyes. The last time we see them, Ruth and Pierre embrace and by that gesture

[13] Frye, *The Secular Scripture*, p. 98.

recall the closing marriage or promise of marriage that ends most comedies. Keller and Vilette have received the wages of their sins. Society's justice and the individual's personal integrity have been realigned, and Larue is allowed at last the role he has always sought, that of Father Logan's ally.

Although some of the conventions have turned toward their darker aspects, the main features of romantic narrative remain. The end of *I Confess* asserts what its earlier movements make possible but delay affirming: human life and struggle is a romantic, not an ironic, quest. We cannot call its vision comic with any conviction, for this film lacks the gaiety that comedy engenders and admits the suffering that it excludes. Its romantic features are finally confirmed; but they are often temporarily equivocal, subject to the sort of parody and reversal of significance that, allowed to stand uncorrected, signal intense ironies.

Any film, however, exists both sequentially and as a whole, fully achieving the latter status after it has been viewed at least once. Considered as a sequence of images and sounds, *I Confess* makes clear only in its conclusion that it represents a universe in which a fertile and sunny world will defeat one that is sterile and dark. Apprehended as a whole in which beginning, middle, and end exist simultaneously, its romantic structure stands out more clearly. In its treatment of character and tone, and in the admission of suffering into its action, it has moved toward a tragic mode, but its narrative retains a romantic shape. Feints in the direction of irony are the standard means for generating suspense in any romantic story and are enfeebled in significance by the ending.

Michael Logan's suffering recapitulates much that is central to the great tragic, romantic myth of Western culture, the story of Christ. That too is a harrowing narrative with a supremely inspiriting ending. *I Confess*, though it accords the powers of darkness and destruction a potency greater than they have in the more comic romances, achieves effects all the grander for its anxiety and seriousness. In Michael Logan we encounter a romantic hero as good and strong as a human can be. The forces he faces are formidable, but he overcomes them and his own weakness. This film does not, finally, embody a discouraging view of human life. It promises that if we remain faithful to the best in ourselves, we will prevail.

The Wrong Man

The tone and structure of *The Wrong Man* share a great deal with *I Confess*. In this version of the falsely accused innocent, however, the balance between romantic fulfillment and ironic bafflement remains extremely delicate through the end of the story proper, and only an appended epilogue assures us that dark malignancy has not achieved permanent equality with brightness. The predominance of designs of darkness and of destructive ironic reversals puts *The Wrong Man* largely into a mode of tragedy and irony, but its ending reverses the dominant modalities of the rest of the movie. The imagery of most of the film is dominated by shadow, its action by pain. In their subterranean quest, the main characters seem fated to remain thwarted and trapped.

From the beginning, night and descending movements dominate light and ascent. Hitchcock makes a prefatory appearance on a set so dark and shadowed that it almost parodies the extreme chiaroscuro of *film noir*, one of the most radically ironic modes in cinema. The tiny, unrecognizable, back-lighted figure whose voice announces itself as Alfred Hitchcock promises that we are about to see "a true story, every word of it." One could hardly ask for a more unequivocal promise of realism. And we shall see, in fact, that the emphasis on small, true-to-life details throughout the film makes good that promise, at least in part. What we are about to view, Hitchcock suggests in his shadowy introduction, will be dark, and frightening as much for its "truth" as for its gloom.

The first shot after the prologue shows the outside of the Stork Club, ominously slanted to the left. After the credits and an establishing title, the camera follows Manny Balestrero (Henry Fonda) home after the club closes, very late at night. This surprisingly long (2:15) sequence achieves a lyric foreboding at the same time that it accurately renders New York City in the small hours of the morning. It appears to have been shot entirely on location. Lighting and sound are ambient, and the footage of the subways has a documentary authenticity.

Yet along with all this *cinéma vérité* and Hitchcock's protestations of "truth," other, intrusively artificial, elements share the opening moments. The stylized opening shot of a tiny, very dramatically photographed figure in the middle of what appears to be a darkened studio implicitly contradicts the words promising unembroidered realism. (We are already being thrust, indeed, into a role as audience that threatens to parallel the role of the unknowingly false witnesses who identify Manny as a robber. How can we be sure that either the voice we hear or, more dubiously still, the minute silhouette we see really is Hitchcock?) The Stork Club itself, the setting of the first sequence, is a place outside ordinary daily life. It represents New York nightlife, ritualized like a carnival, dance, or play.

Authentic as the details of Manny's return home may be individually, they are selected with the undisguised design of creating a feeling of menace. The foreshadowing function of the sequence appears almost excessively transparent. The newspaper ad for a Ford (Manny does not own a car) promising "family fun" and that for "The New York Savings Bank" (Manny has no savings) at once fix the hero's financially strained circumstances for us and provide the police with a convincing motive for Manny's supposed robberies. The two patrolmen who pass by and briefly walk behind Manny as he emerges from the Stork Club also serve to foreshadow his subsequent disaster.

The historical truth or fiction of a narrative plot, as Aristotle showed to most people's satisfaction, is of little aesthetic consequence. Formal qualities, whether derived from real events or from an artist's imagination, determine the meanings that a plot conveys to its audience. The opening of *The Wrong Man*, at the same time that it promises a sort of documentary, also promises the ritual drama that we associate with tragedy. "This is a true story," as Hitchcock announces in the prologue, but it also "contains elements that are stranger than all the fiction that has gone into many of the thrillers that I've made before." The tension between truth and fiction introduced in the prologue gives energy to the whole movie. It will be the sense of fiction, however—highly formal and carefully ordered—that will provide the dominant tone for most of the film.

The careful selection of images of descent and darkness in its first minutes announces that *The Wrong Man* will take place largely in a shadowy underworld. A frequently tilted camera and a profusion of high and low shots further emphasize infernal overtones. A dramatic shot down the stairs to the subway shows Manny disappearing into the bowels of the earth. No parallel shot records his ascent. We know that he has left the subway, but we are not allowed to see him do so. As he approaches his home, an elevated train passes overhead behind him. The visual impression remains one of his being down below. The editing thus joins the camerawork and the selection of images to insist on the hazardous depths of Manny's environment.

By the end of the first movement of the film, which I take to continue through Manny's going inside his home, Hitchcock has invoked a number of related but conflicting artistic energies. Location filming and a documentary style of lighting and sound clash with intrusive editing and cinematography. Manifestly artificial moviemaking disputes claims of truth to life. If the filmmaker proposes to show "life as it is"—stupidly indifferent to human hopes and order—then we will find ourselves witnessing the unprogressive convolutions of an ironic narrative. (In a 1949 interview, Hitchcock defined evil as complete disorder.) If he arranges and controls his materials within a cyclical economy—and in doing so reflects a *spiritus mundi* of similar powers—then we will see a world of romantic renewal, whether comic or tragic. I have already suggested that the film leans toward the tragic; on the other generic axis, *The Wrong Man* achieves a dynamic balance between irony and romance. This poise is disturbed but not fully disrupted by the unequivocally romantic coda that is appended after the action of the narrative concludes. The audience will wonder, I suspect, not so much how the film will turn out as what kind of a film it will turn out to be. These questions, of course, cannot really be separated; but it is worth repeating that such generic tension constitutes a fundamental strategy of Hitchcockian suspense.

Movements downward to darkness, so insistent in the first five minutes, continue to dominate *The Wrong Man*. In few other Hitchcock films does the imagery of quotidian violence and dissolution as thoroughly control the mood. Sirens wail and trains clatter in the background. A motif of elevated "subway trains" carries a subtle suggestion that the underworld is emerging from below to take dominion above. Eerie shadows envelop the front of the Balestrero house. The sound track music that accompanies Manny's quiet inspection of his sleeping sons and silent home mixes equal parts of domestic tranquillity and exotic apprehension. The office of the Associated Life Insurance Company is fretted with the vertical and horizontal shadows that signify, here as so often in Hitchcock's movies, the threat of jail. In this office, Manny is misidentified as an armed robber, and his ordeal begins.

The extreme overhead shots with which Hitchcock optically thrusts characters into a lower world occur frequently during Manny's arrest and indictment. The prefiguring shadow-bars at the insurance office are succeeded by the real bars of the prison cell in which Manny spends the night following his confinement. During his arrest, interrogation, and processing by the police and the courts, the screen often shows only his hands and feet. These shots are sometimes subjective, indicating the direction of Manny's gaze—the result, presumably, of his shame. At all times they reflect the downward gaze of the movie itself. One of the most expressive is a close-up of his hand after he has been fingerprinted at the police station. He looks at his stained fingers, the inklike blood in the black-and-white image. The mark of guilt is on him; but it has been imposed and is no more deserved than the accusation of robbery with which he has also been stained.

After he is released on bond, nocturnal, constraining imagery continues to dominate. With a bridge looming in the foggy night behind them, Manny and his wife arrive at an apartment house in hopes of confirming his alibi. They discover instead that one of the people who could testify to Manny's whereabouts on the day of the first robbery has died. The same news awaits them at their next stop, down by the waterfront where a huge freighter hovers over the scene and foghorns honk dismally in the darkness. Such marine imagery often serves as a symbol of dissolution for Hitchcock. When Rose learns that her husband's second chance for an alibi has also died, she slips into the shadows and begins to laugh hysterically. She will not emerge from the darkness of her breakdown until the epilogue, which tells of her recovery two years later.

The "happy ending," Rose's complete recovery from her stress-induced psychosis, is conspicuously excluded from the action of the film. As was the case for *I Confess*, previous or subsequent good fortune has little place in a story that is essentially about mishap and suffering. *The Wrong Man* chronicles with austere single-mindedness Manny Balestrero's struggle against crushing bad luck, the disintegration of his life, and the threatened loss of his sense of self.

In Hitchcock's comic romances, ascents to love, light, and understanding balance descents to threat and isolation. In *The Wrong Man*, such ascents are largely absent, thwarted, or parodied. Such repressed movement upward takes place when Manny is arrested as he walks up the front steps of his home. When he takes out his latch key to open the front door, he is stopped by the detective who calls him by a name ("Chris") he does not recognize as his own. Manny turns toward the voice. In a subjective shot, he and the audience see three threatening figures materialize out of the darkness below. Frisked and hustled into the waiting squad car, he is sandwiched into the back seat between two of the policemen. It is perfectly clear that he is their prisoner. As he is driven away, the eerie music introduced earlier when he first returned home resumes and confirms its menace.

His ascent up the stairs to his brightly lit home and affectionately waiting family has been canceled, and he is pulled down into darkness and a car full of coldly menacing strangers. To enforce the irony, Hitchcock shows Manny looking across the profile of one of the policemen at his wife busying herself about supper in the cheerful place from which he has been snatched away. This choreography is repeated later at the arraignment when Manny has a brief glimpse of Rose and his in-laws in the courtroom, then is taken back to the cells in the basement. "Put him downstairs, Officer."

When Manny does manage to ascend, he often finds reversals of his hopes—"death's ironic scraping," as Wallace Stevens put it.[14] He and Rose climb the stairs of an East Side apartment building only to discover from a giggling girl that "Mr. Lamacha died, and Mrs. Lamacha—I don't know where she is." Their next ascent produces the same disheartening news: "Marinelli is dead." So is Manny's alibi.

A little later Manny leaves the mockingly festive Stork Club at the end of work and once again walks up the steps to the shadowed front door of his house. Inside he passes the stairs that rise mysteriously from the center of the entryway and that are reflected in a mirror opposite. No one, in the course of the film, ever goes up these stairs. The reflection, the image without the reality, anticipates the disappointment that awaits Manny. He finds his wife awake and acutely depressed in the shadows of their bedroom. Near the end of his concerned conversation with her, she strikes him with a hairbrush, splitting his skin and breaking the bedroom mirror. In it we see Manny's shocked and visually cracked features. Blood marks his forehead as he listens to his wife admit that "there is something wrong with me. You'll have to let them put me somewhere."

The saddest of Manny's disappointing climbs (and, because it appears to be totally gratuitous, the most interesting) takes place after he has been exonerated and has gone to the asylum to bring his wife the good news. He finds there a Rose withered beyond reviving, a wife who shrinks from his touch and who tells him in an emotionless voice, "you can go now." Rose appears to be lost permanently in the world of nightmare and delusion. The demons of irony, if they have not won the contest entirely, appear to have claimed at least half the victory.

As a dispirited Manny leaves the room and goes down a dark hall (but, significantly, toward the light), a written message appears superimposed on his image on the screen. "Two years later, Rose Balestrero walked out of the sanitarium—completely cured. Today she lives happily in Florida with Manny and the two boys . . . and what happened seems like a nightmare to them—but it did happen." As we read this message, the image dissolves from the asylum hallway to palm trees, sunshine, and a prosperous city skyline. A man, woman, and two children walk with their arms about one another along the sidewalk. Together in perpetual summer, Manny and his family live happily ever after.

Given that he immediately reverses its impact, why does Hitchcock include this last, and in many ways cruelest, irony? In part, I think, to

[14] Wallace Stevens, "Peter Quince at the Clavier," in *The Collected Poems of Wallace Stevens* (New York: Knopf, 1964), p. 92.

add a final chapter to the story of Manny's struggle in the night world of malevolent fate. In part to reassert the realism of the movie: psychosis does not disappear with one wave of a verbal wand. And in part, finally, to reiterate the main conflict, one based on repeated setbacks, inexorable descents, and disappointments—all of which Manny survives without losing faith in himself or the world. "I was hoping for a miracle," says the saddened husband. From what we know of him, we can be sure that he will continue to hope. And he will, finally, be justified in his optimism. "They [miracles] happen," replies the nurse, "but it takes time."

The most illuminating religious and archetypal analogue to *The Wrong Man*, as for *I Confess*, may be found in *The Book of Job*. We are likely to remember *Job* as a story of misfortune, but it is perhaps more urgently concerned to report the strength of its hero in retaining faith in God and belief in himself during inexplicable adversity. "Till I die," cries Job in his extremity, "I will not remove mine integrity from me." Manny requires a similar determination. When his mother asks him if he has prayed, Manny replies that he has asked for help. "Pray for strength, Manny," she advises him. In the next sequence, he apparently does. And the sequence following shows us the arrest of the actual robber, an arrest that clears Manny. It is not help but strength—faith, hope, perseverance, belief in his essential innocence—that sees Manny through his misfortunes. And it is at the juncture in his story when he begins to doubt himself and then recovers enough faith to pray for strength that his burdens begin to lighten.

Christopher Emmanuel Balestrero, however, has neither the epic stature of Job nor the extraordinary faith of Michael Logan. He is just average. He and his family, like the Oakleys in *Shadow of a Doubt*, practically define the unexceptional in human affairs. Neither rich nor poor, distinguished or without skills, old or young, Manny (as his familiar name strongly hints) has the stature and situation of the typical citizen, the average guy, Everyman. There is more to his name than Manny, of course, and more to his story than the typical family crisis; but the point I wish to make at the moment has to do with his "like us" stature. He does not have much of the quicker-than-life quality of his counterparts in more romantic films. He does have an admirable patience and a willingness to regard the world as a fundamentally good place. In most respects, however, Hitchcock portrays him, and his surroundings, with an everyday realism that pushes his story toward irony.

As in *I Confess*, horizontal movement by the characters, and to a lesser degree by the camera as well, is restricted and often frustrated.

Manny travels most of the time by subway—a dangerous conveyance for Hitchcock as early as *Blackmail* (1929)—and we often see him being hauled around rather than moving by his own volition. He borrows a Ford from his brother-in-law, the appropriately named Conforti (a name that suggests "with strength and courage," or perhaps "comforter"). It gives him some mobility, if not the "family fun" promised by the newspaper ad. But the car does not really get him anywhere. It leads to dead ends in his attempt to establish an alibi, and he uses it, sadly, to take his wife to the sanitarium. We last see it, standing outside the institution and framed by bare wintry branches, just after Manny has left Rose in the care of the medical staff.

Conforti, who lends Manny the car and raises his bail, represents an unanticipated helper of the sort that so densely populates *Saboteur*. Mr. O'Connor, his lawyer, functions as another. But neither being free on bond nor having the car allows Manny to establish his innocence, and the best the lawyer can accomplish for him is a mistrial. Neither Conforti nor O'Connor can summon the almost magical power of such figures as Pat's uncle in *Saboteur* and old Will in *Young and Innocent*, though they retain the sympathetic aura of those figures. So do the man and his wife who run the resort hotel at which the Balestreros vacationed in the country. But they cannot really help Manny, either. They do not remember what he was doing on the day of the robbery, and the names they provide do not enable him to substantiate his alibi.

If Manny's friends lack the preternatural powers of the helper figures in the comic romances, his enemies lack the demonic exaggeration of the villains. No one attempts to injure or frame him. The police treat him somewhat rudely, and they view the evidence in a way that slants it in the direction of Manny's guilt, but they show no malice toward him. Indeed, it is the less polite and sympathetic of the two detectives who has the flash of recognition that gains Manny his freedom.

The women who bear false witness against him are simply mistaken. They are timid, flustered people who have been frightened and angered by two robberies in their insurance agency in the last year and who are pushed to identify a suspect by the police and by their own anxiety. The prosecutor at the trial is only doing his job; there is none of the indignation against Manny that there was against Michael Logan during the trial sequences in *I Confess*. Toward the end of the trial, the accused man looks around the courtroom as his lawyer is cross-examining a prosecution witness. No one seems to be taking much notice, let alone relishing the prospect of his conviction. The prosecutor and his assistant share a joke; Mrs. Conforti touches up her lipstick; a pair of guards chat, as do a pair of jurors; another juror polishes the lenses of her glasses. The only excitement is occasioned by boredom rather than by intensity of feeling. "Your honor," complains an exasperated juror, "do we have to sit here and listen to this?"

In the films discussed earlier, the truly guilty figures are dangerous both to society and to the innocent heroes who are wrongfully accused of their crimes. In *The Wrong Man*, the real criminal is an ordinary, unthreatening person. He does not at all resemble the enormously wicked and cunning figures like VanDamm, Bruno, or the head of the spies in *The 39 Steps*. When the true thief is captured in the act of attempted robbery by a storeowner and his wife, he cries out rather pathetically, "Let me go! I got kids, I didn't hurt anybody. Let me go!"

The treatment of external artifice and internal ritual, like other formal characteristics, changes between the comic romances and the more ironic story of Manny Balestrero. The artificiality of the filmmaking, its emphasis on conspicuous technique, does not disappear; but it exists in tension, as we have seen, with an opposing documentary plain style. The representation of social ritual within the film turns sharply toward ceremonies of menace. Most such representations center on various aspects of the legal system: the arrest of Manny, his interrogation, the line-up, the booking and arraignment, the trial. All these social formalities must be seen as intensely ironic, since they all lead to the opposite of their explicit objective, the protection of the innocent and the conviction of the guilty. This irony is underlined by the repeated statement of one of the detectives, uttered more as a threat to Manny than as reassurance: "An innocent man has nothing to fear, remember that."

On the contrary, Manny has everything to fear. Justice in *The Wrong Man* looks like that in Kafka's *The Trial*: an arbitrary, incomprehensible exercise in bureaucratic brute force. The combination of power and rigidity in the institutions of the law looks as if it will be fatal for its innocent victim. The chief protector of the comic romances—a lover whose intuition of innocence counterpoises the logic of appearances—has vanished. Manny's wife suffers an acute nervous collapse, and there is no one—except his mother at one crucial moment—to replace her.

What in the more clearly romantic films constitutes marvelous coincidence becomes, again with one crucial exception, ruinous bad luck. The nightmarish improbabilities that conspire against the innocent man are exquisitely timed. That a nearly identical person of Manny's age should commit a series of crimes in Manny's neighborhood, that he should twice rob the office at which Manny purchased his insurance policies, that the impacted wisdom teeth of Manny's wife should cause him to go into the office to borrow against her policy in order to pay the dentist, that the woman who waits on him there should have seen the robber only from a distance and consequently is especially likely to mistake Manny for him and to involve her co-workers in her mistake—these are the coincidences that must occur, all of them, to bring Manny into mortal danger.

They are later compounded by more, equally appalling circumstances. The second time that Manny prints the holdup note for the police, he makes precisely the same mistake that the real gunman made, writing "draw" for "drawer." "That's one of the most remarkable things I've ever seen," says a detective, probably with deliberate sarcasm. "This looks bad for you, Manny," he goes on, "something very strange happened." The police, of course, assume that Manny's mistake duplicates that of the holdup man because they are the same person. And that hypothesis is certainly likely. But in fact the "remarkable thing," the "very strange," has again transpired, as it has repeatedly in order to bring Manny to the point of arrest. The deaths of the two witnesses continue the conspiracy of unlikelihoods that seem destined to subject Manny to a cosmic frame-up.

The fact that the story of *The Wrong Man* "really happened" does not diminish its improbability. Nor does its "truth" alter the fact that such unlikely twists of fate fascinated Hitchcock throughout his career. Virtually all the films discussed so far are rife with such remarkable coincidences. The voice-over that was once slated for the beginning of *North by Northwest* makes a revealing point—perhaps too explicitly for Hitchcock's taste. "Would it not be strange, in a city of seven million people, if one man were *never* mistaken for another . . . if, with seven million pair of feet wandering through the canyons and corridors of the city, one pair of feet *never* by chance strayed into the wrong footsteps? (A pause.) Strange, indeed."[15] With the aid of that canceled voice-over, we can see clearly where banal truth and grotesque improbability meet and merge. In the infinitude of human experience, the strangest of coincidences would be the absence of remarkable coincidences. As Jean-Luc Godard commented in a short essay on *The Wrong Man*, "We are watching the most fantastic of adventures because we are watching the most perfect, the most exemplary, of documentaries."[16] Do the necessary improbabilities of ordinary life manifest any universal design? Or do they exist simply as random statistical artifacts, with no discernible relation to human affairs? A narrative

[15] Lehman, *North by Northwest*, p. 1.
[16] Tom Milne, ed. and trans., *Godard on Godard* (New York: Viking, 1968), p. 49.

that suggests an affirmative answer to the first question will lean toward romance; one that suggests the second alternative almost has to incline toward irony.

The most perfect and exemplary of improbabilities, from a Christian point of view, is the love of God for fallen humanity (Grace) and its full realization in the redemptive sacrifice of Christ. The most remarkable and emphatic of improbabilities in Manny's bizarre story takes place at its moment of clearest confluence with the central miracle of Christianity. This crucial episode is also accompanied, significantly, by the most ostentatious use of artistic contrivance. A collocation of the miraculous, the antirealistic, and the religious thus marks the turning point in Manny's ordeal and the beginning of the solution of the plot. Despite all the ironic structures of *The Wrong Man*, a fortunate miracle gives the movie a final meaning that is romantic.

The enveloping gloom breaks when Manny returns home after a juror's outburst has led to the declaration of a mistrial. Because his wife has been institutionalized, his mother is staying with him to take care of his sons. "I think I could've stood it better if they'd found me guilty," he says. He continues, sounding genuinely discouraged for the first time, "I've brought it all on myself, though. I've been such an idiot, you'd all be better off without me." "None of it is your fault, Manny. You've just had a lot of bad breaks that can happen to anybody," responds his mother, who then suggests that he pray. Manny goes into his bedroom to dress for work. We hear on the sound track an unearthly, quiet air rather similar to that which accompanied his tour through his sleeping home at the beginning of the film. As he puts on his shirt, his eye is caught by a painting of Christ on the bedroom wall. Beside it the shadow of his head and shoulders—a visual simile of crucial significance. The camera tracks forward slowly, then cuts back to Manny, his lips moving, apparently in prayer. It holds on him, and initiates the longest double exposure in Hitchcock's career. For twenty-five seconds we see Manny's face juxtaposed with a street scene in which a man is walking slowly toward the camera. As the man reaches the point at which his face has the same size on the screen as Manny's, and is almost exactly superimposed on it, the image dissolves to the face of the second man. The camera then follows him to his capture when he tries to rob a small grocery.

This sequence has considerable interest as cinematic rhetoric. The shadow of Manny's head and shoulders next to the picture of Christ likens him in his misunderstood innocence to the redeemer of humankind. All similes, however, have a necessary and equally important component of contrast; Manny is *not* Christ, and that too is crucial.

He cannot have the strength or understanding of his role that Christ had. The second visual simile, the superimposition of the real robber's face on Manny's, reverses the precedence of meanings. It conveys first that Manny is *not* that man. But he is *like* that man, a fact that resonates beyond its place as one of the central coincidences of the plot.

If Manny is like Christ, then he is destined to suffer for sins of which he is not guilty. At the same time, the movie carries some suggestions that Manny is like his double in ways beyond physical appearance. Both immediately respond to their capture, for example, with concern about their families. Both have a rather meek bearing. There is a suggestion here of the sort of thinking that begins "there but for the grace of God." Manny is not that man; but as he looks and acts like that man, in some way he *could* be him. Neither Manny nor any other person can ever be entirely innocent of any human crime—nor, perhaps, entirely beyond exoneration.

Manny's religiousness has been alluded to twice before through images of his rosary beads and crucifix. When he is locked up they are found in his pocket; and the last sequence at his trial begins with a close-up of a small crucified Christ hanging from the beads. We are unprepared, nonetheless, for the enormous importance assigned to Manny's prayer during his crisis of self-belief. The suddenly emphatic religious imagery and the break in cinematic style occasioned by the long lap-dissolve give the sequence great intensity. They bring the film as close to an explicit statement of significance as it ever comes, including the introduction by Hitchcock and the written description of the happy ending.

Although religion plays a much smaller part in *The Wrong Man* as a whole than it does in *I Confess*, it has nearly as much importance for its conclusion and its final meanings. Its meanings, indeed, very much resemble those of the earlier film. The MacGuffin, as in *I Confess*, has to do with whether the real criminal will be found. The quest for innocence and identity, similarly, occurs without the providential help of a lover. Nor does the finding and winning of a mate have a crucial role in the establishment or recovery of identity. For a heroine or hero who is already married, the plot may turn on the recovery of a mate or the rejuvenation of a relationship, as in *Rich and Strange*. But with Rose's breakdown, even the reestablishment of the marriage becomes an issue outside the boundaries of the movie. Like the father in both versions of *The Man Who Knew Too Much*, Manny must fight to preserve his family; but he lacks the help of his wife, and the emphasis in portraying his ordeal, as a result, turns to his struggle to maintain the integrity of his own personality. Centrally at issue, in *The Wrong Man* as in *I Confess*, are the faith and personal coherence of the main figure.

Manny must maintain his confidence in his fundamental innocence and the goodness of the world, for that confidence constitutes the essential core of his identity. Like Job, he cannot understand what has brought catastrophe upon him; and a circle of unsympathetic accusers try to convince him to accept the blame for his misfortunes. As in *The Book of Job* again, even his wife accuses him. "You're not perfect, yourself," cries Rose hysterically. "How do I know you're not guilty? You don't tell me everything you do." Manny, Michael Logan, Job, and Christ must all maintain their faith and integrity in the face of overwhelming pressures to abandon it.

If "Manny" suggests something like "humankind," the hero's full first and middle names remind us of the spark of divinity in all people and of their fate to take up individually the burdens of Jesus. Christopher Emmanuel Balestrero, like Christ himself, will wonder in the depths of his ordeal if his God has abandoned him. But, like Christ, he will defeat his own doubt. His triumphant gesture consists of his prayer and of his unbroken faith that even with no hope in sight things will somehow work themselves out. Manny speculates that the real criminal will never be caught, that he may be in jail in some distant state. "What can I do?" he asks. His mother replies, and he accepts her advice: pray for strength. He has the strength of the meek, as does Michael Logan. Not only does such strength suffice, but it is all that could suffice. In Manny and in Michael Logan, we see with particular clarity the Christian archetype behind the quest for identity and self-affirmation in Hitchcock's romantic heroes.

In his more characteristically secular films, love between men and women makes up the principal manifestation of grace, and the shadow of Christ is fainter. But the central conflicts and crises have much the same structure. Even in the semi-realistic *The Wrong Man*, Hitchcock reverts to incredible coincidence and conspicuous artistic manipulation at the moment of greatest anxiety and most intense hope. In doing so, he signals the underlying dominance of a romantic, religious optimism. God is in heaven, and heaven is not inseparably removed from the world. The filmmaker is in control. His desire to rescue his hero and reassure his audience correspond with our need to witness the rescue and receive reassurance. Though the last sequence of the action of the film seems to leave it balanced between Manny's faith and salvation and his wife's loss of hope and continuing confinement, the coda removes most of that anxiety (though not the artistic cohesiveness). When the houselights come up, we, like Manny and his family, may walk relaxed and untroubled into the light and free air. Rose's name, and the pictures of flowers in her bedroom early in the movie, associate her with Persephone. If she repeats the fate of that romantic archetype by being dragged down into hell, she also repeats her fate in being found and returned to the blooming earth.

Frenzy

Frenzy may be seen, structurally at least, as a sort of *The Wrong Man* without the reassuring coda. If we classify Hitchcock's films in terms of relative romanticism or irony, *Frenzy* balances dynamically between the two artistic modes, including both and allowing neither final authority. An enormously rich and complicated film, *Frenzy* recalls the balance of contraries of a famous opening sentence of one of England's greatest novelists. *Frenzy*'s London is the best of places and the worst of places; the movie itself is one of Hitchcock's saddest and funniest, full of heaven's remains and hell's incursions; it is thoroughly modern, of 1972, while it remakes *The Lodger* of 1926; it is romantic and it is

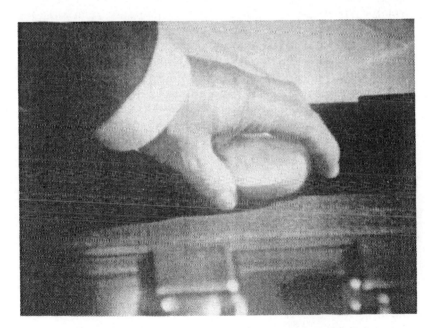

Frenzy: When Rusk picks up Brenda's partly eaten apple and takes an aggressive bite from it, he announces his intention to take possession of her.

ironic; it takes consolation in innocence recovered and mourns corruption triumphant.

To a greater extent than any film I have yet discussed, movement downward and parodies of romantic formulae dominate *Frenzy*. The opening sequence begins with two long, descending helicopter shots: the first starts high over London and comes down to a tracking shot over the river Thames, ending on a tugboat spouting black smoke as it emerges from behind an open drawbridge. The tug provides a curiously dirty, shabby contrast to the ceremonial music that has been on the sound track since the movie started. Even without the surprising intrusion of the boat, a student of Hitchcock's films would have cause to feel a bit wary about the possible foreshadowing of the underworld suggested by the river; for we have seen that in most of Hitchcock's movies, rivers and water carry associations with the night world and/or personal dissolution.

The second shot also swoops toward the river, and the sequence that follows confirms the threatening undercurrent of the opening imagery. With lofty rhetoric and considerable self-satisfaction, a political functionary is proclaiming the Thames officially "clean." He declares that "all the water above this point will soon be clear . . . clear of the waste products of our society." As he ends his speech, the body of a strangled woman floats to the shore: "Another necktie murder!" During the self-congratulatory speech, one member of the listening crowd withholds his applause—Hitchcock himself, dour in a dark suit and bowler hat. He knows more than the politician about the persistence of pollution, and he is about to show us what it is that he knows.

To judge by the reaction of the crowd to the floating body, we are all ready to be amused by such spectacles. As in *The Lodger*, the people on the scene immediately appropriate the tragedy for their own entertainment. "He's a regular Jack-the-Ripper," says one middle-aged woman. "Not on your life," replies a man craning past her for a glimpse of the corpse, "*he* used to carve 'em up. Sent a bird's kidney to Scotland Yard once, wrapped in a bit of violet writing paper. Or was it a bit of her liver?"

In another early sequence, a pair of prosperous men, one evidently a doctor, enter a pub for lunch. There they discuss the latest necktie murder with each other and with the waitress. Their conversation indicts them (and the society they represent) as rather unfeeling and perhaps morally implicated in the crimes. "Our necktie murderer's been up to it again," says one, using a curiously congenial pronoun. "He rapes 'em first, doesn't he?" asks the barmaid. Both men look vastly amused. "It's nice to know that every cloud has a silver lining," returns the doctor. Maisy the barkeeper elaborately signals her delighted shock at his wit.

Since Richard Blaney (Jon Finch) is hovering around the fringe, this conversation operates most obviously to augment the suspicion that we have already conceived watching him tie a necktie of the same pattern as that found around the murdered girl's throat. At the same time, however, it functions as did similar scenes in *The Lodger* to indicate that such crimes are not outside the ordinary sphere of society but are more accurately understood as extreme events within it. Such "sexual psychopaths," the doctor goes on, "appear as ordinary, likable, adult fellows." He hopes, "in one way," that the killer is not soon apprehended. "We haven't had a good, juicy series of sex murders since Christie. And they're so good for the tourist trade." More than the English are implicated. "Foreigners somehow expect the squares of London to be fog-wreathed, full of hansom cabs, and littered with ripped whores, don't you think?" (Such expectations, one might add, probably derive in part from movies like *Frenzy* and *The Lodger*.)

Always economical, Hitchcock has planted a third idea in this conversation. Christie was convicted of a series of sex murders and hanged in 1953. Three years earlier, a man named Evans had been convicted of the murder of his infant daughter and hanged. (He was also suspected, but not convicted, of the murder of his wife.) After Christie's conviction, a special board of inquiry was convened to reopen the Evans case. It concluded that Christie was probably the murderer of both Evans' child and his wife. In 1966, Evans was granted a free pardon, an exoneration that would perhaps have been more gratifying to him had it not come sixteen years posthumously. This widely publicized miscarriage of justice contributed to the sentiment that led to the abolishment of capital punishment in England.

The central character of *Frenzy*, Richard Blaney, undergoes a long slide downhill from which his recovery at the end of the film is only partial. A bit of human jetsam himself, he is being fired from his job as a bartender as the movie begins. But his demotions, apparently, have begun earlier, for his uncivil boss, with pointed sarcasm, calls him "squadron leader." Later we will learn of his broken marriage and failed business ventures. He has been unlucky. "Life," his ex-wife Brenda (Barbara Leigh-Hunt) agrees, "can be very unfair." In the course of the film, life will exercise its penchant for unfairness with increasing savagery, as Blaney loses his job, ex-wife, present girlfriend, old air-force buddy, honor, and freedom. His fortunes, more even than those of Michael Logan or Manny Balestrero, sink almost unremittingly. As he moves downward into an increasingly nightmarish world, he grows more and more isolated from the comfort of human support and social protection.

Camera placements reinforce the descending plot as the film continues; they tend to be high, pushing Blaney down optically. At critical junctures of his story, he often moves or is thrust downward: from his room to the bar where he is fired, down the stairs into prison after his conviction, down the prison stairs to the hospital. A very high subjective shot of him and his girlfriend Babs (Anna Massey) down in a garden fleeing from the police comes from the point of view of the antagonistic wife of his former air-force comrade. Far below, Blaney and Babs talk to her husband. He will offer them sanctuary; but the downward thrusting gaze of the wife dooms the offer from the start. Blaney will not escape the underworld into which bad luck has pulled him.

Nor, as the shot further suggests, will Babs. One of the best-known operations of the downward-looking camera in *Frenzy* follows close upon the shot just discussed and expresses, with a poignancy that direct representation could not match, the murder of Babs by Rusk (Barry Foster), Blaney's false friend and the real necktie murderer. Under the guise of a friend in need Rusk lures Babs to his flat, which he has offered her as temporary housing. Babs is wearing her orange suit, a garment that will later be planted by Rusk in Blaney's duffle bag to incriminate him. Orange on this occasion, as is generally the case in Hitchcock's color films, signals a strong warning of imminent danger. (Yellow tends to serve for Hitchcock as a milder warning color, and red as the announcement of acute crisis.)[17]

With the camera preceding and then pivoting to watch them through the door, they go up the stairs and turn into the flat. Babs enters first. As Rusk follows her, he remarks, "I don't know if you know it, Babs, but you're my type of woman." The last phrase, the same with which he began his rape and murder of Brenda Blaney, tells us that she is doomed. The camera remains focused on the door as it closes, then begins an excruciatingly silent pan and track away from the apartment where Babs will suffer rape and killing. As the camera moves down the stairs, it leaves behind and above it a window that looks out on light, sky, and other buildings. When it reaches the entry hall, the noise of the street begins to come up, growing steadily louder as the retreating camera continues its track out the door and across the busy, raucous

[17] Gorham Anders Kindem, in *Toward a Semiotic Theory of Visual Communication in the Cinema* (New York: Arno Press, 1980), argues that the color brown is also used systematically in *Frenzy*: "the themes of environmental pollution and the human pollution of the environment that infests human relationships, are in part evoked by the repetition of the color brown in specific color objects" (p. 212).

thoroughfare. There may be screams, but nobody is likely to hear them, or take notice even if they are audible. Babs is left alone to die. Rather than protecting her, nearby people drown her out; the camera deserts her—out of indifference or perhaps because it cannot bear to watch. We may feel both helpless and complicit in our own removal from the scene.

Another point regarding Hitchcock's use of color in this sequence is worth taking note of here. As the camera makes its retreat out of the entrance to Rusk's building and across the street, a man carrying a sack of fruit or potatoes moves in front of the camera, effecting a momentary fade to black. After it has passed, the light in the entry hall appears yellow where it was cool and neutral before. The technical explanation for this shift would appear to be that Hitchcock switched film to a stock balanced for outdoor light at this point in the tracking shot, and as a result the tungsten illumination of the hall thereafter registered a warm yellow-orange. A variant of this explanation would be that the cameraman removed a correction filter from the lens as the man went by, thereby in effect switching to filmstock balanced for daylight, but without having to reload the camera.

Trying to explain away the effect technically, however, does not make sense of it. It would not have been difficult to avoid the color shift in the hall of Rusk's building: daylight-balanced illumination of the interior, for example, might have been one solution. We must conclude that Hitchcock both wished the effect and wished it to be relatively unobtrusive. I observed earlier that yellow and orange are often coded as warnings in Hitchcock's color films. The appearance of the yellow light in Rusk's hallway as the camera tracks away, considered as a meaningful element rather than as an unsolved technical fault, reiterates the warning of Babs's orange dress and of Rusk's greeting to her as she enters his flat.

We can better understand the expressive effect of this long up-and-down shot by comparing it with an extraordinary sequence, which reverses its direction and import, from the second *The Man Who Knew Too Much*. The series of shots to which I refer comes near the end of the film, after the attempted assassination in the Albert Hall, when Jo and Ben are in the embassy looking for their son. As Ben anticipated, Jo is asked to sing. In an attempt to fill the building with sound so that Hank can hear her no matter where he may be, she begins to bray "Qué Será, Será." The camera pans slowly away from the ballroom and stops in the hallway. Then come a series of eight very briefly held shots, beginning when the camera reaches the stairs in the hall. In rapid succession follow a reverse shot of the same staircase, a shot of the stair railing near the top, then a second, shorter flight of stairs, a close-up of its ornate banister, a tighter close-up at the top of the stairs, an up-stairs hall, a door, and the doorknob. Finally the camera moves into the room in which Hank is being held.

This rhythmically cut series of shots—stills, in effect—ascends with the mother's voice in quest of the lost child. In tracing the journey of Jo's voice to the ears of her stolen son, the camera becomes the projection of her desire and of the power of her art and, perhaps, of art itself. It goes up to awaken and recover the sleeping, captive Hank and to make whole again the broken family. Like the Prince coming to kiss Sleeping Beauty, it restores, with the same action, the integrity of a society as well.

It is next to impossible to render without unconvincing impression-ism the effect of the series of brief shots that convey us upstairs to the room in which Hank is imprisoned. But however one describes them, their rhythmic, slightly disjunct ascent reverses the smooth, slow descent in the later film as the camera leaves Babs to her fate. The sound tracks also contrast: Doris Day's song accompanying the one, silence and then the chaotic noise of the street the other. At the end of the ascending sequence, rescue and restoration; at the end of the descend-ing one, rape and murder.

A subsequent sequence emphasizes the fatal outcome when Babs ac-cepts Rusk's offer. After cutting away to a dinnertime conversation between Inspector Oxford (Alec McCowen) and his wife (Vivien Mer-chant), the movie returns to the scene of Babs's murder to show Rusk stowing her body on a potato truck. An elevated, wide-angle night shot looks down on the killer as he dollies the body across the street to the truck park—a melancholy crossing to the Land of the Dead. And/or the Land of the Discarded: the potatoes, unsold and unwanted, are being returned to Lincolnshire to be plowed back into the ground.

When the camera follows Rusk and Babs up to his apartment and then makes its sad, solitary retreat, it concludes one of many disap-pointed or parodied ascents to sanctuary, love, or relief. Others prolif-erate. The first time Blaney goes up to see his former wife, his quarrel with her is overheard by her hostile, prissy secretary; the second time, he receives no answer to his knock because she has been murdered by Rusk. He is observed leaving, however, by the secretary as she returns from lunch to discover her employer's body. Her report leads the po-lice to begin hunting him as the prime suspect in the necktie murders.

A little later he and Babs go to the Coburg Hotel, where they are taken up to the "Cupid Room." "Love's little arrows have stuck quite a few 'earts in there, Sir, I can tell you," remarks the porter as he admits them. But beneath the door of this love nest will slide a newspaper, the front page announcing the murder of Brenda Blaney and the search for her former husband. The hotel staff read the same newspaper story. They call the police, who arrive to look out the window of the now empty room into a tangle of descending fire stairs and scaffolding below. Blaney and Babs, fleeing their pursuers, have crept from the Cupid Room by the back stairs. They have been driven back to the lower world of flight and suspicion.

The ironies of this frustrated ascent embrace Babs as well as Blaney. During their brief stay in the Coburg, Babs awakens and gets out of bed to go to the bathroom. Nude, she sits up and draws on her stockings; then we watch her pad into the bathroom, turn on the light, and close the door. This curious little sequence does more than expose Anna Massey's admirable figure. Her next sexual experience will be rape, not lovemaking; and the next time we see her nude body it will be dead and stuffed into a sack of potatoes.

Dick's old squadron buddy Johnny takes him and Babs up the stairs to his posh apartment to hide them from the police; but, as I have already noted, the antagonistic wife (one more Hitchcockian variant on the Terrible Mother) will eventually drive him out. During his stay in Johnny's inept protection, Blaney's life disintegrates further. When he leaves, it is with the knowledge that Babs too has been strangled, and that Johnny and his wife will refuse to help him. What begins as a brave gesture of friendship ends with a cowardly desertion. "But you're my only alibi," Richard points out desperately. "I'm sorry old chap," mumbles Johnny, "I've got to get to Paris today. I can't afford to be kept here."

After he departs the flat of Johnny and his wife, Blaney falls, as did Babs after she left, into the hands of Rusk. The same shot that conveyed Babs up to Rusk's flat shows her lover going up the same stairs to his own catastrophe there. This time the camera follows him into Rusk's "little nest," his home, "the place where," he sententiously tells Blaney, "when you have to go there, they have to take you in. That's what my old Mum used to say." This dreadfully ironic quotation from Robert Frost is delivered as Rusk stands framed between two odd portraits of young women of Indian and/or Oriental descent. These pictures remind us of his alienation from women and of his imperialistic domination and appropriation of them. Babs left Rusk's home as a corpse in a potato sack; Blaney will leave it in the custody of the police, to whom Rusk betrays him.

Related to the motif of ironically reversed ascents are a pair of parodic versions of death and return. The first occurs after Rusk has put

Babs's body on the truck for Lincolnshire and then realized that she must have taken his monogrammed tiepin during the struggle when he throttled her. When he goes back to retrieve it, he is inadvertently hauled away with his victim and the potatoes. During a long sequence of what may be the blackest humor of Hitchcock's career, Rusk struggles with Babs's body for possession of the diamond stickpin. The bouncing of the truck and the rigor mortis that closes its fist make the corpse a frustrating adversary.

Robin Wood has condemned this sequence, noting acidly that "Hitchcock clearly supposed it to be funny."[18] Wood, uncharacteristically, has allowed political preoccupations to unsteady his usually secure critical intelligence. Of course the scene is funny. By making it comic Hitchcock deprives death of its last consolation, its emotional dignity. Babs, a snatched but unrecovered Persephone, can return to the world of the living only in a dreadful parody of resurrection, as a piece of dead meat tumbling among the potatoes in a macabre "Mulligan stew." The last time we saw her nude figure, it was alive and adorable. This time it is a dead thing, with only the mechanical power to feign a grip left from its death agony. The sequence *is* funny, and the more terrible for being so. (Moreover, we take some pleasure, however grave, in Rusk's discomfiture.)

A second action that suggests death and return, Blaney's escape from prison via the hospital, carries complex overtones both of true resurrection and of its parody. The episode begins when Blaney, in keeping with the general sinking of his movements throughout the film, throws himself down a flight of steel stairs in the prison. As he lies unconscious at the bottom, a stream of dark blood emerges from his head. An ambulance carries him away to the hospital. There, in a conventionally comic sequence, he stages an ingenious escape with the help of his fellow prisoners, then sets off in a stolen Rover to avenge himself on Rusk.

We watch him ascend one more time the fatal stairs to Rusk's flat. Letting himself into the apartment, he sees what he takes to be Rusk's red hair on the pillow as he sleeps in his bed. Blaney smashes the top of his concealed face three times with a jack handle from the stolen car, only to watch a feminine arm with braceletted wrist slide from under the covers. He has not killed Rusk but some unknown woman! Inno-

[18] Robin Wood, "Fear of Spying," *American Film* (November 1983): p. 31; reprinted in Marshall Deutelbaum and Leland Poague, eds., *A Hitchcock Reader* (Ames, Iowa: Iowa State University Press, 1986). Further citations to this essay will be to the *Hitchcock Reader* reprinting.

cent before, he is now guilty of the crime for which he has been imprisoned.

But the reversals multiply. When he pulls back the covers he finds the disrobed body of a young woman, garrotted with a necktie. So he is not a murderer after all! The door bursts open. Inspector Oxford enters and sees Blaney with the body. Now it does not matter that he is not a murderer; he has been caught by fate again and will again take the blame for Rusk's crime.

Yet one more reversal remains. The sound of heavy thumping comes up the stairs, and Oxford, signaling Blaney to be quiet, hides behind the door. Rusk enters with a footlocker; sees Blaney; sees Oxford, who shuts the door behind him. "Mr. Rusk," says the Inspector with quiet contempt, "you're not wearing your tie."

The penultimate shot of the film shows the whole room, Rusk between Oxford and Blaney, the murdered girl on the bed in the background right. This brilliant summarizing image wraps up the plot. Rusk drops the trunk, on which the camera moves in close as it falls to the floor. There it lies while the closing credits run and the image fades out. The trunk will not coffin his latest victim; but Rusk will be taking a trip from which, to transplant a quotation that Hitchcock used elsewhere, "no traveller ever returns."[19]

This economical, self-effacing conclusion sums up a good deal of the method and meaning of *Frenzy*. Its series of startling reversals recapitulate similar reversals, mostly with ironic conclusions, that recur throughout the film. That it ends with Blaney's exoneration and with Rusk's capture gives it an upbeat last moment, but the body of yet another of the murderer's victims lies in the background to remind us that most of what has been done cannot be undone. Brenda and Babs, the most attractive characters in the film, exist no more; and Blaney's life has been shattered on the concrete floor of his misfortunes. As the Inspector replies when his kindly wife asks if Blaney will be awarded compensation by the court, "I expect they'll give him some money, but there's no real way to compensate in cases like these."

When the idea of inadequate compensation comes to summarize its action, the meanings of the film take on a dominantly ironic hue. Like Job, and like other Hitchcockian evocations of him, Blaney is an essentially good man upon whom is visited a terrible series of undeserved misfortunes. Unlike Guy Haines, The Lodger, Michael Logan, or Manny Balestrero, he cannot fully recover. Although he survives, he is

[19] The assassins in both versions of *The Man Who Knew Too Much* say this, as does Rico Para in *Topaz*. The line is from *Hamlet*, Act III, Scene i.

left crippled and diminished. He does not emerge with a new wife or even with the recovery of a former prosperity. The worst has happened and it has been only partly retracted. Too much wreckage remains strewn about for us to be left with faith in a benign force that will make sure that all misfortune is repaid with happiness, all tears dried and replaced by smiles.

The empty and violent world to which Blaney returns seems to claim him as one of its corrupted own. The young woman whose skull he crushes does not become his victim only because she has already been murdered. The marks of Blaney's blows are on her forehead. They may be legally and medically irrelevant, but they leave us with an impression of him that recalls the violence and anger we saw earlier: with his wife, in the pub, mashing a box of grapes underfoot after he failed to bet on a horse named—ironically—"Coming Up."

Prominent in the visual design of the last two shots, but iconographically unemphatic at the same time, are two images of the cross. The first comes from the door panels behind Inspector Oxford as he waits for Rusk to enter the apartment. Hitchcock took this cruciform image from doors repeatedly throughout his career, with varying degrees of emphasis but never blatantly. The second image of the cross appears on the top of the trunk over which the closing titles run. Both crosses, and at the same time their relative inconspicuousness, complement the equivocal "resurrection" of Blaney and the convoluted textures of the end of the film. The allusion to Christ is made, but diffidently. Who, if anyone, is associated with the crosses? Blaney, who suffers for the sins of others? Oxford, next to whom the door panels are seen? All four characters—one of them dead—who appear in the final scene? Or do the images of the cross constitute a mocking, a reminder that heaven is empty, or indifferent to human desires? The questions are easier to ask than to answer.

For the movie as a whole, however, religious imagery points toward disappointment and irony rather than toward affirmation. A critical moment in this regard, after which we can no longer hope with any seriousness for the miraculous intervention of a benevolent god or world order, comes during the rape and strangling of Brenda. As Rusk shoves her back in a chair in her office and (possibly) penetrates her, she recites verses five, six and eleven of the 91st Psalm:

> Thou shalt not be afraid for the terror by night; nor for the arrow which flieth by day;
> Nor for the pestilence which walketh in darkness; nor for the destruction that wasteth at noonday.

For he shall give his angels charge over thee, to keep thee in all thy
ways.

As she speaks, we see between her breasts a diamond cross. No aid
descends from a heaven that seems deaf to this eloquent prayer. As
Brenda readjusts her brassiere, we see the cross on her bosom more
clearly. Off camera, again and again, Rusk croaks "Lovely!" In a few
minutes he will strangle his victim. Brenda's last intelligible words are
"O, Jesus, help me, help me." Unlike Michael Logan or Manny Balestrero, Brenda is truly alone, beyond the agency of divine or human aid,
or even benign chance. The last verse of the 91st Psalm, unquoted in
the film, resonates for those who may recall it with dreadful irony:
"With long life will I satisfy him, and show him my salvation."

Against these words Inspector Oxford's description of sexual psychopaths echoes a few minutes later: "In the latter stages of the disease,
it's the strangling, not the sex, that brings them off." An environment
of disease, of human pollution, obliterates one in which spiritual values or moral order have any effective presence. We may not be able to
characterize the world of *Frenzy* as malignant, but it appears to be the
next worse thing, indifferent to human aspirations and fears. Though
the movie will offer some later consolations, it can never, after Brenda
Blaney's unanswered prayer, give any assurance of divine concern or
protection.

During the second dinner sequence, The Inspector makes an observation that illuminates both the hollowness of religion in *Frenzy* and
Hitchcock's remarkable genius for retaining material until he found
the right moment for it. Mrs. Oxford is wondering aloud what the
murderer of Babs might have been seeking in her hand, "a locket, a
brooch, a cross? . . . Not a cross, I think." "I don't see why not," speculates her husband. "Religious and sexual mania are closely linked."
This remark from the most authoritative figure in the film reduces religion still further from an ineffectual superstition to another manifestation of disease.

In many ways, *Frenzy* recapitulates *The Lodger*. Both take a Jack-
the-Ripper series of murders as occasion for their plots, and both create circumstances that nearly convict a man who is at once innocent of
the crimes and their most grievously injured surviving victim. In Marie
Belloc Lowndes's novel, Hitchcock found the idea of a link between
religious and sexual pathology (and very nearly the precise phrase) that
he gives to Inspector Oxford forty-six years later. Its reappearance in
Frenzy confirms the connection between the two films and reminds us
of the astonishing capaciousness and consistency of Hitchcock's mind.

Like those of ascent and resurrection, the romantic motifs of journeying and of miraculous coincidence turn in *Frenzy* largely into parodies. In general, Dick Blaney's status as an emphatically earthbound
former RAF Wing Commander reflects his lack of freedom and mobility. The fluid movement of the opening helicopter shots is reversed by
the progressive entrapment and restraining of the hero in the movie
that follows. The downward motion of the opening shots, rather than
their mobility, will be developed visually and thematically in *Frenzy*.

Of particular importance in Hitchcock's next-to-last film is its par-
odying of yet another set of romantic conventions: the related themes
of artifice and ritual. The first sequence following the credits introduces what will be a pervasive motif in which formal behavior produces conclusions or results that are opposite to those intended. The
politician bids farewell to human pollution on the Thames, as we have
seen, prematurely; when the corpse of the young woman washes onto
the bank, his evocations of pastoral tranquillity only serve to make the
reality of human waste and disease more appalling. Other undercut-
tings and reversals of social rituals follow. The miscarrying of the police as they assemble evidence, and of the judiciary as it draws its errant
conclusions, occupies much of the film. The apparatus that should
maintain social order accidentally promotes error and chaos. Its mistakes are not the mistakes of comedy, startling coincidences that prove
ultimately harmless. Rather they appear inevitable, given the deceitful
way in which the world presents itself. And they are profoundly destructive, not only to the hero of the film but also to the confidence and
safety of society at large.

Frenzy most pervasively subjects to ironic undercutting the social
ritual of eating, the affectionate affirmation of trust that is implied
whenever two or more people sit down to a meal together. It expands
gustatory communion to include the associated apparatus of procuring
and preparing food. "Man does not live by bread alone," nor does one
receive only physical nourishment from eating.

In all his films, Hitchcock is acutely aware of the affirmative rituals
implicit in eating and of the irony of psychologically sterile meals or of
meals shared with enemies.[20] In no other movie, however, does he take

---

[20] The bread and cheese that Erica brings to Robert Tisdall in the old mill amounts to
a first confession of love, and the fact that she leaves her parental table to deliver it
suggests that she has begun to make the transition from her childhood home and family
to an adult one. It is over lunch that Bruno proposes his swap of murders to Guy. The
Lodger and Daisy meet when she brings him his breakfast. In *Shadow of a Doubt*, we
learn of the genesis of Uncle Charlie's murderous psychosis while he eats breakfast in
bed and chats with his sister and niece. In *Psycho* the meal of sandwiches and milk

this tendency to the extremes of *Frenzy*. In this film the motif of food and eating becomes so insistent as to approach the comic. Many of the characters have names that suggest food: Rusk (bread crumbs or crusts in England), who is a fruiterer; Sergeant Spearman, who is once called "positively glutinous with self-approbation"; Babs Milligan, whose surname suggests a stew; Brenda Blaney's secretary "Miss Barley"; Maisie the barmaid; Mr. Asher, his name pronounced to sound like "rasher"; Inspector Oxford and his wife, a novice gourmet cook.

Richard Blaney has a particularly unhappy relation to food and drink, which generally either injures him or serves as a medium through which he expresses his rage. The first four sequences in which he appears all associate him with contentious eating or drinking. He is fired from his job at The Globe for taking a drink before the pub opens, and shortly thereafter he abuses a barman over the size of the brandy he has just purchased with his last pound. (As he does so, the doctor who is lunching in the pub describes the necktie murderer as one of the type of psychotics who are "particularly dangerous when their desires are being frustrated.") He stomps underfoot the box of grapes that Rusk has given him. During dinner with Brenda, he becomes so upset while talking about his failures in business that he breaks his brandy glass in his hand, then snaps brusquely at the waitress who comes to offer assistance.

Food and drink are also associated with Blaney's betrayal into the hands of the police. As Rusk departs his flat, he invites his unsuspecting guest to make himself at home. "There's something to eat in the kitchen. The booze is here. So get on with it, right?" Supposing himself safe for the moment, Blaney helps himself to the offered drink just before the police enter and arrest him. He is not given this day his daily bread; nor is he forgiven, or able to forgive, his trespasses and those who trespass against him.

Hitchcock characterizes Rusk predominantly as a supplier and consumer of bad food. The snake in the latter-day Garden of Eden, Covent Garden, Rusk first appears in the movie eating an emblematic apple. His association with Eden is reiterated when he introduces his mother as living "down in Kent, in the garden of England." During most of his screen time, he either eats or picks his teeth—often both at once. He

---

precedes Norman's murder of Marion. The most arrogant violation of the norms of social respect by the blackmailer in *Blackmail* may be his thrusting himself upon the heroine's family when he coerces her into serving him a late breakfast. The poisoning of Alicia in *Notorious* represents a demonic inversion of the relationship of marriage. And so on. A remarkably large proportion of turning points in Hitchcock's movies takes place around the nexus of food.

jokes about giving short weight at his market, and about Blaney water-ing the gin and "pissing in the beer" at the pub.

During the ghastly sequence of his rape and strangling of Brenda, Rusk is relentlessly portrayed as a fouler of the ordinary human com-munion of nourishment. The sequence begins when he intrudes into her lunch hour, which she is enjoying alone in her office. The violation of her person proceeds in parallel with the appropriation of her meal. Rusk babbles on about how one ought not "squeeze the goods until they're yours" and about taking Brenda out to lunch, but his words entirely misrepresent his intentions. He brags that he has "good points," among them his fondness for "flowers and fruit." His first signs of ungovernable frustration come when he criticizes her lunch as "frugal and mean." When he picks up Brenda's partly eaten apple and takes an aggressive bite from it, he unequivocally announces his inten-tion to take possession of her.

During the rape itself, he repeats in a gravely, insane voice, "Lovely! Lovely!" The obvious connection of this word to the eating motif will be clearer to English audiences than to American ones, for the English cliche of praise for delicious food is "lovely." His grunts accompany his illegitimate consumption of a "meal" that he began when he seized Brenda Blaney's apple. With horrible consistency, he ends as he began, with fruit, taking another bite from Brenda's apple after choking her. As he starts to leave her office, picking his teeth with a stickpin that at once recalls his eating her food and killing her with his tie, he glances back at her desk. Seeing the remains of the apple on it, he returns and drops it into his pocket—like any thrifty patron of a good restaurant who thinks to take the uneaten portion of the meal home.

Rusk represents in the extreme the violence and pollution of the hu-man social order, both in his homicidal sexuality and in his corruption of the symbology of food. He snatches the women from whom he squeezes the life like Pluto dragging Persephone down to Hades. His victims are associated with the "fruit and flowers" that he professes to like; Brenda with her lunchtime apple, Babs with flowers. When he lures Babs to her doom, Rusk takes her through an immense, enclosed wholesale flower market. As they walk among the bouquets, he tells her of his desire to visit the places "where the fruit comes from." But he consumes Babs, as he did Brenda, with little love and no right. After killing her, he stuffs her into a sack of discarded potatoes. Then he returns to his flat where he flops onto his couch to pick his teeth and to enjoy, as it were, a postprandial glass of wine.

Because food and eating represent so much sadness, violence, and corruption, we may be puzzled by the fact that the mealtime interactions of Inspector Oxford and his wife supply *Frenzy* with its sunniest humor. Their comic subplot begins when we see the Inspector unaccountably breakfasting at his desk while he goes over the reports of Brenda Blaney's murder. A moment later, between bites, he reveals the reason for his oddly timed meal: "Sergeant, my wife is currently taking a course at The Continental School of Gourmet Cooking." As his wife does her homework, a succession of unappetizing and unsatisfying examples of her studies present themselves to the meat-and-potatoes Inspector. Oxford tries, with polite good nature, to choke down a "soupe de poisson" in which a brownish, whole squid floats among less identifiable marine remains. A pathetic, scrawny quail occupies his plate next, and he cuts resolutely into it while remarking about the necktie killer that "we've got to find him before his appetite is whetted again." No danger in that regard, so it appears, for the unlucky Inspector.

The next time we see the Oxfords at dinner, the Inspector's wife is assuring him that the wrong man has been jailed and that Rusk, according to her "woman's intuition," must be the real criminal. "What does your intuition tell you I want for dinner tonight?" asks her still good-tempered spouse. "Steak and a baked potato," she replies, accurately. "But you're getting *pied du porc* . . . in the same sauce the French use for tripe." As he tells his wife that Rusk had to break the fingers of Babs's corpse to retrieve whatever he was looking for, she picks up and snaps a breadstick, then absent-mindedly crunches it in her mouth. "It would be so nice to get back to plain bread in this house," the Inspector remarks wistfully. Sergeant Spearman arrives and Mrs. Oxford, to her husband's embarrassment, presses him to accept a Margarita. After he has gone, having produced the evidence that will clear Blaney and implicate Rusk, the Inspector's wife speculates on what might be done to make amends to the wrongly convicted man. "Poor man," she murmurs. "I think the least you can do is ask him round for a really good dinner . . . duckling, with heavy, sweet, cherry sauce." The Inspector, faced with the humiliating spread into public of his private culinary misfortunes, can maintain his good temper no longer. "Well after that jail food he's been having, I expect he'll eat anything." Stung by the sarcasm, Mrs. Oxford gulps the Margarita that Sergeant Spearman has abandoned and totters back to the kitchen.

As Donald Spoto has observed, Hitchcock persistently associates in *Frenzy* the acts of ingestion and sex.[21] (This is nothing new in his directorial career, *Notorious* being the most obvious earlier example of

[21] Spoto, *The Art of Alfred Hitchcock*, pp. 435-45.

such an association.) Discussions of the necktie murderer's sexual proclivities over the Inspector's office breakfast and over dinner at home
inevitably suggest that the Oxfords's mealtime misalignment may reflect difficulties in a more intimate sphere of their marital life. At one
point, over *"caille au raisin,"* the connection becomes almost explicit.
The Inspector's wife is doubting that Blaney is the right suspect: "How
long did you say he was married?" "Ten years," replies her husband.
"Well, there you are. A *crime de passion* after all that time? Look at
us. We've only been married eight years and you can hardly keep your
eyes open at night." "Well that's as may be," he answers, "but I don't
knock you about, either, or make you do degrading things."

This conversation throws a great deal of light not only upon the
Oxfords but upon their place among the complex meanings of the
whole film. They represent an alternative to the brutal, exploitative
relations between men and women that are mostly the norm elsewhere
in the film, and in the context of which Rusk's behavior appears extreme in degree but not different in kind. For men and women, in general, use each other unkindly in *Frenzy*. Forsythe's coarse, dictatorial
tone toward Babs; the evident intention of Mrs. Davidson to treat her
new husband, like her late one, as a housekeeper, stud service, and
cook; the prurient amusement that Maisie and her customers take in
the crimes of the necktie murderer; the abuse Johnny's wife directs
toward her husband as well as toward Blaney; the policeman who
identifies Rusk as being "one for the birds" and who, otherwise hu-
morless, laughs when Rusk characterizes women by saying that "half
of them haven't got their heads screwed on right, let alone know
whether they're being screwed off"—all this expresses, implicitly or
explicitly, relations between men and women that are mistrustful and
condescending and that verge on open hostility.

The relationship between Mrs. Oxford and her husband offers a
plausible alternative to such gender warfare. The Inspector and his
wife collaborate in the true solution of the crimes. They thereby
achieve the sort of insight that crucially operates in bringing the comic
romances to happy conclusions. Mrs. Oxford's experiments in *haute
cuisine*, and her husband's civility about them, show people compromising, being patient, accepting the desire to please as equivalent to
success.

In a world that has fallen as far as the London of *Frenzy*, not many
princes and princesses meet, marry, and live happily ever after. Given
the defects of human nature, however, the Inspector and his wife cope
with the inevitable frustrations of marriage with good humor and mutual respect. Mrs. Oxford seems especially enterprising. After eight

years of lawful wedded bliss, things are bound to get a bit unexciting, at the table as well as elsewhere. Dinnertime may not be the only occasion at which it has occurred to her to introduce continental variations. Neither Mrs. Oxford nor her husband is especially glamorous or without faults; but in a fallen world of human flaws and limitations, they accept each other with grace and affectionate support. They represent an alternative to the all-or-nothing vision of pollution versus pastoral purity that began the film. Their small family may appear frail, but it manages to be loving, orderly, and stable. It contrasts reassuringly with the darkness and chaos that envelop the main plot.

The Oxfords, of ordinary appearance and temper, middle-aged, middle-class, and just slightly stodgy, can maintain nonetheless a life of warmth and interest. Indeed, theirs is the only alternative presented to the diseased or discontented private lives elsewhere shown in *Frenzy*. The Inspector and his wife are doing better than making the poor best of an irremediably miserable situation. Their marriage presents a kind and satisfying response to human needs and limitations. It does not differ fundamentally from the conservative, modest rewards achieved by the heroines and heroes of the comic romances. The cruelest disappointment of their counterparts, both in *Frenzy* and in Hitchcock's even grimmer, more ironic films, often consists of a failure to achieve just such bourgeois emotional stability as that represented by Mrs. Oxford and her husband.

The subplot of the Oxfords imparts an emotional balance to *Frenzy* that keeps it from giving way to unalloyed, sentimental cynicism. Other elements also contribute to its happier side. Innocence and corruption are engaged in a conflict that is not, for all the unfairness and viciousness of the world, wholly one-sided. "Woman's intuition," the affectionate disposition and faith that make the heroines of the comic romances so essential and effective in the cause of good, exists in various ways in three of the four main female characters (the fourth is Johnny's termagant wife). Brenda takes Blaney to dinner, surreptitiously puts twenty pounds in his pocket, and generally behaves with surprising affection for a divorced spouse. Mrs. Oxford never believes in Blaney's guilt, and she wishes to have him over for "a really good dinner" as soon as he gets out of jail.

The most supportive and loving of the good women is Babs. Her presence gives *Frenzy* a sense of hope and congeniality; her murder, therefore, constitutes one of its most painful ironies. She stands up for Blaney to two of the least sympathetic of his persecutors, Forsythe and Johnny's wife. Shortly before her death, she has a garden scene with her lover that could be transposed without dissonance into any of

Hitchcock's luckiest comedies. She and Blaney are in a public garden to which they have fled from the hotel. Babs is half-questioning, half-accusing her lover. "You got that money from her [Brenda], didn't you?" she realizes with damning insight. But the affection of a Hitchcockian heroine gives her faith beyond logic. "Then you believe me?" asks Blaney, a few minutes later. "Thousands wouldn't," replies Babs, nodding affirmatively. They embrace. "I must be soft in the head, letting a suspected strangler put his arms around me," smiles Babs. "Shows you trust me," says Blaney. "I s'pose so," she agrees.

If *Frenzy* were a comic romance, this moment would mark the turning point of Blaney's luck. But the flame of love and belief is almost immediately snuffed. Babs leaves Blaney a few minutes later to return to The Globe; from there she goes to her death in Rusk's apartment. Although Babs dies, she makes an important contribution to the texture of the movie while she is in it. Furthermore, while there is obviously no assurance in the film that such people cannot die, there is no implication that they must always perish, either.

The Inspector, with his sense of duty and order, counterbalances the isolation and loneliness of most of the other characters, and he pursues the case of the necktie murders to a true and just solution. When the police and other agents of social authority become genuinely sympathetic and protective figures in Hitchcock's films, it is a sign of movement toward irony. In the romances, a pair of lovers is characteristically set against the mob, of whom detectives and sheriffs and other social agents are a more organized but equally imbecilic manifestation. As the world decays, and its corruption becomes more evident, official stays against chaos gain increased sympathy. Thus in a movie of comic irony like *Stage Fright* (the target of Hitchcock's satire in that film being very largely his own filmmaking practices), the comforting authority of detective "Ordinary" Smith is set against the deceptiveness of appearances and the real dangerousness of the world. So, too, the Inspector's stature in *Frenzy*. Like Babs's, his presence brightens the otherwise predominantly dusky textures of the movie. He is perceptive, successful, and able, to a degree, to neutralize the forces of death and deceit.

Finally—and this is crucial to the movie—Richard Blaney endures. Although he is partly defeated and considerably brutalized by the world, he continues to seek justice and to entertain hope. He is a person of ordinary stature, but he retains traces of the superior piece of work that a human can be at his best. As an RAF wing commander he was decorated for "inspiring leadership, skill, and tenacity of purpose." The affection of his former wife and the love of his mistress, both unequivocally sympathetic figures, testify to his best qualities; and we see in his refusal to succumb wholly to his misfortunes some of the style and tenaciousness that were cited in the award of his Distinguished Flying Cross. Though he has declined from the man that he was, and though he can never be fully compensated for his misfortunes, he survives at least, and he collects the partial compensation of his exoneration and Rusk's downfall. He may be improvident, forgetful, marginally alcoholic, and unlucky, but he is not evil. And the world, for all that it hounds him to the brink of madness, cannot crush him.

The closing image of *Frenzy*, the close-up of the trunk that Rusk brings to his flat to dispose of his last victim, may appear pedestrian, but it summarizes the complex ambiguities of a vision that Hitchcock sustains throughout the film. It suggests the coffin that it was meant to be; but Rusk is prevented from using it. It carries, as I noted earlier, images of the cross on its lid, and thus at once evokes Christian mythology and recalls the inefficacy of Brenda's prayer. Without promising anything like full happiness or restitution for the beleaguered hero of the film, it does remind us that the antagonist has been apprehended with unequivocally damning evidence in his hands. Further, it evokes some sense of travel and escape from present troubles. If nothing else, it wraps things up, with their complexity undiminished, in a big, faintly mysterious box.

Finally, there is the point we began with, the commonplace quality of this closing image. *Frenzy* is a film of the commonplace—of the banal furnishings of everyday life and, paradoxically, of the intense human desires and crushing disappointments that they reflect. We recall the opening images of the Thames and the politician's grandiloquent claims of present accomplishments and future bliss. The world we know by the end of the movie is smaller, less simple, and less hopeful. But it is also richer and truer. *Frenzy* does not pretend that poisonous "waste products of our society" can be forever banished; on the contrary, it shows human corruption to be fierce and pervasive. But it also shows human life as persistent and capable of islands of love and order in the wash of angry incoherence.

The claim of neat final solutions with which *Frenzy* begins has its own desperate quality. If the more believable portrayal of life that follows is more distressing, it is also, from another point of view, less anxious. In retrospect, the opening promises seem like so many frantic lies. Two hours later we will have witnessed sobering examples of the pollution of human society. But we will also have seen good people, acting with love and kindness, who win at least a few of their battles

with the forces of degeneracy. In the end, such mixed hope and fear
may be less alarming than transparent lies of Eden returned. The former, for all its blend of desire and frustration, is something; the latter,
nothing at all.

ALTHOUGH the outlines of their plots are similar, and although they
resemble each other in numerous details of character and setting,
Young and Innocent and *Frenzy* figure forth very different visions of
human life. The nine films on which the previous two chapters have
focused, all narratives of falsely accused innocents, may be seen as
shading gradually from the optimism and gaiety of comic romance to
the equivocal losses and partial recoveries of ironic tragedy. In their
similarities, and their differences, they display both the coherence and
the fecund variety of Hitchcock's work. In the context of romantic
narrative, and its parodies and negations, we discover much of the conceptual framework through which Hitchcock contemplated the world.

His films vary enormously depending upon his handling of the venerable formulas that he adopted from the first years of his career. The
underlying assumptions about the world, however, and what is congenial or frightening in it, are relatively few and fairly simple. Conservative, conventional prejudices underlie Hitchcock's films. Most of his
fictions embody the kind of straightforward moral attitudes and psychological assurance implicit in popular stories and myths. They are
deeply, if not always obviously, influenced by the Christianity in which
Hitchcock was raised and educated. Like most distinctive representers
of human life, Hitchcock's originality rests not in eccentricity but in an
unsurpassed comprehension of the fundamentals and conventions of
his art. Secure within that understanding, he works manifold variations of texture, tone, and meaning.

The world in Hitchcock's movies always appears in implicit comparison with an ideal of human achievement and recovery that I have
called, in a somewhat specialized sense, romantic. The most tranquil
and optimistic of Hitchcock's movies most closely approximate a full
achievement of simple fairy-tale romantic narrative, updated and
adapted to the overwhelming capabilities of the cinema to create convincing presence. The most alarming and inescapably distressing of his
movies are those that turn the formulas of comic romance upside
down. *Frenzy* persistently develops such tragic ironies, and we shall
see them again in the films to be discussed in later chapters on Hitchcockian irony.

Hitchcock's characteristic and complex use of the conventional tensions and fulfillments of romantic narrative structures constitutes, in

general, the subject of this book. In the movies that I have considered in this chapter, there is a gradual movement from romantic comedy into which considerable elements of irony and destruction have crept (*Strangers on a Train*), through three films that remain romantic in structure but lean increasingly away from comedy and toward tragedy, to the multiple ironies and frequently irremedial sufferings of *Frenzy*. As these films move from a comic toward a tragic sense of action, we observe an increase in the serious pain and misfortune suffered by sympathetic (or partly sympathetic) characters and a decrease in incidental humor. Miriam dies in *Strangers on a Train*; three innocent and attractive young women are murdered on screen in *The Lodger*; Otto and Alma perish in *I Confess*; fate tortures Manny in *The Wrong Man*, and his wife suffers a nervous breakdown from which she recovers only after the story ends; Blaney can never be compensated fully for his anguish in *Frenzy*, and both his former wife and his present companion are raped and murdered.

When Hitchcock's films move away from romance and toward irony, their romantic conventions do not disappear but transform into versions that are disappointed, frustrated, or parodied. Ascents to truth and love lead instead to falsehood and hostility; the adventurous travels of the romances are progressively restricted and constrained; in place of episodes of disappearance and return, repeated descending actions suggest a world spiraling entropically downward. The clarity of issues and the distinctions between sympathetic and unsympathetic characters grow increasingly complicated by qualifications and complexities. In the social themes of *The Lodger* we may see something of this tendency; in *Frenzy* it additionally informs characterization and setting. The core romantic plot of fall, purging quest, and redemptive triumph is persistently distorted, in more ironic films, into a failed approximation or a parodic reversal.

As a result of Hitchcock's tendency to organize his vision of life, positively or negatively, in relation to the expectations embodied in romantic narrative conventions, we find consistency of desire in his films but great variety in the extent of its gratification. The ideals of happiness—love, trust, personal and social coherence, familial stability—remain unchanged; the degree to which the movies suggest that such happiness may be possible varies radically. *The Trouble with Harry*, for example, portrays a world in which human desire and natural process synchronize almost perfectly: death is as fecund as life itself, fall promises the next spring, aging leads to rejuvenation, and isolation is a precursor of connection. In a film like *Topaz*, on the other hand, the implicit goals of human life remain what they are in romantic films, but the world cannot accommodate them. Human interactions at every level of magnitude from international relations to families and lovers are pervaded by deceit and betrayal. The movie's vision of the way things are, moreover, persuades us that such isolation and double-dealing are inevitable. Reality does not allow mutuality of interest, let alone love and trust, between men and women, among families, within organizations, or among nations.

The conception of the good, then, and the substance of desire remain largely constant in Hitchcock's universe. The ability (or perhaps inclination) of fate and nature to accommodate human hopes differs sharply from film to film. As it does so, the treatment of comic and romantic formulae varies proportionally. At the extremes, lucky coincidence opposes malignant fate; larger-than-life characters of cheerful resolve face mean, embittered little people; and unmistakable truth confronts a miasma of conflicting and mutually exclusive viewpoints. In practice, Hitchcock's films, like other fictions, rarely swerve entirely to one extreme or the other. They may often be most clearly understood, however, by observing how closely they approach the pure dream fulfillment of the comic romances or fall away toward the nightmare negations of tragedy and irony.

CHAPTER FOUR

Do Not Presume: Irony

Blackmail: Cyril Ritchard and Anny Ondra. *Blackmail* insists that no one can be either entirely pure or wholly inexcusable. Virtually all its action takes the shape of collaboration.

IRONIC films need not be bitter. They may be thoroughly comic, in which case we will generally call them something like "satire," "travesty," or "parody." The central structural features of irony do not primarily concern how happily or ill its actions turn out but rather its parodies of romantic conventions and reversals of romantic expectations. As we have seen, however, ironic realism has a general affinity for destruction and tragedy. Unless its tendencies toward disappointment and reversal are carefully controlled, they lead to real pain and destruction, which are incompatible with comedy. Of the five films discussed in this chapter, only one, *Mr. and Mrs. Smith* (1941), is unequivocally comic. *Rich and Strange* (1932) and *Secret Agent* (1936) cut their laughter with heavy doses of anxiety and suffering. *Blackmail* (1929) and *Topaz* (1969) end in ironic whimpers that, if they avoid the protagonists' deaths that conclude most tragedies, also lack tragedy's frequently redemptive sense of justice, closure, and grandeur.

The more ironic Hitchcock's films become, the more relentlessly they undercut the conventions of romantic narratives. Protagonists ascending to what in romantic films would be occasions of love and clarification encounter instead intensified conflict and perplexity. Rather than helping, fay-like minor characters impede the hero or heroine. Time is neither progressive nor cyclic but linear, repetitive, and sterile. When it does cycle, it returns to the paralyzed confusion of winter, not to the regenerated clarity of spring. Pretensions to adequacy on the part of heroes and heroines—to say nothing of the larger-than-life quality they have in the romances—leak slowly away. They descend to the underworld, but they often fail to return. If they do make it back, they have been stained by suffering and terror, and they can never be wholly free of their experience of the demonic. In Hitchcock's ironic narratives, artifice and ritual do not metamorphose into truth but remain no more than fakery. Journeys lead nowhere. Miraculous coincidences degenerate into malign conspiracies or unlucky accidents.

Characterization increases in complexity. At the same time, the audience's response may be confused or ambivalent, divided among equivocal central figures who do not have the sympathetic clarity of their counterparts in romantic fictions. Viewers' feelings grow increasingly ambivalent. An "on the one hand . . . on the other" response becomes almost inevitable.

Hitchcock's ironic films center on the same issues and conflicts as his romances, but the development of characters, plots, and imagery mocks the conventions of the myths and fairy tales that lie behind the romantic movies. Distressing experience, with its deflation and corruption of idealized dreams, prevails over innocence. In Hitchcock's ironic comedies, this movement leads to a debunking of illusions that concludes in a sort of wry shrug. As the films move from comedy toward tragedy,, however, the thematic and emotional conclusions grow bleaker until they are summed up in the image of the death's head that is briefly superimposed on the last shot of *Psycho*.

Samuel Beckett once remarked, "There is a wonderful sentence in Augustine. . . . 'Do not despair; one of the thieves was saved. Do not presume; one of the thieves was damned.' That sentence has a wonderful shape. It is the shape that matters."[1] For Hitchcock, too, such shapes matter. The movement of his films toward or away from innocence and redemption determines most powerfully their meanings, the kinds of stories they finally tell.

His romances counsel against despair. The indefatigable protagonists of the comic romances hardly admit the possibility of defeat and seem congenitally incapable of despondency. Their playful, optimistic energy protects them from the fear and discouragement that might lead them to abandon their sometimes horrific quests; and it finally drives offstage the cynical demons whom they oppose. The less comic romances—such films as *Jamaica Inn, Rebecca, Suspicion, Dial M for Murder*, and those discussed in the previous chapter—admit the possibility of despair but finally overcome it. Their central figures, often stressed almost to the breaking point, find enough resiliency in themselves and sufficient mercy in the world to scramble to happy endings and reject the temptation to despair.

The ironic films, on the other hand, counsel against presumption. It is this fictive moral for which Hitchcock is perhaps best remembered, in part because it formed the dominant message of his enormously popular televison series, and in part because of his public persona—a shrewd, droll fatman whose humor was almost always sardonic, constructed of ironic premises and postures. The best known of his films, moreover, is probably *Psycho*, one of the most profoundly ironic of his movies, but also one of the extreme ends of the spectrum of his career.

Of course, even Hitchcock's gayest comic romances bear with them occasional overtones and threats of irony. Genre labels describe tendencies, not immiscible essences. Conversely, the five films discussed in this chapter have moments of romantic clarity, but they remain predominantly ironic, evoking images and episodes typical of romance only to reverse the significance and disappoint the hope. Yet it is worth

[1] Harold Hobson, "Samuel Beckett, Dramatist of the Year," *International Theatre Annual* 1 (1956): 153. The source in Augustine of Beckett's quote has not been identified.

repeating that Hitchcockian irony always assumes as the normative and desirable conditions of life the same outcomes that are sought in his romantic narratives. When Hitchcock operates as an ironist, in short, he operates as a disappointed—sometimes embittered—romanticist. The heart of a romantic storyteller still beats behind his sourest ironies; the intensity of their cynicism testifies to the eager anticipation of happy prospects and to the fervor of regret. When Hitchcock's movies lead us to gloomy conclusions, they do so by raising and dashing optimistic hopes. The pain and fright of films like *Blackmail, Topaz, Vertigo*, or *Psycho*; the cynicism of *Rich and Strange* and *Secret Agent*; the zany incoherence of *Mr. and Mrs. Smith*—all develop in direct proportion to the ability of the movies to encourage and disappoint hopes of innocence, pleasure, security, and love.

Blackmail

Like the films of Murnau and other German directors who were Hitchcock's main cinematic influences, *Blackmail* embodies much of its meaning in expressionistic imagery. A good deal of this predominantly ironic imagery consists of romantic motifs, the ordinary meanings of which are reversed or otherwise parodied. Some of its images, on the other hand, straightforwardly emphasize the themes of confusion and threat that dominate the film: obscuring, infernal smoke, vision-blocking curtains, and the stripes that so often for Hitchcock evoke the bars of jail cells.

Characters ascend insistently in *Blackmail*, but when they go up in this ironic film, they do not escape their woes or clarify their confusion but only discover or cause further misfortunes. The first ascent comes in the prefatory documentary-like episode of arrest that precedes the main action. The detectives mount a flight of stairs, then turn into the bedroom of the man they are seeking, disarm him, and take him away under arrest. All movements upward in the main plot will end in similar violence and/or restraint.

The initial ascent in the main plot appears innocuous, but it leads eventually to the murder of the artist, Crewe (Cyril Ritchard). The central couple, Frank (Johnny Longden) and Alice (Anny Ondra), after a petty quarrel at the police station, arrive at a restaurant in central London. They are unable to get into a crowded elevator, so they take the steps up to the next floor, where they are told that the lower dining room of the restaurant is full and are asked to continue to the upper level. When the boy at the door is distracted by more arrivals, they slip inside despite his attempts to stop them. Once inside, they have predictable trouble finding a table, go through some undignified struggles with other diners, and are briefly separated.

Because she and Frank have insisted on the lower level dining room, and because they quarrel over whether to go to the movies, Alice is in a position to allow herself to be picked up by a man (Crewe) with whom she has flirted there before. The equivocal, even dangerous, quality of ascent is established for the main plot as it was for the introductory subplot. It is in the nature of the irony of *Blackmail* that the action of ascent is itself rendered ambiguous. Is the dining room to be taken as an upper room or a lower one? Obviously, it is both. Does the fact that they must take the stairs rather than the elevator emphasize or qualify their going up? Such ambiguity will characterize *Blackmail* at every formal level: imagery, plot, the motivations of its main figures.

Alice says with naive self-justification before entering Crewe's building, "I think a girl knows instinctively when she can trust a man." Her incautious acceptance of the artist's invitation to see his studio is followed by a series of ascents. The camera follows them up the stoop. Once inside, it turns for a radical shot up a flight of stairs in response to the artist's announcement that "I'm right up there . . . top." A conspicuous crane or elevator shot then follows Alice and Crewe up four-and-a-half flights of stairs. As the two walk up the shadowy staircase, the music on the sound track ascends as well, in a faintly comic aural emphasis of the rising action of the characters and the camera.

Alice's ascent to the artist's room seems at first to be leading to something like a prince's castle. Crewe's studio is decorated with a fanciful hood over the fireplace, an ornate candle stand, heavy curtains, and exposed ceiling beams. Crewe proves, however, to be not the ideal mate and rescuer of fairy tales but a masher whose attempted rape leads to his killing, Alice's loss of childish innocence, and Tracy's (Donald Calthrop) blackmailing of her. As she creeps out of the artist's studio after stabbing him, Alice recrosses the landing—its heavy shadows having been foreshadowings indeed—and begins to descend the stairs. The stairs are now photographed from above, the camera looking straight down the stairwell to the black and white tile floor of the entrance hall. This downward-pointing shot reverses the earlier ascent and underlines the deceit of its romantic promise. The camera now acknowledges the horror of the murder as it watches Alice go down into a night world of terror and guilt from which she will never emerge, even after her blackmailer dies at the end of the film. As she walks the dark streets of London in a daze, Hitchcock cuts to an extremely high shot looking down on the Thames, a shot that places Alice in an underworld cut in half by a black river. The characters of *Blackmail* rise only to fall, or to be pushed, below the point at which they began. The truths they encounter during their unfortunate ascents, far from setting them free, compromise and disillusion them.

Later ascents lead to analogous disappointment and catastrophe. After Alice returns home, Hitchcock shows her going up the stairs to her bedroom; but instead of the sleep she pretends to have had, she has spent a night that was a waking nightmare. Tracy flees the police by climbing the towering central dome of the British Museum, only to fall through its glass to his death.

Images of hands, a symbol Hitchcock habitually employs to signify the coming together of lovers, also has ironically reversed connotations in *Blackmail*. Again, associations with accusation and confinement are established during the introductory sequence. The suspect's hand shoots out from behind his newspaper to grab for his gun but is intercepted by the arresting detective's hand. At Scotland Yard, he is identified in the lineup when a young woman places her hand on his shoulder (a gesture that Hitchcock uses again during the trial sequence of *The Wrong Man*). Close-up shots of the suspect's hands being forced onto an ink pad and paper to record his fingerprints—another anticipation of *The Wrong Man*—continue to parody the comforting associations of hands and touching. The opening arrest ends with a long sequence in the lavatory, during which the police wash their hands— of the grime of the day and, perhaps, of their responsibility for the legal miseries of their fellow creatures.

During her irritating restaurant meal with Frank, Alice briefly loses one of her gloves, a detail that anticipates her forgetting them in the studio after she has stabbed Crewe and that is connected to the threatening imagery of hands throughout the film. The limp hand of the artist signals his death when it flops out from behind the bed curtain. Later, a series of subjective shots renders Alice's indelible horror at the memory of the artist's dead hand—a memory that is reinvoked when she walks about London by the upraised hand of a policeman directing traffic and by the dangling hand of an unconscious drunk.

As with other central symbols in *Blackmail*, the meanings associated with hands are slippery and sometimes reverse their dominant connotations. When Frank recognizes one of Alice's gloves in the slain artist's apartment just after the police have arrived, a tight close-up shows his hands enfolding the incriminating bit of evidence with tender protectiveness. He provides in Alice's absence the sheltering affection missing when she was with him. At the end of the film, as they leave the inspector's office together, Frank repeats his shielding gesture when he takes Alice's right hand in both of his. The last shot of a hand in

Blackmail, however, reiterates the sense of hostility. In close-up, the jeering jester painted by the dead artist points an accusing finger at Alice and Frank while hollow laughter echoes in the background.

Along with imagery in which ordinarily comforting romantic meanings are negated, *Blackmail* uses visual motifs that are conventionally demonic or express menace. Stripes composed of alternating bright light and deep shadow, suggestive of prison bars, insistently raise the threat of arrest. Obvious uses of this shadow-pattern appear on the stairs and in the hall leading to the suspect's room in the prefatory episode, on the stairs to the artist' studio, and on those that lead to Alice's bedroom. The stripe pattern also appears in the shadow moustache on the face of the aroused Crewe before he attacks Alice, in the fence behind the bobbie who obliviously strolls by during the attempted rape, on the striped sweater worn by the woman who gossips about the stabbing the next morning, and in the wrought-iron fence and the architectural columns of the British Museum during Tracy's attempt to evade the police.

The white-fringed dark coat that Alice wears during her first appearance in the film anticipates her association with images of stripes later.[1] After killing Crewe, she dazedly holds the knife, which alternately flashes bright and dark in the light—another association of the heroine with the stripe pattern, and an anticipation of the flashing electric signs that she will see while she walks through London. As she emerges from the artist's studio, the conspicuous shadows that earlier streaked her assailant's face now darken her own.

The stripe imagery reappears during the parallel cutting between Tracy fleeing the police through the British Museum and the conscience-stricken Alice in her parents' home. The sun through the window casts dark lines on the wall behind her as she agonizes over whether or not to confess killing the artist. Just after Tracy falls to his death, Hitchcock cuts back to Alice. She is signing (too late now) a letter that ends, "I am going to give myself up. I cannot bear the thought of that man being accused of something I have done." She underlines her name—another quiet evocation of the stripe motif—and then rises to stand by the table. Her movement brings the shadows of the windowpanes onto her face; they look like a rope and noose around her neck—the eventual outcome, as she supposes, of her confession. At Scotland Yard a little later, a shadow seems to point at Alice as she awaits the chief inspector. The motif of dark bars is picked

[1] Hitchcock used a similar image, a striped coat, for similar symbolic purposes, on the heroine of *The Ring* (1927).

up by the windowpanes out of which Alice gazes as if at a world from which she will soon be locked away.

Windows and mirrors in *Blackmail* also evoke suggestions of threat and tension. The suspect in the opening episode first sees the police in a thin mirror; and we later see him in the reflection of the Scotland Yard plaque as he is being taken into the building for interrogation. At the end of the film, Hitchcock photographs Alice in the same distorting, accusatory mirror.

The atmosphere of danger and obscurity is reinforced by suggestions of the demonic. In front of the doorway to the artist's building, a mysterious figure stalks; and Crewe's flat is guarded by an enigmatic white mask that lurks in the darkness. The presiding spirit of the studio is the painting of the malign jester. After the killing, all London takes on an infernal air, with the high shot over the Thames and shots of fog in a deserted Trafalgar Square. The gigantic, dramatically shadowed head that watches impassively as Tracy climbs down a rope at the British Museum recalls the mask by the door of the artist's studio. Like a prison guard or a guard at the gates of hell, it seems to bar any return from the underworld into which the desperate man is sinking.

Tobacco smoke insistently suggests something like the heat and menace of hell seeping into the upper world. The suspect in the opening movement is first seen smoking in bed, and a little later Hitchcock indicates the passage of time during his interrogation by a close-up of an ashtray full of cigarette butts. Tracy extorts a cigar from Frank, then lights it ostentatiously while he smiles malignantly at the frightened couple. When Frank pays for his tormentor's Corona, the blackmail is implicitly established. The smoke issuing from Tracy's mouth recalls Alice's steaming breath as she walks the streets of London after the killing. This imagistic association between Alice and Tracy expands to include Frank a little later: when the police are coming to arrest Tracy, the detective lights a cigarette as he looms over the now terrified blackmailer. The connection between smoke or fire and danger finds its way into the dialogue when Tracy pleads with Alice, "Look here, Miss, you tell him. Tell him that he's playing with fire, and (pause) and we shall all of us burn our fingers."

The opening image of the film, the spinning circle of the wheel hub on a police van, introduces another important ironic symbol that will be repeated at the end of the movie, as the detectives pursue Tracy. Images of circles in shots of telephones and police communications equipment further associate circular imagery with the pursuit of criminals. Circles also appear twice in clock faces, as Alice waits for the artist in the restaurant and as she walks through the night after stabbing him. Similar imagery of circles figured heavily in *The Ring* (1927) and in the turning mill machinery that Hitchcock used to suggest the inexorability of justice in his previous film, *The Manxman*.

The sound track, Hitchcock's first and one of the first in the history of British cinema, contributes its ironies with precocious sophistication. Like visual imagery, aural motifs both reverse the meanings of sounds normally associated with comfort and communication and exploit those that intrinsically lend themselves to suggestions of confusion and threat. The ironic use of music is conspicuous. The three central male figures, Frank, Crewe, and Tracy, all whistle or sing at moments of crisis. Their melodies are far from reassuring.

Disquieting music figures prominently in the miscalculated seduction that leads to the death of the artist. As Alice explores his studio, Crewe, like an amorous songbird, whistles off camera. While she disrobes to model a tutu for him, he sits at the piano singing a song about liberated, modern young womanhood. "They say you're wild, an awful child, Miss Of-Today," begins the chorus, which proceeds to assert that "there's really no harm/ In the beautiful things that you do./ You've a heart of gold, so let them nag and scold—/ You're absolutely great, Miss Of-Today." Concluding his song, the artist turns to Alice, who now stands before him in the scanty ballet costume, and remarks, "And that's a song about you, my dear."

Despite her apparent encouragement of Crewe's advances, these lyrics thoroughly misrepresent Alice's fundamentally conservative character. Crewe again plays the song, at a more frenzied tempo, just before he drags Alice to his bed, and the sound track after Alice knifes him is occupied by strangely ethereal variations on the same melody. As the closing title comes up, the sound track once more repeats the chorus of Crewe's song.

With an irony that cannot be known to Frank but that will not be missed by many of the audience, the detective recalls his dead rival's musical penchants as he whistles abstractedly while looking out the studio window. Like Crewe when Alice was inspecting the same apartment, Frank strolls about whistling as he looks for clues to the killing. Later Alice's pet bird chirps exuberantly while her mother chatters about "the murder last night round the corner." Tracy sings "Corona, Corona" as he prepares to light his expensive cigar. Then he happily whistles "The Best Things in Life are Free" while he eats the breakfast that he has exacted from Alice.

Mocking laughter echoes disturbing music. The suspect in the opening episode laughs scornfully when Frank jumps out of the way of a stone that flies through the window from the hostile crowd below.

Leaving the station with Frank for their dinner date, Alice laughs heartily at the attendant's joke in order to make her coldness to Frank more pointed. In Crewe's studio, she laughs when she first sees the painting of the jester, which will soon become an emblem of the hollowness of laughter throughout the film. Her flirtatious tittering a little later encourages advances that are immediately repelled when made.

The wounding laughter of *Blackmail* culminates during its last sequence. The door attendant makes a rather feeble joke about Alice taking away the detective's job, and all three laugh—the guilty lovers with painfully forced jocularity. Alice's laughter dries up when she sees the torn painting from Crewe's studio. As the two men continue their banter, Hitchcock cuts to a close-up of the demonic, corrupt face of the laughing jester. The laughter grows louder and more hysterical as a policeman carries off the painting along with a second canvas on which Alice childishly painted her own version of a smiling face. The two paintings are carried together down the hall as the screen fades to black and the laughter rises to an insane crescendo. Like song, laughter in *Blackmail* only derides the happiness and human community it evokes.

The ironically reversed significance of sounds like music and laughter is amplified by aural motifs that emphasize further the violence and human isolation of the world portrayed in *Blackmail*. Like the warning yellows and reds that Hitchcock later used in his color films, the clamor of honking traffic rings alarms throughout this black and white movie. Hitchcock may be recycling a crucial moment in Murnau's *Sunrise* when cars honk at Frank and Alice immediately after Alice abandons the anger she was cherishing over having been kept waiting. A similar encounter with passing traffic in *Sunrise* marks the reconciliation of the estranged husband and wife. If the allusion to Murnau is made, however, it undergoes ironic reversal in *Blackmail* when Alice and Frank quarrel in the restaurant a little later.

Thereafter, the honking of auto horns always announces concealed hazards, missed connections, and violence. In front of Crewe's building, a horn sounds when Tracy overhears Alice tell the artist about her father's newsstand, and it sounds again at the moment Alice agrees to go inside. Another horn honks off camera when Crewe turns in response to Tracy's call as he and Alice are mounting the stoop. After Crewe is dead, a horn sounds in the street outside, and more blaring horns haunt Alice as she walks through London. When she comes back after her night of wandering, the same ugly sound of modern chaos punctuates her return to the home that can no longer offer her rest or safety.

Honking vehicles are part of a larger theme of noise and chance mistakes. Human connections and the purposive quality of human behavior are obscured in *Blackmail* by intrusions of random interference and haphazard confusion. When the Landlady calls the police to inform them of her tenant's death, a highly stylized shot puts the old woman, shown only from her mouth to her waist, on the left side of the screen holding the speaker of a telephone. The police operator, the front of his face sliced off by the edge of the frame, holds a receiver to his ear on the right. These two truncated figures, within inches of each other on the screen, have ludicrous difficulty making themselves understood.

POLICEMAN: Who did you say it was?
LANDLADY: Mr. Crewe.
P: Mr. Who?
L: No! Crewe, I tell you! It's all over!
P: Alright, don't you worry, I'll send round straight away. What number did you say, seven or eleven?
L: Thirty-one.
P: Thirty-one?
L: What?
P: Thirty-one, I said.
L: No, no, thirty-one.

This dislocated vaudeville patter not only emphasizes the inability of the Landlady and the policeman to communicate but replaces the decisive high-tech (1929-style) response of the police in the first episode with comic futility.

Instruments of communication appear increasingly ineffective as the movie continues.[3] The interruption of the Chief Inspector's telephone prevents Alice's confession; and the investigative apparatus of the police leads them not to the truth but to hounding an essentially innocent man to his death. By the end of *Blackmail* we are left with little faith in the legendary efficiency of Scotland Yard. Indeed, we may wonder retrospectively if the man arrested in the first episode might be as fundamentally innocent as Tracy.

Intermittent trivial mistakes characterize action itself as random and meaningless. As the motif of obstructed messages turns the tenuous audibility of early sound systems into an expressive resource, that of banal stumbling does the same with the difficulty of postdubbing and reshooting of scenes with fluffed cues. Lest we suppose that the mis-

[3] The discussion of *Blackmail* in Marsha Kinder and Beverle Huston, *Close-Up* (New York: Harcourt, Brace, Jovanovich, 1972), pp. 52-58, is largely devoted to the "failure of various kinds of communication."

takes in *Blackmail* are production flaws, however, we should notice that they occur, like scrambled communications, at significant junctures. The first moment of such random, banal awkwardness comes during Hitchcock's cameo appearance, when a small boy on the subway train tugs annoyingly on the hat of a passenger portrayed by the director. The Landlady, a patron muse of clumsiness, stumbles on her words when she tells Crewe that the person who left him a message was "the same gent what called yes . . . different time." Frank's repeated, unsuccessful attempts to signal a waitress at the restaurant is the sort of insignificant annoyance that life is full of but that movies usually exclude. Yet that small frustration contributes to the irritability of Alice and Frank that provokes their fatal separation.

The motif of the blunder becomes most prominent during the sequence in the artist's studio, an episode that can be seen in its entirety as a sort of terrible mistake. When Alice postures in front of the artist's easel, she accidently makes a mark on the blank canvas. The artist, in his nervousness, stutters when he tells her to draw something; and Alice trips and bumps against him as she begins to do so.

The inclusion of such mistakes undercuts any sense of order or purpose in the world of the film. It reverses the implications of conspicuous artificiality in Hitchcock's romantic movies, in which the intrusive hand of the maker assures us that everything is under control and signals that what we are watching carries particular denseness of meaning. The occurrence of trivial, ordinary awkwardness suggests the opposite. It reduces the sense of significance and implies that the maker has no more control over his little world than anyone else does over the world at large. If the director of *Blackmail* cannot wholly guide his own creation or deliberately allows misleading mistakes to deceive his characters, he imitates a universe the powers of which are either impotent or malicious.

Characterization in romantic films, as we have seen, leans toward fairly clear polarizations, especially in terms of audience sympathy. As Hitchcock edges toward irony, this clarity, along with the sense of order in the fictive universe, becomes obscure. In *Blackmail*, the audience will find Alice more attractive than Tracy; but much of the action of the film, like the imagery of stripes that associates these two apparently opposed figures, works to soften the lines of moral distinction between them, and between Tracy and Frank as well. By the end of the movie, we are likely to see all three as victims of a world where romantic contrasts between the innocent and the guilty have been blurred to uncertain distinctions between the guilty and the guiltier.

Hitchcock's characterization of Alice works insistently toward contradiction and compromise. Though the movie does not suggest, for example, that the artist's attempted rape is anything but deplorable, it does make clear that Alice's behavior contributes substantially to the course of events. We see her self-indulgent, deceitful behavior with Frank at the restaurant when she tries to rid herself of his company so that she can pursue a meeting with Crewe. In the artist's studio, her flirtation is easily interpreted from the man's point of view for something more promising. In addition to agreeing to go to his room with him late at night, she behaves coquettishly once there. When he attaches a nude female body to the head that she daubs on the blank canvas—a reasonably clear indication of what is on his mind—she responds with a giggle and an enticing, "Oh, you *are* awful." A little later she initiates the idea of putting on the tutu, holding it up and coyly asking, "I say, how would I do for one of your models?" The artist accepts the invitation, of course, working on Alice's vanity when she hesitates. Seductively, she has Crewe "do it up," a request that gets her a predictable—and from Crewe's viewpoint an unexpectedly rebuffed—embrace. The pattern of approach-avoidance flirting that has characterized her behavior from the moment she allowed Crewe to induce her into his building obviously both confuses and encourages the artist, and his eventual attempt to rape her may be seen as a misreading of the mixed signals that she has sent him throughout the scene.

Hitchcock's point (and mine) is not that Alice nearly got what she was asking for. Nor that Crewe plays a guiltless part. Until Crewe loses control and drags Alice to his bed, however, the dynamics of the whole episode have been those of a mutual seduction. Division of the cast into spotted villain and virginal heroine is not supported by the action. The sequence gives the lie to the melodramatic, shadowy, handlebar moustache that appears on the impassioned Crewe's face; it opts finally for a pattern of characterization that links the two figures in mutual guilt. The shadows on Alice's face as she leaves the apartment not only mark her shame and terror but also associate her morally with Crewe.

Alice, most of the audience will feel, is a decent, conventional young woman with a tendency toward flirting. After she tries to give Frank the slip at the restaurant, she thinks better of her behavior and attempts a reconciliation, which he rebuffs. The note of confession she writes to exonerate Tracy—despite his contemptible blackmailing of her—suggests that she does have "a heart of gold" beneath her surface defects.

But unlike the world of the comic romances, that of *Blackmail* does not forgive even peccadilloes. The imagery associated with Alice underlines her inability to escape moral pollution once it has touched her. After she has killed the artist, Alice claws at the recently finished painting of the jester. In tearing it, she stains her hand. When she blacks out her signature on the painting that she and the artist made together, the Alice White who came up to Crewe's has been darkened forever; she does not leave as the relatively innocent girl who entered, even though she has preserved her virtue in some narrow sense. The London she walks about after the killing is not the London she knew before; it everywhere proclaims her crime and Cain-like isolation from the rest of humanity. Advertising signs take on ironic, accusatory meanings: "white purity," "A NEW COMEDY," "good cocktail." The derisory laughter at the end of the film reflects Alice's unhappy understanding of her own guilt.[4]

Psychologically, Alice accompanies into confinement the paintings that she watches being carried into the depths of Scotland Yard. She has joined the jester as a captive in the world of sin, a world that permanently claims those whom it touches. Alice's suffering for her flirtation may seem excessive to us, as may the deaths of the amorous artist and the pathetic Tracy. But *Blackmail* portrays a world in which the penalties for misbehavior are wildly out of proportion to the misbehavior itself. Far from being redeemed by grace and forgiveness, its inhabitants are hounded by the vindictive opposites of such forces. A heart of gold is no assurance of innocence, and everybody has flaws sufficient to implicate him or her in human corruption and crime.

Blackmail insists that no one can be either entirely pure or wholly inexcusable. Missteps and catastrophes alike always come about through the actions of at least two characters. Alice lies to Frank about why she does not want to go to the movies, but she then apologizes and promises to accompany him after all. He refuses to accept her apology and stalks out. Outside the restaurant door, however, he pauses and evidently has decided to return and make up when Alice emerges on Crewe's arm. The responsibility for Alice's entering the artist's studio is divided also: Alice hesitates, Crewe presses her, Alice

---

[4] The question of Alice's guilt or victimization during the attempted rape and afterward has been much discussed. For a careful analysis of these issues (and a thorough summary of other critics' views), see Tania Modleski, "Hitchcock's *Blackmail* and Feminist Interpretation," *Publications of the Modern Language Association of America* 102 (May 1987): 304-15. Modleski argues that the "subtle and prolific" ironies of the movie do not support the polarized views about Alice's innocence or Hitchcock's misogyny that *Blackmail* has frequently attracted. I am very much in sympathy with both her specific understanding of *Blackmail* and her skepticism about Hitchcock's putative antifeminism.

consents. Virtually all the action of *Blackmail* takes the shape of collaboration.

Frank, Alice, and Tracy act in bad faith and commit crimes, but extenuating circumstances make their behavior seem less reprehensible. Frank suppresses evidence, but he does so from motives of love. Tracy pleads that he was driven to blackmail: "Why, I'm not so bad really ... things have gone wrong lately, and ... one's got to live, you know." And Alice, most convincingly: "You don't know. He tried ... oh, I can't tell you! It's too terrible! I was defending myself, I didn't know what I was doing, and then. ..." Yet despite their excuses, all remain to some extent culpable.

The sense of shared guilt is emphasized by Hitchcock's repeated blending together of the identities of his figures. Alice and Tracy are connected by their common association with stripes. Tracy's name, and his behavior as a sort of free-lance detective, connects him with his ostensible foes, the police. A dissolve that gradually replaces the face of the chief inspector with Tracy's emphasizes their surprising similarity.

Like his guilt or innocence, Tracy's hair color shades into intermediates: "You couldn't say he was blond, and you couldn't say he was a brunette. He was a bit of both." From Alice's point of view after she has killed Crewe, a related blending of opposite roles takes place when she looks at the photograph of Frank on the wall of her bedroom. Her lover and protector has become a possible agent of exposure and conviction. While Alice, Frank, and Tracy await the coming of the van from Scotland Yard, they are photographed like a romantic triangle, with its complex attractions and antagonisms. In the last shot of the film, Crewe's devilish, technically accomplished painting and Alice's childishly scribbled head are carried off together. Like all the contrasting characters and actions of the film, these dissimilar pictures are joined by intricate, unpredictable, and indissoluble ties. Oppositions do not remain clear in *Blackmail*. Few, indeed, even remain in opposition, as they metamorphose into far more complicated, mutually implicating relationships.

The distinction between art and the objects it portrays threatens to disappear in the homogeneous ironic fog. At dinner, Frank declares that he would like to see a moving picture called *Fingerprints*. "It's about Scotland Yard. It might be amusing; bound to get all the details wrong." "I don't see why," Alice retorts, "I hear they've got a real criminal to direct it so as to be on the safe side." (Who could know more about institutional justice than criminals?) Intricate lab work as the Landlady searches the police mug shots—rendered as prismatically multiplied rotating images, analogous to the multiple images of the motion picture itself—suggests that the process of detection and the process of movie making are akin. The usual relation between real crimes and fictional thrillers is reversed when Alice responds to Frank's self-importance by declaring, "You and your Scotland Yard, if it weren't for Edgar Wallace, nobody's ever heard of it." Crime and its foes, by such reasoning, are not represented by thrillers like *Blackmail* so much as they are created by them. Without Edgar Wallace, nobody would ever have heard of Scotland Yard. Without Alfred Hitchcock, Alice's infidelities, Crewe's assault, the knifing, Frank's betrayal of his professional integrity, and Tracy's death would not exist. The director, too, is one of the criminals.

Such aesthetic logic contributes to the sour, melancholy tone that dominates the film. Mutual responsibility for crime and conflict at once joins people and separates them. After Frank has led Alice out of the commissioner's office, he asks her why she came to Scotland Yard. "I did it," she whispers. "I know," he replies, taking her hand as she tries to explain what happened. "My dear," he murmurs emotionally, and the two walk down the hall toward the front door. As they walk, Hitchcock cuts to a rear view. We see Frank drop Alice's hand. They continue to walk together, but their weary figures look stiff and de-jected. They have a secret to keep for the rest of their lives, a point emphasized when they encounter the waiting room attendant, who im-mediately jokes, "Did she tell you who did it?" Forced laughter fol-lows. Frank and Alice can never relax in the confidence of uncompro-mised personal, or mutual, integrity. They have shared in two murders; and though neither was premeditated or entirely unjustified, neither was necessary. The bond of their painful, guilty secrets will hold them apart as it ties them together.

Like the heroes and heroines of the comic romances, Frank and Alice are united at the end of their adventures. The enemies to their love, though gone, can never be forgotten; and there remain the disintegra-tive forces between the lovers that separated them and made the kill-ings possible in the first place. Unlike their counterparts in the ro-mances, the protagonists of *Blackmail* have no chance of living happily ever after. Their unforgiving world, their unresolved pasts, and stained human nature itself prevent such an ending. Indeed, *Blackmail*, like many intensely ironic works, does not really end at all. It breaks off, but its problems mostly remain. Those that are solved, moreover, are replaced by others that result from the very solutions.

The end of *The Manxman*, the silent film Hitchcock made just be-fore *Blackmail* (though its release was delayed until after the success of *Blackmail* in 1929), strongly resembles that of the sound film it preceded. Like *Blackmail*, *The Manxman* is a deeply ironic film, with similar complexities of character and motive, intense moral ambiguities, and repeated reversals of romantic expectations. Its conclusion is by no means cheerful, but its central lovers, who have been exposed and expelled from society, walk away from a jeering crowd into a pastoral landscape and a sky of mixed clouds and light. They are carrying the baby that they have at last been able to acknowledge as their own. At the same time that their public denunciation ruins them socially, it liberates them from the suffocation of living a falsehood.

Their situation, wretched as it is, hints at a hope for forgiveness that Alice and Frank are denied. Alice has been released from the threat of official suspicion; but she has been condemned, at the same time, to the loneliness of someone burdened with a past that must be concealed at all costs. Nor can she be liberated from having to live with the knowledge of two deaths for which she was largely responsible. She is isolated from the comfort of society and from all other persons but one. That she shares her secret with Frank may perhaps console her; but the end of the film shows such consolation to be deeply ambiguous, both for her and for her companion in guilt.

Rich and Strange

Released three years after *Blackmail*, *Rich and Strange* conforms in most respects to Hitchcock's ironic practice in the earlier film. Its characters are perhaps slightly more polarized than those of *Blackmail*; but its ethical issues are quite as intricate. Its dense texture develops by a series of similar thematic and imagistic associations, reversals of expectation, and blending of apparent opposites.

The plot is elaborated through the kind of reversals and rereversals that we colloquially describe with the adverb "ironically." It begins eight years into an unexceptional marriage, when the excitements of courtship have become memories of memories and the couple —at least the man—are growing restless. Aggravated beyond patience by the banal frustrations of his middle-class routine as an impecunious accountant, Fred (Henry Kendall) is liberated from his quotidian rounds by a large gift of money from a sympathetic uncle. He and his wife Emily (Joan Barry) set out "to experience all the life you want by traveling." What he experiences, "ironically," consists to a considerable degree of the same sort of irritations and frustrations that he set out to escape. Little things do not go right. As Fred was queasy on the subway coming home from work, so he is nauseated on the ships that cross the

Rich and Strange: Joan Barry. Their return from the brink of death parallels the return of their marriage from the brink of dissolution. First Emily, then Fred, emerges from their porthole like a pair of very large newborns.

channel and the Mediterranean.[5] He is an irritable and bored sightseer in Paris, Port Said, and Colombo. His new experiences only provide new occasions for the kind of blundering bad luck that manifests itself in his balky umbrella and floppy newspaper in the first sequence. Finally, he returns home the same self-absorbed, dissatisfied, and crabby child-man that he was before leaving. His journey to "experience life" produces neither excitement in exotic places nor any richer appreciation of his home.

To the extent that his life of travel differs from his life in London, it differs for the worse. He is acutely seasick for days at a time, is hit in the eye by a flying ring on one ship, and is clobbered by a washbasin on another. He is duped and bilked of a thousand pounds by an ersatz Princess whose "father kept a cleaning shop in Berlin." His affair with her could just as well have been the predictable liaison of a bored young office worker with a secretary from his office. The black cat that

[5] This emphasis on seasickness, and the central idea of voyages and adventures that lead nowhere and yield no significant self-knowledge, are repeated from *Champagne*, released four years earlier in 1928.

disgusts him by getting on the table in his flat reappears cooked up with rice aboard a Chinese junk. He narrowly avoids drowning when the ship carrying him and Emily back home is wrecked in the fog. Worst of all, he nearly abandons, or loses to a more appreciative rival, his undeservedly loving, patient, protective wife.

Unlike the retributive ironies of *Blackmail*, however, those of *Rich and Strange* are mostly comic and essentially harmless. If his quest for "life" leads to nothing constructive, it does not cause him any lasting pain or serious loss, either. (The emotional adventures of the voyage are of more consequence for Emily.) Although the movie constantly deflates Fred's pretensions, puts various sorts of banana peels under his feet, and gives him seasickness in place of excitement on the high seas, it never allows him to suffer irreversible damage.

Furthermore, Fred ordinarily bumbles about so ineffectively that he cannot seriously harm himself or anyone else, despite his most foolish attempts. He displays this side of his character quite clearly during a scene with Emily at the end of their outbound cruise. The Princess, having compensated herself with his thousand pounds, has escaped "the pleasure of [his] company." "Well," he says by way of justifying his intent to go to Australia with his royal companion, "you were going to run away with your precious Gordon." "But I didn't!" Emily heatedly points out. "Well, did I?" he responds self-righteously, entirely missing the point that his wife chose to come back to him and that he had to return to her because his paramour gave him the slip. As the exchange ends, his ineptness in all matters great and small is underlined again. "Wish I'd never come on the trip!" he exclaims petulantly, kicking at a wastebasket. But instead of blasting the unoffending object across the room, Fred gets his foot stuck in it. He is as ineffectual as he is childishly selfish. He thoroughly deserves to be stuck with his sham Princess; but she will not have him, and so he escapes her clutches.

Like such great comedians of the early sound era as Stan Laurel and Oliver Hardy, Fred is chronically out of step and at odds with a world in which he cannot find a comfortable place. His umbrella will not open until it is no longer needed; he cannot maintain his balance on the underground train; the only program on the wireless when he turns to it for distraction is "Mr. Baker's twelfth talk on accountancy," precisely the maddeningly mechanical activity at which he has spent his miserable day. Waiting to leave for his voyage of adventure and discovery, he tries to light a cigarette; the lighter will not catch. The trip itself continues to multiply Fred's petty misfortunes. Even The Princess's seduction of him is delayed for an excruciating half-minute while he fumbles at her veil.

The discontent that drives Fred to long for more "life" is so overstated, and his desires so trivial, that his quest must fail for want of a significant goal. "Are you satisfied with your present Circumstances?" asks a newspaper headline rhetorically. As Fred rides the underground, the posted advertisements tease his economic ego: "Clothe your wife at Garridges," "Dine tonight at the Majestic." Manny Balestreros reads similar ads in the subway on his way home during the opening sequences of *The Wrong Man*, but unlike Fred, he is only mildly affected by them. He knows, as Fred never does, how fundamentally fortunate he is and how insubstantial are the pleasures that his straitened circumstances make him forgo. Because Fred is tired of eating steak and kidney pie at home instead of dining at the Majestic, he declares to his wife that "the best place for us is a gas oven." Valetudinarian that he is, this discontented office worker responds excessively to every frustration and temptation to egotism and greed. He is a robot of grumpy hypochondria, on the one hand; on the other, an automaton of covetousness.

Fred's fellow workers share his comic rigidity. *Rich and Strange* opens with rows of accountants bent over their columns of figures like so many adding machines, or insects. When six o'clock arrives, the workers, mechanically obedient to mechanical time, pop two by two from the office building. In paired synchrony, they open their umbrellas and go to join the hoards in the underground.

On the back wall of the office, appropriately, appears a shadow that suggests a spider web (an image that Hitchcock uses to very different effect in *Suspicion*). Similar intersecting lines appear on the clock face in the railroad station and through the viewfinder of Fred's camera when he tries to take a picture of Emily on the pitching deck of the ferry. The web-like shadow is repeated more exactly in the Singapore hotel room, first as Fred announces his intention to leave Emily for The Princess, and again when he returns to admit that The Princess has sucked a thousand pounds from him.

In the opening sequences of *Rich and Strange*, only Fred, alone and struggling with his broken umbrella, is out of phase with the other human machines. But he is driven by clockwork quite as mechanically as his co-workers, even if his unreliable machinery often fails. His defiance of the clock in the train station gives way to his drunken attempts in a Paris hotel to reset his watch by the elevator floor indicator. Fred persists in his irritable bungling. Sending machines to sea does not, it appears, turn them into reasonable human beings; it simply changes the furnishings into which they rigidly run themselves.

The combination of reversed romantic expectations in its plot and of relatively harmless mechanical rigidity in its characters makes *Rich and Strange* at once ironic and comic. But along with the satire largely associated with Fred, another plot develops. This second set of actions, only intermittently connected to Fred's missteps, centers on Emily and generates partially fulfilled romantic adventures, the eventual disappointments of which come about in more subtle ways than the deflation of her husband. It is Emily who has the real adventures on their voyage, who gains self-knowledge and insight into Fred, and who changes. This outcome involves a good deal of irony itself, for Emily does not share the restless discontent of her husband as the movie begins. She responds indignantly to his hyperbolic self-pity: "To talk about gas ovens when we've a roof over our heads, food, beds, oh, and lots of things!"

At the beginning of their voyage, Emily joins her husband in exporting a blundering middle-class English style to the continent. They struggle across the choppy channel (a title proclaims, "To get to Paris you have to *cross the Channel*"); they act the part of overwhelmed tourists in the crush of the French capitol ("To get to the Folies Bergere you have to cross Paris"); they get drunk and navigate the hotel lounge as awkwardly as they did the previous stages of their journey ("And to get to your room you have to cross the hotel lounge"). At the Folies, they are shocked by the scanty costumes of the chorines. "The curtain's gone up too soon," squeaks Emily in alarm, "they're not dressed." After they manage to return to their hotel room, they play out a small domestic farce when Fred drunkenly trips trying to get into bed. Emily sees him kneeling on the floor—to pray, she supposes—and so she kneels herself; then Fred sees her and follows suit with his own devotions.

Up to this point, Fred and Emily seem perfectly matched in their provincial, bourgeois awkwardness. When they begin their trip to the Orient, however, another bout of seasickness removes Fred from Emily's side; chance replaces him with the handsome, gentle, and urbane Commander Gordon; and her real adventure begins. Although she and Gordon first meet when he accidentally brushes her with his coat, their time together is passed without any sign of the short-tempered awkwardness that characterizes Fred. Between them there is a relaxed mutuality that gradually deepens into the love of two people who are superbly well suited for one another.

But their growing love is accompanied, almost from the first, by complicating undertones that vary from the ludicrous to the elegiac. For Emily is married, and that most constraining of circumstances cannot but cast its long shadow over her tender relationship with the Commander. Soft music wraps Emily and Gordon in romantic promise as they converse at the ship's rail the first night out. A title, "Night at sea," introduces the sequence, which begins with Emily standing alone at the rail, her hair glowing in the delicate light. The moon glimmers bewitchingly through the clouds. A parallel cut, however, moves the camera to Fred, who is lying in extravagant discomfort which is increased by the unwelcome sight of a menu brought to his room by a solicitous steward. Then back to Emily and Gordon, slowly walking arm in arm along the empty deck. The insertion of Fred into this sequence anticipates the insistence with which Hitchcock will complicate his portrayal of Gordon's and Emily's affair of the heart.

The next day, as Emily and Gordon sit chatting, he gets out some photos of his home. One of them shows him sitting on his porch, an empty chair opposite. As elsewhere in Hitchcock's movies, the pair of chairs functions as a symbol of marriage. Emily asks if she may draw on the photo, and to Gordon's amusement inserts the figure of a woman into the unoccupied chair. Immediately, the dialogue hints at their suitability for each other. "I could sit and listen to you all the afternoon," the Commander remarks contentedly. Emily replies in the same vein, "Funny you should say that, because I always find it so difficult to talk to people . . . but not to you, I find it quite easy, much easier than I could to my husband. . . ."

The two are sitting in chairs shaped very much like those in the photo that Emily has just altered. The table between them also repeats the photo. Their places are reversed as in a mirror, but otherwise they essentially duplicate the scene of domestic congeniality that Emily has sketched on the picture of the previously solitary Gordon. The sequence of images suggests that she is suited to do in life what she has already done on the photo. A moment later, she ends her remarks upon the difficulty of love by hoping that her companion will "be sure you get the right girl. It would be a crime if you were wasted." She appears to make her remark·innocently, but its possible applicability to Emily herself is not lost on Gordon, who begins to be disturbed. The sequence ends by reiterating its dominant theme when a fellow passenger greets the Commander and, seeing Emily, remarks affably, "And this, I presume, is Mrs. Gordon." As Gordon and Emily look rather ambivalently at each other, the image fades to darkness.

Even as the closeness of Emily and the Commander grows, however, we are repeatedly reminded of Fred's obstructing influence; the sequence just discussed began with a shot of Fred languishing in bed. The next sequence, which leads to Emily's and Gordon's first kiss, starts with a similar shot of the miserable husband, and it includes an unwelcome intrusion from the Old Maid of the cruise who interrupts Emily and Gordon on the pretext of providing a plaster that might cure Fred's seasickness.

After fleeing the Old Maid, the Commander and Emily once again find themselves at the deck rail, gazing over moonlit waters. In one of the most striking sequences of this astonishingly inventive film, the camera follows their legs as they walk down a flight of steps and cross a lower deck, stepping over several lengths of heavy chain and past a coil of rope. We then see them in a middle shot that includes in the background a group of crewmen playing cards. After they mount another flight of steps to overlook the ocean again, Gordon turns back toward the superstructure. "Like to see a ship we were once passengers in?" he asks with a prophetic nostalgia. She calls him "Gordon" for the first time, and a moment later they are in each others' arms with soft music in the background. Fragments of lyrics are audible: "throughout the years . . . my heart. . . ." Startlingly, on a dissonance the music stops. An agitated Emily declares that they should go back. As they descend to the lower deck, the card-playing crew members are quarreling. They cross again the chains and ropes that, if we take them as images of Emily's marital ties, have proved to be less easily stepped past than the first crossing seemed to promise. The sequence, so amorously charged in the middle, ends on a note of weary disappointment. Emily leaves the Commander to return to her sleeping husband. As she bends down to give Fred an affirming kiss, she is stopped by his sleepy muttering. "What's for dinner, Em?" he mumbles querulously, "Steak and kidney pudding? Again? Every other night it's steak and kidney pudding." (We might remember the culinary variety that the Inspector's wife in *Frenzy* tries to introduce into another eight-year-old marriage.) As Emily stands sadly and pensively, her husband continues to complain in his sleep, and the screen fades to a gloomy black.

Another title introduces "The last night of the voyage," and Gordon and Emily once more stand at the deck rail in the moonlight. The Commander repeats his earlier remark, "Like to see a ship we were once passengers in? It's running away from us now." He pleads with Emily to marry him. This time the intercut of Fred seems to argue for Emily's freedom; for her husband and his bogus Princess are talking about their future together, and The Princess is coarsely reassuring Fred that "if a woman cannot hold her man, there is no reason why he should take the blame."

The elevated affection between the Commander and Emily contrasts with the boorish philandering of Fred and The Princess. As in Hitchcock's romances, the selfless quality of true love is set against the self-indulgent egotism of mock-love. The Commander is unoffended by Emily's innocent assertion that he, unlike her husband, is not "terribly clever." In contrast, Fred will later complacently explain to The Princess that "she [Emily] never really understood me. I was a bit too much for her." During the shipboard carnival, Emily and Gordon embrace. To spare Emily's feelings, and in deference to her married state, Gordon explains away the lapse by announcing, "I'm drunk, Emily." "No, you're not," she replies. Then, "If you're drunk, I am too." "Exactly," he murmurs, and walks slowly away from her and from their temptation. Immediately preceding this hard-won victory of marital fidelity over love, Fred—without an apparent thought of Emily—has gone into The Princess's cabin to consummate their affair.

Gordon's protectiveness is often aroused by Fred's mistreatment of Emily. At Port Said, he sees her walking the streets alone while Fred, in full view of his distressed wife, passes with The Princess. Gordon's immediate instinct is to go to Emily's side to distract her from her dismay. He later accompanies her ashore at Colombo after Fred has again deserted her in favor of The Princess.

Ironically, it is Gordon's long withheld denunciation of Fred as a childish fool, after Emily has apparently agreed to marry him, that sends the tenderhearted wife back to her loutish husband. Like Gordon's, Emily's love is essentially selfless, and when she sees that her husband needs her, she is unable to leave him, even for a greater love. "I recognized your faults, whereas before I'd always dressed you up in all kinds of silly virtues . . . I saw that I was a wife for you, that without me you'd be lost." Fred, unable to understand such devotion, thanks Emily sarcastically, and departs to elope with The Princess. He returns only because The Princess has run away without him, a betrayal that raises not only the rebuffed adulterer's indignation but also—comically, touchingly—that of his loyal wife.

Gordon, because his own love is selfless, can understand the same quality in Emily's otherwise inexplicable attachment to Fred. "Knowing you," he writes, "I accept your verdict. You have made your choice and I see the way of it. I don't know much about love, how long it lasts or what the remedies are, but I love you, Emily, so much that I can't write any more—only blessings and prayers for you." The note from him that Emily reads after Fred has left her alone in the hotel room marks a moment of real anguish in *Rich and Strange*. Not only have

Emily and Gordon denied themselves to each other, but it appears that they have done so to no purpose whatsoever.

The mention of "remedies" gives us some hope that the Commander may eventually recover from his loss; but for the moment everything seems to have come out wrong. *Rich and Strange* looks very much like an entire inversion of the fairy tale it started out to imitate. Gordon has been consigned to loneliness; and Emily, her wishes for her friend reversed in her own life, has not wound up with "the right person" but will continue to be "wasted."

As Emily tearfully finishes reading this message, she gazes at the waves breaking on the beach outside the hotel room window. They recall the waves that broke against the bow of the ship, reflecting the tumult of her feelings as she and Gordon stood at the rail just before their first kiss. But the discord that ended that scene turns to hopelessness in this one. The waves are diminished from passion to steady grief, and she looks at them not with Gordon but alone in an alien land. If their melancholy rhythm offers any consolation, it comes from the fact that waves are also associated with the seasickness of her faithless husband. We may consequently be reminded that Emily, although she has evidently lost Gordon, is at least rid of her ridiculous mate.

Though such a thought may please the audience, it cannot much console Emily, who has devoted herself to her marriage. Her commitment, in contrast to Fred's idle restlessness, appears in comic foreshadowing during their stay in Paris. When Fred gives Emily a sexy nightie, she is reluctant to wear it because "people will think that we aren't married." Fred chuckles with drunken satisfaction, "Don't feel a bit as if we are."

Unlike Fred, Emily understands the disappointments and reversals of love; and as a result, paradoxically, she values her marriage enough to make extraordinary sacrifices to preserve it. We may recall her profound little speech to the Commander on their first afternoon together. "Love is a very difficult business, Mr. Gordon. You'd be surprised. It makes everything difficult and dangerous. You know, I don't think love makes people brave, like they say it does in books. I think it makes them timid. I think it makes them frightened when they're happy and sadder when they're sad." Nowhere in Hitchcock's work does the ironic reversal of romantic assumptions about love and adventure appear more explicitly than when Emily contrasts the reality of love with what "they say . . . in books." What she says—ironically again—does not so much apply to her love as it does to her husband's. Fred is, as Gordon says, "a sham." His blustering aggressiveness comes not from self-confidence or happiness but from the fact that he is "frightened" and "sad."

After The Princess eludes Fred and he—like a timid, homesick child—is forced to return to Emily, the pattern of romantic renewal reasserts itself. It is here that one sees most clearly, I think, the deep influence on Rich and Strange of Murnau's magnificent Sunrise, albeit that Hitchcock finally parodies the outcome of the earlier story of a marriage almost lost and then revived. Both films contain a husband seduced away from his wife by a sophisticated vulgarian, a wreck at sea immediately after the reconciliation of the married couple, and a return from the brink of death to revived life and fertility.

As is common in romantic narratives, the line of action in Rich and Strange turns sharply upward after its low point, dips to face death itself, and reascends to resurrection and multiplied triumph. In Hitchcock's inversion of those formulae, however, the triumphs will prove to be fleeting, or at least mixed. But the moment of ironic reckoning lies beyond the renewing adventures of the voyage home—a voyage in which Fred at least partly seems to discover who he is and what Emily means to him. In the shipwreck he faces the loss of his newly retrieved marriage and his very life; and he is miraculously spared to gain a deeper sense of affirmation and renewing fertility.

After their fog-bound steamer begins to sink, Emily and Fred are trapped in their cabin. They face apparently certain death as the listing ship is abandoned and silence replaces the sounds of panic and flight. The porthole is blocked by waves—with all the symbolic complexity that they have acquired during the movie. As they prepare to die, Fred admits that he is frightened. His wife cradles him in her arms. "Em, I'm sorry," he says in a sort of deathbed repentance; "there's only been you, there's only ever been you." The water creeps under the jammed door and the screen fades again to black—funereally. But their return from the brink of death parallels the return of their marriage from the brink of dissolution. The screen brightens to a dazzling sun shining into their cabin, and the camera pans to the sleeping couple as Emily awakens to realize that they are still alive. Amusingly, a shot from outside the ship shows first Emily and then Fred emerging from their porthole like a pair of very large newborn infants.

Their subsequent adventures on the Chinese junk expand these lessons about the value of life and love to the human condition at large. Fred and Emily watch one of the crew members of the junk drown when he is trapped on the steamer, as they almost were. Then they witness the birth of new life: the wife of the master of the junk delivers a baby who is anointed with the waters of the sea that has recently served to bury the ship and the Chinese sailor caught in its rigging. Emily weeps with emotion over the birth while Fred puts his arms around her and says comfortingly, "There, there, don't cry, Em old dear. . . . We're alright, Em, we've got each other." A few moments later, the idea that they, too, might have a baby clearly enters their minds. As they hold each other, Hitchcock cuts first to shots of the sun breaking through clouds, then returns to Emily and Fred kissing, Emily's hair glowing in the light as it did on the night when she and Gordon first embraced. The camera returns once more to the fertile image of swelling clouds and the warm, life-giving sun.

Were *Rich and Strange* to end at this point, its ironies would be far less pointed than they actually are. But we have already had some clear hints that the romantic renewal and deepening of love that Emily and Fred experience aboard the junk will be adulterated by other, more ironic, strains. The small, unglamorous defects of both the protagonists and of life generally are not suppressed in the romantic epiphanies aboard the junk. The shipwrecked pair's enjoyment of their first meal ends in nausea when they realize that the meat mixed with the rice is the remains of the cat that Emily rescued from the sinking steamer. Just before the birth of the baby, Fred helps his wife to a seat on a raised deck only to put her down indecorously on a knot of rope. The two then discuss defrauding the insurance company by telling it that the thousand pounds stolen by The Princess went down with the steamer. Fred's comforting, affectionate remarks after the birth are punctuated by others of his usual insensitivity: "These damn Chinese breed like rabbits. . . . Gosh, isn't it [the infant] ugly!"

As a result of such dissonant undertones, we are not entirely surprised when the last shot of the sun and clouds cuts smoothly into one of nocturnal London. Its flashing advertisements recall the underground signs that aggravated Fred's discontent in the first sequence. The old irritations of bourgeois life, and Fred's inability to respond to them with any grace or perspective, return in a rush. Their landlady (played by the same wonderful comic actress who played the Landlady in *Blackmail*) greets them with a welcome-home meal of, alas, steak and kidney pudding. The black cat that aroused Fred's wrath in the opening of the movie, and whose cousin he unwittingly ate and regurgitated on the junk, gets on the table again, to disgust him by licking a spoon. The wireless, which offered Fred the annoyance of "Mr. Baker's twelfth talk on accountancy" when he came home from work at the beginning of the film, now revives unwelcome memories of his seasickness with reports of "strong northwesterly gales all coasts of the British Isles. . . . Channel crossings extremely rough."

As if reminded of the diverse tempests of the cruise from which they have just returned, Emily and Fred embrace before their cozy fire. Fred walks to the front door and thoughtfully gazes up the hall. "I was wondering," he remarks to Emily, "if we could get a pram down that passage." So far, so good. But the wanderlust that struck Fred at the beginning of the film seems to capture his wife in a domestic way at the end. Emily asserts that she will want a bigger, nicer house after Fred gets a new job. Fred demurs, "What do you want to move for? We've been here all these years." As the two quarrel, the movie ends on the ironic notes that have emerged as dominant throughout.

This husband and wife will live, it appears, contentiously ever after. There is nothing terrifying about their fate; *Rich and Strange* remains comic, and neither will suffer too much or too poignantly. Nor, on the other hand, is there anything heartening about their prospects; *Rich and Strange* remains ironic. Fred and Emily return only slightly changed to circumstances essentially unchanged. They are a little older, they may have a baby. Emily understands Fred better and will both protect and dominate him as she could not have done before. But in gaining insight and self-confidence, she has lost some of the innocent diffidence that made her such an appealing figure. Ultimately, Emily and Fred have not gone very far toward self-discovery and they will not go much farther. If they are too comfortable to despair, they have no cause for presumption, either. Life, and they, will go on—getting nowhere, for there is nowhere for them to get—equally without great pain or great joy.

They have each other, poor things in some respects, but their own. As the title figure muses at the end of one of John Mortimer's television plays, "Because however awful it is . . . they can't stand to be alone . . . they'd rather have war together than a lonely peace" ("Rumpole and the Married Lady"). Such a conclusion does not apply quite equally to the dependent, self-centered Fred and to the more generous Emily, but it summarizes in a rough way the mild consolation to which the adventures of *Rich and Strange* finally lead. The alternative, an unfulfilled single-blessedness, appears in the fate of the Commander, despite our sense that he may recover from his disappointment. It is portrayed, at once more sadly and less sympathetically, in the satiric lampoon of the stereotyped creature The Princess calls "the gossip woman."

If the mutual strutting of Fred and The Princess inverts the love of Emily and Gordon, the lonely presence of the scrawny, middle-aged spinster counterpoints their love by love's absence. The Old Maid intersects the two true lovers at every turn. She interrupts them before and after their first kiss. She appears, solo as always, as a peeping Bo

Peep to intrude briefly into the *ménage à quatre* at the Carnival. The last night of the voyage, she cheers alone in the festive company, out of sync and ludicrous as always. On deck in the moonlight, the four lovers, mismatched as they are, nonetheless are paired. Each has someone, whatever the difficulties, with whom to celebrate or mourn the end of the voyage. If the outcome of the lovers' adventures prevents us from overrating the consolations of having a mate, the insistently pathetic appearances of the Old Maid suggest that we ought not to dismiss them entirely.

In Hitchcock's romantic movies, love redeems the present and resolves the past. In movies of mixed genre like *Sabotage* or *Foreign Correspondent*, love tempers the pains and lightens the trials of a difficult but not hopeless world. In *Blackmail* and *Rich and Strange*, the multifaceted aspects of love are as shifting, hard to resolve, and ambiguous as the ironically ambiguous world. Love in such films neither reforms life nor creates a haven of consolation. Like everything else, it remains subject to vicissitudes and uncertainties, thoroughly tangled in the degenerative, unprogressive movement of a linear time that repeats without renewing.

If Fred and Emily have learned anything, it is not that there's no place like home, but that every place is home. For Emily that conclusion is perhaps more comforting, and certainly better understood, than it is for Fred. Looking at Port Said, she remarks pensively, "To think that place has been there all these years! All those strange people, having their babies, dying, cooking their funny meals. Strange, it's been there all these years." Fred, contemptuous as always, snaps back, "Well, you don't think they built it specially for us overnight, do you?" Later they will quarrel in Singapore as they quarrel in London, while a Salvation Army band (to reappear in *The 39 Steps*) marches past outside their window, with a familiarity and an artistic appropriateness that is, like everything else in *Rich and Strange*, multiple.

The irony of the title can hardly be missed. Indeed, Hitchcock enforces his point by quoting the phrase in its well-known Shakespearean context between the opening domestic sequences and the departure of Fred and Emily on their voyage. On an otherwise empty screen appears: " 'Doth suffer a sea change/ Into something rich and strange.'/ *The Tempest*." But nothing changes. For the uncomprehending Fred, nothing is strange. At home or away, he is continuously "all at sea." For his brighter, more sensitive wife, everything is remarkable. But neither one discovers a magic isle where life can be renewed and the past made right through radiant, never-diminishing love. Nevertheless their world is not corrupt or painful. It is moderately comfortable, in fact.

It simply remains—in pointed contradiction to the promise of the title—imperfect, often irritating, and routine.

Mr. and Mrs. Smith

Mr. and Mrs. Smith repeats, in its wacky way, the story of a marriage almost lost, then recovered. Like *Rich and Strange*, its ironies are fundamentally comic; but unlike its predecessor, they are practically unalloyed with real pathos. The pain and conflict it contains, indeed, are portrayed as a form of pleasure for the central couple and as a necessary psychic nutrient in their relationship.

The oddity of such a theme and the status of *Mr. and Mrs. Smith* as Hitchcock's single screwball comedy have led critics to treat it as an aberration in its director's career. Hitchcock himself seemed to take a similar view, dismissing the movie in *Hitchcock/Truffaut* as no more than "a friendly gesture to Carole Lombard," and agreeing with his interviewer that making it had been "a waste of time."[6] Rohmer and

Mr. and Mrs. Smith: Gene Raymond and Carole Lombard. The ironic films counsel against presumption. The visible part of the sign on the parachute makes the allegory explicit. It reads, simply, "Life."

[6] Truffaut, *Hitchcock/Truffaut*, pp. 139 and 314.

Chabrol, on the other hand, regard *Mr. and Mrs. Smith* as a project that Hitchcock took "very seriously."[7] They identify the films with which it has the clearest affinities as *Champagne* and *Rich and Strange*. Though they misremember some of the details of the film, they have, I think, an accurate understanding of its place in Hitchcock's career. Among Hitchcock's later movies, *The Trouble with Harry* comes closest to reproducing the antic comedy of *Mr. and Mrs. Smith* and occasionally reverts as well to the rapid, zany dialogue style of the earlier work. *The Trouble with Harry*, however, is as radically romantic as *Mr. and Mrs. Smith* is ironic; in every detail, the later film reiterates its central theme of renewal. *Mr. and Mrs. Smith*, like *Rich and Strange*, returns to the point of its beginning with only a slight sense of regeneration.

Of the Hollywood comedies of remarriage that Stanley Cavell discusses in *Pursuits of Happiness*, the darkest one, *His Girl Friday*, has most in common with *Mr. and Mrs. Smith*. Both end not with the rediscovery of a marriage but with the confirmation of old habits. Those habits—the instincts for journalistic predation that join Walter and Hildy and the libidinal biting and clawing that bond Mr. and Mrs. Smith—land both films worlds away from the restorative self-creation-in-love of romance. Among other Hitchcock movies, *Suspicion* and *The Paradine Case* could be called comedies of remarriage without laughter. Like most of the movies Cavell examines, their marriages have failed in consummation or have somehow become unconsummated. Their couples must discover or rediscover each other and consecrate their vows anew. The conclusion of *Mr. and Mrs. Smith*, however, only confirms its protagonists in their abrasive, peculiarly comfortable marriage of antagonism controlled by rules.

Mr. and Mrs. Smith deviates from Hitchcock's other ironic works chiefly in the undiluted quality of its humor. Its main themes, and the ironies it constructs around them, are entirely consistent with Hitchcock's career-long preoccupations. *Mr. and Mrs. Smith*, in brief, may be odd Hitchcock, but it is not tangential. It is a particularly exuberant *scherzo* in the diversely unified cycle of romantic stories and their ironic counterparts that make up Hitchcock's career.

The opposition between true and false love, or love and lust, which is central to Hitchcock's romantic work, disappears in *Mr. and Mrs. Smith*. Egotistical desire no longer opposes emotional generosity but replaces it. The possessive sexuality that remains to represent love in *Mr. and Mrs. Smith* can be contrasted only with simple absence of

7 Rohmer and Chabrol, *Hitchcock*, p. 62.

passion. The relatively selfless love of Commander Gordon in *Rich and Strange* has disappeared in *Mr. and Mrs. Smith*. The libidinal egotism of Fred and The Princess remains, and its foil becomes the deprivation of love exemplified in the earlier movie by the Old Maid, and in *Mr. and Mrs. Smith* by the capon-like gentility of Mr. Smith's (Robert Montgomery) southern law partner, Jefferson Custer (Gene Raymond).

"You're in one of your romantic moods again. That's been the trouble since the beginning," declares David Smith to his wife when she complains that "all you ever think about is yourself." Given the ironic psychological dynamics that shape the relationship between him and Ann (Carole Lombard), David has reality on his side when he scornfully dismisses his wife's idealization of Jeff as "kind, and simple, and gentle." Possession is nine-tenths of the law of love as well as of property. "You're mine and you belong to me," he will later assert. "You couldn't have anything to do with that pile of southern fried chicken." His wife will declare him right. As she begins to be won back to her husband by his alternately imperious and prostrate courtship, Ann explains to Jeff, "You know the real reason he keeps chasing me? He's still so much in love with me. He's such an egotist, he can't bear the idea of letting someone else kiss me." Love is not separated, as in the romances, from ownership or control.

Ann takes offense not at her husband's treatment of her as a possession but at his failure to renew the form (their invalid marriage license) that legitimizes his dominion. David, for his part, responds to the news that he is technically unmarried with the excitement of Fred in the Paris hotel room when his drunkenness and the sight of Emily in a sexy nightie make him feel as if he is not married. Preparing to bed what he thinks is his unsuspecting "new mistress," he preens himself and whistles with an erotic satisfaction that appears to be based entirely upon his perception that he is about to reap a sexual harvest to which, in some superficial way, he is no longer entitled. He is getting something for nothing; and as a result his lawful wedded routine takes on the allure of illicit possession. The incongruous fact that the prospective victim of his seduction is his wife in no way cools his predatory ardor.

Love in Hitchcock's romances combines personal esteem and a protective impulse with desire; but in *Mr. and Mrs. Smith* attraction thrives on conflict. Like a pair of minks, Ann and David require the foreplay of violent battle rather than gentle wooing. An opening pan over a chaos of dirty dishes reveals a beardy Mr. Smith playing solitaire in his bathrobe and looking apprehensively toward a bed in which Mrs. Smith tosses petulantly. Their three-day war, however, soon leads to an affectionate reconciliation. The last sequence of the movie parallels the first, when their sexual reconnection is preceded by even more protracted battling. A pair of crossed ski-tips, the final image of the film, symbolizes at once their union and the conflict necessary to it. Upon such concupiscent brawling depends the continued stability—such as it is—of their marriage.

Set against the alley-cat amorousness of Mr. and Mrs. Smith is the sexless gentility of David's partner. A former Alabama fullback who does not drink liquor, never breaks training, and eats "four vegetables a day," Jeff's manliness is cool and stilted. Ann praises him for his restraint, but his disinclination to conquer and hold a mate does not finally recommend him as a suitor, especially for a woman like Ann. In the world of *Mr. and Mrs. Smith* "consideration" betokens abnormally low libido rather than selflessness. However excessive Ann's denunciation of Jeff as "a lump of jelly" may be, there is a lack of ardor in his decorous chivalry. In the absence of any alternative model of love in this movie, Jeff's stiff courtesy appears more sterile than gentle. He is also childlike, still very much the earnest son of proud, overprotective parents. Adult love between men and women (so far as anyone in *Mr. and Mrs Smith* qualifies as an adult) is compounded equally of sex and venial violence.

Mutual healing and need in love, an idea central to all Hitchcock's romantic films, diminishes to a comic parody. The central characters injure themselves; they are not hacked at by injustice or bad luck. The image of Mr. Smith hitting himself in the nose in order to escape his embarrassment at the Florida Club sums up the self-inflicted origins of his woes. His faked collapse and Ann's caring for him at Lake Placid further parody the motif of the healer and the healed.

His "delirium" induces Ann back to a position of intimacy, as she shaves and cares for him. We may be reminded at this point of a familiar Hitchcockian premise, of which Ann's unnecessary nursing of David is a comic variant. Men and women, put in proximity and some need of each other, will come together, fall in love. No such coming together results from David's quickly uncovered charade; but his attempt to regain physical intimacy with his wife by faking illness reminds us of situations in other Hitchcock films where the sickness is real, the stakes much greater, and the outcome more elevating, or dire.

Other familiar romantic motifs reappear in *Mr. and Mrs. Smith* in the ludicrous or eviscerated versions characteristic of ironic comedy. Infernal depths are realized in the smoky kitchen of the decayed restaurant where David takes Ann and in the sweaty steam room of the Beefeater's Club, a comic hell to which Mrs. Smith exiles her husband.

There he encounters a feeble version of a damned soul and tempter in Benson (Jack Carson). Moments of discovery (equivocal, as one might predict) take place in toilets with clanking plumbing and on trips during which the fresh country air is sharpened by the fresher excretions of the horse pulling the sleigh. David's quest for love leads him to the Florida Club, his vulgar blind date, and a self-inflicted bloody nose. Ann's leads her to the same club and then, in a mock romantic ascent, to the top of a parachute ride that maroons her with Jeff in a rainstorm.

The soaking that Ann and Jeff suffer at the carnival represents the final diminution of the tremendous storm that Murnau made the climax of *Sunrise* and that Hitchcock first adapted to comic and ironic uses in *Rich and Strange*. The absurd plight of Ann and Jeff reflects both an inversion and a comic shrinking of the romantic convention it parodies. A more dangerous inversion, as I observed earlier, occurs in *Strangers on a Train*, during the carnival sequence that culminates in Miriam's murder.

Complex interplay between artifice and reality and a tendency for make-believe to prefigure or express deep truths characterize acting and pretense in Hitchcock's romantic comedies. Pretense in ironic films, on the other hand, has no underlying layer of truth; it remains self-interested fakery. In *Rich and Strange*, The Princess simply molts her borrowed feathers and turns back into the cleaner's daughter that she was all along. None of the elaborate charades in which David engages in *Mr. and Mrs. Smith* leads to much besides embarrassment. His ruse of shutting the door and pretending to be gone in the first sequence does produce the desired reconciliation; but similar deceptions later in the film are ineffectual. The companion of the beautiful woman he pretends to be with at the Florida Club threatens to beat him up, and his performance at Lake Placid has only temporary success. In an ironic world, the surface of things is their significance. Reality has no more meaningful underbody. Pretense, therefore, can only be false; it cannot shadow a deeper truth beneath superficial appearances.

The comedy of *Mr. and Mrs. Smith* is based upon familiar principles, the pervasive rigidity and the infantility of characters who fail to achieve emotional maturity appropriate to their station in a grown-up world. As may be appropriate to a lawyer's wife, Ann has a passion for rules. The three-day marital siege that ends during the first sequence has resulted, we learn, from one of the rules that the couple has adopted: "you are not allowed to leave the bedroom after a quarrel unless you've made up." The affectionate resolution of their spat suggests that this rule may make sense, and the audience is not prepared to disagree with Ann's self-congratulatory proclamation that "we must never change that rule. You know if every couple had it there'd never be a divorce." A few minutes later, however, a second rule, evidently that Ann should ask and David should answer an intimate question every month, raises the first specter of the protracted separation that occupies most of the film. Ann asks her husband whether, if he had it to do over again, he would marry her. His "no" tensions the emotional spring that will release its energy when she learns of their invalid marriage license.

That legal technicality has the same kind of mindless rigidity that their domestic rules threaten to impose. No one ever suggests that their marriage is truly dissolved by the invalidity of the license, unless Ann wants it to be. The functionary who brings David the news, in fact, is quite explicit: "Oh, you really are married, and everything, but there's a little technicality. . . ." Despite its essential inconsequence, the "little technicality" unravels the fabric of their marriage. That it should do so—or that Mr. and Mrs. Smith should allow it—reflects the mechanical slavery in which they are held by rules. Similarly legalistic, Ann's mother, apprised of the news, earnestly cautions her daughter "not to," as if Ann were a naive virgin rather than a woman married for three years.

As eccentric, abrasive, and rigid as Mr. and Mrs. Smith are both individually and within their marriage, they fit each other well, and their bizarre rules seem to suit them as well as they suit each other. The fact that David is a lawyer implies that he, too, has a penchant for technicalities. "It's possible," says Jeff to Ann near the end of the film, "it's more than possible, that as peculiar as David is, you couldn't be happy without him." *Mr. and Mrs. Smith* portrays marriage as a state of adaptation, of being accustomed to someone. It accommodates the inflexibility of its partners. Such a conception is not very inspiring, but within the ironic assumptions of the film, it is reasonably comfortable. And it is probably the best anyone can expect to do. Retreating from his injurious answer to Ann's question about whether he would marry her again, David replies with as much truth as comic sinking, "I love you, I worship you, I am used to you."

The childishness of Mr. and Mrs. Smith (and of Jeff) amounts to another sort of rigidity, a refusal to respond to the passage of time. Such arrested development can be seen as a comic variant of the injurious past that haunts more sober movies. The problem of time in *Mr. and Mrs. Smith* results not from a trauma that enslaves the protagonist to the past, but from the willful refusal of the central figures to grow up. David and Ann are more closely related to the lost boys of *Peter Pan* than to the characters of "Sleeping Beauty."

The dialogue is soaked with the childishness that is evident in the characters' tantrums and stubbornness. David calls Ann a "great kid" and "my little girl," the latter an epithet that her mother applies to her as well. "Annie, you haven't changed a bit from the little girl that used to go runnin', in and out of the house. I'd a recognized you in a minute," declares Mr. Devers. Ann's first date after she throws David out of the apartment is with a man old enough, as the saying has it, to be her father.

Her husband appears scarcely less juvenile. "Now can I go to work?" David asks his wife after their argument, like a chastened boy asking if he can go out and play. He and Jeff talk about Jeff's days as a football player as if such youthful concerns were still at the center of their lives. His dependency upon his wife for shaving and laundry and his childish ploy of playing sick to gain Ann's sympathy add to our impression that he, along with his wife and most other adults in the movie, are essentially big, affluent children.

Time passes; but Mr. and Mrs. Smith resist any change. Ann cannot understand why the "little blue dress" has shrunk, even though it has not been out of the closet for three years. Mama Lucy's restaurant has altered, as has Ann's expanding figure; and "Mama Lucy" herself has turned into a scruffy, cigar-chomping man. The "place has changed a little," as Ann and David admit with considerable understatement. Nonetheless they try to act as if it—and as if they—have remained the same. Their amusing, humanly understandable refusal to respond to the mutability of life is another form of the rigidity that governs them.

Such obdurate inflexibility, the movie implies, may be found not only in its title characters but in humankind generally. The title of the movie suggests "Mr. and Mrs. Everybody," and the question that sums up the real subject of the film—"if you had it all to do over again, would you have married me?"—is one that any married person must at one time or another contemplate. Contrary to what Ann asserts, she and David *do* have a marriage that is basically "just like other people's." The visible part of the illuminated sign upon the parachute ride where Ann and Jeff are soaked makes the allegory explicit. It reads, simply, "Life."

Genres in *Mr. and Mrs. Smith* combine in a way that is extremely unusual for Hitchcock. Although its radical irony rules out the profound optimism of the romances, its unadulterated comedy so thoroughly excludes serious danger and pain that the movie nonetheless retains its good cheer about life. *Mr. and Mrs. Smith* returns its silly but harmless creatures to a state of comfort. If their lives lack transcendent meaning, the universe in which they dwell remains essentially benign, its linear time full of entertaining scuffles that come out alright. We do not have the sense of grace and renewal in love that we have at the end of Hitchcock's more romantic films, but nothing in the film makes us regret the lack of a deeper meaning. Life passes like a spring day in *Mr. and Mrs. Smith*, and the movie ends long before any hint of evening raises so much as a shadow of night and darkness.

Topaz

As Hitchcock's films shift toward anxiety and nightmare, emotional values attached to the political and social institutions represented in them grow more positive. A detective may embody much of the authority and human sympathy present in such movies—despite the general truth that Hitchcock usually presents police as cold and threatening. Larue in *I Confess* and Inspector Oxford in *Frenzy* exemplify such figures. The policemen achieve their attractive status because their sympathy and professional scruples contrast with the indifference to

Topaz: Politics shatter love. At the beginning of their escape to the West, the Kuzenov daughter deliberately smashes a figurine of kissing lovers.

truth and human suffering of the characters surrounding them. Although Larue and Oxford make mistakes about the guilt of a central figure, their basic competence and generosity set them apart from the meanness of the villains and the ineptitude or selfishness of most of the minor figures. Decent, honest men, they stand out against the human wickedness and egotism that their profession assigns them the task of trying to restrain.

Detective "Ordinary" Smith (Michael Wilding) in *Stage Fright* actually becomes the romantic lead, rescuing Eve (Jane Wyman) from the demonic clutches of Jonathan (Richard Todd) and carrying her off through a sort of theatrical sunset of spotlights to what we assume will be marital happiness. Ted the detective comes to the aid of Sylvia and establishes himself romantically with her after the death of Verloc at the end of *Sabotage*. In the last few minutes of *Notorious*, the hitherto emotionally crippled Dev plays a similar role. In all three movies, a romantic pattern finally submerges an ironic one that has dominated for most of the earlier action. But the ironic structures have such power that they can be challenged only from within. Disorder and deceptive appearances necessitate an alliance of romantic forces with institutional structures that would not be required in a world more wholly controlled by efficacious love and miracles.

Before turning to *Topaz*, of all Hitchcock's films the one that perhaps most clearly exemplifies the characteristic connection between politics and irony in his work, I would like to establish a context for it by looking at the conclusion of *Secret Agent* (1936). At the end of this earlier film, practical, "realistic" social structures confront the romantic growth of love and personal rebirth that has shaped the relationship between the two central figures. Neither mode dominates. The plot is resolved by realistic-ironic politics and a sort of rebirth that exist together in acute tension. *Secret Agent* thus concludes not by presenting a preeminent world view but with a deadlock between alternatives that are mutually exclusive. It shows with particular clarity the opposing visions of human life embodied in the competing ironic and romantic energies of its story.

The short final sequence of *Secret Agent* begins when stirring martial music strikes up and camel troops gallop toward the camera. The music, triumphantly upbeat, accompanies images that consist mostly of lap-dissolves of advancing infantry, newspaper headlines announcing victory, and the Chief of Intelligence shaking hands at a celebratory gathering of high officers. The final shot is a double exposure of a post card and the smiling faces of Ashenden (John Gielgud) and Elsa (Madeleine Carroll), heads together and evidently married. The card reads, somewhat ambiguously, "Home safely but Never Again. Mr. and Mrs. Ashenden." The smiles of the happy couple are wan.

The clichéd movie celebration of military triumph embodied in the ending of *Secret Agent* is profoundly inadequate as a closure for the complex and sometimes sordid narrative that precedes it. Quite remarkably, Hitchcock has put his foil at the end of the movie rather than at its beginning. The standard happy ending of political good vanquishing political evil offers the audience only momentary satisfaction. The viewer will eventually remember that the friendly, innocent Caypor is dead and his gentle wife widowed. The General and Marvin, insatiable lechers and unhesitating killers both, are morally indistinguishable in their murderousness; and Ashenden and Elsa are deeply implicated in a war that kills bystanders and combatants alike. The human costs of the victory loom too large for us to exult comfortably in the closing spectacle of battles won.

But we are not, at the same time, allowed to shrink with simple moral revulsion from all war. The two sides do not have an equal claim to our sympathy. The moral authority of Ashenden and Elsa aligns the audience with the British. The war at issue, moreover, is a matter of history—history told in this film from the winning side's point of view. When Elsa and Ashenden confront the apparent necessity of murdering Marvin just before the train wreck, their exchange summarizes the inescapable dilemmas that arise when political necessities and love clash.

ELSA: I'd sooner see you dead than let you do this [kill Marvin].
ASHENDEN: Do you realize this might be the end of our forces in the East?
E: What difference does that make to me?
A: His life against the life of thousands.
E: What do I care about them? What do I care about him? He's done. We're not going to have this on our conscience.

The successful attack of the Royal Air Force at this moment constitutes an ironic *deus ex machina*, a celestial intervention that resolves the argument in the only way that it can be resolved, by force. The advocacy of Elsa for love and innocence and of Ashenden for "the life of thousands" conflict absolutely and irreconcilably. Before the bombs fall, however, the movie has made clear that both Elsa and Ashenden may have to accept death in some form as the cost of winning the point. Ashenden will murder Marvin on behalf of the British armies in the East, and Elsa "would sooner see [Ashenden] dead" than let him execute Marvin.

"The entire film," as Yacowar writes, "is a disturbing experience. It challenges our complacent assumptions about the possibility of purity or heroism in war."⁸ Worse, it offers no alternative. Paradoxes and ambiguities make its characters what they are individually and constitute its world collectively. Wars cannot end. Mr. and Mrs. Ashenden's marriage has a past before it begins, literally and figuratively. So does human society. That past condemns the present and future to compromises and dilemmas. Humankind is condemned to make war at the same time it is allowed to make love. If love offers some consolation for the killing, it cannot quell the human appetite for death or even wholly escape participating in it.

The "Never Again" of the Ashendens' post card seems a noble but faint hope for them, for humankind, and for the Europe that in 1936 was looking back at one seizure of massive carnage and drawing itself up for another. As it recalls The Great War, *Secret Agent* looks ahead to the next social *grand mal*. The terrifying deterioration of the world after 1932 presents itself as an obvious explanation for the turn in Hitchcock's work toward a melancholy irony. In no other period of his career is he so consistently and centrally political. A brief recitation of titles and dates indicates clearly enough Hitchcock's preoccupations during the middle 1930s: *The Man Who Knew Too Much* (first, 1934), *The 39 Steps* (1935), *Secret Agent* (1936), *Sabotage* (1936), *The Lady Vanishes* (1938).

The last sequence of *Topaz* strongly resembles that of *Secret Agent*, but *Topaz* makes its point more directly. It begins with a headline on the *New York Herald Tribune* announcing "Cuban Missile Crisis Over." This shot is followed by a series of dissolves to the low points of the preceding narrative: the Mendozas (sympathetic agents) reduced to human ruins by torture, a dead leaker of NATO secrets lying on the roof of his car, Juanita (Karin Dor) dying in her murderer-lover's arms, Devereaux (Frederick Stafford) grieving silently after learning of her death. As the sequence ends, two men walk arm in arm toward the Arch de Triomphe. From behind, one looks like Khruschev. The shot suggests a confusing collaboration between putative enemies that recalls the shifting alliances throughout the film.

The missile crisis may be over, but the collage of dissolves sums up the devastating expense of the espionage that contributed to its solution. The deadly spying, moreover, has affected the outcome of the crisis only slightly. When Mike (John Forsythe), the American agent, gets the intelligence André Devereaux has obtained at the cost of at least four lives, he remarks that it "confirms our information from

⁸ Yacowar, *Hitchcock's British Films*, p. 201.

other sources, including the U-2 photos." If the combatants have not died entirely in vain, they have given their lives only to reinforce information already gained elsewhere. In *Secret Agent*, the gathering of intelligence was probably not necessary either; the bombing of the train occurs independently of Ashenden's or Elsa's efforts. That implication, however, is not emphasized in the earlier film; in *Topaz* the relative inconsequence of what happens in the main plot is explicit.

The simple patriotism and moral rectitude that *Topaz* eventually overwhelms in political ambiguity and personal betrayal are implicit in an opening title superimposed on the May Day parade in Red Square. "Somewhere in this crowd is a high Russian official who disagrees with his government's display of force and what it threatens. Very soon his conscience will force him to attempt an escape while apparently on a vacation with his family." This opening promise of personal conscience triumphing over political loyalty however, progressively gives way to ironic reversals and uncertainties. Global opponents mingle until we can hardly tell who is on which side. Hitchcock dissolves his usual distinction between the corruption of public life and the romantic redemption of private love. Freedom constrains, information obscures as much as it reveals, and global travels lead to equally unfaithful bedrooms everywhere. By the end of *Topaz*, the opening title has become as inadequate to the action it introduces as the closing sequence of *Secret Agent* is to the complex story it pretends to conclude.

The image cuts from Red Square to Copenhagen. The camera looks down on the confluence of two rivers traversed by bridges, which suggest in retrospect surprising connections between the opposing political sides. By the end of *Topaz*, the four countries whose conflicts occasion its plot will have been conflated. Their agents appear practically interchangeable, as do their ethics. The rhetoric of the film begins to run them together early, when a high shot of the Soviet flag introduces the Russian Embassy in Copenhagen; a little later, a pointedly similar high shot of an American flag gives us our first view of the American Embassy. The allies of the United States and the Soviet Union, France and Cuba, are drawn into the same pattern of indirect identification. The first shot of the French Embassy in Washington comes from another elevated camera looking down past the French tricolor to the street below. The red, white, and blue Cuban flag is conspicuous at the beginning of a Castro rally.

All four intelligence organizations share a mentality of authoritarian repression. Before they defect, the Russian family is under surveillance continuously, and the Soviet Embassy is a compound behind locked gates. The White House in Washington also appears behind defensive gates, and the agents at the safe house greet the Kuzenovs with high-handed bossiness. André is called back to France with dictatorial abruptness. Juanita complains that Castro has made Cuba "a prison."

The identification of apparently opposed political entities is intensified by symbolic color schemes. Spoto asserts that *Topaz* "tells its story entirely in terms of specific colors and color relationships."[9] Such a statement deliberately exaggerates; but the systematic use of color does generate much of the complex meaning of this very complex film. Among other Hitchcock works, only *Vertigo* and *Marnie* use color as expressively.

Red is strongly associated with the Soviets from the first shots of Red Square and of the flag over their embassy. This association will continue throughout the film, largely in connection with their allies, the Cubans. The bodyguard of the Cuban leader Para has flaming red hair. At the Hotel Theresa, Uribe is bribed in the midst of bright red signs and panels. The documents detailing the Cuban-Russian agreement are kept in a red attaché case. Juanita, when she appears at her house with Para, wears a bright red dress.

The red, white, and blue associated with the United States and with its NATO ally France repeats the colors of the flags of both countries. Blue is especially emphasized. After his successful espionage, Dubois returns to his shop to drape a blue banner on a white floral cross. The U.S. agents and those working with them usually appear in blue suits. When André meets his family at the airport in New York, a prominent TWA advertisement greets them in red, white, and blue. After André replaces Para at Juanita's side in Cuba, she changes from her red dress to a white nightdress that she wears sitting in front of a blue curtain the next morning.

France, as Spoto points out, is also associated with yellow: in the furnishings of André's house in Washington, in the color suggested by the words "Columbine" and "Topaz," in the yellow smock of the French agent Dubois. With few exceptions, however, yellow is curiously absent from sequences in France itself, which is characterized by neutral grayish tones and blacks and whites.

Both red and yellow may often be better understood not as signifying one country or another but as participating in another system of symbolism, one found in all Hitchcock's color films. In many contexts they are associated with their conventional public meanings: "Danger!" for red, and "Caution" for yellow. The yellow flowers that Mike

⁹ Spoto, *The Art of Alfred Hitchcock*, p. 424.

brings to André in New York serve both to warn of difficulties ahead and to reiterate his association with the French. The autumnal yellow of the trees through which the Kuzenovs are driven suggests their wariness of their new protectors; and warning yellows are combined with the reds of danger (and of Communism) outside the Hotel Theresa.

When André's wife Nicole learns that Jacques, her lover and an old family friend, is a Soviet spy, she exclaims, "Horrible! Horrible!" Her husband infers from her cry a personal betrayal along with the political one. He responds by bowing his head in front of a bouquet of yellow and orange flowers. Nicole, in a black dress, stands before a white curtain. The black and white suggest—here and elsewhere—moral clarity and political neutrality that always prove impossible to maintain. "No one is neutral," André tells his wife when she tries to persuade him not to get involved in quarrels between the Russians and the Americans. His words return to haunt him and Nicole in this scene; black and white give way to yellow and red.

The red associated with the Russians in Red Square is also associated with the real danger of their military might. When André shows Juanita how the Geiger counter works, a red lamp on the bedside table warns against using it. Red is associated with danger most obviously when, as in *Marnie*, it is figured as brilliant blood, often on a white background: when the Mendozas are apprehended because of the wife's bleeding wound, when André's son-in-law is shot, when Jarre is found on the roof of his car, and when blood seeps from under Juanita's body.

Complicating the color symbolism in *Topaz*, in addition to the interaction of two different associative patterns, is the fact that contrasts of all kinds insistently metamorphose into identifications. The opposing meanings of reds, blues, whites, and yellows become confused, just as political and personal oppositions run together. The flags of the U.S.S.R., the U.S., France, and Cuba have obvious similarities. All use red; three have stars; and three are red, white, and blue. Cuba, the political nexus of the movie, serves also as the visual crossroads; its red, white, and blue, single-starred flag combines important elements of the flags of the other three countries. Like the countries themselves, their distinguishing political emblems are as similar as they are different.

Visual equivocation reinforces ambiguity of action and dialogue. After the Kuzenov family escapes from Copenhagen, a long shot follows their U.S. airplane as it rises into a spectacular red-orange sky. Does the red recall the Communist country from which the Kuzenovs have fled? Or does it anticipate the country to which they are going?

Does it warn of impending danger? Or is it a more personal symbol, marking for the Kuzenovs the end of one life (its sunset) and the beginning of another (its dawn)? All seem to be appropriate interpretations, despite their partial incompatibility.

Two similarly equivocal shots occur after Para has killed Juanita. The first, from an overhead camera looking straight down, recalls the moment of courtroom catastrophe in *The Paradine Case.* As Juanita's body slips from Para's arms, her blue dressing gown flares out like an immense flower. Hitchcock cuts away from this image to focus on one of Para's subordinates talking on the telephone with the airport security agent who has been obliged to let Devereaux through customs. Then the camera is back on Juanita and Rico Para, a medium shot at eye level this time. Para stands still and silent at the feet of Juanita, from beneath whose body blood wells into dark red pools.

The shots of the murdered Juanita exemplify one way *Topaz* makes its dense and ambiguous meanings. As the neutral blacks and whites behind Nicole yield to the oranges and yellows that frame the face of her stricken husband, so the black and white tiles of Juanita's cool marble floor are impinged on by her blue robe and her red blood. Dead in the cause of one lover who is working not for his own country but for its ally, she is killed by her other lover, who is also working as much for Russia as he is for his own land. Everyone is implicated in her death.

Para's murder of Juanita is also partly an act of cherishing and mercy. At the beginning of the sequence that ends with Juanita's death, Hitchcock inserts a familiar image. As Juanita hurries past Para, he catches her by the wrist. In close-up his hand draws hers toward him. The allusion to the penultimate shot of *North by Northwest* seems unmistakable. It shows as clearly as any single moment in Hitchcock's career the difference between his romantic and ironic modes and their similarity. Whereas Thornhill gripped Eve to save her from falling, Para pulls Juanita into an embrace that ends with her shooting. The commitments of romance lead to the renewal of life; the entanglements of irony end in death.

Topaz takes place in settings that often give the impression of having sunk below the normal, everyday world. An elevated, downward-looking camera frequently accounts for this depressed atmosphere. Moments of crisis, in particular, tend to be pushed downward optically. When Kuzenov lies in denying any knowledge of "Topaz," Hitchcock cuts to a camera angle that looks down sharply. Extreme overhead shots show Uribe taking Dubois's bribe and betraying the Cuban–Soviet accord. Other examples of elevated camera placements are consistent with these and give political activity—especially that which involves lies or threatens violence—a subterranean quality.

Near the end of *Topaz*, the camera elaborately rises and falls when Mike Nordstrom exposes Jacques Granville as a spy. This remarkable shot, nearly two minutes in duration, recalls the famous crane shot that leads to the twitching eyes of the disguised murderer in *Young and Innocent*. Both involve a long descending movement forward, and both climax in a close-up of a guilty man who is about to be unmasked.

The shot begins at eye level from inside the conference room, the screen filled with the image of a pair of ornate double doors. These swing open and the combined French and American delegations come in, Jacques Granville in the center. The camera draws back and slightly upward, including in its field of vision the entire conference room, as Mike and the head of the American delegation identify Jacques. When Mike leaves the small American group to walk toward the French, now split in half with Jacques on the left and Mike approaching the group on the right, the camera ascends again. It reaches its apogee as he delivers his message. Then, as the head of the French delegation approaches Jacques with the news that will send him to his suicide, the camera descends to eye level and tracks toward the now isolated traitor. It stops on his face and pans slightly to follow him out the same doors that began the shot. They close behind him. Hitchcock cuts to another closing door, that of Jacques's home, and a few seconds later we hear a gunshot. In *Topaz*, as in *Young and Innocent*, the sense of a man trapped and driven back into the underworld is intensified by camera movements that isolate, expose, and finally push him down. The downward-looking camera that first appears over Red Square and then gazes down on Copenhagen and the Soviet, American, and French embassies, which records critical turning points in the political action, and which follows the fall of the murdered Juanita, looks down again on the exposure of Jacques Granville.

As high camera placements visually push *Topaz* down, shots with lenses of long focal length distance its characters and action from the audience, which is put in the position of voyeur or spy. In addition to an elevated camera, the early shot of the Soviet Embassy uses a very long lens, which gives the impression of covert observation from a remote point. The sense of spying is immediately confirmed by two shots of the Kuzenovs being watched in a concealed mirror as they leave the embassy and are shadowed by a trio of Russian agents. Similar long shots of Dubois at the Hotel Theresa and of Mendoza taking surreptitious photographs of the Soviet missile ships further associate telephoto cinematography with the idea of spying. Though some long

shots represent the point of view of identifiable observers, others have
an impersonal perspective. The spy in those shots is the camera itself;
and the audience, insofar as it depends upon the camera to establish
its relationship to the action, is urged toward a feeling of looking in
(and down) from a remote place. Such a point of view weakens the
tendency of an audience to identify with the characters it is watching
and encourages the sort of circumspect detachment that we sometimes
call "ironic distance."

Within *Topaz* an analogous detachment among the characters reinforces the sense that looking is spying and that trust and empathy are
largely illusory. Shifting, confused personal connections parallel unstable political ones. The French nominally remain neutral, but André in
fact puts French Intelligence at the service of the Americans against the
Cubans who are in collusion with the Russians. On the other hand,
some of the French are also working for the Russians, and against
NATO, of which France and the United States are members. Para and
the Cuban cause are betrayed by Uribe. André pretends to be a commercial attaché when he is in fact an intelligence agent. He is married,
but at the same time he is deeply involved with Juanita de Cordoba in
Cuba—an affair that he denies having when his wife confronts him
with her suspicions. While he deceives his wife, the Cubans, and his
own government, he is being deceived himself both by the members of
his government who work for the Russians and by his wife, who is
having an affair with his old friend.

André's espionage impinges continually upon his family life. When
we first see Nicole, she is complaining about the dangers of André's
job. In response to Mike's suggestion that she must be accustomed to
her husband's intelligence work, she replies, "a wife never gets used to
it." A little later, Mike will appear in the Devereaux's hotel room in
New York to take André away from an eagerly anticipated family hol-
iday.

As a result of what he learns in New York, André decides to go to
Cuba and thereby precipitates a bitter argument with his wife. "André,
I don't want you to go," pleads Nicole, "I'm afraid for you, for your
career, for your life." She is also afraid for herself and her marriage:
"There is a woman in Cuba, isn't there, named Juanita de Cordoba?"
How does she know? Domestic espionage. She heard it from Claire
d'Arcy who got it from her husband who got it from the office in Ha-
vana. This household intelligence, the intersection between home and
politics, nearly leads to the destruction of André's and Nicole's marriage. She walks away from him in anger as he is leaving, and he returns to find her gone without explanation. It is also possible, and per-

haps suggested by the analogy of the names, that she begins or resumes her affair with Jacques because of her suspicions about Juanita.

Politics shatter love. To create an opportunity to use a telephone at the ceramics factory, the Kuzenov daughter deliberately smashes a figurine of kissing lovers. The strains that André's political involvements put upon his marriage impinge also on his affair. Scarcely have he and Juanita concluded their passionate reunion before they are quarreling about his failure to send word of his visit, the difficult time he has picked to come in the midst of tightened security, and her relation to Rico. "Maybe we ought to start all over again," André says. They kiss and, presumably, forgive.

But in *Topaz* neither Juanita nor André, nor any person or nations, can simply make up. The past, with its residual resentments and its complex layers of loyalty and betrayal, cannot be left behind. The love of Juanita and André collides with his marriage, her affair with Rico Para, and the politics of four countries. By the end of the movie she is dead and André's wife has implicitly confessed her own affair with a man who, unknown to her, was betraying his loyalty to their country as well as to her husband. The last shot of the Mendozas, torn and battered by torture that has forced them to expose Juanita, may serve as a summarizing image of the unstable compounding in *Topaz* of love, politics, family loyalty, and espionage.

The sharing of meals, a symbol of great importance for Hitchcock, reflects in *Topaz* the fragility of both personal and political loyalties. In his romantic films, eating together brings people together—even when the meals appear contaminated by anger or bad faith. This symbol of trust and social bonding is inverted most radically in *Frenzy*. But *Topaz* is not far behind. The conflict between political and family loyalties leads to an aborted dinner party that was to have consisted of André and Nicole and their daughter and son-in-law. All that we see of it is a brief shot of the latter three sitting forlornly in the otherwise deserted lounge of the restaurant, waiting while André goes about his business of spying on the Cubans. For the rest of the film, meals are associated with espionage. In Para's hotel room, a half-eaten hamburger languishes on a grease-stained official document. Dubois, escaping from the Cubans, bounces off the canopy over a "Chock full o' nuts" restaurant. During breakfast, André shows Juanita a radio-controlled camera for spying on the Russians. Intruding on dinner later, Para reveals to Juanita and André that he has killed Uribe and that he has learned André's real profession. The Mendozas go on their spy mission with their cameras and telephoto lenses concealed in sandwiches for a sham picnic. Their film is returned to Juanita's home in the cavity of a chicken and developed in a darkroom behind the pantry. A relaxed Kuzenov will offer coffee and cigarettes to his new countrymen as he reveals his former connection with the spy ring. Finally, when André meets for lunch with a group of his friends, two of them are traitors to France and enemies to him and a third repeatedly tries to absent himself rather than get involved on André's behalf.

Images of flowers, another insistent motif in Hitchcock's romantic movies, are also reversed in significance. Spoto's remarks are illuminating: "Every set is ablaze with floral arrangements, and the image suggests a ubiquitous and massive funeral, since each locale has the faint redolence of death."[10] Irony inverts romance. The ordinary association of flowers with abundant life and rebirth reverses to persistent invocations of peril and death. Mostly yellow and red, the flowers intersect with patterns of dangerous color symbolism.

Romantic adventures commonly take the form of quests, but traveling in *Topaz* tends to be constrained and ineffectual or even deadly. Para announces that Uribe has left on "his journey . . . a journey from which no traveler ever returns." André's departing telephone call from the airport reveals that Para has sent Juanita on the same journey. André makes it back to Washington; but his homecoming is a hollow one, for his wife has left him and his superior arrives to order him back to Paris to face a board of inquiry.

The urgent journeying that criss-crosses the rest of the film is not quite so dismal in its results, but the trips from Copenhagen to Washington to New York to Cuba to Paris do not lead to any decisive resolution of either political or emotional tensions. The Cuban missile crisis may be over, but the suspicion, intrigue, and betrayal that accounted for it, and for the instability of personal life as well, remain. There is no sense at the end of *Topaz* of ascent or renewal. The dead remain dead. The living will continue to jet about in the illusion that they may be able to gain political advantages that will be lasting or even significant.

Topaz develops the political content that in *North by Northwest* exists as a relatively unemphasized secondary theme. Triumphant love and realized identity in the earlier film ultimately push the indecisive maneuverings of superpower intelligence into the background. In *Topaz*, politics, not love, dominates the action; and victories, as in all Hitchcock's ironic treatments of society, are not easy to distinguish from defeats.[11]

---

[10] Spoto, *The Art of Alfred Hitchcock*, p. 430.

[11] The special historical circumstances of *Foreign Correspondent* and *Saboteur*, works

HITCHCOCK's ironic films tend to start in public locations and move toward more private spaces. More romantic films are more likely to begin in the midst of intimate actions. Exceptions exist, but the general tendency nonetheless reveals one of the distinctions between Hitchcock's dominantly romantic and ironic works. The former use public (usually criminal or political) actions chiefly as MacGuffins. In the ironic works, the anonymous world eventually dominates the individual, and the chance of personal realization or redemption is crushed by indifferent, accidental forces.

We tend to associate "reality" with ironic fictions not so much because their assumptions about human life have a more solid empirical basis than romantic ones, nor even because their conventions are more familiar and comfortable to us, but because such stories reject the energies of the miraculous. When André is first told that Henri Jarre has been leaking NATO documents, he remarks that it may be "possible." "It's more than possible, it's true," Kuzenov responds drily. Later André imparts the same information to his government colleagues in the restaurant in Paris. "This is a fairy tale," murmurs one of the men. He means that there can be no truth to it. But André's information is accurate, and *Topaz* is no fairy tale. That deflating fact is precisely what finally so discourages the viewer about the nasty, dangerous world the film portrays.

The saving providence that underwrites the heroines and heroes of Hitchcock's romantic narratives is largely absent from the ironic ones. Romantic clarities are replaced by equivocal coincidences, compromises, trade-offs, double-edged swords. As a result, ironic fictions invite the sort of elaborate rhetorical and philosophic analysis that shows every gesture and statement to contain and even draw attention to its opposite.

Ironic plots and conventions can hardly be shown to be more true to life than romantic ones, but they can be shown to be more complex and involuted. They can also be shown, as a general rule, to be worked out in opposition to romantic expectations. The opposite position—that romance may be seen as a parody of irony—cannot be argued with the same conviction; for both set as goals much the same ends of human self-creation and fulfillment. When ironies are reversed again, however—a circumstance that we occasionally see in Hitchcock's movies—the romantic can be reestablished as a sort of parody of irony. Such a return from ironized to restored romance constitutes the central

that were made in the shadow of World War II, may account for their generally un-Hitchcockian combination of emphatic political content and romantic fulfillment.

structural principle of *Rebecca*, in which the opening Cinderella story turns into an ironic nightmare only to reverse once more into another fairy tale when the true love of the peasant maiden breaks the spell of depression and self-hatred that an evil witch (Rebecca) has cast over the enthralled prince. Films that prolong the balance of ironic and romantic energies may declare their predominant genre only in their closing moments, when the protagonists rise and find themselves or when they are at last exiled from the possibility of renewal. *Notorious* provides an especially powerful example of such protracted instability.

Hitchcock's fifty-three feature films conclude considerably more often with romantic closure than ironic uncertainty, but none is without elements of both. Not only are the central tensions of Hitchcockian irony and romance the same, but their endings must be apprehended in similar ways—as threats escaped (for the romances) or hopes denied (for the ironic films). Few of Hitchcock's ironic movies finish in irredeemable catastrophe. (*Easy Virtue*, *The Skin Game*, and *Vertigo* have perhaps the direst conclusions.) None ends in clear resolution, either. At the conclusion of *Rich and Strange* and *Mr. and Mrs. Smith*, nothing very awful has happened, but nothing has changed. At the end of *Blackmail* and *Topaz*, crueler actions have been accomplished. But nothing fundamental has changed in those films, either, except for the diminution of hope that anything can change for the better. In *Rich and Strange* or *Mr. and Mrs. Smith*—both comic films—little pain attends that loss of hope, which pertains more to the audience than to the characters within the works. The loss of the hope of redemption in *Blackmail* is located pointedly in the characters themselves. At its end, Alice and Frank have left forever the illusive Eden of youthful innocence. During the recapitulation of images of destruction that concludes *Topaz*, death's ironic scraping grates in the ears both of the central figure and of the audience. Nothing has been revealed by its outcome except to shatter the supposition that political right and wrong exist in essential distinction from one another. The destruction of such hopeful illusions contains the central point of *Topaz* and, in diverse ways, of most of Hitchcock's ironic movies.

By my count, about three-quarters of Hitchcock's films have predominantly romantic tonalities and resolutions. Most of the rest are ironic; and a few—*Lifeboat*, *Shadow of a Doubt*, and *Rear Window*, for example—remain poised between the gratified hope and desire of romance and the resignation, dismay, or inconclusiveness of irony. The juxtaposition of the dialogue between Young Charlie and Jack with the ironic, clichéd sonorities of the memorial service for Uncle Charlie at the end of *Shadow of a Doubt* strikingly balances hope and cynicism. The simultaneous political inadequacy and romantic satisfaction of the end of *Secret Agent* achieve similar equilibrium.

With the exceptions of *Vertigo* and *Psycho*, however, few of Hitchcock's ironic films are generally regarded as central to the body of his work. Hitchcock is not just the "master of suspense" but the master of resolving suspense. And such resolution in his movies more often than not takes place with a decisive confirmation of romantic hopes and obliteration of ironic anxieties. *The Lodger* seems more typical of its director to most Hitchcock fans than do *Easy Virtue* or *The Skin Game*; *Rebecca* and *Family Plot* feel more Hitchcockian than *Mr. and Mrs. Smith* or *Topaz*. Hitchcock's ironic movies are less shown, esteemed, or understood than his more common romantic ones; for despite the popular conception of Hitchcock as a somewhat morbid ironist, most of his audience instinctively expects the witty, slightly unbelievable, regenerative conclusions to which his predominantly romantic work has accustomed them. They tend to be more comfortable with *The Lady Vanishes* than with *Sabotage*.

This chapter, and the discussion of *Vertigo* and *Psycho* that follows, should not be understood to retreat from my earlier argument that Hitchcock is at heart chiefly a maker of romance. Rather it attempts to establish his ironic films as an integral part of his work, to show that they, too, are Hitchcockian. Of course, I am aware that many commentators feel that only his ironic movies are centrally Hitchcockian. Robin Wood articulates that view with eloquent clarity: "the films of these directors [Hawks, Renoir, McCarey] are centered on values of generosity and affection between people, on the possibility of contact and reciprocal relations. In contrast, the characters of von Sternberg, Antonioni, Hitchcock are, typically, trapped, isolated, unable to communicate." Later in the same essay he writes, "The problem with Hitchcock is that the movement [toward normality] seems always blocked."[12]

These formulations describe accurately one of the directions of Hitchcock's work. My own discussions of *Blackmail*, *Topaz*, and *Vertigo* largely agree with and expand accounts like Wood's. But to take

---

[12] Robin Wood, "Retrospective," reprinted in Deutelbaum and Poague, eds., *A Hitchcock Reader*, pp. 33-34, 38. Frank McConnell, in *Storytelling and Mythmaking* (New York and Oxford: Oxford University Press, 1979), p. 170, articulates a contrary view that is close to my own. "However brutalized or tarnished by the circumstances that imprison them, Hitchcock's characters always try to fight back toward the 'normal' state of society, the 'normal' state of their own lives in which they can continue to function as citizens, husbands, wives, etc. For Hitchcock, in other words, the ordinary is also the optimal."

such films as typical is to ignore or dismiss a far larger group that affirm and gratify Hitchcock's, and our, profound need for "generosity and affection between people" and for faith in a universe that heals the corruptions of time and experience. The stakes are equally high in Hitchcock's romantic and ironic movies because they are the same. The casting of his loaded dice more often turns up sevens and elevens than double ones. Significantly, even in Hitchcock's most painful films the hope of a redemptive outcome is sustained until the end. All irony may perhaps be understood as reversing romantic conventions; but Hitchcock's ironic films usually also evoke anguish, chagrin, or startled horror. If one thinks of the work of more consistently ironic film-makers—Antonioni, Bergman, Fellini, Godard—the pervasiveness of cynicism is greater, the outrage diminished. When Hitchcock creates ironic fictions, he does so, in a manner of speaking, under protest. We feel that his movies are shocked at their own ironies, that they resist ending in catastrophe or stasis. The world should not be that way.

CHAPTER FIVE

"I Look Up, I Look Down"

Vertigo: Kim Novak and Jimmy Stewart. Mirrors in *Vertigo* warn us of the incompleteness of what we can see directly. Scottie's image joins Judy's in a shot that recalls Elster and Madeleine.

Vertigo (1958) and *Psycho* (1960), Hitchcock's most admired films, subvert most thoroughly the romantic plots, images, and structures that recur throughout his work. Though these two movies are held in special esteem—the taste of many Hitchcock critics running to the pleasures of irony—they are not particularly characteristic of Hitchcock's films in general. They mark one of the extreme ends of the spectrum of his work, with such relatively unalloyed romances as *Young and Innocent* and *To Catch a Thief* occupying the other. The great majority of Hitchcock's films have elements of both romance and irony, with outcomes that usually favor romance. *Vertigo* and *Psycho*, however, constitute practically homogeneous ironic exercises. They doggedly frustrate and reverse any romantic impulses toward clarity and fulfillment.

The central figures of *Vertigo* and *Psycho* struggle to understand and resolve destructive personal histories, both their own and those of allies and antagonists encountered in their quests for happiness. They fail. Their defeats reflect the unforgiving necessities of Hitchcockian tragic irony. The gay-hearted playfulness of the comic romances is overwhelmed in *Vertigo* and *Psycho* by moral inexorability. Retribution replaces forgiveness. Confusion and ambiguity baffle resolution. Both films give centrality to human illness and decay, not healing. *Vertigo* names a condition (as we are told in the film itself) that results from an unconquerable fear of heights; "psycho" is Fifties and Sixties slang for the violently crazy, the psychotic. In both movies, the disease of the past is incurable.

Crucial to most romances—and therefore at the center of the failure of romance in *Vertigo* and *Psycho*—is the confronting and overcoming of a voracious, enervating past. The cyclic, regenerative time that energizes romantic narrative returns from fall and winter to spring and summer. In ironic fictions time is linear, an unprogressive succession of days stopping in the endless winter of death. Romance and irony thus clash in their understanding of time's regenerative or entropic powers. The heroes of Hitchcock's romantic and ironic films both set out—as St. Paul puts it—to "redeem the time, for the days are evil." World and time in romance are sufficient and cordial to such an enterprise; in ironic narrative, paths of glory lead but to the grave.

In most of Hitchcock's films an oppressive past infects the protagonists; or, if it does not infect them directly, it casts a freezing shadow upon the happiness and hopes of their world. The malignant past event may be proximate—a crime that takes place at the beginning of the movie (as in *Saboteur*) and that must be publicly accounted for in order to release the hero from the onus of false accusation. Alternatively, the quest to clear the hero's or heroine's name may wind back to a more distant and complicated past, as it does in *To Catch a Thief* and *I Confess*.[1]

Exorcisms of past sins restore the fertility of the present and thereby make a future possible, but they are fraught with risk as well as charged with hope. The recovery of personal history may require a descent to the World of the Dead, from which return is no certainty; or it may reveal, as in *Oedipus Rex*, unbearable truths about the seeker. A lethal past triumphs over desperate attempts to confront and set it right in *Vertigo* and *Psycho*; the central quests of both lead to disillusionment and/or death. In the time-oppressed but more romantic films discussed in the next chapter, attempts to uncover and detoxify the poisons of bygone horrors are largely successful. The intersection of past and present, the fight between the living and the bloodthirsty dead, is unusual in the movies discussed in these two chapters only in its insistence and explicitness; the realignment of past and present is an issue of enormous importance for all Hitchcock's works. In the romantic closures common to the majority of his films, rebirth, the recovery of innocence, and prospects of a fertile future predominate. The ironic *Vertigo* and *Psycho*, however, conclude with death and sorrow.

Vertigo and *Psycho* also develop in opposition to other romantic conventions, which they raise only to disappoint or reverse. Plots spiral away from rather than circle back to central moments of restoration; and insofar as circling actions or images do appear, they tend to be broken or to repeat acts of destruction, not creation. Descents dominate ascents. Death obliterates human identity and continuity, whereas in more romantic movies it is a preface to rebirth. Disappearance does not precede but prevents discovery. Purposeful romantic quests give way, in *Vertigo* especially, to mere "wandering." The characteristic romantic furnishings of flowers and helpful strangers tend to worsen things rather than meliorate them. Selfish desires contaminate the love of even good figures. The comedy of *Vertigo* and *Psycho*—and both

[1] Numerous fictions of all kinds, of course, depend for their central conflicts upon the impingement of the past into the present. Fairy tales are full of heroes and heroines who undertake or have forced upon them projects that require them to understand and undo the catastrophes of the past; so are a great many of the monuments of Western literature, from *The Iliad* and *The Odyssey* through *Paradise Lost* and a high proportion of novels. The Fall of Adam and Eve is a version central to Christian culture; the reverberations of their action will end only with the end of time itself, a "happily" that obliterates the "ever after." The classical myth of a Golden Age from which humanity has declined into an era of "lead" or "stone" is another widely occurring version.

are often very funny movies—is black comedy, humor without reassurances against its potential to frighten and destroy.

Vertigo

Hitchcock's films can be revealingly grouped according to their dominant vertical directionality, their ratio of downwardness to upward-
ness. As its title promises, *Vertigo* embodies, more insistently than any
other Hitchcock movie, the physical and metaphysical fear of falling.
Its predominant movement is a spiraling downward. What few ascents
it manages end uniformly in disappointment and the reassertion of the
power of the fall. All effectual forces in *Vertigo* finally conspire to draw
its figures downward to darkness.

The first sequence after the titles portrays a struggle to stay up, an
unsuccessful attempt to avoid falling. It also hints at the perverse desire
to let go, to cease resisting the fall and so to free oneself from the anxiety that attends the struggle. The latter desire is Scottie's (James Stewart); but the subjective camera that embodies it identifies it as well with
the audience, humanity in general.

As he hangs on to the bending gutter and the policeman returns to
help him, Scottie looks down between the buildings. A track-in and
simultaneous zoom to wide-angle (not, as is usually asserted, a track-
out and zoom-in) exaggerates the perspective and stretches the apparent distance to the street. "Gimme your hand," says the uniformed cop
who is trying to help Scottie to safety. A close-up of his reaching hand
is followed by his fall from the roof to his death.

The parallels and contrasts with similar shots at the end of *North by
Northwest* are illuminating. "Give me your hand," says Roger Thornhill as he stretches down for Eve Kendall. She reaches up for him in
return, and a close-up of their meeting hands is soon followed by the
famous dissolve into the upper berth of the 20th Century Limited. *Vertigo* has the same words and the same shot; but the hands do not meet
because Scottie, almost fainting from his acrophobia, cannot reach for
the proffered help.

Vertigo is a movie of trying not to plunge into the abyss, and failing;
North by Northwest, equally, is one of trying not to be dragged down,
and of finally succeeding in going up. Few first-time viewers of *Vertigo*,
I would guess, expect the fatal fall that ends its opening sequence. We
do not usually anticipate such unequivocal rejection of our hopes in a
film, especially at its beginning. Thornhill's miraculous escape from his
drunken drive downhill in "Laura's Mercedes" reveals the presence of
an artistic guardian angel for the hero of *North by Northwest*. *Vertigo*

announces unequivocally in its opening action that we cannot expect such lucky miracles in its world. In doing so it warns us both of the kind of movie it will be and of the painful consequences that must follow from that fact.

Downwardness in Hitchcock's movies is almost always associated with an imagery that suggests infernal regions, the land of the dead. As Scottie shadows Madeleine Elster (Kim Novak) during the first part of the movie, his descending excursions lead him to dark passages and other settings suggestive of entrances to the underworld. On the first morning, Scottie drives downhill behind Madeleine's Rolls Royce to enter a slightly sinister alley and then a back passageway, dark and mysterious. She leads him next through a dark, old church in which an unseen organist plays a fragment of a fugue, and thence into the yew-filled graveyard behind. Afterward she again drives down, turns left, drives downhill once more. This time she goes to a museum (the Legion of Honor), where Scottie spies on her from the shadows while she sits in front of the portrait of Carlotta Valdes, whose grave she had visited in the churchyard. From the museum she goes to the "McKittrick Hotel," where she disappears like a ghost and eludes her startled pursuer. When he returns to her apartment building, he finds her auto in the parking lot. On its dashboard lies the bouquet she bought at the flower shop, a token of the reality of Scottie's strange journeying.

At the florist's and at the McKittrick Hotel, Scottie is photographed from inside the door as he enters. By awaiting him in this way, the camera suggests a power of foreknowledge, an understanding of the inevitability of outcomes and possibly some control over events by the observing presence in the movie. The observing presence itself is thus associated with the mysteriously descending Madeleine and with the nether regions to which she leads the detective.

Scottie's next shadowing of Madeleine leads to another series of descents and dark passages: down past a grove of trees to the museum again, through gates into a dark wood, through another fence, and along the bay to the Golden Gate Bridge. There Madeleine jumps into the water. Scottie saves her, and, as it eventually works out, loses himself. When he leaps into the bay after Madeleine, Scottie suffers a fall as devastating as that which threatened him in the first sequence. Though he has not literally died, subsequent events will make clear that he has been lured into a realm of shadows and doubtful, shifting realities.

When he next follows Madeleine, the descent becomes still more marked; she goes down ten hills before she parks in front of Scottie's flat. After they begin to wander together, the scenes have a fragrance of death about them. Among the shadowy redwoods of John Muir Forest, Madeleine briefly disappears again. Then she and Scottie kiss by the sea, the crashing waves at once repeating their stormy emotions and threatening dissolution. Very high angle shots look down on the car they drive along a dusky road through another forest to San Juan Bautista with its arched walk of shadows and its gloomy stable. There Madeleine and Scottie undergo a last descent; Madeleine plunges from the bell tower and Scottie is destroyed psychologically. The detective will return much later with Judy to free himself from the past, to stop "being haunted." But though he thinks for a moment that he has climbed out of the abyss, that he has "made it," the overpowering downwardness of the place and of the movie will triumph again when Judy falls to her death.

As is always true of Hitchcockian irony, the physical descents of the characters are matched and intensified by camera placements that push them down optically. A very high angle shot follows Madeleine and Scottie as they drive along the coast the first time, and a similar high tracking shot follows them as they leave Scottie's apartment to go to San Juan Bautista. Another high shot of the car driving along in the evening, very much like the earlier one, follows Scottie and Judy again to the same place.

High shots looking downward from Scottie's point of view emphasize his descent from the bell tower after Madeleine falls to her death. They are followed by an elevated shot pointed nearly straight down at Scottie when he emerges far below and disconsolately walks away. (This shot is in effect repeated in *North by Northwest*, just after Townsend's death at the UN, when a radically downward-looking camera watches Thornhill emerge from the UN building into a half-comprehensible world of flight and pursuit. A similar shot, in a similar context of terrible knowledge and misfortune, looks down on Young Charlie as she comes out of the library after having confirmed her appalling suspicion about her uncle in *Shadow of a Doubt*.) Another high shot follows Scottie at the conclusion of the cruel inquest into Madeleine's death. This shot dissolves into one of him visiting the dead woman's grave; Scottie has been absorbed fully into the world of the dead. When Midge (Barbara Bel Geddes) later visits him in the sanitarium, he simply is not present to her. He lives somewhere else, with "someone dead." The high shot of San Francisco that introduces the action after Scottie has left the hospital should warn us that he has not yet returned to the land of the living. Indeed, he will continue to seek the shadow of Madeleine in her old haunts.

Vertigo comes from a fear of heights and from the simultaneous horror of falling and attraction to letting go that occur in many people on high places. The film has to do with trying, and being unable, to go up and stay up. It portrays the forces that pull one down, forces that are partly external but that are also within oneself. John Belton writes of "the vertiginous pattern of near-simultaneous attraction and repulsion."[2] On the one hand Scottie desires to go, or stay, up—in the realm of light, stability, and love. On the other, he is terribly responsive to the pull from below. He sometimes seems driven—especially in the anguish that follows losing Madeleine—to let go and fall, as Ingrid Bergman says in *Under Capricorn*, "down, down, down to where I can go no further; down, to where nothing can hurt me anymore."

The dominant geometric figure of *Vertigo*, the spiral, expresses the tendency to fall apart emotionally. The spiral is an unstable alternative to the circle. Turning "in a widening gyre," as Yeats wrote in another ironic "Second Coming," "things fall apart/ The center will not hold." The twisting spirals of the title sequence disappear as they approach and recede from the camera. The affliction they symbolize comes from within human beings; all the spirals originate, like the title of the film itself, from the center of the deep eye that the camera pans up to at the beginning of the title sequence. As Marian Keane writes, "its [*Vertigo*'s] figures possess the causes of their bereavement within themselves."[3] The music that accompanies the credits, and that will characterize most of the rest of the movie, spirals and wanders like the images it accompanies. Neither melodic nor atonal, it consists chiefly of a seemingly endless succession of chords that never find resolution.[4]

Further spiral imagery, more or less prominently, pervades the rest of the film. The position of the dead policeman on the street after he falls, his arms and legs partly extended and partly bent, makes of his body a spiral figure. His fall itself suggests a spiral, for he turns horizontally while dropping vertically. The body of the dead Madeleine on the mission roof hints at the same spiral figure in the same way. The spiral suggested by the small bouquet of flowers and the hair of Carlotta Valdes, Madeleine, and Judy constitutes another crucial instance. The complex camera movement during the kiss after Judy's full physical transformation back into Madeleine also suggests spiral motion, again intensified by the repeated prominence of the spiral curl in the

[2] John Belton, *Cinema Stylists* (Metuchen, N.J. & London: The Scarecrow Press, 1983), p. 54.

[3] Marian Keane, "A Closer Look at Scopophilia," in Deutelbaum and Poague, eds., *A Hitchcock Reader*, p. 346.

[4] For this formulation, I am indebted to Royal Brown's discussion of music in *Vertigo* at the conference on "The Rereleased Hitchcock" at Pace University, June 15, 1986.

back of Judy/Madeleine's hair. The shots down the staircase in the bell tower at San Juan Bautista generate further reiterations of the spiral figure. The final evocation of the spiral may be the most important. It occurs at the end of the movie when Scottie stands, arms slightly bent and extended, in an attitude that recalls the bodies of the policeman and of Madeleine.

Associated with descending movements and spirals are images of transition, passageways that lead to darkness, disappearance, and death. "Portals of the Past" and other such images, as we have seen, are significant features in the landscapes of Madeleine's wanderings. They frequently lead to her temporary disappearance—when she enters the graveyard of the Mission Dolores through the shadowy church, when she vanishes from the McKittrick Hotel, when she leaps out of Scottie's field of vision into the bay, and when she disappears among the redwoods into the dark forest.

Such a shadowy passageway recurs as a symbol of death in the dream she relates to Scottie: "When I come to the end of the corridor, there's nothing but darkness and I know that when I walk into the darkness that I'll die." A little later she does, apparently, come to the end of the darkness at San Juan Bautista. There a shadowed passageway leads to a darker livery stable and finally to the obscurity of the bell tower stairs and Madeleine's death. At the same location later, Judy seems to take the nun who materializes from the shadows as Madeleine's ghost. She falls to her death backing away in terror from this spirit of vengeance, which comes as much from her own conscience as from the world outside her mind. Given the action that precedes the nun's entrance, Judy's terror is particularly ironic. Scottie appears to relinquish his vindictive rage and move toward forgiving Judy at the very moment when her own guilt surges up to extinguish for both lovers any future that they could have had.

The insistence upon Madeleine's obscure wanderings and Scottie's implication in them (wandering is his "occupation") constitute ironic parodies of the purposeful quests of romantic narratives. In an abstract way, the wanderings also reiterate the dominant motif of the spiral. Responding to Midge's question, "Where do you go these days?" Scottie replies, "Oh, just wandering." When Midge persists, Scottie's second evasion evokes quite literally the spiral shape that his shadowing of Madeleine has traced: " 'Round about." In a film as profoundly ironic and essentially tragic as *Vertigo*, the characters can only wander. Quests lead into mazes with neither centers nor exits. There is finally no place to go, no possible outcome besides death. So they pass the time wandering instead of questing, dreading but helplessly sinking toward the inevitable blackness at the bottom of the spiral.

As we have seen, Hitchcock's romantic films are organized around quests that lead, whatever the MacGuffin, to the creation (or recovery) through love of the protagonists' personal and social identities. The miscarrying of that search constitutes the central frustration of *Vertigo*. Though Scottie's coercive dismantling of Judy's personality and his attempt to force her to be Madeleine is the most frequently discussed attack on identity, the failure of Scottie to discover himself in love has a thematic centrality that dominates the whole film.

Like the heroes of most of Hitchcock's movies, Scottie at the beginning appears to be a somewhat overaged adolescent. He is too old and eligible not to be married, but he is still sheltering behind maternal skirts. Throughout the film, he displays that slight retardation of psychological development characteristic of Hitchcock's heroes at the beginning of his films and outgrown and resolved by the end of the romantic ones. But Scottie, lost in the disorienting convolutions of *Vertigo*, will not find his adulthood in the arms of his proper mate.

Though he complains of Midge's motherliness during his first sequence with her, Scottie seems content to maintain just that sort of relationship with his former fiancée. He asks her what a sketch of a brassiere represents and gets the predictable maternal response that "You know about those things. You're a big boy now." That is just what he seems to be—a big boy, not a man. He is still "available Fergusson," content to question Midge about her love life and plans for marriage rather than pursue either himself. When Scottie tries to overcome his acrophobia on Midge's stepstool, he faints into her motherly embrace and her consoling "Oh, Johnny, Johnny." The impression of Scottie's immaturity is reinforced at the inquest when the presiding magistrate reprimands him as if he had been a bad boy.[5] At the psychiatric hospital, Midge continues to mother her charge as she assures a catatonic Scottie that "You're not lost. Mother's here." But he is lost. In discovering and losing his love he not only has not found his adult identity, but he has lost even the youthful personality he had before.

The beleaguered heroes of Hitchcock's happier films find their helpmates and their grown-up identities with young women who, beginning with Daisy in *The Lodger*, typically carry the vernal imagery of

---

[5] The casting of Stewart as Scottie may also contribute to our impression of his youth. As Wood comments, "we habitually think of James Stewart as young, even in middle age, 'boyishness' being one of the basic components of his star persona." Robin Wood, "Male Desire, Male Anxiety," in Deutelbaum and Poague, eds., *A Hitchcock Reader*, p. 227.

Persephone with them. Often lost themselves, they return to bring renewed life to rescuers who must also be rescued and sometimes resurrected after their descents to figurative Hades. But just as Scottie cannot manage to be reborn into his mature identity and station in the world, so Judy/Madeleine turns out to be a failed Persephone, unable to return from the kingdom of Pluto to give new life to a forlorn lover.

The imagery of flowers and other vegetation that is persistently associated with Judy/Madeleine evokes the Persephone archetype; but the film finally fails to validate it, leaving the heroine in the land of the dead and the hero and his world unredeemed. From the first time Scottie sees her at Ernie's, flowers surround Madeleine. When he begins following her, she leads him first to a flower shop, then to a flower-strewn cemetery. Madeleine carries about a bouquet of roses that duplicates the one in the "Portrait of Carlotta." She will, significantly, tear apart the flowers and throw their petals into the bay just before she leaps in herself. The shattering bouquet reappears as the first image of Scottie's nightmare after Madeleine's death.

When Madeleine tells Scottie her name after he pulls her from the bay, she pronounces it to sound like "Aster," a daisy-like flower. Disguised, Judy/Madeleine is appropriately "Elster." (So is Gavin, the evil genius who literally "elsed her" and who, mysterious and demonic, comes from "elsewhere," presumably below.) As "Aster," Madeleine reminds us again of her association with flowers and with an ultimately inadequate Persephone.

Midge cannot replace the failed Persephone of Madeleine: the flowers she brings to Scottie's room are as ineffectual in reviving him as her music (she is perhaps a failed Orpheus also). Midge has no fertility, no power to rescue or bring back to life. The spirited erotic potency of Hitchcock's romantic heroines has decayed in her into sophisticated passivity. Her only decisive gesture, the satiric painting of her bespectacled face on her copy of the "Portrait of Carlotta," fails woefully. All amorous energy remains with the ultimately demonic Madeleine.

The association of Judy/Madeleine with flowers is reasserted after Scottie leaves the hospital. He encounters Judy as he looks up from a flower shop window in which Carlotta's bouquet is displayed. Like Persephone, so it at first appears, Madeleine might return as Judy to the surface of the world in floral splendor. On the wall of Judy's room, over her bed, is a painting of flowers that recalls the bouquet; in the short hall that leads to her room is a similar painting. As Scottie and Judy walk about the city, vernal and floral images proliferate. Like Madeleine, Judy is also associated with trees; and much more than Madeleine (whose characteristic color tends to be red) Judy is often seen dressed in green or bathed in green light. For Hitchcock such green, as Rothman points out, "is the color of dreams, fantasies, and memories."[6] It is also the color of Persephone, who brings with her the miracle of spring and rebirth.

But if Hitchcock's romantic heroes and heroines fall to rise, his ironic protagonists rise only to fall. The dreams in *Vertigo* turn to nightmares, the fantasies and memories are largely falsifications. The green associated with Judy only "links her ironically to the *sequoia sempervirens*, 'always green, ever living.' "[7] Judy, like Madeleine before her, looks up from the car window at the trees overhead as she and Scottie drive to San Juan Bautista and death. These shots give the impression that the heroines are far below the trees, looking up from a perspective that is practically subterranean. As the Judy section of *Vertigo* approaches its catastrophe, her predominant greens begin to mix with Madeleine's reds—a dangerous hue in all Hitchcock's color films. The close-up of Judy's (and Madeleine's and Carlotta's) ruby pendant culminates this shift toward red.

When Scottie attempts to leave mother Midge for lover Madeleine, he is stifled by the incredible reality of the murder plot in which Judy has enlisted. Judy/Madeleine cannot save either herself or Scottie. Neither character achieves the personal coherence attained by the protagonists of Hitchcock's more romantic films. In *Vertigo*, shots that suggest breaking apart or incompleteness symbolize this unannealed fragmentation of personality.

The most emphatic of these shots comes at the beginning of Scottie's nightmare, as his memory of Madeleine's bouquet flies to pieces. The fragmentation of the female face in the initial images of *Vertigo* prefigures the psychological coming apart that is to follow. The frequent profile shots of Judy/Madeleine—and one crucial one of Scottie in Judy's hotel room—also express the theme of incompleteness. Where Hitchcock's romantic protagonists make themselves whole in finding each other, Scottie and Judy/Madeleine lose both each other and their coherence individually.

Flower petals are scattered on the surface of San Francisco Bay when Madeleine makes her fake suicide attempt. In Hitchcock's films, water more often conveys a threat of dissolution than a promise of new life. In *Vertigo* it is predominantly associated with death. The Golden Gate Bridge, like similar bridges in other Hitchcock films, looms like a thoroughfare across the Styx.

[6] Rothman, *The Murderous Gaze*, p. 359.
[7] Wood, "Male Desire, Male Anxiety," p. 227.

Occasions on which people drink together in *Vertigo* continue the menacing symbolism of water. More important, they also mock what should be a moment of human trust and communion. In Gavin Elster's company the first day, a suspicious Scottie refuses a drink. But later, having swallowed the bait of Gavin's lies and Madeleine's perform-ances, he lifts a glass of whiskey with an enthusiastic "Boy, I need this!" At Midge's, his drinks are interrupted or unfinished, like their courtship. He has time only for a hasty gulp as Midge takes him to see Pop Liebel to learn the story of Carlotta Valdes; and he leaves another drink unfinished after she has angered him by painting her face on a copy of the "Portrait of Carlotta."

(Though Midge later visits Scottie at the hospital, her jealous joke effectively ends their faltering relationship. The satiric painting ap-pears to mortify Scottie by mocking his credulousness about a ghost story to which he responded with rational scorn himself when he first heard it from Elster. At the same time it seems inspired by something approaching self-hatred in Midge. It underlines her lack of sex appeal or mystery in comparison to Madeleine. Midge's grotesque self-por-trait appears as much an acknowledgment, perhaps unconscious, that she can never attract Scottie as an attempt to bring him back to his senses.)

The most potent drinks in *Vertigo* are those Scottie gives to Judy/ Madeleine. He offers them as potions to calm and soothe. In doing so, he puts himself into the role of her comforter and protector, a role that in Madeleine's case he would seem to usurp from her husband. When he insists on giving Madeleine a cup of coffee at his apartment to warm her after she has jumped into the bay, we have the first clear indication that he has fallen in love with her. His hand rests on hers and he begins to stroke it. A ringing telephone, a call from Elster, the concerned hus-band, amplifies the adulterous harmonics of his first furtive embrace.

The pathos and irony of this moment need little explication. Scot-tie's desire to comfort and heal and the love that follows from his per-ception of Madeleine's need for help (a fundamental sequence of emo-tions in Hitchcock's movies) are exploited as part of the murder plot that will play Scottie for a helpless sucker. It is worth noting that Judy's letter/voice-over later says, "I made the mistake, I fell in love. That wasn't part of the plan." Evidently it *was* part of the plan, however, that Scottie should fall in love with her—the unforgivable part.

Twice we see Scottie offer Kim Novak brandy at his apartment: first when she comes as Madeleine to tell him new details of her recurring nightmare, and later when he is trying to calm the distraught Judy after making her shop for clothes. Scottie uses the same phrase both times:

"it's like medicine." Again the impulse to heal, to comfort. And again Scottie is in the dark. First he is being manipulated to play his unknowing role in Elster's murder plot, then he is trying to recreate Madeleine in Judy, without knowing that she really is/was Madeleine already.

No greater horror can occur in a Hitchcock movie than the failure or exploitation of the instinct to love and heal, on which the recovery of innocence ultimately depends. The apotheosis of this humane impulse occurs in Christ. We have seen that Hitchcock in more romantic films displaces and eroticizes Christian doctrine by associating it with the redemption and rebirth that his heroines and heroes achieve through their love and faith in each other. In *Vertigo*, Christian symbolism, like other romantic motifs, is inverted. It is diminished to one more ironic sign of the irremediable human condition.

Throughout the film, Christian references are associated with anguish and frustration. Scottie suffers for the sins of others; but unlike Christ, he agonizes in vain. Hanging from the gutter in the first sequence, he looks down, then rolls his eyes as his head sags to his left arm. This gesture anticipates the more obvious posture of crucifixion that he assumes on the bell tower in the last shot. Other images with Christian overtones also attach to Scottie in contexts of deception or pain. In the Mission Dolores a telephone pole forms a cross in the upper background as Scottie watches Madeleine visit Carlotta's headstone. Two sidewalks cross at the base of the bell tower as he emerges after Madeleine's death. In his nightmare, his head is caught at the center of a web (of lies, conventionally, but also related to cruciform images); the dream ends with him falling in a full silhouette that anticipates his posture on the bell tower.

There is particular irony in placing the two appalling deaths of Madeleine and Judy in the mission of San Juan Bautista. Not only does the Christian setting in general mock the antiredemptive outcomes of the two visits there, but the evocation of John the Baptist has a particular inverted appropriateness. The first and second comings of Judy/Madeleine lead not to rebirth but to death. She descends but does not arise. She does not gain the everlasting life that baptism promises but the total extinction of a life and identity already hollow and incoherent.

Judy/Madeleine's association with Christian images is parodic in the broad way of her association with Persephone. She leads Scottie through the church of the Mission Dolores, and a church is conspicuous in the background near the McKittrick Hotel where she also leads him. She floats with her arms out forming a cross when she leaps into the bay. Another utility pole, in the upper right corner of the screen, adds the image of a cross as she and Scottie talk on the porch of his apartment. Her last words are "Let me go into the church, alone." ("Whither I go, ye cannot come," says Christ to the Disciples in *John* 13.) In none of these scenes is Madeleine a redemptive figure; on the contrary, in all of them she is leading Scottie to damnation.

The last words of the film are uttered by the nun who startles Judy: "God have mercy." At the very moment when Judy has attained or is about to attain the power to heal Scottie and herself through love, a terrible *deus ex machina* enters to prevent redemption. Though Scottie attempts to deny the possibility of any repair of their past, Judy begs him to "keep me safe," and he takes her into his arms. As they are kissing—both in full knowledge of who the other is for the first time in the film—the nun enters and Judy falls to her death. Neither God nor Hitchcock has mercy. The quality of mercy, indeed, hardly ever appears in *Vertigo*. The nun's words, and the Christian imagery that Scottie's pose in the last shot culminates, only confirm the crushing absence of grace.

The emptiness at the center of life that inversions of Christian imagery express is reiterated by representations of artifice and such related motifs as mirror reflections and dreams. *Vertigo* begins not with an image but with the abstract, expressive art of music. A simple, repeated figure and unstable chords accompany an empty screen. The musical score of *Vertigo* will in general echo the suspended quality of its characters and action.

More stable, conventional music, whether it occurs environmentally or on the background sound track, does not provide the resolution that it promises. The J. C. Bach that Midge has on the phonograph in the second sequence makes Scottie dizzy, like his vertigo. Midge tells the doctor after Scottie's institutionalization that she does not think "Mozart's going to help at all." Judy/Madeleine is often associated with relatively stable, melodic music; but the contexts for such interludes, retrospectively, are invariably ironic: the tranquil fugue in the Mission Dolores; the extravagantly lush romantic score that joins the crashing waves during the first kiss of Madeleine and Scottie (a shot so clichéd and overproduced that we can hardly take it seriously, even at first viewing); the sunny harp music and rich violins that accompany the high shot of San Francisco immediately after Scottie's release from the hospital; the similarly scored, even more romantic music as Scottie and Judy stroll through the park. All these scenes, and the reassuring music that accompanies them, will later prove to be undermined by falsehood. Less deceptive are the sounds of warning that arise frequently, either in ominous music or in cautionary foghorns and bells.

As art and its analogues in Hitchcock's romantic films reveal essential truths, and sympathetic deceptions transform into actualities, the opposite dynamic controls ironic films like *Vertigo*. Gavin Elster lies even about lying. "I'm not making it up," he assures Scottie, "I wouldn't know how." Wood notes that "Madeleine is presented in terms of the 'work of art,' which is precisely what she is. Her movement through the doorway suggests a portrait coming to life, or a gliding statue; when she pauses and turns her head into profile, the suggestion is of a cameo or silhouette, an image that will recur throughout the film."[8]

But a silhouette withholds as much as it shows; it allows us to see only half of what it portrays. The other side is completely concealed by the profile that we do see. Most two-dimensional art—the "Portrait of Carlotta" and Hitchcock's *Vertigo*, say—have the same constraints as a conventional silhouette; it can show only one side of things, 180 of 360 degrees.

Mirrors in *Vertigo* remind us of the other side. They warn us of the incompleteness of what we can see directly. Gavin and Madeleine are conspicuously doubled by a mirror the first time Scottie sees Elster's putative wife. Later in the flower shop, it is unclear whether Scottie is watching Madeleine directly or in a mirror (a hint, perhaps, of the difficulty of separating image and substance). Shopping at the beginning of his project to convert Judy into Madeleine, Scottie's image joins Judy's in the mirror in a shot that recalls Elster and Madeleine. Waiting for her to return from the beautician's shop, Scottie fidgets in front of Judy's dresser mirror in her hotel room. The last two images suggest that Scottie is losing what remains of himself in his desperate attempt to recover Madeleine. Like the woman he is trying to bring back from the dead, he is becoming a reflection without an original.

It is Scottie's sight of the other side of the Carlotta necklace that he notices in the mirror as he helps Judy dress that confirms his intuition about her true identity. Yet what he discovers deductively gives him only another surface understanding. It blocks him from the profounder knowledge that he approached moments earlier when he seemed to guess Judy's real identity. Though they give Scottie, and us, glimpses of "the other side," mirrors in *Vertigo* are like the fragments of mirrors hanging on the walls in Madeleine's dream. The "truth" they offer is incomplete and potentially deceiving. At best, mirror images are like the whole Madeleine fabrication as Judy describes it in her letter: "part made up, part true."

[8] Wood, "Male Desire, Male Anxiety," p. 228.

Dreams figure forth in *Vertigo* a truth/falsehood as equivocal as that of art and of mirror images. Madeleine's dream, though it reveals much of the woman who relates it, is probably made up and certainly deceives Scottie. Scottie's dream is real enough, but it is largely composed of images that are, at bottom, lies: Carlotta's bouquet, her portrait, her empty grave. At the center is Scottie, caught in a web of deceit, then endlessly falling. Hitchcock uses obtrusive special effects throughout this sequence, not to indicate essential truth as would be the case were *Vertigo* a romantic film, but to show pervasive equivocation.

From the beginning of *Vertigo* Hitchcock emphasizes the power of the artist to withhold rather than to reveal facts and contexts. The blank screen that opens the movie is a radical declaration of the director's power to show us nothing beyond what he wishes. The fragmentary face that begins the credit sequence has much the same effect. Who is this woman? Where is she? Why is she alarmed? What does it mean that spirals within spirals come from the depths of the pupil of her eye? Why are we presented with such a bewildering introduction? The next shot hardly clarifies things: a close-up of a bar that we do not know to be a bar until it is grasped by hands, for the moment equally unknowable. What we understand best after the first few minutes of *Vertigo* is how little Hitchcock has allowed us to understand.

But increased information does not lead to full comprehension. One of the characteristics of ironic fictions is a tendency toward self-deconstruction, the running together of apparent oppositions and the incorporation in every proposition of its contrary. This tendency of things to shift ground constantly and recombine in new patterns is part of the vertigo of the title and of the unresolving motion of the schematics of the film as a whole. The unusually large number of dissolves in *Vertigo*, many of them not especially economical, suggests the fluidity of reality. Different truths, different ways of looking at things, swirl together even while they remain unreconciled.

Ironic assumptions about art and reality imply that Madeleine's story (or Gavin Elster's) not only is not, but cannot be true. The significance of its falsehood, however, runs still deeper. The dead, in this logical and finally realistic film, cannot be reborn or resurrect themselves within the living. They can only wait, certain of their final victory, for the living to join them. They have a status and a magnitude—like the foredoomed hero and heroine of *Vertigo*. But their substance is illusory or evanescent. As the sculptor William Parry writes, "Things touched by shadow are aggrandized and devoured."[9]

---

[9] William Parry, "What is Shadow?" unpublished statement, 1986.

Another work of art within the larger work, Midge's painting of her head on Carlotta's portrait, expresses the jealousy of Scottie's former fiancée and her skepticism about Madeleine's mystery. As in *Topaz*, everyone in *Vertigo* seems to be spying on everyone else; and as in the later film, love is shot through with deceit, jealousy, and manipulation. Midge fuels the amorous envy that leads to her baiting of Scottie by undertaking her own private investigation of him. Her most jealous moment, and the apparent cause of her misjudged joke, comes when she witnesses Madeleine leaving Scottie's apartment at night. "Well now, Johnny-O," she murmurs bitterly, "was it a ghost? Was it fun?"

Scottie investigates Madeleine as an employee of her husband and falls in love with the wife he is supposed to be following and protecting. At the same time, Elster and Judy are keeping Scottie under observation and insinuating him into their murder plot. But like Scottie, Judy is falling in love with the person Elster has employed her to control. The erotic overtones of personal espionage are often emphatic, as when Scottie watches Madeleine take off her jacket in the window at the McKittrick Hotel, and in a host of details during and after her plunge into San Francisco Bay, of which his unshown but nonetheless emphasized undressing and bedding of her is only one. The emotional connections that come out of all this snooping is mostly Hitchcockian bad love, anxious and possessive. Pathetically, like most bad love in Hitchcock, it tries to be better but cannot.

The graphic motif of the arch, in Hitchcock's romantic movies an anticipation of union between heroine and hero, reappears ironically in *Vertigo* to underline broken promises. The mission of San Juan Bautista is introduced with an establishing shot of its arched walkway; and the shape of arches will generally dominate there, both during Madeleine's death and during the return of Scottie and Judy. Arches are prominent behind Madeleine as she takes leave of Scottie in the courtyard with her speech about the impossibility of their love: "Even if you lose me, then you'll know I loved you and I wanted to go on loving you." Through an arch the detective sees Madeleine's body plunge to the roof below. The subsequent inquest begins with the same shot of the arched walkway as the sequence that led to Madeleine's death.

With Judy, arches also figure as emblems of the frustrated hopes of love. On their first morning together, she walks with Scottie past embracing lovers with an arched memorial across the water in the background. When Scottie takes her back to San Juan Bautista, he pulls her from the car in front of the same row of arches through which he walked with Madeleine. In the last shot of the film, Scottie stands framed in an arch of the bell tower, a fitting image of love and religion whose failures are linked throughout the film.

Judy/Madeleine is unable to love because she is possessed by Elster as Judy and by Carlotta Valdes as Madeleine. Scottie is thus twice wrong when he cries out, just before Madeleine's death, "No one possesses you." At the end of the film, Judy will fail to win Scottie as he failed to win Madeleine, because he has been captured by the past, by "someone dead." After she has allowed him to fully remake her, Judy embraces him and declares, "Oh, Scottie, I do have you now, don't I." But in a little while she will fall from the tower and Scottie will be possessed by two dead lovers, neither of whom was ever quite alive.

In tearing up her confession and trying to win Scottie for herself, Judy breaks faith with her love. She gives in to the desire to have Scottie and puts him, and herself, at terrible risk. She is not telling the truth when she says, "I don't care anymore about me." The lines that precede that utterance give it the lie, make her prostitution of herself and her desire to possess Scottie painfully clear: "If I let you change me, will that do it? If I do what you tell me, will you love me?"

In a way, Judy deserves what she gets. But in a way, she does not. It is partly true to say that "The revelation [of Madeleine's deception] immediately exposes the entire 'romantic love' project of the first two-thirds of the film as a fantasy and a fraud."[10] Additionally, however, we must take into account the tone and context of the revelation, which are tender. When we witness Judy writing her note and hear her voice-over, we are given a powerful invitation to identify and sympathize with her. She writes to Scottie about how she loves him and wants him to be at peace. She is undoubtedly sincere, and one could even argue that by offering herself to him as Judy she might help him lay to rest the ghost of Madeleine. But wanting him for herself, she will both lose herself and deprive him of any possible future peace.

Pretending to fall in love with Scottie, Judy/Madeleine falls for real. This motif, so common in the solutions of Hitchcock's romantic comedies, recurs in the ironic tragedy of *Vertigo* as a long step toward catastrophe. If playing at love has created real love, it has also barred its fulfillment. It is a remarkable part of the achievement of *Vertigo* that its structure and rhetoric, like those of other great tragedies of Western culture, make us at once concur in and bitterly regret the logic and the justice of its outcome.

All this is not to say that Scottie is simply an innocent victim of the diabolism of Elster and the weakness of Judy. Like everyone else in *Vertigo*, he contaminates with egotism his desire to love and be loved. In Scottie, preeminently among the characters of *Vertigo*, the urge to

---

[10] Wood, "Male Desire, Male Anxiety," p. 230.

"know" takes on a Biblical resonance in which emotional or sexual possession confirms dominion. With the exception of the last minute of the film, Scottie does not appear to be capable of trusting the prescient understanding that lovers have for each other in Hitchcock's romances. Instead he depends upon the sterile and deceptive knowledge of facts and logic.

As he embraces her by the sea, Scottie tells Madeleine, "I've got you." Then, just before her death, "No one possesses you. You're safe with me." His obsession with transforming Judy into Madeleine entails controlling her to the point of subjugation. When he confronts her with what he has inferred of the truth, his sexual jealousy and sense of violated ownership fuel his rage as much as his sense of betrayal. "You played the wife very well, Judy. He made you over, didn't he? He made you over just like I made you over." This remark aligns him in miserable company with the "free" and "powerful" men who have used up women since the rich man who kept and then discarded Carlotta Valdes. A moment later, he is even more explicit about Gavin Elster's prior ownership of Judy/Madeleine. "And then, you were his girl, huh? Well, what happened to you? What happened to you? Did he ditch you? Oh, Judy, with all of his wife's money and all that freedom and that power and he ditched you—what a shame."

Elster and Scottie, and presumably the rich man of nineteenth-century San Francisco, all use women and take their things from them. Elster "marries into" the shipbuilding business, then discards his wife. Scottie woos Judy, then tries to discard her for his recreation of Madeleine. And the forebear of both of them corrupts Carlotta only to abandon her and take her child.

Although such exploitation of other persons is associated explicitly with men, Judy/Madeleine does not escape the disease. As Madeleine, she emotionally takes over and uses Scottie; as Judy, she wants to possess him for herself. Like Scottie, she too suffers jealousy—hers, ironically, directed at her former self, the false Madeleine. She wants to be loved as Judy, not because "I remind you of her." In one of the more pathetic scenes in the film, she is stung by a longing look that Scottie bestows on a woman who walks by while they are eating in Ernie's, a woman who reminds him of Madeleine.

In the world of *Vertigo*, where time leads to decay and loss rather than to renewal and recovery, such possession as Scottie desires could never occur. Even if Madeleine were real, Scottie could not freeze her in an eternal present of protective, encircling love. His most hubristic utterance comes at the climax of the scene by the shore. "Don't leave me, stay with me," begs Madeleine. "All the time," Scottie vows. In saying so, he as much mistakes the possibilities of life and time as he does the reality of Madeleine's love. The past, a vampire, preys on the present. It renders all therapeutic hope and love "too late."

The desire to possess one's love forever is closely bound in *Vertigo*—again preeminently with Scottie—to a passion for knowing, for formulating and fixing reality. Scottie's involvement with Madeleine begins when Elster tells him that he has "to know" what his wife does during the day. Before long, however, Scottie has fallen in love and the desire to know has become his own. He tells Madeleine, "I'm responsible for you now. You know, the Chinese say that once you've saved a person's life you're responsible for it forever. So I'm committed. I have to know." When he shifts the terms of his relationship to Madeleine from being "responsible" to having to "know," Scottie moves from nurturing toward controlling and possessing.

During this sequence the word "know" is uttered ten times by Scottie and Madeleine; during the same sequence and the preceding one among the redwoods, the significant homonym "no" occurs another nine times. The knowledge that Scottie seeks will prove to be nullity. It leads, as Madeleine says, only to "explaining it away." Love, as Hitchcock's romances show positively and *Vertigo* negatively, requires not explanations but miracles.

When Scottie first encounters Judy, the same nasty desire to possess by knowing reappears: "I just want to know who you are." As he forces Judy to shop for clothes that will make her look like Madeleine, Scottie draws a wry tribute from the head salesperson: "The gentleman seems to know what he wants." He does and he does not. "Why are you doing this?" asks Judy, "What good will it do?" "I don't know, I don't know. No good, I guess. I don't know." The dialogue continues to pivot on the same deadly word:

> JUDY: I wish you'd leave me alone. I want to go away.
> SCOTTIE: You can't, you know.
> J: No, you wouldn't let me. (Pause) And I don't want to go.
> S: Oh, Judy. Judy, I tell you this, these past few days have been the first happy days I've known in a year.
> J: I know. I know. . . .

Scottie and Judy need love, not knowledge. Twice it appears that Scottie will accept a loving intuition, but both times the chance is snuffed by an immediately subsequent event. The first comes when he kisses Judy after she has finally acquiesced in the last detail of her transformation, the arrangement of her hair with its Carlotta spiral. She emerges through a green haze into Scottie's arms. His impossible dream almost fulfilled, he begins to kiss her. Apparently, he senses at some level the truth of what has happened, because he looks up as he remembers the last moments with Madeleine in the livery stable. Then, despite his disturbing intuition, Scottie returns to the embrace. He accepts in some way that he has Madeleine in Judy and seeks no further explanations.

But a few moments later comes the destructive revelation of the necklace. The miracle is shattered, and Scottie knows the essential fact. Love, like Madeleine's possession by the ghost of Carlotta, is explained away. As Alex Sebastian's mother exclaims when she learns the truth about Alicia in *Notorious*, so Scottie now realizes that he "knew, but didn't see."

He will have one more chance to accept his redemption, to declare his faith. In the last sequence, Scottie starts to come to terms with Judy's love and his own despite his full comprehension of the sorry details of the past. As his rage is replaced by grief, he chokes, "I loved you so, Maddie." The past tense of the verb seems to suggest that he is cured, free. His "Maddie" occurs only on this one occasion; it is neither "Madeleine" nor "Judy" but an amalgam, a new being, both and neither.

His utterance brings Judy out of the shadows, repeating his words, "I loved you so." She begs, "Oh Scottie, please. Oh Scottie, you love me, keep me safe." "Too late," he says in anguish as Madeleine had earlier. "It's too late. There's no bringing her back." But at another "please" from Judy, Scottie takes her into his arms and kisses her. For a moment, love seems to have conquered all knowledge and all resentment. There can be "no bringing her back," and still Scottie embraces Judy. In doing so, he implicitly accepts both her love and his own for her.

But only for a moment. Even if Scotty and Judy briefly transcend themselves, the artistic logic of the film is too powerful for them. A specter rises out of the shadows, Judy shrinks back, and we hear her scream as she falls to her death. The pull of the downward has again triumphed. Freedom, safety, and love prove fleeting or illusory. In the vengeful, entropic fictional universe of *Vertigo*, no mistake goes unpunished. What goes up must come down, and what is gained cannot be held.

Freedom, an insistent value throughout the film, is revealed as hollow and even oppressive. As masculine power, freedom manifests itself in the abuse of women—an abuse that leaves the men who exercise it (if we can judge by Scottie) isolated and forlorn. When we first see Scottie, he is declaring that "tomorrow'll be the day. . . . I'll be a free, [as he waves his cane the gesture hurts him and he catches his breath] free man." Returning with Judy to San Juan Bautista, he returns also to the idea of freedom: "One final thing I have to do, and then I'll be free of the past." And a little later, "when it's done, we'll both be free." He is right, but in a way that he (and we) understand only after the final catastrophe. Freedom, apparently, is composed of loss and desolation. For a brief time, one may hang suspended above the abyss, but the downward pull is continuous and will eventually prove too strong for mortal resistance. The freedom one achieves cannot be avoided; but it comes at the cost of human comfort and love, one's own identity, and finally life itself.

Wood observes that "Scottie is left hanging (we never see, or are told, how he gets down). Metaphorically, he is suspended for the remainder of the film."[11] This brilliant formulation describes the existential anguish that proves to be the ironic reality behind the fantasy of freedom in *Vertigo*. But Scottie does, at least once, fall. During the dream that precedes his madness he falls and falls, and it is at the end of his falling—parallel to Madeleine's description of entering the darkness at the end of her dream—that he cracks up. His posture in the last shot of *Vertigo* repeats his posture at the end of his dream; he is once more broken, fragmented, fallen.

The "mistake" that initiates his long descent consists of his falling in love with Madeleine. The rest of his misfortunes follow. In Hitchcock's romantic films, falling in love marks the moment at which the hero's or heroine's fortunes begin to turn upward. In *Vertigo*, Scottie's recovery of his love ruins him. Not only does he convert Judy into Madeleine, but he regains Madeleine herself. Precisely by realizing his dream, however, he loses it. For if Madeleine was really Judy, if she still exists, then she never existed, never was really anyone. With his regaining/losing Madeleine, Scottie discovers that he loved a fiction. Since what is left of his own identity is defined by his love, he loses himself again, as he did the first time Madeleine "died." But with her second dying he loses himself more finally and desperately because he loses not only Madeleine but his memory of her and probably his belief in her possibility. His past has been canceled along with his future.

Hitchcock's romantic movies show us protagonists who triumph not in freedom but in the creation of self and in making a permanent connection with a true lover. In the ironic Hitchcock, the failure to achieve self-realization and a return to innocence corresponds with a

11 Wood, "Male Desire, Male Anxiety," p. 225.

failure to achieve love. *Vertigo* may remind us of the closing lines of Arnold's great antiromantic poem, "Dover Beach":

> . . . the world, which seems
> To lie before us like a land of dreams,
> So various, so beautiful, so new,
> Hath really neither joy, nor love, nor light,
> Nor certitude, nor peace, nor help for pain;
> And we are here as on a darkling plain. . . .

The fate of Scottie and Judy/Madeleine has an even more desperate conclusion. Arnold's speaker begins his melancholy declaration with "Ah, love, let us be true/ To one another!" In the downward swirling, time-tortured world of *Vertigo*, the lovers cannot be true. At worst, they use and abuse, lie to and deceive each other. At best, they try and fail to make themselves havens of safety in each other's arms. But being true to one another does not seem possible. Nothing seems possible in *Vertigo*, and only nothing.

Psycho

A woman's eye dominates the opening of *Vertigo*. From it come the titles of the film and the twisting spirals and to it they return. At one of the climactic moments of *Psycho*, blood-stained water spirals down the drain of the tub in which Marion (Janet Leigh) has just been murdered. Then, with the help of a very precise dissolve, the camera enters the drain only to emerge, now spiraling slowly itself, from the pupil of the eye of the dead woman.

The startling similarity of these central images signals an equally close relationship between the films in their entirety. In both, the inexorable forces of past sins and mistakes crush hopes for regeneration and present happiness. Love is desperately desired and painfully withdrawn, and symbolic rebirths turn into abortions. In each, Hitchcock removes a central character a little more than half way through the film—an even more disorienting and unexpected event in *Psycho* than in *Vertigo*, which has, in Scottie, a second center of interest and identification left to the viewer. Both are intensely ironic movies, with the attendant reversals, frustrations, and inversions of romantic motifs and ideas.

Psycho is Hitchcock's best-known and most popular movie, and commentators have made it his most intensively analyzed one. My interest in it will be largely confined to those aspects that illuminate the cinematic grammar and vocabulary of Hitchcockian irony. I will thus

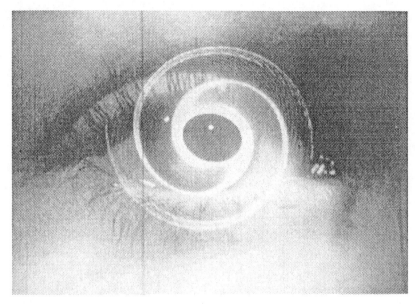

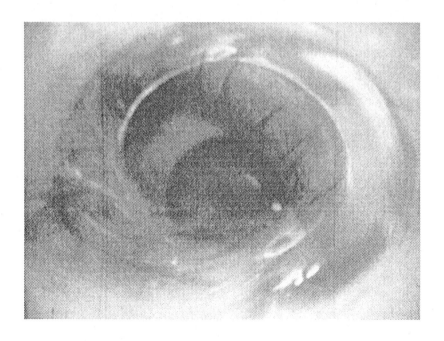

be concentrating my attention on the descents to a dark, dank world of terror and dissolution; and on the characters' defeated attempts to achieve love, a place among other people, and a secure understanding of themselves.

Like *Vertigo, Psycho* takes place in a world haunted and finally consumed by an unappeasable past. The power of the absent and the dead that Sam (John Gavin) bitterly complains of in the first sequence will prove to be far greater than he realizes: "I'm tired of sweating for people who aren't there. I sweat to pay off my father's debts, and he's in his grave. I sweat to pay my ex-wife alimony and she's living on the other side of the world somewhere." Norman's mother, a person who literally is not there, will eventually dominate the lives of everyone in the film.

As is always the case in Hitchcock's antiromantic films, forces impelling the protagonists downward overwhelm ascents and the power of the characters to resist the pull of ironic gravity. *Psycho* takes place in a lowered setting from which it never effectively rises. The opening sequence begins with the camera descending from a high, bright viewpoint over Phoenix to a dim hotel room, and so establishes the locus of action for the rest of the film as downward and dark. At crucial moments, high angle shots reemphasize the downward look required to see into *Psycho*'s world: the shot of Marion's car, with her body in the trunk, sinking into the swamp; the extreme overhead shot that follows Arbogast up the stairs where he finds death rather than the truth he hopes for; the nearly identical shot in which Norman Bates (Anthony Perkins) carries his mother to the fruit cellar; three very high shots looking down on Marion early in the murder sequence and another later as Sam and Lila (Vera Miles) search the motel bathroom.

The characters in *Psycho*, on the other hand, move downward less often than is generally the case in Hitchcock's ironic movies. The reason, I think, is that the opening shots of *Psycho* firmly place the rest of the film below some normative point of view. A few especially sad or dangerous actions, however, take the form of terrible descents. Marion's life blood swirls down the tub drain, and a little later her body is sucked into the swamp with her car. (When Lila arrives in Fairvale, she unwittingly emphasizes Marion's death as descent by remarking to Sam that she hopes "to get Marion out of this before she gets into it too deeply.") Arbogast stumbles backward down the stairs during his murder. Lila, searching for Marion like Demeter for her lost Persephone, descends to the Hades of the fruit cellar for its awful revelation.

From *The Lodger* onward, Hitchcock associated his heroines with

Persephone—as parodic versions in the movies that tend toward irony. The hints of Persephone that attach to Marion in *Psycho* are transformed into distortions or frustrations of their original model. Marion disappears as if snatched away. The flowers that Persephone was picking and dropped on the ground during her abduction reappear in the floral wallpaper of Marion's room in the Bates Motel. But though Hitchcock's camera emphasizes them, the printed flowers generally are not photographed directly but reflected in mirrors, as images of images—twice removed from reality.

The substance of the Persephone myth will be rendered as falsely as the flowers in the room where Marion spends the last minutes of her life. Rothman notes that at the end of the murder, "the eye's emergence from within the drain is an image of birth."[12] But like the eye of the amorphous sea creature at the end of Fellini's *La Dolce Vita*, it marks the birth of death, an emblem of final hopelessness and corruption. In the last shot of *Psycho*, Marion's car and body are retrieved from the swamp. She is dead, and spring will not return. Marion, the failed Persephone, is also a bird who will not be reborn from her ashes, certainly not in Phoenix, Arizona. Where Hitchcock's romantic heroines are at once rescuer and rescued, healer and healed, Marion both causes fatal illness (Norman's final displacement by "Mother") and dies herself.

Marion may also remind us of the Hitchcock heroines and heroes who struggle to establish their real innocence and to find love. But she will find death instead. Her attempt to marry will be frustrated from its inception. Her boss will see her fleeing town, a policeman will witness her trying to conceal her identity by switching cars and license plates, and the "private island" she seeks will turn instead into a "private trap" from which there can be no escape. Once she has "gotten off the main road," she can never get back. The "long drive . . . all the way back to Phoenix" will become instead that journey "from which no traveler ever returns."

Nor will vernal life return to Norman's mother. When she comes back to possess her son, she brings "a chill" of death with her—a point made emphatically by superimposing a skull on the last shot of "her" (within the body of Norman). Wood notes the ironic importance of the fact that Norman's mummified mother is kept in "a fruit cellar—the fruit is insisted upon in the mother's macabre joke about being 'fruity': the source of fruition and fertility become rotten."[13] When Marion asks Norman why he does not "go away," he replies that he cannot

---

[12] Rothman, *The Murderous Gaze*, p. 308.
[13] Wood, *Hitchcock's Films*, p. 120.

leave his mother. "She'd be alone up there. The fire would go out. It'd be cold and damp, like the grave." Later we will hear his mother protesting against going to the "dark, dank" basement. But the last shots of Norman/Mother make clear that he/she has not escaped the darkness, or the dank chill, or the grave. In *Psycho*, as in *Vertigo*, no one finally can.

As *Psycho* begins, the white bars of Saul Bass's title designs repeatedly wipe to black; the camera then pans high across a sun-baked Phoenix only to descend and enter a dark hotel window. Inside, Marion and Sam appear as bright figures against the dimness of the room. But for Marion that personal brightness will almost immediately begin to fade as she slips into darkness.

Her movement into shadow begins—literally 'and figuratively—when she encounters a devil of temptation in the form of the amorous, self-important Cassidy. As she leaves her boss's inner office to put the money in the bank and then, so she says, "go straight home," she has probably already conceived the plan of her crime. Her return to the outer office is preceded by her shadow on the door frame and filing cabinets; Hitchcock has subtly begun to darken her. Marion's entrance into her bedroom is again announced first by her shadow. She left the office in a light blouse and skirt, and we may remember that she was wearing a white bra and slip in the hotel room. When she comes into her bedroom, she is wearing black underwear. Having conceived her design to steal Cassidy's $40,000, she has swerved from the light of the main road and joined the creatures of shadow and blackness.

Her flight with the money is imaged as a journey deeper into darkness. While she drives out of Phoenix, the shot of her anxious face dissolves into lowering clouds and a darkening landscape. It dissolves again to her driving at night, then fades out. The next shot fades in on a sunny morning; but suddenly Hitchcock's most famous policeman intrudes, with his black sunglasses like malevolent blanks of eyes. Later, Marion drives through gathering dusk into rainy darkness, out of which appears the sign for the Bates Motel. Behind the motel looms the spooky house, in silhouette with clouds scudding through fragmentary moonlight. Marion's blood swirling into the black void of the tub drain ends the descent into darkness that began when she decided to make off with Cassidy's cash. The broader descent into darkness that is *Psycho* ends with a reprise of the opening titles, but with the tonalities significantly reversed: black bars come together across the picture, then blackness fills the screen and the movie ends.

Bright light, the ironic equivalent of darkness in *Psycho*, serves to blind rather than to illuminate. When Sam raises the window shades in the first sequence, no clarification accompanies his gesture. The glare of the oncoming auto headlights through the rainy night dazzles and confuses Marion. Along with the neon sign of the Bates Motel, light is associated indirectly with her murder through Norman's pleasantry that "We just keep on lighting the lights and following the formalities." The murderous brightness of the motel culminates in the glaring white of the bathroom tiles as Norman rinses Marion's blood from them.

The bare lightbulb illuminating the corpse of Norman's mother in the fruit cellar continues the association of harsh light with death. It swings eerily as Lila stares in horror at the mummified body, then as Sam overpowers Norman, who has entered in a dress and wig. "Again and again," as Rothman observes, "a lamp will be associated with the mother, becoming her surrogate in the frame and—like the ceiling lamp in *The Lodger*—the emblem of her mystery."[14]

Bright lights in *Psycho* provide complicated, rich, always dangerous imagery. As symbols of dissolution, they parallel the blank white in the background at the end of Scottie's nightmare in *Vertigo*. They often generate the "white flash" that Rothman observes to be characteristically associated with violence and danger in Hitchcock's films. In some contexts, they suggest theater lights or the projection lamps of the cinema.[15] The swinging light bulb in the fruit cellar, and the alternating bright and dark it produces, also recall the positive/negative picture of a woman's face that sums up the irreducible ambiguity of *Rear Window*. For despite the rough plausibility of the psychiatrist's explanatory narrative, its emotional inadequacy and intellectual omissions are so great that the mysteries of *Psycho* finally remain irresolvable.

As light in *Psycho* fails to illuminate, water fails to refresh. It blurs, dissolves, and drowns. Introduced by the rain that smears the window of Marion's car before she turns into the Bates Motel, water is associated with death and disintegration throughout the film. The sound of Marion's shower at the beginning of the murder sequence repeats the sound of the rain. When her baptismal cleansing runs with blood, the true figuration of water is fixed. The camera's slow track down the tub with the blood-stained water, Norman's cleaning of the bathroom, and the burial of Marion's car (and body) in the swamp, confirm that water brings death rather than new life. In the last shot of the film Marion's car emerges from the muck of the swamp, the dark and damp of her

---

[14] Rothman, *The Murderous Gaze*, p. 277.

[15] "Now the flickering caused by the swinging bulb makes the inner chamber of the fruit cellar into a movie theatre—a stand-in for the room in which, even now, *Psycho* is being screened." Rothman, *The Murderous Gaze*, p. 327.

grave. *Psycho* thus ends on a watery parody of rebirth that is also an ironic ascent and a repetition of what might be called, from its appearance in *Vertigo*, the "too late" motif.

Immediately after Marion's death, the camera moves slowly away from her eye. We see a few drops of water caught near the corner, like tears shed for her own death. But Marion's tears not only have no power of catharsis; they are probably not tears at all. They are only water, as indifferent to her fate as the shower that runs heedlessly on after she has been killed.

The broken lines and cracked letters of Saul Bass's opening titles suggest fragmentation, as do partial, depthless images in mirrors that are used systematically throughout *Psycho* to prefigure the shattering of its characters' personal coherence. As she complains to Sam about meeting in hotel rooms, part of Marion's back is reflected in a mirror behind her. In her bedroom she looks at herself while she seems to hesitate about stealing Cassidy's money. Her image is slightly cropped by the left side of the mirror as she does so. The morning after leaving Phoenix, she watches the trailing policeman in her rear-view mirror. When she takes the damning step of spending some of the money, she is radically bisected by a downward looking shot and a mirror in the washroom where she takes the cash from her purse. As the moment of her murder approaches, we watch Marion and a series of her mirror reflections converse with Norman Bates. (It is worth observing in passing that Norman reverses the role of the helpful strangers who emerge to aid the heroes and heroines of Hitchcock's comic romances—figures like the Crofter's wife in *The 39 Steps*, Old Will in *Young and Innocent*, and the insurance agent in *To Catch a Thief*.)

In the second half of *Psycho*, Arbogast, Sam, and Lila are shown in mirrors that appear in contexts similar to those associated with Marion in the first half. We see Arbogast's back in the mirror by the registration desk (in which Marion was also reflected) as he questions Norman. Sam twice appears in the same mirror, again in conversation with Norman. Searching for Norman's mother in the old house, Lila startles at her reflection in a pair of aligned mirrors. This moment constitutes Hitchcock's most explicit suggestion that his characters are experiencing—and we are watching—not something weirdly outside ordinary experience, but the expression of a potential for personal distortion and violence that is the other side, the mirror image, of human normality.

All that Marion wants, after all, are the humble treasures of love, marriage, home, and family. For Hitchcock these are the basic materials of human happiness and fulfillment and—their banality notwithstanding—the highest stakes any person can play for. The deprivation of such fulfillment, or its realization in twisted forms, leads to the deepest human unhappiness and psychological leprosy. Marion wants to stop meeting in cheap hotels, to have family dinners on Sunday afternoons, to get married. Nothing more remarkable. Nothing less crucial.

Her unattractive fellow secretary has "Teddy" and a solicitous mother; the daughter of the vulgar Cassidy will be married and have a house from her father as a wedding gift. Modest and equivocal as the happiness of such people may be, it is more than has fallen to the lot of Marion or Sam. The opening scene depicts their lack of money and their personal isolation, as they make love in an anonymous room in a hotel of the sort that "aren't interested in you when you come in, but when your time is up." Sam's father is dead, and Marion has no mother—only a picture that hangs on the dining room wall. Any place, any small family, would nourish the emotionally starved Marion. As she desperately assures Sam, she would be happy to live in a spare room behind the hardware store in Fairvale and to "lick the stamps" on the alimony payments for his ex-wife.

What we see of families in *Psycho*, however, suggests not only that Marion loses her dream in trying to find it, but that such fantasies of domestic happiness are unlikely in their very origins. Among Norman, Cassidy and his daughter, Marion's co-worker and her "Teddy" and mother, and even the rather frigid, irritable, and divorced Sam, no one promises much in the way of familial warmth or stability. Only the minor figures of the Sheriff and his wife cast a tiny glimmer of contrasting emotional light.

In one of the grimmer clusters of ironic jokes in *Psycho*, Marion's dreams of domestic fulfillment half come true, but only after she dies. Sam writes her a letter that seems to agree that they should get married now, as she pleaded. But his letter is being written immediately after we have watched her car/coffin disappear into the swamp. Later, Lila will play out with Sam the sort of domestic scenes that Marion hoped to buy with Cassidy's money and for which she paid with her life. Working with Sam to solve the mystery of Marion's disappearance, Lila's relationship with him becomes increasingly connubial. Like Hitchcock's protagonists in the comic romances, they struggle together to unravel a mystery, to reclaim innocence. They pose as husband and wife, as Hannay and Pamela do in *The 39 Steps*, but as Marion will never be able to do, in falsehood or in truth.

If the lack of a family and a place is crippling, the perverse realization of them is worse. Norman's wretched "more than happy" childhood has left him with an infantile and divided personality. The respectability of his "following the formalities" conceals radical personal incoherence. The staid Victorian mansion preserves not just skeletons in closets but whole rooms full of them. With its center in Mrs. Bates's bedroom full of old-fashioned, sentimental knickknacks, the illness of the past has all but consumed the present. By the end of the film, its contagion will have erupted to absorb present life entirely.

Marion's desire to marry and to establish a family and a place draws its energy from the same psychological needs as Norman's pathological clinging to his dead mother and his childhood home. Although Marion is driven to grand larceny by her frustration, Norman's illness is obviously more profound. He, more than Marion, resembles one of his stuffed birds, a denizen of the night world, frozen in time. His room retains its toys, its stuffed animals (a childish affection transformed, as taxidermy, into an adult obsession), its cot in the corner. The imagery suggests Eugene Field's sentimental "Little Boy Blue," with its stopping of all motion in the dead child's room symbolized by dusty toys. Norman rises angrily to the bait when Sam incites him by asserting that "If you saw a chance to get out from under, you'd unload this place." "This place?" Norman retorts incredulously, "This place happens to be my only world."

It may be, as the psychiatrist asserts, that Norman kills Marion because of his sexual attraction to her and "Mother's" consequent jealousy. But it may also be that she sets off his murderous impulses when she threatens to encroach on his fragile sense of place and to force the present into his past. Only when she suggests that Norman leave his home and put his mother "someplace," does he display overt hostility to her. At that point, he leans aggressively forward and challenges her officious euphemism, "People always call a madhouse 'someplace,' don't they?" He continues to rage at her, despite her apologies, about "people who cluck their thick tongues" and about "the laughing and the tears, and the cruel eyes studying you" inside an institution. Manacled to the past, his place is with his sick mother, as hers is with him. "Someplace" for Norman is where his delusions of love, home, and family are declared invalid and exposed. Marion's suggestion that he might go out to seek his own life threatens the disease that has flourished in him; it may also evoke in "Mother" an anxiety about her postmortem survival quite as powerful as any sexual envy.

The central poverty of human life in *Psycho*, and the source of much of its miserable comedy and deep pessimism, derives from the inability of its characters to make contact. The inadequacy of human community is expressed partly by the barrenness of one of Hitchcock's favorite symbols of social affection and coherence: the act of eating together. The first words of *Psycho* direct our attention to food. "You never did eat your lunch, did you?" says Sam, as the camera cuts to a shot of Marion's untouched sandwich. Her appetite for love, we gather, was stronger. Marion's uneaten lunch will be the first of a number of aborted or defective meals, and the unhealthy competition between food and sex will continue throughout the movie.

When Sam urges her to stay longer in the hotel room, she replies that "these extended lunch hours give my boss excess acid." Miserable about meeting Sam in cheap hotel rooms where she and her lover "steal lunch hours," Marion declares that "this is the last time." Continuing the verbal imagery of eating, Sam asks if he can see her next week, to "have lunch, *in public*." "Oh, we can see each other," Marion replies, "we can even have dinner. But respectably. In my house, with my Mother's picture on the mantle, and my sister helping me broil a big steak for three." But the rivalry between food and sex (an analogue perhaps of the rivalry between open married love and furtive lovemaking) arises again. "And after the steak," interjects Sam, "do we send sister to the movies, turn Mama's picture to the wall?"

When she returns to the office, the eating motif continues: Mr. Lowry is lunching with a client. Caroline, the other secretary (Patricia Hitchcock), offers Marion one of the tranquilizers that she got from her mother's doctor on the day of her wedding (further indication, perhaps, of the conflict between sex and ingestion). Mr. Lowry and Cassidy enter on Cassidy's line, "Wow! It's as hot as fresh milk." A little later, he declares that he is "dying of thirstaroony" and goes into Mr. Lowry's office for a drink. When Caroline offers her tranquilizers again, Marion declines: "you can't buy off unhappiness with pills." But as poor excuses for the communion of eating together as the pills and business drinks and lunches of the office may be, they are, like the marriages spoken of there, better than the nothing Marion has. Later, in the ironic working out of Marion's relationship with Sam, with Lila taking her sister's part, the Sheriff's wife will invite the couple to the Sunday dinner Marion longed for in the hotel room.

The theme of eating, of sharing meals, strongly recurs during the sequences just before Marion is murdered. Norman approaches her with a shy invitation to share his milk and sandwiches. In doing so he appeals at the same time to her sense of place: "I don't set a fancy table, but the kitchen's awful homey." Again sex will be both associated with food and put in competition with it. From the dark house on the hill, Marion overhears an old woman's angry voice: "No! I tell you, no! I won't have you bringing strange young girls in for supper; by candlelight, I suppose, in the cheap erotic fashion of young men with cheap erotic minds." She repeats Sam's question about what would follow Sunday dinner: "And then what?" Mrs. Bates knows what, as did Sam, and forbids both the meal and the sex she supposes will follow it: "Go tell her she'll not be appeasing her ugly appetites with my food, or my son." Even her coarse taunting uses imagery related to eating. "Or do I have to tell her 'cause you don't have the guts? Huh, boy? You have the guts, boy?"

Poisoned before it begins, the miscarried meal shifts from the kitchen to the lesser intimacy of the office parlor, where Norman does not eat at all and where Marion, among stuffed ravens and owls, only nibbles at her food, "like a bird." After the meal that Norman's fancy made the beginning of a romance, Marion sits alone at the desk in her motel room. Norman returns alone to the kitchen whose homeyness Marion never saw. An untouched apple rests on the corner of the table, suggesting both uneaten food and unconsummated desire.

As Marion begins her shower, she repeatedly opens her mouth to let the water run in, a gesture in keeping with the surrounding imagery, at once ingestive and sexual. The half-aborted meal and the wholly aborted erotic fantasy lead directly to Marion's murder, which the context suggests is also a symbolic rape and consuming of her. (We can look ahead to the similar conjunction of eating, rape, and murder in *Frenzy*.) Norman has dessert later. He gags when he discovers Marion's body, but as he sinks it in the swamp, he chews a bit of food nervously. During Arbogast's questioning, he munches on candy.

As Marion is dying at the end of the murder sequence, Hitchcock gives her a gesture that recalls some of the most important moments of human connection in his work. Slipping down the tiles on the bathroom wall, she stretches her hand toward the camera for support, or help. In *Young and Innocent* and *North by Northwest* that expressive reaching out leads to the clasping of lovers' hands and escape from the void. Even the villain is saved by a similar grasp in the comic, romantic world of *To Catch a Thief*. It is an indication of the traitor Frye's having cut himself off from his countrymen that the joining of hands will not hold in *Saboteur*, and he falls to his death. Marion, alone not so much because of her crime as because she exists in a world in which everyone is alone, reaches out to nothing more supportive than a shower curtain that gives way, like the stitching on Barry Kane's sleeve, and lets her fall down dead. The camera, if we take her gesture as partly directed toward it, offers no more help or consolation.

Failures of language become in *Psycho* one of the central symbols for the distortion and miscarrying of affectionate connections. The misuses of language signal not only the inability to make contact with other people, but also the degree to which characters have lost touch with themselves. The world of the film evades the descriptive capabilities of words. Language stutters in *Psycho*, in eloquent inarticulation expressing the frustration and bewilderment that its characters cannot find the words to describe.

A few occasions of fluency exist; for example, Cassidy's veiled propositioning of Marion at the beginning of the film or the psychiatrist's speech at the end. But language at such moments appears transparently manipulative or else well meaning but obtusely inadequate, explaining away rather than comprehending. Like the sterile, possessive "knowing" that obsesses Scottie in *Vertigo*, the futile attempts of the characters of *Psycho* to articulate who they are and what they want only deepen their confusion. Their utterances are compromised from the moment of formulation, connected half-consciously to frustrated needs for affection and sex. When the characters of *Psycho* speak, their sentences typically seem divided against themselves, at once trying to reveal and to conceal the speaker.

The titles that begin *Psycho*, "Phoenix, Arizona . . . Friday, December the eleventh . . . Two forty-three p.m.," among their various functions, indicate the inadequacy of linguistic and numerical labels to summarize significantly the complex reality to which they are attached. The tragedy that will follow those bald, factual signs can in no way be predicted or explained by them. Another set of labels, the license plates on Marion's two cars, prove equally empty of significance. Her attempt to cover her escape by changing cars (and thereby license plates) is aborted in its very inception by the hovering policeman. Moreover, he never appears in the film again; so his knowledge of Marion serves neither to protect her nor to apprehend her killer. Marion's burial begins with a close-up of the license plate as Norman drives her car to the swamp. Her public identity, which she died trying to escape, disappears with her. It has been as useless to protect her as it was impossible to evade. Only in death can she escape the meaningless label that nonetheless so alarmed her. As the car is dragged up in the last shot of the picture, the telltale but insignificant plate is wholly obscured by the mire.

Other public labels equally fail to conceal or disclose the people to whom they are attached. Words in *Psycho* have a slipperiness that destabilizes their meanings and suggests an amorphous or Protean quality in reality itself. Marion signs in at the motel as "Marie Samuels," an alias that does not deceive Norman for long, but that does associationally register her never-to-be-realized desire to marry Sam. Lila addresses the counter boy at the hardware store as Sam; then she later takes Marion's place at Sam's side when they "register as man and wife" at the Bates Motel. Both misnamings suggest a sort of inter-changeability of people and what they are called. Lila's stereotypic characterization of the supposed Mrs. Bates as "a sick old woman" is related to the motif of labels that are not quite pertinent. Mrs. Bates does, and does not, exist. She is, and is not, either an old woman or a sick one. How can words, the currency of rational discourse, possibly be adequate to such an impossible reality?

The second half of *Psycho* is unusually talky for Hitchcock; only two or three arresting images interrupt a plot solution that depends otherwise mostly on a steady flow of words. Yet we continually sense the feebleness and even irrelevance of the language and reasoning being brought to bear on figuring out what has become of Marion. We have, after all, seen the appalling, irrational events of the first half. If we do not yet know the whole story, we know enough to understand the inadequacy of public labels and formulations to what actually hap-pens in the dark places of this world.

One sign that characters are out of control of their lives is that they are often slightly out of control of their words. Small distortions of meaning are most common in Norman's speech (along with the more obvious difficulty of his stuttering), but they occur also with Marion, especially when she is under emotional pressure. Struggling to come to some clearer understanding of her future with Sam, she tells him, "You make respectability sound, (pauses) disrespectful." We know what she means, but "disrespectful" is not quite right; "unrespectable" would be. She is not quite able to articulate, or to understand, what bothers her about Sam's explicit reference to their sex life. Sam, not respecta-bility, is "disrespectful"—of her unhappiness and of her desire to change the terms of their relationship.

Trying to fend off Cassidy's advances in the office, she produces an-other small oddity of speech. Cassidy asks, "Do you know what I do about unhappiness? I buy it off. Are, uh, are you unhappy?" Marion replies, "Not inordinately." By which she really means, one guesses, "None of your business." But the idea that she has no more unhappi-ness than is suitable for her seems strange. Surely most people regard any ongoing unhappiness as "inordinate"; and we know that Marion is very unhappy indeed.

She will pull back from Norman's sympathetic movement toward her in much the same way. "You've never had an empty moment in your life, have you?" he asks. Again her mixed impulse to show a little and hide much leads to a slightly peculiar reply, "Only my share." How much emptiness would be her share? But again we know otherwise. Marion's life is, and evidently has been for a long time, terribly empty.

Norman's malapropisms and stuttering also come on occasions of emotional stress; and they often occur, like Marion's, in some kind of sexually charged context. He is unable to bring himself to say the word "bathroom" when he is showing Marion her cabin; and he does not find the right word later when he tells her that "eating in an office is just, (hesitates) just too officious." Like Marion's "disrespectful," "officious" is off the mark, but a good deal farther—just as his lonely madness has gone a good deal farther than hers.[16]

Of course, Norman may be joking. We are often not quite sure if he is, and, if he is, for whom his jokes are meant. Is he conscious of his play on words, for example, when he announces to Marion that "M-mother, m-my Mother, um, what is the phrase? She isn't q-quite herself today." However we take his intent, his words expose a dysfunction in Norman's ability to establish contact with other people. His stuttering and his little errors of syntax and meaning provide our first hints of the horrible incoherence that lies behind his diffident exterior. In his eagerness to be ingratiating, he says less and reveals more than he wishes.

"Mother," interestingly, is always perfectly forceful and clear in the vulgar aggressiveness of her speech. But we should perhaps not be too surprised by that fact, for Norman—blandly odd as he may be—nonetheless possesses a wit and linguistic self-consciousness largely missing from the other characters in a film that is often talky but, uncharacteristically for Hitchcock, rarely eloquent. It is Norman who responds most strongly to the words of others ("someplace," for example) and who has an awareness of language that is signaled by such characteristic interlocutions as "let me put it this way." The aptness that reverses his inarticulateness is most evident in the fact that he—much more than the rather pedantic psychiatrist at the end—gives a convincing account of the central themes of *Psycho*. We remember him as its truest spokesman in such formulations as "We all go a little mad sometimes. Haven't you?" In his remarkable speech to Marion about "traps," he comes close to comprehending fully the world in which the characters of *Psycho* struggle with so little success to find happiness. "We're all in our private traps, clamped in them. And none of us can ever get out. We scratch and claw, but only at the air, only at each other. And for all of it, we never budge an inch." The only other character who ever

---

[16] In "Psychosis, Neurosis, Perversion" (reprinted in Deutelbaum and Poague, eds., *A Hitchcock Reader*, pp. 311-31), Raymond Bellour distinguishes between Norman's "psychosis" and Marion's "neurosis" as failures—different in degree but similar in kind—to achieve "a final equilibrium between desire and the law."

approaches such articulate understanding is Marion, especially when she follows Norman's intellectual lead in the parlor: "Sometimes we deliberately step into those traps."

And then, of course, there's "Mother." In her/Norman's last words, she/he reminds us of the importance, deceptiveness, and inadequacy of language throughout the movie.

It's sad when a mother has to speak the words that condemn her own son, but I couldn't allow them to believe that I would commit murder. They'll put him away now, as I should have, years ago. He was always *bad*. And in the end he intended to tell them I killed those girls and that man. As if I could do anything except just sit and stare, like one of his stuffed birds. They know I can't even move a finger, and I won't. I'll just sit here and be quiet, just in case they do suspect me. They're probably watching me; well, let them. Let them see what kind of a person I am. I'm not even going to swat that fly. I hope they are watching. They'll see. They'll see and they'll know, and they'll say, "Why she wouldn't even harm a fly."

Her/his collection of clichés is as true and false as most of the equivocal words in *Psycho*. Everything "Mother" says is true, as long as we accept the premise that "she," at once dead and alive, is speaking. Otherwise, everything Norman says is false. "Her" speech is also notable for its inconspicuous but pervasive linguistic self-consciousness: "speak the words," "tell them," "be quiet," "they'll say." Like everyone else in *Psycho*, "Mother"/Norman tries to find, or create, or fix in words a reality that corresponds to needs and wishes simpler and happier than the universe of the film can accommodate.

The interior monologue of "Mother"/Norman at the end of the movie is only one of a number of occasions during which the characters of *Psycho* shape fantasy scripts. Imaginary dialogues are not abnormal or even unusual behavior, of course; but in the absence of love and a stable social identity, they can begin, like Norman's hobby, not to pass the time but to fill it. They have entirely overtaken Norman.

They threaten to overtake Marion as well. The extent to which she has allowed her fantasies to replace the actual world is not clear, but her impulsive, hopeless attempt to steal Cassidy's money and flee to Sam suggests that she is no longer wholly under the guidance of a reality principle. She persists in her unlikely scheme despite two events that should have persuaded her to give it up: her boss's seeing her as she drives out of Phoenix and the suspicion of the policeman the next morning. Instead she listens to voices in her head: her imagining of Sam's surprise at her arrival in Fairvale, of a conversation between the cop and the used car salesman, and of the reaction of Mr. Lowry, Caroline, her sister, and Mr. Cassidy to her absence on Monday morning.

If we intensify and extend Marion's actions and fantasies, we arrive at the full lunacy of Norman, who supplies not only his mother's voice but her person as well. Once his nether world is entered it is empowered. To return to ordinary reality is at best difficult and uncertain, perhaps impossible. Marion's response to Norman's statement that "we all go a little mad sometimes" will comprehend the outcomes of *Psycho* better than she knows: "Sometimes just one time can be enough."

In a world without grace or forgiveness, Norman and Marion fail in their struggles to find identity and a place among other people. They die or are replaced (by "Mother" for Norman and, in a way, by Lila for Marion). No rebirth, only obliteration. At the end of *Psycho*, the failure of language is associated again with broader futility. During the psychiatrist's explanatory summary, he tells of Norman's attempt to resurrect the mother he murdered. "She was there, but she was a corpse. So he began to think and speak for her, give her half his life, so to speak." But Norman cannot speak life back into his mother, and the psychiatrist's explanation cannot bring Marion back to be forgiven and to marry Sam. If one compares the end of *Psycho* with that of even as equivocal a romance of the past recovered as *Marnie*, its resigned and hopeless vision of human possibility becomes apparent. Unearthing the past in *Psycho* allows us nothing more than a partial understanding of its ravages; we cannot cure or undo them.

For all the psychiatrist's fatuous manner, much of what he says is plausible enough. He does not, as some commentators have noted, address the central questions of the movie as a whole, but we can hardly expect him to. After all, he has not seen the movie or even participated in more than a minute fragment of its complicated unraveling. What Rothman calls "the mystery of the real identity and nature of 'Norman Bates,' " cannot be explained by examining Norman Bates alone. It has to do with the nature of human identity itself, and with the capabilities and inadequacies that allow us to imagine what we might hope to become at the same time that we are unable to attain the self-recreation that we crave.

Like the mystery of Madeleine/Carlotta in *Vertigo*, which in being solved is finally only deepened, the psychiatrist's explanation of what happened to Norman Bates and Marion Crane only leads us to profounder questions. Marion does not have a chance to ask in her final agony, as Scottie does, "Why me?" But the question applies to her, and to all humans, all equally unfortunate because equally condemned to sickness and death. It constitutes the final, unsolvable mystery at the heart of *Vertigo* and *Psycho*. Both movies ask, but can never answer, two overwhelming questions: "Why?" and "Why me?"

Rothman writes that *Psycho* "decisively demonstrates . . . a truth we already know: we have been born into the world and we are fated to die."[17] The grief at the center of such films as *Vertigo* and *Psycho*, however, shows that Hitchcock, like his characters, cannot reconcile himself to the inevitability of a long, meaningless spiral into oblivion. Even in Hitchcock's uncompromisingly ironic works, the quest for rebirth, or innocence, and for a better, more whole self realized in love, remains enormously powerful. No one in Hitchcock's movies goes gentle into that good night or accepts without horror the "fal-fal-false-falsity" of the human vision of Eden regained.

Hitchcock's romantic films deny that God, or the gods, have brought us into the world only to abandon us to wandering, loss, and death. They affirm our quest to redeem time and recover innocence. They also confirm the benevolent presiding of another god, the filmmaker, who at once imitates and creates life. The romances do not invalidate such ironic films as *Vertigo* and *Psycho*, nor are they repudiated by them. Hitchcock, like most of us, must have fervently hoped that rebirth in love should be the way of things, and dreaded that it might not be. His life's work, in sum and in most of his movies individually, expresses that hope and that dread.

[17] Rothman, *The Murderous Gaze*, p. 341.

CHAPTER SIX

Bygones be Bygones

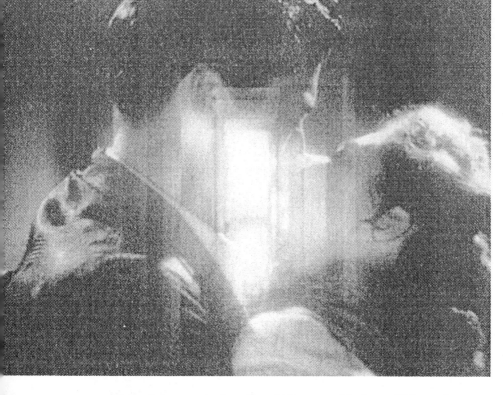

Spellbound: Gregory Peck and Ingrid Bergman. The love of John and Constance is as improbable as the filmmaker's technique.

THIS chapter returns to films that are constructed largely within the traditions of romantic narrative. Like *Vertigo* and *Psycho*, all have protagonists who undertake quests to uncover and resolve bygone events that are casting a freezing shadow upon present happiness. Identifying and coming to terms with the old source of present infection constitutes the first, and often the hardest, step in restoring health.

Struggles with the unsleeping dragons of days gone by have obvious parallels with the psychoanalyst's search for the cause of neurosis in the emotional remains of prior traumas. Modern romantic narratives that turn on the poisoning of the present by the past, therefore, often have more or less explicit psychoanalytic coloring. The dangers threatened in such stories suggest the anxieties of psychiatric patients, who exhume a past that may be injurious if unexamined, but that they fear will be fatal if exposed. *Spellbound* (1945) and *Marnie* (1964) explicitly develop their quests for innocence as psychoanalytical searches. *Under Capricorn* (1949) does not take quite the same form, but it incorporates the same assumptions about the ongoing effects of unresolved psychological stress.

Freudian psychoanalysis and similar theories of human psychological development, from the point of view implicit in Hitchcock's films, may be understood as modern versions of ancient cultural strains. Far from breaking with traditions, they are recent developments of a conception that stretches back to the beginnings of culture. History itself, especially when it is studied with a view to illuminating current conditions, could be said to represent another variation upon the assumption that the deformations of the present may be remedied only when their causes in the past are known.

Embodied in Hitchcock's films, this view of psychology is less belittling than commentators often suppose. Hitchcock pokes fun at psychologists who fancy themselves to be dealing in new goods—most obviously in *Spellbound* and *Psycho*—but his amusement is good-natured and the figures he caricatures are portrayed as naive, not vicious. His reduction of psychoanalytic theory and practice to its baldest ideas and patterns—again most obviously in *Spellbound* and *Psycho*—does not serve satire as much as artistic economy. Dr. Brulov's remark when he undertakes a crash analysis of the amnesiac John Ballantine (Gregory Peck) in *Spellbound* applies to the representation of psychoanalysis in Hitchcock's movies generally: "this is a shortcut, but we haven't much time."

Hitchcock uses psychoanalysis as another version of the romantic quest for identity. He finds its central assumptions, if not its scientific pretensions, wholly congenial. Since he has no particular interest in psychoanalysis as science, Hitchcock need not worry about his stylized condensation of the usual course of therapy or his excessively simple (from a realistic viewpoint) representation of the process of gaining access to the unconscious. Movies are life with the dull bits cut out. Psychotherapy, like anything else, consists mostly of slow, dull bits to be cut out.

Not only does Hitchcock radically condense the process of psychiatric self-discovery, but he explicitly attacks parts of its scientific framework, notably its emphasis on an ultimate professional impersonality and its dependence on deductive procedures. The explicit psychologizing in *Spellbound* and *Marnie*, and similar, implicit ideas in *Under Capricorn*, have led some viewers to expect a scientific world view that all three films in fact undermine. These movies do not represent exercises in dramatized psychology. Only superficially different from Hitchcock's other romantic adventure-thrillers, all establish an obtrusively unrealistic mode early. And all become conspicuously artificial at crucial moments: the Dali-designed dream sequences in *Spellbound*, for example; Henrietta Flusky's (Ingrid Bergman) highly theatrical revelation of her past in *Under Capricorn*; and the suffusion of the screen with red in *Marnie*.

Certain other romantic elements attain particular importance because of the prominence of the past. Characters who suggest wicked parents or obstructive siblings figure conspicuously and require a lover-rescuer who must deliver his or her future mate from such oppressors. The idea of the healer healed is prominent in all three movies. The search for identity, lost or blocked by previous misfortune, becomes explicit. In its most benign manifestation, the past in Hitchcock's narratives consists of little more than a parent or family that must be outgrown and replaced with a lover or spouse. At its most malignant, it corrupts the present like an incurable cancer. "The dead," James Joyce once wrote, "envy the living." In Hitchcock's movies, a wounded past envies the present and prevents its rejuvenation.

Also easily adapted to a psychological emphasis are other characteristic romantic elements: demonic descents, actions of death and return, and the usual Hitchcockian dichotomies between true and false love and between hope and cynicism. Representations of formal ritual and an emphasis upon conspicuous moviemaking artifice suggest that psychoanalysis is a sister to cinematic art rather than a competing science. This implicit conception has given particular offense to viewers with realistic prejudices, and it may be useful to address some of their objections by starting with this issue.

Highly theatrical, *Spellbound, Under Capricorn,* and *Marnie* have been flayed as clumsy, naive, and unbelievable by viewers repelled by obvious special effects and crude pseudopsychoanalysis. Others have taken a more enthusiastic view of the same elements, praising the films for apt expressionism and psychological subtlety and conviction. Like most radical disputes about taste, this one derives at least in part from clashing perceptions about what sort of thing is being discussed, and therefore about what expectations one might reasonably bring to it. As I have indicated, I think it a mistake to regard these films as infused by scientific realism or literary naturalism. Their insistence upon their own artifice, and upon the internal representation of formal ritual—the very tendency that their detractors find most offensive—indicates what kind of stories they embody. We will understand them most accurately if we take them as they announce themselves: romances with an emphasis on psychologizing rather than psychological case studies with a narrative sugar coating.

The antirealism of *Spellbound, Under Capricorn*, and *Marnie* functions as it does in other Hitchcockian romances: it elevates grace and protective order over heartless logic, malignity, or randomness. *Under Capricorn*, with its dramatic sound track, histrionic voice-over, and obviously painted backdrops immediately announces itself as something both made up and having a historical basis. "And now," ends the introductory narrator, "our story begins." What begins the story, significantly, is a ceremony almost as artificial as the sets, music, and theatrical voice that introduces it. Elaborately attired in dress uniform, the new Governor arrives, accompanied by shouted orders among the attendant soldiers and by a military band. As he begins his speech to a somewhat restive audience, the internal formality of his arrival echoes in yet another way the framing formality of the movie itself: it is not wholly polished or plausible. His stiltedness draws attention to itself. The Governor attempts an authoritative bearing that he does not fully achieve. This theme of almost-convincing pretense will recur. Like feigning in other Hitchcock movies, it expresses truth as well as falsehood.

A similarly obtrusive musical sound track, rather more portentous, accompanies the opening credits of *Spellbound*. A fall wind strips the leaves from a tree that is outlined against a large, ragged cloud. The voice-over of *Under Capricorn* becomes in *Spellbound* a written disquisition, preceded by a quotation from *Hamlet*. At the end of its brief explanation of psychoanalysis, the language deviates from its previously scientific tone. "The devils of unreason are driven from the human soul." Like the opening minutes of *Under Capricorn*, those of

Spellbound insist upon the made-up, fictional quality of what is to follow. The story will be a parable; a pattern of life, not a slice.

Marnie begins with the same sort of highly charged musical sound track. The credits emphasize the "storiness" of what is to follow by appearing on one of Hollywood's most hackneyed title props, turning book pages. The opening shots are enigmatic and serve to make the audience aware of the manipulations of the filmmaker. We see an unexplained close-up of a woman's large yellow handbag under a tweed-suited left arm. (The yellow color that first appears here will, as is usual for Hitchcock, signal "caution, be alert" throughout the film.) The camera tracks in extreme close-up for a few seconds, then drops back to reveal the back of a dark-haired woman carrying a suitcase in her other hand and walking along a deserted railway platform. It follows her for a few more feet, then stops as she continues, sets down her suitcase, and looks expectantly up the track. Cut to a close-up of an angry, shouting, rather stodgy businessman. "Robbed! Cleaned out!" Cut to an open safe, its top shelf empty. Now we know what the first sequence was about. We have also been reminded of the degree to which our knowledge is controlled by the presentational decisions of the filmmaker.

A little later, we see Marnie (Tippi Hedren) riding her horse Forio against a rear projection so obvious that it often draws laughs from first-time viewers. That shot cuts to another, equally obvious in its artificiality, of the waterfront neighborhood of Marnie's mother. Along with this cinematic fakery, *Marnie* indicates internally the importance of feigning and falsehood. We see Marnie's face for the first time just after we watch her rinse brunette dye from her hair and emerge as a golden blond. What she really is is very different from what she at first appears to be.

As the stories of all three movies unwind, Hitchcock reasserts their artificiality and/or conspicuously obtrudes his own hand at moments of intense significance: critical plot turns, revelations of character, apparently ruinous cul-de-sacs, and final solutions. A famous (or notorious) instance of such contrivance in *Spellbound* occurs when Constance (Ingrid Bergman) and John Ballantine (Gregory Peck, at this point masquerading as Dr. Edwardes) first embrace. "Something has happened to us," says Dr. Edwardes to Constance. As they approach the admission that they have fallen in love, alternate close-ups of the faces of the two lovers become tighter and tighter until the last two shots are of Gregory Peck's eyes and then Ingrid Bergman's. Hers close. Violins swell while the image dissolves to an opening door. Through it appears another door beyond; and that one opens on another door, which opens on another, which opens on a brilliant light as the image dissolves back to the embracing lovers.

With this subjective, expressionistic dissolve (though from whose point of view is hard to say), the film abruptly turns self-consciously cornball. It is tempting to laugh at Hitchcock's literal rendering of the cliché for self-discovery in love. At the same time—and especially during viewings after the first—one's laugh is likely to be more sentimental than derisory. The miracle of love is as outrageous and improbable as the filmmaker's technique. It is, as Gregory Peck says, "like lightning striking. It strikes rarely." As is usually the case when Hitchcock's protagonists fall in love, the dialogue, music, and images collaborate to emphasize not the plausibility of that occurrence but its wonderful unlikelihood.

Other crucial sequences share this emphasis on artificiality or unlikeliness. The obvious rear projection of Constance and John skiing precedes his recovery of his memory and his identity. The horrible reversal of his good fortune a few minutes later is rendered with virtuoso compression and stylization. Ballantine is arrested and detained; Constance testifies at his trial; Ballantine is convicted and incarcerated; and Constance returns brokenhearted to Green Manors. All this occurs in the course of seven consecutive dissolves and less than forty-five seconds of screen time.

The last shots of the movie, which show Constance and John about to depart on their honeymoon, conspicuously repeat an earlier sequence. The newlyweds recognize the conductor at the gate as the same one who was puzzled when they continued together previously after an apparent goodbye kiss. As he watches again, even more puzzled, they kiss and continue together once more. The camera tracks in to his blankly bewildered face and the film ends on the note of amused improbability that tempers many of its most intense moments.

When Ballantine relates his dream to Constance and Dr. Brulov, his description is illustrated by a succession of expressionistic sets designed by Salvator Dali. Discussing this dream sequence, Hitchcock said that he wished to do dreams not in the misty style usually favored by Hollywood but with hard edges and the sharpness of daylight.[1] (Filming outdoors had to be abandoned, however, as too expensive.) Such photographic clarity intensifies the disjunctive surrealism of the dreamer's images. Dali's distinctive painting further underlines the close relationship between the compression of meaning in dreams and the similar compression in art.

[1] Truffaut, *Hitchcock/Truffaut*, pp. 163-64.

The sequences just discussed illustrate two important points. First, turning points are frequently produced by astonishingly unfortunate or lucky coincidences in the plot and are accompanied by an increase in the conspicuousness of filmmaking artifice. A conjunction of improbability and artificiality emphasizes the close relationship between moments of intense significance in life and the ways in which art reveals order in the chaotic-looking world. Second, Hitchcock goes to considerable pains in *Spellbound* to emphasize antirealistic qualities. At its beginning and end, and at the most important junctures of its narrative, it insists on its dissimilarity to ordinary reality, on its status as a story, a made-up thing, a concentration of meaningful artifice.

Under Capricorn opens and closes with manifestly painted sets. The Governor's Mansion and Flusky's (Joseph Cotton) house, settings for crucial sequences, exhibit the same painterly artificiality. For some viewers, the remarkable mobility of the camera will also draw attention to the technique of the film; and for all audiences, the costume drama aspect will have the same effect. At one of the moments of greatest anxiety and revelation, when we discover that Millie has been using a shrunken head to terrorize Hattie, Hitchcock inserts a thunderstorm. Like that at the beginning of *Young and Innocent*, the symbolic storm in *Under Capricorn* simultaneously underlines the intensity of the moment and its theatricality.

Marnie begins more realistically, but it quickly becomes intensely stylized and expressionistic. Marnie's self-recovery, as much Mark's (Sean Connery) achievement as hers, is associated throughout the film with conspicuous formal devices: suffusions of red, flashbacks, zooms, eerie music, obvious artificiality of sets, and conspicuous rear projection. This attention-getting artifice paradoxically signals again an intensification of truth and significance. It indicates that the story has reached a moment at which veils are drawn back and actuality revealed.

The first moment of obvious artifice occurs after the opening sequences, when Marnie arrives at the "Red Fox Tavern" and goes to ride Forio. The sexual overtones of her relation to her horse receive immediate emphasis. "Ah, there's my darling!" she exclaims as the horse is brought from the stables. "That big, old spoiled baby of yours knew something was up," says the owner of the stable, "tried to bite me twice already this morning." Marnie smiles, embraces the muzzle of the horse, and murmurs ardently, "Oh, Forio, if you want to bite somebody, bite me!"

During a brief long shot of her cantering, the music rises as it did when she washed the dark dye from her hair. The shot then changes to a close-up of Marnie riding against an obvious rear projection of woods. Hitchcock then abruptly cuts, while continuing the same musical theme (generally associated in *Marnie* with revelation) to an overhead view of a cab arriving on what is obviously the studio set of a waterfront neighborhood.

What connotations are attached to this sequence? It follows Marnie disposing of the remains of her false identity by putting a suitcase in a station rental locker and kicking the key down a grate. Her previous identity resists discarding; the key does not drop easily from sight but must be forced by Marnie's shoe. Immediately afterward we see her on Forio, looking happier and more relaxed than she manages to be almost any other time in the film.[2] The context immediately preceding this sequence suggests that we are seeing the real person—for the moment happy, relaxed, affectionate. Why "the real person" should be presented in an especially artificial manner is a question that I will address shortly. The point I wish to make here is that the association between unconstrained truth and conspicuous artifice of presentation is established very early.

Abrupt cutting and the uninterrupted music on the sound track make the succeeding episode at Marnie's mother's seem almost like a continuation of her riding. This smooth transition has considerable appropriateness, for the essential subject of the sequence with Marnie's mother is again revelation of "the real person." But now we see a different side: an anxious, infantile woman haunted by phobias and nightmares.

When Marnie sees a vase of red gladiolas set against a white window curtain, she experiences a terror that is rendered subjectively by eerie music and a startling red suffusion that tints the screen without obscuring the image. After Marnie goes up to her bedroom to rest, the same portentous musical motif and the flash of red are repeated as she has "that old dream again . . . when the cold starts." As in the sequence before, Hitchcock's conspicuous technique is associated with revelations of the real person behind the respectable, carefully turned-out manikin.

The red flash recurs, accompanied by the same music, after Marnie has gotten a job at the company of Mark Rutland and spills a drop of red ink on her white shirt-sleeve. A little later, during a scene of great importance, the red suffusion and its associated musical motif occur

---

[2] The constraint of Tippi Hedren's performance is something for which she has been consistently criticized. Given that her stiffness reflects the tension in the personality of Marnie, however, and is therefore entirely appropriate to her role, this criticism seems misplaced.

again. Marnie has come in to type for her boss on a Saturday afternoon, and during events that follow, her employer falls in love with
her. We can identify, I think, the precise moment. Its details establish
the crucial fact that Mark falls in love with "the real person" and not
with Marnie's façade. He falls in love when he first sees Marnie's illness and need and simultaneously recognizes that she is capable of responding to his love.

The sequence begins by emphasizing the clinical, behaviorist interest
Mark has had in Marnie since he first thought that he recognized her
as the woman who robbed Strutt. A zoologist who has been forced to
leave the scholarly world to patch and bail the foundering family business, Mark asks Marnie to come in on Saturday to type a paper he has
written on "Arboreal Predators of the Brazilian Rain Forest." Once
again, a thunderstorm is brewing. Before it breaks, Mark treats Marnie
as another zoological object. His paper, he tells her, "deals with the
instincts of predators, what you might call the criminal class of the
animal world. Lady animals figure very largely as predators." He follows these suggestive remarks with a complacent smile, a raising of
eyebrows. We can infer what he admits later: at this point he views

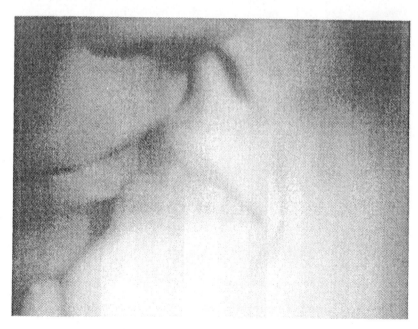

Marnie: Sean Connery and Tippi Hedren. Mark's study of instinctual behavior
is replaced by the behavior itself. He falls in love.

Marnie as a particularly interesting example of predatory behavior and has employed her in order to observe her as he presumably did the jaguarundi that he trained to trust him. (It is a suggestive parallel to Marnie's affection for her horse Forio that the widowed Mark should have framed on his desk, in the spot usually reserved for a picture of wife and children, a photo of this big snarling cat.)

Then the storm breaks, Marnie gives way to her crimson terror, and the study of instinctual behavior is replaced by the behavior itself. Mark falls in love. Paralyzed by the lightning and the red she sees suffusing the white curtains, Marnie begs, "The colors, stop the colors!" When a branch smashes through the window, her panic is complete. At this moment, while she trembles in his arms, Mark leans down to kiss her. The camera moves in to a close-up that approaches the ludicrous; Mark's lips and Marnie's lips and nostrils entirely fill the screen. The storm ends; the kiss ends. "All over. You're alright." She will be alright someday, perhaps; for, however involuntarily, she has taken the necessary first step on the way to recovery: the loving connection with Mark. It is a connection that her sickness will make her resist most of the time. At the height of the storm, however, stripped of her defenses and expressing the personality that she normally conceals and represses, Marnie responds to Mark's embrace.

Mark, in need of a healing love himself, takes a fragment of statuary from the damaged remains of his dead wife's collection and tosses it to the floor. "Well, we've all got to go sometime." Since he has already told Marnie that these objects were all of his dead wife's things that he had kept, his gesture implies that in Marnie's arms he has been able to let go of his bereavement.

The theatrical thunderstorm, the exaggerated close-up of the kiss, the flashes of red and their accompanying music, all emphasize the miraculousness of falling in love, its simultaneous truth and implausibility. It is crucial that the technical motif of the red flashes has already been linked to the underlying reality of Marnie's true self. We see again in this sequence the profoundly optimistic view of human love and need that informs many of Hitchcock's movies. Marnie may be beautiful, intelligent, and mysterious, but those qualities only pique Mark's scientific interest; they do not cause him to fall in love. His insight into her weakness inspires his desire to hold and protect her. His own need and loneliness, moreover, make him ready for loving. The opening of the doors will be slower and more painful than in *Spellbound*; but it begins with the same coming together of two people who want each other more than either knows—two people who should not, by the very nature of things, be alone. Their coming together begins with the same intensification of both truth and artifice that underscores in Hitchcock's romantic films the rare, ordinary miracle of love that gives life hope and resonance.

The seed planted in the storm has a long gestation before it buds, and it will not blossom during the movie. Marnie's resistance to Mark, her attempted suicide, and the threat of prosecution for her past crimes intervene before the renewal of hope at the end of the film. The promise of the ending, however, is unequivocal; and in its formal dazzle it repeats much of the sense of miracle and parting of veils that characterized Mark's falling in love during the storm. Exhuming and confronting the past during the last sequence of the movie, Marnie and Mark recover the expectations raised by their first kiss.

Marnie's return to her catastrophic past begins with another storm. An overhead shot, suggestive of the depressed world in which Marnie is trapped, shows Mark trying to drag her like a reluctant child out of his car and into her mother's flat. A drenching rain is falling. The most intense, and formally startling, sequence of the film follows. As Mark struggles with Marnie's mother, who is demanding that he get out of her house, Marnie pipes in with a high, childish voice, "You let my Mama go, you hear. You let my Mama go. You're hurtin' my Mama." The camera dollies in to an extreme close-up of Marnie's face, then cuts to a shot—evidently representing her field of vision—of a couch in her mother's apartment. The plain, somewhat worn sofa reminds Marnie of the still plainer flat of her childhood, in which the violent death of a sailor occurred twenty years ago. It was that event, though she retains no conscious memory of it, that emotionally crippled her.

While she looks at the couch, the shot dissolves to the tunnel-like living room of her childhood home, in which a young woman in a loose housecoat prepares a bed on an armchair while a sailor (Bruce Dern) stands aside waiting for her. The shot that follows is a strikingly strange track-in. The effect of these shots is at once to draw our attention to the technical virtuosity of the sequence and, by their disorienting quality, to represent memories that have the impact of immediate experience.

Bernice, Marnie's mother, goes into a bedroom and rouses a child (Marnie), whom she leads to the chair and covers with a blanket. She and the impatient sailor then go into the bedroom. The sailor slams the door carelessly behind him. The image changes at that moment back to the adult Marnie's face, her mouth and eyes opening in terror at the crash of the door slamming, which is also the sound of the thunder crashing in the present and on that night long ago. The camera holds on Marnie-present for only a moment, then cuts back to the little girl who is Marnie-past, as she screams (which replaces the scream that Marnie-present was about to utter) and throws herself forward on the easy chair where she has awakened during the storm.

As the storm continues to rage in present and past time, and the image continues to alternate between the present and the past, we learn the truth about Bernice's "accident" and about the death of the sailor. "Marnie, Marnie, help me," sobs Bernice in the past, when the sailor falls on her leg. "I got to help my Mama," cries Marnie in the present. The image cuts back to the past, as the child strikes the sailor with a fireplace poker. The screams of Bernice-past, of Marnie-past, and of Marnie remembering in the present blend into one as the camera pans up his blood-soaked white tee shirt. Then, with a dissolve back to the present, it duplicates and explains the red suffusions that have signaled Marnie's breakdowns throughout the film.

The rest of the film occurs in the present; there are no more red suffusions or flashbacks. The past has not been excised, precisely, but it has been recaptured. It has been rendered conscious and perhaps controllable. More revelations follow from Marnie's mother: her concealment of the truth of the sailor's death, the attempt of the social authorities to take Marnie away from her, the tawdry, sad circumstances of Marnie's conception. As Marnie and Mark leave Mrs. Edgar's apartment, the children who were skipping rope and chanting when she first visited are doing so again. "Mother, mother, I am ill,/ Send for the doctor over the hill." Marnie is not yet cured, but her recovery is possible now. The storm that was breaking as she and Mark arrived has blown away. The sun is shining on the still wet pavement as she and her husband drive off into a proverbially brightening future. As if to emphasize the conventionality of the happy ending, a high angle shot gives us another view of the painted set of the Baltimore waterfront while the car turns a corner and disappears.

The possibility of freedom from the tyranny of past crimes applies as well to Marnie's mother. As Marnie and Mark leave, a battered-looking Bernice wearily murmurs from her chair, "Goodbye. Goodbye, Sugarpop." The epithet, as we have learned in the flashback, is a pet name for her child from before the "accident." Like her daughter and (less overwhelmingly, to be sure) most of the other characters in *Marnie*, Mrs. Edgar has long struggled with the weight of an oppressive past. In wishing goodbye to her "Sugarpop," she gives Marnie the freedom of adulthood by acknowledging the past that she has hitherto concealed from her. At the same time, she escapes that crushing past herself.

The virtuosity of camera work, cutting, and sound in this sequence;

its highly artificial, almost clichéd conclusion; and the stylized acting of Tippi Hedren and Louise Latham (Bernice Edgar), fittingly climax and resolve a film in which exaggerated formal characteristics have consistently been associated with what is most true and significant. The final sequence thus exemplifies, with an intensity unexceeded in Hitchcock's work, his characteristic expenditure of formal dazzle on the most critical moments of plot and revelations of character.

Hitchcock's handling of Marnie's story suggests that art has a curative role to play in helping us to bring our personal pasts into harmony with the present. The intensification of significance in dreams, in movies and other works of art, and in vividly reexperienced memories signals the kinship among all of them. All winnow from the undifferentiated mass of daily experience—which paradoxically they transform and disguise—the essentials of truth and meaning. What Hitchcock's movies represent is not the flux of ordinary life but the essential meaning underlying that flux, which can be comprehended most universally in the intensifications and stylizations of art.

Marnie herself, though she intends sarcasm, turns to a self-consciously artistic formulation to describe what is happening to her. Having awakened from her recurring nightmare, she is trying to put off Mark's attempts to get her to talk about herself. But Mark persists. "You're really dying to play doctor, aren't you?" she finally remarks irritably. "Okay, I'm a big movie fan, I know the games."

Her supercilious mockery has a surprising outcome. Drawn into "the game" of free association and through it back into a fragment of her past, she ends clinging to Mark and sobbing, "Oh, God, somebody help me." Her acceptance of Mark's embrace and her admission that she needs help are hopeful auguries. We should not forget that these first twitches of her "poor, paralyzed little legs" come during an episode that begins on Marnie's side as a parody of psychoanalytic melodrama. *Marnie*, one need hardly say, has already shown itself to be a particularly theatrical version of just such a thing.

Set against the art of the movie itself are frequent instances of "internal artifice": pretense and deceit of all kinds, and social rituals like receptions and fox hunts. Such actions are generally associated with the forces that are preventing Marnie from knowing who she is and from breaking the cycle of compulsive behavior in which she is trapped by her unremembered past. Most occurrences of internal artifice raise the crucial issues of the film, but they characteristically obscure or misrepresent rather than clarify them.

Marnie's disguises and false identities constitute the most obvious example of internal artifice. Like the behavior of many criminals, her thefts are rationalized by a profit motive but originate in deep personal anguish. Herself unable to know who she is, she cannot possibly present a truthful identity to the world. Only when riding her horse or when jolted by events that evoke her past is she herself; and those occasions, as we have seen, are associated not with internal artifice and ritual but with the conspicuous artificiality of the movie itself.

The honeymoon cruise, the reception after Mark and Marnie return, and the fox hunt all force Marnie to play roles that cause her acute pain. The unsustainable pretenses on the ocean liner lead to her attempted suicide; the reception honoring their marriage exposes her to the fury of Strutt and the threat of jail; and the fox hunt, which is presented as an exercise in sophisticated savagery, ends with Forio dead and Marnie reverting to her identity as a thief.[3] Her marriage to Mark, at first, amounts to little more than a "façade." He underlines the hollowness of their situation when he instructs her about connubial behavior the first morning after their honeymoon: "This is a drill, dear. Wife follows husband to the front door. Gives and/or gets kiss. Stands pensively as he drives away. A wistful little wave is optional." Such charades in life deceive; they mislead and injure both the actors and their audiences. The pretenses of art, in contrast, reveal. In *Marnie* they are associated with freedom and healing.

Similar sorts of pretension in *Spellbound* and *Under Capricorn* receive similar treatment. The elegant civility of Dr. Murchison in *Spellbound* conceals murder and leads first to the unjust conviction of John Ballantine and then to the death of Murchison himself. The same pattern of deceit covering violence and self-hatred appears in small in the opening episode of the movie, in which the psychotic patient Mary pretends to seduce and then claws the attendant who is taking her to Constance. Her conversation with Constance makes it clear that her

---

[3] Critics often assume that Mark rapes Marnie and that his violation of her leads to her suicide attempt. This assumption strikes me as unwarranted and unnecessary. The sexual threat contained in Mark's stripping Marnie's nightie from her would be quite sufficient to terrify her to the point of suicide. She has already complained about the duration of their stay on "this boat, this trip," a situation more like prison than a honeymoon for her, and one that she escapes, in fact, by the strong message she sends by her attempted suicide, which ends the voyage. Mark, moreover, has given her his word earlier that he "wouldn't," a promise that it would be out of character for him to break, even when a bit drunk. However that may be, the sequence is photographed and edited to make what happens or does not happen beyond ascertaining. We do not know what Mark does or does not do to Marnie, and the film pointedly makes it impossible for us to know. Speculations, including the one I argue for above, are thus somewhat counter to the spirit of the sequence itself, which withholds knowledge beyond Mark's initial loss of self-possession and subsequent apology and kiss.

hostility includes herself as well as the men she professes to despise. The deceptions of Ballantine, who is trying to pass as Dr. Edwardes, are the symptoms of his illness, symptoms that are more dangerous to himself than to others. Like Marnie, he has lost himself. He cannot show, or live, an identity that he does not possess.

Internal artifice in *Under Capricorn* leads to the same inferences. The hollow welcoming ceremonies at the beginning of the film are as scanty of true human cheer as the dinner at Sam Flusky's house a little later. The Irish Society ball, for all its surface of community spirit, is shown to be less an occasion of social harmony than of hurtful exclusion. The deceptions of Hattie and Flusky, like those of John Ballantine, are symptomatic of their illness and victimization. Caught in their collaboration to conceal the real killer of Hattie's brother, neither can speak to the other of the debts that each feels to be beyond possible repayment. Both are easy marks for Millie, who uses them in a manner somewhat analogous to the way Dr. Murchison exploits Constance and John in *Spellbound*. Like Murchison, Millie practices vicious deceptions; she attacks both the marriage of Flusky and Hattie and the very life of the latter.

Because he is fooling himself as well as others, Charles Adair practices the most complex deceit in *Under Capricorn*. His wish to help Hattie becomes indistinguishable from his unholy desire to prize her away from Flusky. As in *Marnie* and *Spellbound*, achieving freedom and escaping from threatened captivity is gained in *Under Capricorn* at the same time that truth is revealed. "Help me now," pleads Hattie. "Tell them that they must set Sam free. Tell them what happened." After a brief struggle between his angels and his devils, Charles tells how he came to be wounded. By doing so he frees Flusky from the threat of imprisonment and makes it possible for Hattie and Sam to renew their marriage.

He also escapes the self-deceptions that led him to try to undermine Hattie's union with her husband. He leaves New South Wales with a self-knowledge and maturity that he lacked when he arrived. As Hattie and Flusky are free at the end of *Under Capricorn* to resume their long-interrupted marriage, Charles is free of his rather charming but juvenile egotism. The end of *Under Capricorn* returns to the patently fake waterfront set of the beginning. Its artificiality, like that of *Spellbound* and *Marnie*, is consistently intensified at its critical moments.

Even the internal artifice and deceptions of these films sometimes uncover, despite themselves, essential reality. Marnie's lies contain a measure of truth. The tale she tells Mark about her childhood with "Mrs. Taylor" in California thinly displaces numerous details of her actual situation. Constance and John become the newlyweds they pretended to be earlier. And Charles achieves in the conclusion of *Under Capricorn* the role of a truly disinterested friend to Hattie. Such transformations of lies into truth occur only with sympathetic characters, however, and then somewhat unusually. Internal representations of fiction-making, lies, and empty social rituals are more often associated with falsehood.

The linking of truth with art and artifice in *Spellbound, Under Capricorn*, and *Marnie*, and their implausibility as realistic documents, affirms rather than weakens their claim to significance. Most indigestible to the "plausibilists," and most important for the films themselves, the abrupt and astounding "cures" of central figures insist upon the centrality of the miraculous. With only a few days of psychological poking about to prepare him, John is hauled up a mountainside by Constance and skis down to discover in a flash of memory who he is, why he is so vulnerable to self-accusation, and what actually happened on the day of Dr. Edwardes's death. The exposure of Millie, and Charles's enlistment on the side of the good and true, clear away all the accumulated anguish, confusion, and rage that years of imprisonment and mutual alienation have created in the marriage of Hattie and Sam. And Marnie, on one busy day, loses control of herself at a fox hunt, must destroy her beloved horse Forio, reverts to her identity as a thief, recaptures her lost past, and bids fair to live happily ever after. It is not hard to see why complaints about unbelievability have attached themselves to all these works. They are, from the outlook of everyday experience, implausible. But as I have argued, astonishment itself certifies a kind of human significance.

Even from a realistic perspective, however, these films accommodate considerable defense. Rapidity of sequence—compression, in another word—is a form of metonomy, the representation of the whole by the part in time rather than in space. The abruptness of the cures of John, Hattie and Sam, and Marnie are not necessarily serious claims that psychoanalytic processes can be accomplished in a few weeks.

The cures themselves, moreover, are complicated in various ways. The first miraculously neat solution of *Spellbound* has hardly taken place before it is reversed. Constance and John are warming up after their galvanic skiing (the next day, presumably, but the cutting makes the events feel immediately sequential), when the detectives who have been pursuing them enter, announce that a bullet has been found in the back of Dr. Edwardes's corpse, and arrest John. What seemed too good to be true is shown to be too good, indeed, to be true. The romantic fantasy hits a realistic bump and flies off the rails of wish fulfillment onto a track where things do not happen as we would like them to but as they are likely to. This irony is itself ironized back to romance, but the emotional satisfaction of the final happy ending is irrevocably complicated by our memory that the first happy ending was canceled.

If Hitchcock's inclusion of what are in effect three alternative endings for *Spellbound* does not finally make the film more realistic, it does make our apprehension of it more complex. Hitchcock invokes and acknowledges the power of the realistic mode that first appears to overthrow romance and is in turn overthrown itself. In one way, this sequence of endings gives the final romantic conclusion extra force. In another, however, it includes the realistic mode and acknowledges its legitimacy. *Spellbound* refuses to vanquish finally the hardheaded perspective that has been represented throughout the movie by Constance's colleagues at Green Manor, the police, and, most sympathetically, Dr. Brulov.

One of Dr. Brulov's speeches, which occurs when he is consoling Constance in the interim between John's conviction and her discovery that Dr. Murchison is the true murderer, presents a moving and eloquent consolation for those who must give up the dream of loving and living happily ever after. "It is very sad to love and lose somebody. But in a while you will forget, and you will take up the threads of your life where you left off not so long ago. And you will work hard. There is lots of happiness in working hard, maybe the most." The lonely Dr. Brulov is probably speaking for himself as much as he is comforting Constance. *Spellbound* will soon reassert its triumphant romanticism, but the inclusion of this speech broadens the film's depth and humanity.

Like that of *Spellbound*, the ending of *Under Capricorn* elicits mixed emotions. Most viewers' affection for Charles will erode as they witness the increasingly destructive direction he takes in "helping" Hattie. When he acknowledges the priority of the love of Hattie and Sam for each other, and suppresses the claims of his own feelings, he regains our full sympathy. His self-imposed exile back to Ireland is both noble and melancholy. "Don't forget me," says Hattie, still innocent of the depth of Charles' passion for her. "I won't ever forget you," he replies. As he leaves he tells Winter that Australia, big and full of opportunity as it may be, is "not quite big enough."

We glory in the achievement of long delayed happiness for Sam and Hattie and in the selfless gesture that makes it possible; but we must feel some sadness for Charles, now the odd man out. He plays a role, at the end, rather like Dr. Brulov's. He reminds us that fate does not grant everyone a clinching of love and a tranquil future. Some must carry on without such final consolations. The poignancy of his departure is increased by the fact that his last words are spoken to Winter, who has himself been exiled to Australia because he "got a girl into trouble." For Charles, as for the aptly named Winter, the possible spring of love lies in an uncertain future.

The complication of tone at the end of *Marnie* comes not from the lingering unhappiness of a figure like Dr. Brulov or Charles Adair, but from its acknowledgment of the profundity of its heroine's injuries and the difficulties that still lie ahead. As Wood has pointed out, "Nor are we given grounds for believing Marnie 'cured' at the end of the film: a start has been made, but the hopefulness of the last shots is offset by the reminder, through the mother, of the difficulty of outgrowing habitual attitudes."[4] Though the storm has lifted for the moment, and Marnie's recent tears have dried, the children still chant "Mother, Mother, I am ill." If Marnie's growing acceptance of Mark shows that she has come a long way toward emotional recovery, it hardly counts as a full fairy-tale declaration of love when she tells her husband that she would rather stay with him than go to jail. But it does, at the least, signify trust. As for Sophie the jaguarundi, learning to trust anyone is a great accomplishment for Marnie.

The ends of these three films, then, are not simple explosions of roses and violins. But for all that one can mount some defense of them in terms of realistic complications, they remain wondrous. They all portray, with self-conscious stylization, therapeutic miracles of extraordinary clarity and suddenness. The healing love of Constance in *Spellbound* and of Mark in *Marnie*, and of Hattie, Sam, and Charles in *Under Capricorn*, makes possible the wonderful solutions of terrible difficulties. The transforming power of love in these films confirms them as variants of Hitchcock's comic romances. As much as *Young and Innocent* or *The Lady Vanishes*, they redeem dangerous or evil days through the grace of women and men in love.

Spellbound, although it has the most pervasive psychoanalytical framework of the three films, features a protagonist whose emotional disturbance is presented as being relatively superficial. The cure of John Ballantine's amnesia may best be regarded as the MacGuffin of what Rohmer and Chabrol called "a great film about love."[5] The true healing in this film consists of correcting in John and Constance their unmarried state. The dialogue in the lodge, just before John's arrest,

---

[4] Wood, *Hitchcock's Films*, p. 154.
[5] Rohmer and Chabrol, *Hitchcock*, p. 81.

recapitulates the concerns of the movie in ascending order of importance:

> JOHN: How does it feel to be a great analyst?
> CONSTANCE: Not so bad.
> J: And a great detective?
> C: Wonderful.
> J: And madly adored?
> C: Very wonderful!

As usual, we should regard the MacGuffin as something more than an inconsequential excuse for the real concerns of the film. The cure of John's memory loss and the insight of Constance into his illness and innocence make up an important part of the central action of the quest for love and identity. In their mutual self-discovery, Constance and John at once remember and learn who they are. The MacGuffin provides the urgency the film requires, but it does not provide, nor does *Spellbound* have, the deep anguish of acute illness. (This is not to maintain that amnesia is a trivial complaint in real life, only that its medical seriousness is minimized in *Spellbound*.) John and Constance need to be married. And to each other. What is wrong with them may be superficial in the framework of abnormal psychology; but it is profound, and, from the romantic point of view on which Hitchcock built most of his films, no more wrong than right. Their need for love signifies their health as much as their lacking it puts them at risk.

Early in *Spellbound*, the amorous Dr. Fleurot puts before us the idea that Constance is frigid, or at least hopelessly repressed. Her work, he tells Constance, is "brilliant but lifeless. There's no intuition in it. You approach all your problems with an ice pack on your head." Because he says such things while unsuccessfully trying to make love to her, however, we are not likely to take his analysis too seriously. We are, on the other hand, exposed to the suggestion that Constance has attained the age for leaving single young womanhood. Like Lina in *Suspicion* or Melanie in *The Birds*, it is time for her to leave the attachments and timidities of girlhood and to give her heart as a woman.

Dr. Murchison and Dr. Brulov supply the figures of parents ready to be outgrown. The former must be unmasked and rejected; the latter behaves as a good father, who will be reassigned to a different position in Constance's newly extended family. Brulov himself announces his eagerness to undertake his new role when he declares, somewhat incongruously, "any husband of Constance's is a husband of mine."

Constance's refusal at the beginning of the film to believe in love comes from youthful inexperience, not from a fatal absence of emotional capacity. When she declaims against poets' "filling peoples' heads with delusions about love," she expresses a perfectly conventional skepticism that narrative artists have routinely assigned to the heroes and heroines of love stories. In defying Eros and Aphrodite, Constance does not realize that she is asking for the amorous awakening she will shortly undergo; but the audience should. Her resistance to the idea of love both invites her fall and testifies to its force when it comes.

She is contrasted, not likened, to the man-hating, emotionally incoherent patient who at the beginning of the movie calls her "Miss Frozen Puss." The sexually diseased Miss Carmichael, seductively clinging to every male who comes near her, emits cold, dangerous flashes, like an electric eel. When Constance and John fall in love, their conjunction comes, as he says, like lightning.

In a reversal of apparent authority characteristic of Hitchcock, the unattractive, self-interested analysis of Dr. Fleurot turns out to be at least partly accurate. Constance's clinical exterior really does conceal "a sweet, pulsing, adorable woman underneath." But John Ballantine, not the idly flirting Fleurot, awakens Constance's responsive femininity. Chattering happily at Ballantine as they ride the train, a transformed Constance confesses, "I've always loved very feminine clothes, but never quite dared to wear them. But I'm going to after this. I'm going to wear exactly the things that please me, and you."

As the natural health of Constance's feelings contrasts with the neurotic teasing of Miss Carmichael, so the seriousness and spontaneity of John's love are set off by the triviality of Fleurot's willful passion. John, like Constance, has no amorous history of any consequence. Like his future spouse, he needs to discover himself in a love that comes unbidden. His amnesia resembles the burn he received in the war; it is painful but not terribly deep. Essentially innocent and healthy, he has been bruised by his unhappy childhood accident and by his unwitting involvement in the feud between Edwardes and Murchison.

As a character in his own right, he has only modest presence. Both Murchison and Brulov have as much personality and resonance as the mild-mannered figure who becomes Constance's lover. His amnesia and psychological collapse may account, to a degree, for his lack of personal heft and depth. Another explanation is aesthetic: *Spellbound* is Constance's film, more than it is the story of Constance and John equally. It presents a young person who discovers herself in recovering her lover; and her lover, for all that he must be decent, attractive, and in need of her aid, exists as her artistic appendage, not quite as her partner. The proportions between Constance and John in *Spellbound* resemble those between Barry Kane and Pat in *Saboteur*. Like Constance's John, Barry's Pat is an agreeable occasion for the main figure's affections but lacks a subtly or extensively drawn personality of her own.

The relatively selfless love between the protagonists is partly defined in *Spellbound*, as in most Hitchcockian romances, by contrast with the lecherous or egotistically self-interested affections of other characters. Dr. Fleurot's abrasive, jealous hankerings after Constance provide one such contrast. Dr. Murchison's willingness to sacrifice the happiness of his intellectual daughter to his own security represents another. Constance's devotion to Murchison is conspicuous, and he treats her with a paternal affection that hypocritically promises reciprocal admiration and solicitude.

The contrast between true love and its egotistical or purely libidinal counterfeit is sounded in a comic key as well. Two clownish passers-by lighten the texture of Constance's desperate trip to the Empire Hotel to find the fugitive "J. B." The first arrives in the harmlessly horny person of a drunken businessman from Pittsburgh who tries to pick her up in the lobby. The second is the self-congratulatory house detective who comes to her aid and whom she enlists to help her locate her patient and lover. The detective guesses that she is looking for her husband (in which he is not far wrong) and replies to Constance's feigned amazement at his perspicuity that he is "a kind of a psychologist. You know, you gotta be in my line." Beaming at her praise of his cleverness, he helps Constance to find her lost "husband" and answers her thanks with obtuse self-satisfaction: "I'm glad to be of service; I'm a married man myself and I know how it feels to have a wife come chasing after you to apologize." Later, after Constance and John have fled the hotel, the bellboy shows the detective a newspaper story that reveals who John and the heartsick little "wife" really are. The camera cuts to a close-up of the detective's face as the truth dawns and his complacency turns to angry, belated understanding. An oboe tootles.

The treatment of character in *Spellbound* is of a piece with Hitchcock's practice in his other romantic stories of selfless, curative love. Constance has a confidence in her eventual mate's innocence that only love can provide. She answers Dr. Brulov's impatient dismissal of her "women's talk" with an eloquence that speaks for most of Hitchcock's lovers as they try to convince a stolid world of the innocence that heart's intuition can know but eyes and logic cannot. "The mind isn't everything. The heart can see deeper sometimes. . . . I couldn't feel this way toward a man who was bad, who had committed murder. I couldn't feel this pain for someone who was evil."

"We both know," declares Dr. Brulov irritably, "that the mind of a woman in love is operating on the lowest level of the intellect." But as later events disclose, love discovers what Dr. Brulov's science cannot, and Constance's intuition triumphs. Psychoanalysis fits into the fairy-tale plot like any other system of miracle-denying logical deduction. Considered as part of the structure of *Spellbound*, the illness of John Ballantine has its primary significance not as a medical syndrome but as a story element similar to the curse of the evil sorcerer in *Sleeping Beauty*. It is an enchantment to be overcome by a heroic kiss.

In comparison with those of *Spellbound*, the central figures in *Under Capricorn* suffer more intensely and have been more deeply deformed by bygone catastrophes. Their past has a social as well as a personal dimension, and the wounds of guilt and old suffering are deeper and slower to heal. Besides their own misfortunes and mistakes, Hattie and Sam (and, as an unpropertied younger son, Charles) are burdened with the injuries inflicted by culturally transmitted snobbishness and injustice. They must overcome not only their personal pasts but the societal past that persists in the infant nation of New South Wales.

Under the pressure of grief and regret, Hattie's marriage to Sam has long been falling apart. The breach in their union comes about not because of mutual incompatibility, but because of their individually unhealed wounds. Hattie has lost her nerve, or thinks she has. Her years of suffering and her guilt over being the cause of Sam's imprisonment have left her vulnerable to Millie and to the drugs and alcohol that her virulent nurse dispenses. Her alienation from the warmth of friends and acquaintances increases her depression and weakness. "I had courage, long ago," she tells Charles, "but I lost it."

Recalling years of impoverished waiting for Sam, she reveals the toll of her degradation: "It is part of me. Even now I sometimes long to go down, down, down to where I can go no further, down to where nothing can hurt me anymore." Hattie cannot regain the confidence that allowed her to marry Sam in the first place, in defiance of class and family. Guilt overwhelms her. "He's [Sam] suffered terribly. I've done him many and many wrong. Wrong to love him. Wrong to marry him. No children. A burden when he was trying to save his soul in this new country. Why should he not hate me?"

Similar guilt has rendered Sam powerless to express his love. His very strengths—pride, fortitude, uncomplaining independence—leave him at the mercy of his pain and seal him away from his wife. Even the energy and shrewdness that account for his material prosperity seem ultimately to throw up barriers between him and any sympathy. The luxury that he provides Hattie only increases her guilt. He remains overwhelmed by the past: his wife's superior social class, the poverty and suffering that her marriage to him caused her, the refusal of "polite society" to readmit either of them. Like Hattie, Sam takes the guilt for his spouse's suffering upon himself: "I meant to make it up to her, you see, for all she'd been through. But it didn't work out that way. We weren't the same people after all those years . . . I had my work, of course, but she had nothing." An extraordinarily attractive man delivers this speech, a man of humility, toughness, and devotion to his wife. But the very virtues that make him so attractive have been turned around by his sufferings, and his wife's, to force a separation between them. He is too good to forgive himself, too generous to allow his wife to pay off the debt of guilt that she feels toward him.

Another of his virtues, his personal honesty, leaves him susceptible to Millie's schemes to ignite his jealousy. Without deviousness himself, he does not suspect it in Millie. She chaffs his most tender scar, his socially inferior origins, when she urges him to let his wife return to Ireland without him. "Once her ladyship's gone, you'll be able to get some peace. . . . You'll be done for if you go. You're somebody here, you'll be nobody there." And then, as dangerously as possible, "She'll have her friends. They won't do anything to an Earl's daughter. Leave it to her lords and ladies . . . Mr. Adair . . . she'll be alright."

But for all of Millie's adroit reopening of his lacerations, Sam will not turn against his wife. His love is stronger to preserve his marriage than the forces of past and present to bring about its dissolution. The excesses of guilt and self-sacrifice that have kept two decent people from accepting each other's help are at last dissipated. In part, the renewal of their marriage results from the exposure of Millie and the liberating testimony of Charles. Equally, however, it comes about as a result of Hattie's public confession that she, not Sam, killed her brother, and from Sam's realization that the cycle of mutual self-sacrifice must be stopped. He will not corroborate her confession. "No!" he declares, "sacrifice, sacrifice, all along we've sacrificed ourselves for each other. There must be an end to it. The law said a killing was done; the law said a killing was paid for. Why must they go on and on and on at it?"

The idea of too much selflessness in love is an unusual one for Hitchcock, who customarily contrasts the other-directedness of true love with the egotism and possessiveness of love's demonic mirror image. In *Under Capricorn*, in fact, the mutual devotion of Sam and Hattie is set against the selfish, possessive desires of Millie and, when he is at his worst, Charles. Both Millie and Charles (again, less egregiously) betray what is for Hitchcock the most sacred of human trusts, the comforting

and embracing of those who are in need. Both are antinurses, carrying
death and despair where they promise to heal and bring hope. They
are driven to do so by the grasping passion that desires to control and
possess.

Yet Millie and Charles are not subjected to untempered criticism.
Their viciousness is shown to arise from misfortunes not far different
from those that afflict Hattie and Sam. But unlike Hattie and Sam they
have not the love, and Millie lacks the strength of character, to maintain their goodness and their moral health. In curious and complicated
ways, Millie and Charles form a sort of parallel couple to Hattie and
Sam. They contrast with the central pair, but they also resemble them.
They too are victims of an arbitrary, unfair social hierarchy; they too
carry in their hearts loves they cannot fully express. Charles describes
himself as "the youngest son of an Irish Peer, into a very bad bargain."
Millie is condemned, a bit like Sam, to love someone out of her sphere.
She complains to Sam, with a bitterness for which we must have some
sympathy, "Oh no! *Mr.* Flusky, I'm not good enough for you; I know
that. I'm only good enough to work for you, and slave for you, and
look after your, your drunken. . . ."

But our sympathy is limited by the recognition not only of Millie's
murderousness but of her emotional corruption. "What kind of love,"
Hattie asks, "drives you to make such horrible things, to do such? I
don't understand that kind of love. [to Sam] When you and I speak of
love, we, we don't mean the same thing." Earlier in the film, as Charles
is telling Hattie that she must "beat back the shadows and be queen
again in your own kingdom," Millie passes. "Brrrr!" he exclaims, "I
felt as though somebody walked over my grave." Charles's insight has
penetrated the essence of Millie's identity. She is a spirit of death. The
"medicine" she provides Hattie stupefies and addicts her. Her loving
kindness is lethal. She rules the servants with brutality, beating them
continually. (When Hattie takes over the house after Millie's departure, her first act is to go to the kitchen and burn Millie's whip.)

In contrast with Sam's honest piety, Millie's self-righteousness
serves her own ends, as she strives to put asunder the marriage bonds
between Sam and Hattie. After Millie returns to Minyaga Ugilla following the shooting of Charles, she readdicts Hattie to the witch's
brew of opiates and alcohol. Finding Sam seated in front of the fireplace one evening, she insinuates herself into the chair facing his, Hattie's. (The symbolism of the pair of connubial chairs goes back in
Hitchcock's movies at least as far as *The Farmer's Wife.*) Millie's usur-
pation of Hattie's place functions symbolically like her appropriation
of the household keys—another Hitchcockian symbol of domestic rule

and order. Certain that Sam's wife is about to return to Ireland and leave her in control of the house and its master, Millie complacently remarks, "The Lord works in a mysterious way, His wonders to perform. It'll all turn out for the best. Once Her Ladyship's gone you'll be able to get some peace."

Millie, of course, is providing the Lord considerable assistance in performing "His wonders." She parodies the marriage vow by telling Sam that if he stays behind when his wife leaves, she (Millie) will "work to the death" for him. Later, exposed as the murderess she would be, Millie reinvokes her demonic piety. "I know the Lord's way when I see it." "Millie," asks Hattie, "I don't understand. Are you in love with him?" "Don't dare to say that," responds Millie. "The Lord will never forgive you for saying that." And finally to Sam, "The Doctors said it would come to this in the end. The Lord's punished her!"

The connection between true love and grace—and between false love and damnation, a strong undercurrent throughout Hitchcock's work—rarely surfaces more clearly. At the end of the scene in which she is exposed and thwarted, Millie rushes down the stairs and disappears into the darkness—a specter from the underworld fleeing back to hell. The enemies of love and the enemies of grace are coextensive.

Hitchcock emphasized connections among personal enmity, class hatred, and self-serving piety in *The Manxman, Easy Virtue, The Skin Game, Rebecca*, and *The Paradine Case*. In these films, something like Original Sin is expressed by a corrupt and unjust class system and is accepted and exploited by the antagonists of the film, who are themselves its victims but who aspire to become its privileged guardians. Such is the case in *Under Capricorn*. Millie, an unregarded servant in love with her master, is another victim of social bigotry. Her merciless righteousness internalizes the prejudice that excludes her from polite society. By adopting such values, she finally excludes herself from the possibility of forgiveness and self-acceptance.

Unlike Millie, Charles in the end manages to resist the devil's offer to exchange his soul for the hope of forbidden love. The severity of his temptation is measured by the distance he falls toward succumbing to it. But at the last moment, Charles becomes a true lover of Hattie. He simultaneously restores her marriage and cures himself.

Hitchcock choreographed with eloquence and subtlety the critical episode in which Charles finally puts his selfish desires behind him. Hattie is pleading, in vain, with Sir Richard to release her husband, who has been arrested because of the shooting of Adair. Without knocking, Charles himself enters the room and crosses toward Hattie. As he approaches her, the camera dollies slightly toward the right until he stands facing her in profile. In the background, playing a crucial if silent part, is a portrait of a man, its head slightly above the faces of Charles and Hattie, and its gaze directed at Charles. This portrait, I think, stands in for the imprisoned Sam during the exchange between Hattie and Charles that follows.

The camera holds its position for most of their conversation, in the course of which Charles realizes what his love for Hattie requires of him. Between Hattie and Charles is the image of the portrait, separating them, turned with Hattie in appeal to the man who can restore her husband to her. As she tells him why she has come, Hattie moves closer to Charles. The camera dollies in so that the three figures—Hattie, Charles, and the painting between them—are not only on the same visual line but in the same pose, in profile from the chest up. "You've helped me," says Hattie. "More than anybody knows. Help me now. Tell them that they must set Sam free. Tell them what happened. They must set him free! Give him back to me, Charles."

As he understands that he has the power either to restore Sam to Hattie or to put him out of the way forever, Charles turns slightly and gazes into the distance. His movement brings his face into three-quarter profile, the precise angle of the portrait in the background, but facing the opposite way. When Sir Richard asks for his nephew's account of the shooting, the camera turns toward Charles until Lady Hattie disappears from the screen. At the same time, it dollies in so that the portrait in the background goes out of focus. The moment of truth, this shot suggests, is for Charles to face alone. Though Sam's freedom and Hattie's happiness depend upon his declaration, the highest stakes are for Charles himself. He must either honor the integrity of his love and his own soul, or abandon himself to the lies of possessive egotism.

As he recounts the events that led up to his shooting, Charles walks toward Sir Richard and the Crown Prosecutor. The camera pans and dollies after him until a new triad is established: Sir Richard and a bit of States Attorney Corrigan make a composite figure of authority on the left of the screen; Charles Adair stands in the middle; and Hattie sits on the right. Where the portrait intervened visually between Charles and Hattie earlier, Charles now stands between Hattie and the societal forces that are on the brink of ruining her and Sam. After a few moments of suspense, Charles speaks the words that will set Sam free and doom forever his own hopes of winning Hattie for himself. In a question rich with meaning beyond the speaker's comprehension, Sir Richard asks his nephew, "On your word of honor, as a gentleman, is that all that happened that night?" The unintended ironies do not escape Charles. He smiles, "As a gentleman." Hattie takes his hand and kisses it gratefully.

The camera dollies in to Charles and Lady Hattie, who has risen, still holding his hand. They look into each other's eyes with nothing, now, between them. When Hattie releases Charles's hand and moves toward the door, the camera pans so that the portrait enters the picture when Charles leaves it. As the understanding between Hattie and Charles is now clear, so can it be clear again between Hattie and Sam.

On a low chest beneath the portrait rests a small statue of a mounted knight slaying a dragon. The gallant knight Charles has come to the rescue; the gentleman of honor has made those words refer to something other than a rigid system of snobbishness that casts out such worthy people as Hattie and her husband. In setting Sam free of the false accusation, Charles restores some luster to the idea of gentility. Most important, he releases himself from the demonic possession that threatened to make him Millie's masculine counterpart.

Charles's dilemma gives the present an equal claim with the past in creating suspense in *Under Capricorn*. *Marnie* gives centrality to old psychological scars. Although Mark's upper-class sister-in-law Lil (Diane Baker) combines many of the features of Millie and Charles, she does not finally have their importance. More simply than *Spellbound* or *Under Capricorn*, *Marnie* turns on the uncovering and detoxifying of the past.

As its title promises, the central character of *Marnie* constitutes its subject; the recovery of her past is the object of its action. A rich and sympathetic figure, Mark, takes on himself the role of chief investigator and interpreter of Marnie's lost childhood. As a result, his point of view often predominates. The depth of his character, however, does not mean that he shares center stage with Marnie, for his importance comes chiefly from his relation to the heroine.

In profound ignorance of her past, Marnie has no real identity and consequently no future other than meaningless movement through time. She needs to find herself and a spouse, a way of being and a reason to be. The opening sequences establish the fluidity of her physical appearance and her lack of attachment to places, which, with the exception of the inn near Garrett's Stable, seem equally indifferent to her. Other than her mother and her horse, no one figures emotionally in her sterile life. Her relation to her mother, moreover, appears haunted and constrained. It is characterized by an infantile anxiety on Marnie's side that is pathetic and incongruous in an otherwise mature, sophisticated, and self-confident young woman. No core supports the manikin-like surface of her manufactured identity. Herself unknown to herself, she cannot respond to other people except to deceive and rob them for motives that she does not understand.

The offspring of her mother's juvenile prostitution, Marnie constructs a finishing school persona that contrasts radically with the poor uneducated woman who reared her. Despite her artificiality, however, she genuinely transcends her origins and reveals traces of an affectionate woman behind her glacial exterior. An exceptionally fine person, at least potentially, lies concealed beneath the camouflage of her illness. Though she is no Robin Hood, her crimes do not seem entirely self-serving. We learn at the end of the film, in fact, that their chief object has been to buy the love of her mother. Marnie is ill, but she is neither vicious nor personally deficient.

Fortunately for Marnie, Mark both loves her and sees through her elegant disguises. On their first outing together at the race track he asks if she had "a tough childhood." She denies it, but he answers his own question more accurately: "I think you did. I think you've had a hard, tough climb. But you're a smart girl, aren't you? The careful grammar, the quiet good manners—where did you learn them?"

In Hitchcock's other romances of false accusation, the role played by Mark tends to go to the feminine lead. Mark's love, his intuition of Marnie's essential innocence, and his discovery and making public of the way in which she has been injured replicates in most essentials the roles of characters like Erica in *Young and Innocent* and Constance in *Spellbound*. Mark protects Marnie and restores her wholeness. Perhaps more than coincidentally, his name recalls the Gospel that gives particular emphasis to the healing powers of Christ. He embodies forgiveness. "Will I go to jail?" Marnie asks him at the end of the sequence in her mother's flat. "No, not after they hear what I have to tell them," he assures her—and the audience as well.

Just before Mark gives Marnie this assurance, Hitchcock assigns Sean Connery a gesture that expresses his character's relation to Marnie by contrasting it with her mother's. Early in the film, Marnie reveals herself to be jealous of her mother's affection for "little Jessie," the neighbor girl whom Mrs. Edgar takes care of during the day, and who looks conspicuously like a juvenile version of Marnie herself. At one point, the girl brings a hairbrush to Mrs. Edgar. Marnie has seated herself on the floor by her mother, affectionately resting her head on her lap. "Marnie, mind my leg," her mother says when she sees Jessie waiting. Mortified by Jessie's gloating smile of victory, Marnie moves away to a chair. Mrs. Edgar lovingly attends to the child and muses, "When Marnie was a little girl, I didn't have time to brush her hair."

After Marnie's recovery of her memory of the murder and Mrs. Ed-

gar's further revelations, Marnie has again seated herself on the floor
with her head in her mother's lap. Mrs. Edgar looks down at her
daughter's hair and tries to touch it, but she is unable to bring herself
to do so. "Get up, Marnie, you're aching my leg," she says. Again Marnie retreats. This time, however, Mark gently straightens and smooths
her hair. "Now," he murmurs, "that's better." His expressive gesture
summarizes a characteristically Hitchcockian aspect of the conclusion
of *Marnie*. Like many of Hitchcock's protagonists, Marnie finally
leaves a parent who is no longer adequate (in Mrs. Edgar's case, never
was) and turns to a partner with whom she can find adult love and
make a home of her own.[6]

Marnie's heroine and her rescuer are both pointedly alike and
sharply different. In certain details, Mark's past and present resemble
those of the woman with whom he falls in love. He has a father but no
mother. She has a mother but has never known a father. He has lost
his wife; she pretends to be a recent widow. More important, her life
has been deeply touched and shaped by death. Her childhood continues to constrain her adult life, as Mark's does his. "What about your
tough childhood, Mr. Rutland?" she asks him. "The old, sad story,"
he replies with self-mockery, "promising youth blighted, dragged
down by money, position, *noblesse oblige.*"

Despite his refusal to take his comfortable misfortune seriously, he
has suffered from the sins of his father, who neglected the family company until it was "about to go down for the count." As a result, he had
to abandon his career as a biologist and spend his time among business
and society people for whom he obviously cares little. His condition is
far from being as desperate as Marnie's, but Mark lives a rather lonely
and isolated life. He shares Marnie's antipathy for the self-satisfied
world of conspicuous consumption in which he is stuck by birth and
from which she, by the same cause, has been excluded.

His misfortunes, however, have not crippled him as Marnie's have
her. His acceptance of his wife's death is grave and straightforward.
Mark's first name may carry overtones of healing; his second, "Rutland," suggests what he calls "wholesome animal lust." In love with
Marnie, he cheerfully admits that he is a "sexual blackmailer" with an
ardent desire to take her to bed. His attraction to Marnie makes up
part of his love; her inability to love him is associated with her dread
of any physical contact, with her nauseated horror of "disgusting, animal" sex.

When Marnie reveals (on their honeymoon night) that she "can't

[6] Wood, in *Hitchcock's Films*, p. 161, makes a similar point.

bear to be handled," Mark, as usual, comes right to the heart of the matter: "Why? What happened to you?" We do not know yet what happened to Marnie, nor does Mark, nor does she (consciously), but what happened to her was her childhood—not only the murder but terror of the sex that came into her home to disturb her nights as her prostitute mother entertained clients.

Mark's love, aided by his training as a behavioral biologist, will eventually bring to light Marnie's crippling secrets. He is a zoologist, but instead of studying places of confinement, "zoos" (as Marnie supposes in making one of the few blunders that reveal her imperfect education), he trains animals to trust him. His love for Marnie works to the same effect. He does not imprison her; he teaches her to have confidence in him and to understand herself, and in doing so he sets her free from the cages of her past.

Hitchcock sets against Mark's liberating love, as usual, the lust, envy, and possessiveness of a group of antagonists who attempt to keep Marnie in her psychological jail. Among them is Strutt, the bantam accountant whom Marnie has just robbed as the movie opens. This initial episode strongly hints at connections among Marnie's criminality, her striking beauty, and her sexuality. "A pretty girl without references," she has played on Strutt's attraction to her to gain access to the office and, eventually, its safe. "The little witch!" Strutt ejaculates to Mark, "I'll have her put away for twenty years. I knew she was too good to be true." He will have an opportunity to make good on his threat later in the film, when Lil maliciously invites him to the reception at the Rutland home the night before the fox hunt. There he again shows the real motives for his rage. It is not money but masculine pride that impels him to pursue his revenge. As his comically apt name indicates, Strutt combines lechery and egotistical self-importance. At the same time, he is mean-spirited and priggish. He embodies, in his fantasies at least, the nastiness that Marnie mistakenly supposes a part of the character of Mark and all other men, whom she dismisses as "filthy pigs."

Marnie's more formidable enemies profess affection for her and in their distorted ways even feel it. They are also, significantly, women. Her deadliest foes are not the men whom she fears and despises, but the women who would keep her away from men generally, or from Mark in particular. Lil Mainwaring (another suggestive name), Mark's sister-in-law, has been living in the house of her late sister's husband and patiently waiting to inherit the man himself. Though she admires Mark and probably loves him, her affection comes with the desire for self-gratification that characterizes all Hitchcock's bad lovers. Dark-haired and fair-skinned, Lil has close generic ties to such terrible women as Mrs. Danvers in *Rebecca*, the priestess in the first *The Man Who Knew Too Much*, Millie in *Under Capricorn*, and Mrs. Paradine in *The Paradine Case*. Slightly more distant branches of her family tree are occupied by the stepmothers of Snow White, Cinderella, and Hansel and Gretel. Lil will not gain the sympathy of many viewers, yet there remains some real pathos in her sorrow at losing her brother-in-law. When Mark observes that she has reached the age for marrying, she ruefully admits, "I was waiting for you."

The most formidable, fond, pathetic, and smothering of those who oppress Marnie in the name of love is her mother. As Millie does, Mrs. Edgar convinces herself that God's will and her own desires are congruent. "I thought when she lost her memory of that night it was a sign of God's forgiveness. I thought I'd been given another chance, to change everything, to make it all up to her." Such "forgiveness," however, sets neither Marnie nor her mother free from their past crime. Marnie remains trapped by the hole in her conscious memory; her mother, for her part, cannot forgive or forget. Along with her affection, she hates her daughter, in part perhaps as a result of the murder charge she faced on her behalf. During her first visit to her mother's apartment, Marnie asks tensely, "Why don't you love me, Mama? . . . What's wrong with me?" Mrs. Edgar will not tell Marnie what's wrong with her, as much to preserve the pious fiction of her own life as to spare her daughter. Such love is diluted in considerable measure by neurotic self-deception, and that dilution poisons Marnie.

Mrs. Edgar's mother love is also compromised by a possessiveness that becomes explicit in the last sequence. Hitchcock presents Bernice Edgar with compassion, but he does not conceal her desire to own and control. Marnie is conceived when her mother barters her virginity for "Billy's basketball sweater." "I still got that old sweater. An' I got you, Marnie. An', after the accident, they tried to make me let you be adopted, but I wouldn't. I wanted you. An' I promised God right then, if he'd let me keep you, an' an' you not remember, I'd bring you up different from me—decent."

The tears streaming down Mrs. Edgar's face confirm Marnie's realization that "you must've loved me, Mama." But Mrs. Edgar's love, both in its origins and in its continuation after the "accident," is compounded too much of falsehood and covetousness to reassure or nourish her daughter. Bernice Edgar's confession strongly suggests that she was victimized by her own impoverished and loveless childhood. Marnie's mother, however, had no Mark to fall in love with her and make possible the forgiving of old debts. She suffers, and passes on to her daughter, the disease of life without love. She also passes to Marnie its symptoms, attempts to fill emptiness and lack of self-esteem with possessions and a self-justifying consciousness of being "decent." Only at the end of the movie do we understand just how great an absence is described by Bernice's answer to Jessie's question, "Didn't you all have a daddy either?" "No, we didn't," she replies emphatically. "We surely did not."

In *Under Capricorn* and *Marnie*, distortions of love in the past have transmitted their woes to the present. In *Spellbound*, past events weaken Ballantine and make him vulnerable to the disturbed Dr. Murchison. In all three, redemption comes from love, as amazing and providential as the grace of which, in most of Hitchcock's movies, it is the earthly counterpart.

Notorious (1946), a film made around the same time as *Spellbound* and *Under Capricorn*, shares with them a central theme of love redeeming the ongoing waste and evil of the past. We are not given any details, but Dev (Cary Grant) has evidently been hurt badly by a woman at some former time. As a result, for most of the film he can neither offer nor accept the love that would save and cure Alicia (Ingrid Bergman) and himself. Only at the very end, when he comes to carry her out of the den of Nazi dragons in which she is being slowly poisoned to death, can he acknowledge both his love for Alicia and his fear of love. "I couldn't see straight or think straight. I was a fatheaded guy, full of pain. It tore me up, not having you."

The sickness inflicted on Alicia by her past—her discovery that her father was a German spy, her despairing slide into sensuality and alcohol, the public disgrace of her father's trial—requires the medicine of love. Until Dev can come to terms with his love for her, she is forced to accept the poisonous, possessive lust offered by Alex Sebastian. Alicia may be the strongest and most affecting of all Hitchcock's heroines. Desperately ill and misunderstood herself, she faces dreadful enemies and public disgrace without help or understanding. Her lover is himself too crippled to act on his love or to trust his knowledge of her essential innocence. Only when Alicia's unfailing truth and strength bring Dev to "see straight or think straight" can he return to carry her away, have the poison flushed out of her, and live with her at long last.

In *Notorious*, as in *Spellbound, Under Capricorn*, and *Marnie*, the past afflicts the present. Although bygone catastrophes play unusually large roles, these films fundamentally repeat the narrative structures and dominant imagery of Hitchcockian romance. All lead to the achievement of identity and an establishing or recovering of innocence. Their cure for the loss of self and station also repeats the romantic

pattern around which Hitchcock organized the majority of his films:
on a metaphorical white horse, true love—armed, generous, and confident—rides to the rescue.

In accord with their romantic structures, the three films of this chapter associate the diseased past with demonic imagery and downward
movements. Descents to the underworld reappear emphatically. In
these movies, however, they take the form of returns to and confrontations with the past. What Rohmer and Chabrol say about *Spellbound* applies equally to *Under Capricorn* and *Marnie*; all pivot
around "a theme dear to Hitchcock and which might be formulated as
follows: 'It is necessary to descend twice, to follow the path a second
time.' "[7]

Descents and the high camera angles that visually force characters
down are associated in *Spellbound* with threats of disaster, memories
of past catastrophes, and dangerous developments in the plot. Ballantine, posing as Dr. Edwardes, collapses at Green Manors in a subterranean operating room among a crowd of ghostly, white-gowned figures. The incident that left him with his crippling guilt, his inadvertent
killing of his brother, occurs at the end of a slide down a stone banister.
His psychological impairment is evidently reactivated when he is
forced to bail out of a burning airplane. Just before he is arrested and
sent to jail, when he is celebrating what he thinks to be the recovery of
both his identity and his innocence, he is photographed from high camera placements that foreshadow the reversal that occurs when the detectives enter. Fleeing the police earlier, he and Constance appear far
below the camera in Grand Central Station, then scurry downstairs to
the train. The recovery of the repressed memory that has been haunting Ballantine comes when he is able to stop his descent as he and
Constance hurtle toward a precipice.

Similar imagery generates similar suggestions in *Under Capricorn*.
The name of Flusky's mansion, "Why Weepest Thou," labels it as a
storehouse of past sorrows; and the actions and images that we see
inside confirm its connection to an underworld. The smoky kitchen,
with its whip, fire, and screeching women, appears like an outpost of
hell. We initially see Hattie, the camera moving slowly up from her
bare feet, as she descends the stairs to a dinner party at which only
men occupy the table—their wives unwilling to come to a place so disreputable. The shrunken head with which Millie has been terrifying
her distraught mistress looks like an apparition from the land of the
living dead.

[7] Rohmer and Chabrol, *Hitchcock*, p. 82.

When she tells Charles the story of her elopement with Sam, Hattie summarizes her years of penury and despair while waiting for her husband to come out of jail. Her narrative evokes a descent into an underworld. Like Persephone, she has partly incorporated her degradation into her very being, and as a result she can never fully escape: "All that hot misery, it became me . . . it is part of me." Recalling his wife before her decline, on the other hand, Sam describes her as "a holy blessed angel" and tells Charles how she would ride "at a fence like it had the Kingdom of Heaven on the other side." Sam's quotation from the Bible about the "great gulf" that has separated him from Hattie invokes a context that refers specifically to the distance between heaven and hell. The title of the movie itself, finally, insists upon the imagery of descent. *Under Capricorn* takes place on the other side of the globe, beneath the civilized world, in a land to which are shipped, as the opening narration has it, "prisoners, many of them unjustly convicted."

The imagery of descent in *Marnie* similarly suggests a lowered, harrowing level of existence. After her robbery of Rutland & Co., Marnie sneaks down the stairs of the office as she makes her escape. Riding Forio in the next sequence, she looks down at the furious figure of Mark who, like an avenging spirit, has somehow followed her to Garrett's. He makes her dismount from her horse and walk back to the stable, consigning her for much of the rest of the film to an existence both spatially and psychologically depressed. Water, frequently a symbol of dissolution in Hitchcock's movies, combines with descent and high camera placements when Marnie tries to kill herself in the swimming pool of the honeymoon ship.

The most catastrophic of her falls occurs at the conclusion of the fox hunt when she must shoot Forio, who breaks his leg when he fails to clear a high stone wall. At the beginning of the sequence, Marnie gallops away in horror from the fox hunt where the hounds are tearing their prey to pieces and the hunters are chatting and laughing in red jackets. Again she is stricken by her mysterious red suffusion. When Forio falls, fragmentary, rapidly cut close-ups recall the demonic imagery of plunging horses on the merry-go-round at the conclusion of *Strangers on a Train*. The broken leg of the horse, and Marnie's desire to put Forio out of his misery as quickly as possible, anticipates the revelation of how Bernice Edgar's leg was broken, and how the child Marnie killed the sailor who had fallen on her mother. After she has killed Forio, an overhead shot shows the shattered Marnie crossing the front hall of the Rutland mansion on her way to get the combination to the company safe as she reverts to her identity as a thief. Camera angles remain radical—high, low, slanted—while she leaves the house

and arrives at the office. There the expressionistic cinematography culminates in an exaggerated, subjective zoom-in zoom-out when Marnie
is unable to bring herself to remove the money.

Another very high shot introduces the arrival of Mark and Marnie
at her mother's flat. Marnie rushes across the entry hall and half collapses at the bottom of the stairs. Only after having relived the horrors
of long ago can she arise from her illness and support herself—as she
said in ironic mockery earlier—on her "poor, paralyzed little legs."

Opposed to the downward forces of destruction and disintegration
are movements up toward love, truth, and release. *Spellbound* and *Under Capricorn*, movies in which the troubles of the central figures are
unambiguously solved, show persistent tendencies toward such elevated epiphanies. In *Marnie*, which ends less decisively, ascents more
often appear subdued and equivocal.

Throughout *Spellbound*, Constance and John go upward to discover
love and to unravel the secrets of the mysterious past that threatens to
keep them apart. They fall in love during their walk along a hilltop
road high above a pastoral landscape. As Constance stoops through a
barbed-wire fence, she stumbles and John helps her to her feet. A bit
of sentimental comedy follows, cluing us to what has happened emotionally. "Lunch, lunch. What'll you have? Ham or liverwurst?" asks
her enamored companion. "Liverwurst," Constance breathes lovingly,
as romantic violins in the background swell. That evening she will ascend the stairs to Dr. Edwardes's quarters and admit more conventionally and consciously, despite her earlier assertion that such things do
not happen, to having fallen in love. At this second moment of amorous epiphany, Hitchcock repeats the passionate comedy of the afternoon, with a symphony orchestra on the sound track and the exaggeratedly clichéd opening doors of the lovers' first kiss.

Constance will pursue her fleeing lover up to a hotel room in New
York. Later she takes him upstairs to another bedroom on their "honeymoon night" at Dr. Brulov's. Together she and John ascend the
mountain above "Angel Valley" to discover the cause of his amnesia.
Finally, we watch Constance again walk up the stairs from her room
in Green Manors to the chambers of the director, where she confronts
Dr. Murchison and elicits the confession that will set the wrongly convicted Ballantine free. The shots of her ascending nearly duplicate the
earlier ones when she went upstairs to confess her love. But her second
ascent, as it rescues Ballantine, drives Murchison to a suicide's hell.
Hitchcock emphasized the demonic overtones of Murchison's death in
the original release prints by inserting a flash of red into this black and

white movie at the moment that the real murderer pulls the trigger of the gun he has turned against himself.

The fluidity of camera movement in *Under Capricorn* emphasizes the unbroken connections between past and present for the central characters of that film. The vertical direction of camera movements also amplifies symbolic movement toward damnation or innocence. The camera follows Charles as he goes through Government House and mounts the stairs to defy his cousin's proscription against associating with Flusky. It follows him again as he scales the vines outside Hattie's window after she has locked herself despairingly in her room. (This ascent leads to love, but of a questionable sort. From the moment that he kisses Hattie in her bedroom, Charles begins to stray from his role as her healer to that of the amorous rival of her husband.)

Under Capricorn reaches its happy ending via a series of liberating incidents that occur in elevated settings. On the night when Millie's wickedness is finally exposed, Sam goes up to Hattie's bedroom twice. The first time follows his revelation that he plans to resign his wealth and influential station in New South Wales to return to Ireland with his wife. He tucks Hattie into bed and attempts to soothe her fears. He returns in response to her cries for help, after she has discovered that Millie is trying to murder her. A little later, he refuses to provide evidence to corroborate his wife's confession that she killed her brother. After he tells Hattie what he has done, he and his wife reach a loving understanding. "Nobody can hurt you. I'm safe with you now. We shall always be together," Hattie sobs. "Shhhh. Don't talk," Sam says reassuringly. "Tomorrow will look after itself." Arms about each other, they walk slowly up the stairs. Though the threat of arrest still shadows them, bygones have at last truly become bygones. For the first time in the movie the future can be trusted to "look after itself."

Because it marks the closing of the old wound that has separated Sam and Hattie for so long, their loving ascent constitutes the emotional climax of *Under Capricorn*. Though important actions remain, and take place in elevated settings, the sense of upward movement will be less emphatic. Hitchcock does not try to surpass the moment of connubial reunion. Although Hattie must go upstairs in Government House to plead for her husband's release, we do not see her ascend. While Charles is delivering his liberating explanation, however, the camera gazes through the windows overlooking the bay. For Charles, this is his moment of truth, and it is appropriate to emphasize the elevation of the setting from his point of view.

Leaving at the end of the film, Charles descends to the skiff that is waiting to take him to a homeward-bound ship. The camera follows him down to the water, then pans up to look at Sam and Hattie where they stand arm in arm on top of the sea wall. They have been restored to one another and exonerated in the eyes of the law, and their station high above the camera emphasizes that they have finally been released from the hell in which they dwelled since the ill-fated beginning of their marriage. At the end of the film, we know the answer to the question asked by the name of their house: "Why Weepest Thou." We know also that they need not weep any longer.

Ascending movements in *Marnie* occur less frequently than in *Spellbound* and *Under Capricorn*, and they are more equivocal. Marnie goes up the stairs to her bedroom in her mother's home, but there she suffers her old nightmare. The ascent to love in Mark's office when he kisses her for the first time involves also the destructive thunderstorm and her panic. Painful as they are, however, these heavily charged intrusions of bits of her unresolved past anticipate the eventual recovery of the whole horrible story and the prospect that in remembering it Marnie may be free of its constriction. The temporary reversals do not finally contradict the hopeful overtones of the movement upward that precedes them.

But living together will require continuing good luck and hard work. The last shot of the car driving away is elevated, so that the protagonists move in a visual plane beneath the camera. The explosive revelations of the day have made Marnie's cure and the clearing of her criminal charges strong possibilities, but neither she nor Mark has yet left the lower world, with its not entirely resolved past and its future hazards.

The frequent journeys associated with romantic quests and heroes appear in *Spellbound* as the pastoral stroll when Constance and John fall in love, their escapes to New York and Rochester, and their trip to Angel Valley. *Under Capricorn* begins with shots of disembarking prisoners and of the new Governor's arrival. It ends with Charles's departure for Ireland. In between, there is a good deal of movement from the city to Minyaga Yugilla and back. Thanks to Hitchcock's frequent use of an extremely mobile camera, even sequences in interior settings convey a strong sense of movement.[8]

Beginning with the shots on the train platform, *Marnie* depends

---

[8] Stanley Kubrick's *The Shining* provides a similar example of ordinary movement made to suggest a romantic quest through an underworld of past horrors. From its opening shots, the film is characterized by fluid camera work of the sort that Hitchcock pioneered in *Rope* and *Under Capricorn*. In the tracking shots of the boy on his low-slung tricycle, in particular, Kubrick attains an impression of great distances traversed to reach an eerie world beyond the reach of everyday experience and ordinary natural law.

heavily upon images of going and coming, flight and seeking. Marnie rids herself of her past identity in the rental locker of a bus or train terminal, takes a station wagon to the Red Fox Inn, goes to Garrett's to ride Forio, enters Philadelphia via a striking shot of two trains pulling into the yards side by side (suggestive, perhaps, of Marnie's double identity), takes a cab to Rutland's, is driven by Mark to the races, and is grilled about her past in the same car when he has caught her after she robs the company. They honeymoon on an ocean liner, and Mark's unsuccessful attempt to make connections on that trip is reflected by their early return, via airplane, to the Rutland mansion. The fox hunt and the subsequent drive to Baltimore lead to the climax of Marnie's unwilling quest for her past. The last shot of the film again emphasizes the theme of going somewhere, as Mark and Marnie drive toward the ship-filled harbor. The dominance of imagery of travel reminds us how closely *Marnie* approaches films like *The 39 Steps* and *North by Northwest* in its underlying concern for the discovery of truth and innocence.

Closely connected to the power of the past are two other central features of Hitchcockian romance: actions suggestive of death and resurrection, and connections among love, faith, and innocence. *Spellbound, Under Capricorn*, and *Marnie* pivot on loss and recovery, or descent and reascent; and all three have at their centers a return to the past that involves death or a partial loss of self. All end with a present made brighter, and a future made possible, by triumphant confrontation with the blocking forces of a haunting past.

Actions of self-loss and recovery in *Spellbound* center on Ballantine. His amnesia is brought upon him by a series of encounters with death. The accidental killing of his brother leads to an unstable repressed memory. His guilt lurks in his psyche as a structural flaw that only needs a triggering episode to bring his personality crashing down. After another confrontation with death, the shooting down of the plane in which he is flying, he witnesses the murder of Dr. Edwardes on the ski slopes. The foundations of his personality crack, and he literally loses himself in guilt. In addition to the disintegration of personality, the threat of his physical death is raised explicitly. As Dr. Fleurot says after Ballantine has fled Green Manors, "An amnesia case of that sort with the police after it's an obvious suicide." His recovery through exhuming his memory of childhood catastrophe becomes a sort of resurrection.

The prosecution Ballantine faces as a result of his inability to remember the circumstances of Edwardes's murder associates the threat of imprisonment with his struggle to recall his past. He can be cleared of the accusation against him by discovering what really happened to Dr. Edwardes, but that knowledge is locked in his damaged memory. As a result, he goes to jail. After his conviction, shots of locking jail cells reverse the shots of opening doors when John and Constance first kiss. Constance's discovery of the truth, and the release of her lover from prison, culminate another action of symbolic death and resurrection.

As in *Spellbound*, symbolic death and rebirth in *Marnie* are tantamount to the recovery of memory and excision of old psychological scar tissue. Such actions are generally associated with descent and reascent, the imagery of which often depends more on camera placements than on physical movement. The most literal of Marnie's resurrections comes after Mark finds her unconscious in the swimming pool of the ship and revives her by artificial respiration.

Of the actions suggesting death and return in *Under Capricorn*, one occurs in the fictional past and is told by Hattie rather than portrayed in flashback: Hattie's shooting of her vengeful brother, Sam's assumption of his wife's guilt, his imprisonment, Hattie's following him to New South Wales, and their eventual reunion. In the present of *Under Capricorn*, each of the three central characters suffers a near death or loss of self, followed by a recovery. Charles is critically wounded by Sam's horse pistol and regains his health only after hovering on the brink of death. His spiritual recovery follows immediately upon his physical one and redeems him from an affliction as potentially mortal as the pistol shot.

Because of that accident, Sam is accused of attempted murder and arrested with the promise that he will be returned to the chain gang. His release comes about as a result of Charles's account of the incident; and it is associated, like Charles's physical recovery, with a spiritual resurrection. Sam's spiritual rebirth, however, precedes his arrest, when he rescues his wife and frees himself at the same time from Millie's machinations.

The central action of descent and rebirth in *Under Capricorn* is Hattie's. Before she achieves final liberation from her own demons and from Millie's persecution, she makes several futile efforts. She undertakes a prefatory attempt when she comes down from her room to join Sam and his guests at the dinner party. Pathetically trying to play her proper part as hostess, she arrives drunk and shoeless, and manages to stay only a few minutes before returning to her bedchamber of horrors. There she suffers an episode of apparent alcoholic delirium that Charles brings to an end by shooting her imaginary "rat." At the urging of Charles when he comes to live at Minyaga Yugilla, she again attempts to regain control of her home and herself. She is thwarted by Millie, who shames her in front of the kitchen staff, and she retreats once more. With Millie temporarily out of the way, she begins to recover again, only to be thrown back by the disaster of the Irish Society Ball. Her permanent return to light and sanity comes during the climactic epsiodes of the film: Millie's exposure, Hattie's reconciliation with Sam, and Sam's clearing by Charles.

Hattie must overcome the unresolved grief of years gone by. As the thunderstorm rages outside her bedroom, she begs Sam, "Please make it go away." "It's all in your mind, Hattie," Sam assures her, "there's nothing there." He is both right and wrong. "It" *is* mostly in her mind—the more formidable for that—but something exists outside her imagination as well. After her husband tucks Hattie in bed and leaves, she gets up and turns back the covers. The screen is abruptly filled with a gaping, mummified, shrunken head. A long peal of thunder rumbles in the background as Hattie sinks to the floor.

Thunder continues while the camera pans across the room to a rain-streaked bedroom window, then dissolves back to a close-up of Hattie's face. The light catches a tear at the corner of one of her closed eyes, an image that rhymes visually with the raindrops on the window. In a moment, she will open her eyes and discover Millie preparing to poison her, and her enthrallment by the spirits of the underworld will be broken. But in the instant before her crucial discovery—a typical sequence of events for Hitchcock—she falls into her deepest hopelessness and isolation.

Early in *Under Capricorn*, Hitchcock prepared for this climactic image by having a disreputable sailor try to sell Sam a nearly identical shrunken head. Sam shoulders him to the street, and we have a glimpse of the ghastly trophy before the sailor picks it up and calls Flusky "the son of an old shark" and a murderer. Our first sight of this savage artifact is thus associated obscurely with the oppression of the past and Flusky's murder conviction, to which the sailor's curse is the first allusion. A few moments earlier, Charles rather cavalierly inquired of the manager of the Bank of New South Wales as to Flusky's past crime. "What did he serve his time for," Charles asks pleasantly, "bank robbery? Or is he just a murderer?" "Stop, Mr. Adair, stop," urges the banker. "We do not discuss such matters in Sydney. A man's past is his own business. Out here, we let bygones be bygones." Unabashed, Charles continues his raillery, "Oh, can you do that? It's a thing we never learned to do in Ireland." This conversation casually introduces the very heart of the suffering and conflict in *Under Capricorn*. When

we see the shrunken head again, its associations with bygones that refuse to be bygones already have been established.

The second appearance of the head constitutes one of the great moments in Hitchcock's work. Beyond its power to shock (which is considerable), the close-up of the contorted face summarizes most of the
central issues of the film. The greasy death's head embodies at once the
terrible refusal of the past to go away, the pain and victimization that
it memorializes, and its demonic horror. We understand at a glance
how Millie has used the shrunken head to make her mistress appear
half-mad, and how unfairly Hattie has suffered from everyone's assumption that she is hallucinating. Most sadly, it conveys the depth of
Hattie's helplessness and suffering. In her half-stupefied state, the
ghastly head must be horrifying indeed, and her inability to convince
anyone of its existence leaves her alone and deserted.

Like most of Hitchcock's heroines, Hattie evokes Persephone. The
head carries her down to a sort of hell in which she seems beyond the
reach of human comprehension or rescue. Her unsuccessful attempts
to escape the underworld into which the past and Millie have thrust
her recall her mythic predecessor. Floral imagery reinforces the association. She is wearing flowers in her hair when she descends the staircase to greet her husband's dinner guests; and she is dressed in a floral
bonnet and has a flower on her bosom when Charles urges her to begin
what he calls her "reincarnation." Attired in another flowery, heart-
shaped bonnet, she tries to visit the wounded Charles, only to be re-
fused admittance and denounced by her husband when she comes back
home. All these occasions end in catastrophe and her return to the exile
of her room.

When she emerges forever from her private Hades to plead with the
Governor for Sam's freedom, however, she wears again the flower-
decked bonnet. She wears a similar hat when she comes to the waterfront in the last sequence of the movie. A fresh breeze is blowing, and
the sound track is full of vernal birdsong. The romantic pattern prevails. Persephone is back from hell; spring and Hattie have returned.

The happy outcomes of Hitchcock's romances express an optimism
about the goodness of things, a faith that constitutes the ultimate message in these films. The sun will eventually pierce the clouds; the truth
will out; evildoers will receive their just deserts and the good will be
rewarded. John Ballantine recovers his memory and is proved innocent; Sam and Hattie recover each other and their happiness, while
Charles discovers the true worth of his own character; Marnie learns
to trust Mark. Such faith in a benign world appears most simply in
Hitchcock's comic romances. It is realized with more complication in

more generically mixed films; and its failure constitutes the deepest stratum of doubt and bitterness in Hitchcock's ironic movies. In *Spellbound* and *Under Capricorn*, the welling up of this deep faith is finally expressed quite unequivocally. The vision of a happy future at the end of *Marnie*, as we have seen, is a bit less certain; and the sense of triumphant vindication consequently appears more tentative.

Constance is convinced that John Ballantine could never be a murderer. She maintains her belief in the face of assurances to the contrary from all her colleagues, the police, the courts, and even her old teacher and emotional father Brulov. Love, as usual in Hitchcock's movies, sees deeper than the most brilliant empiricism. John proves to be a gentle, affectionate, sane man whose innocence is unequivocal. Constance's first name underlines the importance of her unflagging faith in her lover's innocence; her second name, Peterson, may contain a faint Biblical allusion with a similar reference to faith and grace.

More radical in his trust and forgiveness, Mark believes in Marnie's fundamental goodness. The woman he falls in love with has in fact committed the crimes of which she is accused. Yet she does not bear responsibility for them. Once the details of her past have been discovered, she is safe from jail. The tribunal of poetic justice—the audience of the film—after it witnesses the flashback to her childhood cannot possibly deem her guilty, either. She has been "a cheat, and a liar, and a thief" by compulsion, not choice. At bottom, despite her own belief to the contrary, she remains "decent," a word that she uses ironically, but which the broader context of the movie ironizes again back to its undiminished meaning. Embraced by Mark's healing faith in her, Marnie is cleared of crimes forced on her by the assaults of her past.

Mark's belief in the innocence of his reluctant wife makes him one of the most heroic of Hitchcock's faithful lovers. He achieves an almost divine ability to understand and forgive. He does so, what is more, while facing the hostile, determined resistance of Marnie against his efforts on her behalf, a resistance that originates partly from her deep conviction of her own guilt. In *Notorious*, Alicia asks her lover to believe that she remains "a nice, unspoiled child, full of daisies and buttercups." But until the last minutes of the film Dev is unable to allow himself that trust. In *Marnie*, by contrast, Mark insists on Marnie's underlying innocence and eventually restores to his wife the ability to bestow such charity upon herself.

In *Under Capricorn* the theme of belief is more complicated still. Both Sam and Charles, each with the trust and intuition of love, retain faith in Hattie's "innocence" in respect not to any alleged crime but to her condition of chronic drunkenness and depression. Charles's faith in Hattie's unspoiled identity very much resembles Mark's belief in Marnie. Despite Hattie's assertions that she has lost her courage, Charles insists that she can regain her old joy and self-confidence. But his belief in her becomes entangled with an adulterous desire to possess her. His last-minute refusal to ruin Sam not only restores to Hattie her husband, but it reflects his understanding of her essential goodness and fidelity. If Hattie were even a little faithless, Charles might have been very much so. His love for her gives him an insight into her virtue that enables him to overcome the temptations of his own desire.

Commitments to faith and love, as usual in Hitchcock's films, distinguish the figures who can return to a state of innocence from those who cannot. The fallen characters of *Spellbound, Under Capricorn,* and *Marnie,* even relatively well-intentioned ones, have ceased to believe in miracles. They "know" that they cannot hope for a better world, and that they must live with the consequences of a past that has permanently compromised human existence. Lacking love to set them free, they are indeed prisoners of the past. Dr. Murchison has only his power as head of Green Manors to validate his existence; Millie struggles to escape her low social status by stealing Sam from Hattie; Lil waits for Mark to drop into her lap. Though less extreme in their wretchedness, they recall Uncle Charlie in *Shadow of a Doubt,* for whom the world was a "foul sty." Such figures cannot receive, nor give, the faith and hope of a love that chiefly desires good for another and that sees in the beloved an image of unspoiled humanity.

Such love constitutes, for Hitchcock whose psyche remains religious even in creating secular entertainments, the way to truth and resurrection. It also constitutes the only possible awakening from the nightmare of history. As *I Confess* and *The Wrong Man* clarify the importance of an underlying vision of Christian grace in Hitchcock's work, *Spellbound, Under Capricorn,* and *Marnie* highlight another, equally insistent mythic/religious theme, the infection of the present by the past, and the need to confront and send back to hell the unclean spirits of old crimes.

Ballantine slides into an underworld of darkling guilt when, as a child, he accidentally knocks his brother onto fatal iron fence spikes. Hattie's suffering from past misfortunes is intensified by social prejudice. Respectable society has no warmth or concern for her, and the sanctimoniousness of Millie reverses the loving grace it mimics. Marnie falls sick and is prevented from recovering by forces like those that oppress Hattie. Her mother's religious fervor may not be as hypocritical as Millie's, but it is no more healing. Mrs. Edgar and her daughter, moreover, are both victims of a society that tries to condemn them to its lowest levels and is more eager to convict than to embrace them.

In *Spellbound* and *Marnie*, the entrance of a dedicated lover signals a turn toward the cleansing of the past and the restoration of happiness in the present. Though the disposition of characters is more complicated in *Under Capricorn*, the outcome is the same. All three movies, like Hitchcock's other romantic fictions, incorporate a conception of human life that is ultimately optimistic and redemptive. Their emphasis on overcoming the past gives them a particular thematic center, but they do not deviate sharply from the patterns of plot, character, imagery, and movement typical of Hitchcock's filmic storytelling elsewhere.

They all contain, as well, an emphasis on their own artifice that is also characteristic of Hitchcock. In other Hitchcockian romances, emphatic implausibility and contrivance underscore the miraculousness of the resolution. Such intrusive artificiality implies that works of art reveal essential significance by condensing and cutting through the haze that makes up most of daily experience. *Spellbound* and *Marnie* have been criticized for not representing the process of psychoanalysis realistically; but I hope that my argument has shown that such criticism misses the point. All three have been called "talky" or "theatrical." Again, I hope that my analyses have shown that these films generate their meanings in ways that are always as visual as they are verbal.

The poisonous pasts detoxified in *Spellbound, Under Capricorn*, and *Marnie* are archetypal as well as particular to the films and their characters. All humankind is haunted by its mortal history; all persons must face and overcome their pasts. Through the words and stylized actions of art, we confront our past and make possible its present redemption. As we watch these three films, we see our own tarnished and unfortunate histories and discover the possibility of our own forgiveness. In the public privacy of a darkened movie theater, we find ourselves on the screen and shed tears of sympathy for the projected shadows who suffer on our behalf. The entire activity could hardly be more corporate and formalized; at the same time, it could hardly be more personal and private. The same statement, we might note, applies to psychotherapy.

The compact, stylized psychoanalytical romances of *Spellbound, Under Capricorn*, and *Marnie* contain quests for identity and redemption that take place chiefly through journeys of words. Words in the ironic *Vertigo* and *Psycho*, by contrast, are ineffectual and recalcitrant. All five films remind us of hereditary inadequacy and guilt, wrong turns taken, injuries unhealed. They look back to a past that must be recovered and overcome. Stuck physically in the present, we can move back in time only through profoundly energized memories. Hitchcock had great sympathy for psychoanalysis, in which he perceives much of the same power that art and ritual have to distill human reality to its essences and return people to emotional first causes. But psychoanalysis alone cannot finish the journey it begins. It must be accompanied by love and grace, and it must at some point turn from logic to miracles. Only miracles of love—like those represented in the stories we call romances—can redeem our past, heal our wounds, and make us new.

CHAPTER SEVEN

"Love's Not Time's Fool"

ALTHOUGH Hitchcock occasionally indicated that *The Trouble with Harry* was one of his favorite films (thereby showing unusual fondness for a commercially disappointing venture), most commentators have taken only a slight interest in it. It is generally regarded as a pleasant but insubstantial and, for Hitchcock, rather anomalous performance. The understanding of Hitchcock's career that I have presented in this book suggests, I hope, the opposite. *The Trouble with Harry* stands out among Hitchcock's works chiefly because it insists overtly upon a theme usually more implicit in his films but almost always central to them: that of descent and return, of death and rebirth. Its unbroken comic mode bears a similar relation to the comedy of other Hitchcock movies: it is atypical only in its insistence and uniformity.

The Trouble with Harry sets forth with unequaled bluntness and economy the romantic vision of innocence and immortality that informs the greater part of Hitchcock's work. In their triumphant conclusions, the comic romances fulfill that vision; as Hitchcock's films move toward irony, the anxiety over the impossibility of redemption in a corrupt world increasingly dominates the faith that it can be achieved. Whether romantic or ironic, however, Hitchcock's other films admit the existence and power of evil. Only *The Trouble with Harry* incorporates from its beginning conditions that all Hitchcock's movies assume to be the highest good fortune. Its world is in essential alignment with the needs of its characters. The tensions and alarming suspense that shape Hitchcock's other works are therefore largely absent. *The Trouble with Harry* is composed of nearly pure nectar, the Hitchcockian *summum bonum* unadulterated.

Actions suggestive of rebirth, usually sublimated into relatively realistic forms, are of crucial importance in most of Hitchcock's movies. They pervade *The Trouble with Harry*. From the opening credits, virtually every detail figures forth the renewal of the natural and human world. Death itself enlists in the creation of life. This thematic basis is embodied so fundamentally that the continuous rejuvenations of the movie occur with little excitement or even emphasis. Re-creation is something to be expected, as basic a fact of nature as gravity or heat. Urgency would be misplaced in this film, for resurrection may be safely assumed. Death passes and life renews without effort or anxiety. The bland tone of *The Trouble with Harry* constitutes more than comic technique; it results from a profound confidence that death lacks the power to destroy and that hope can scarcely help but prosper.

Hitchcock's pastoral comedy takes place in a New England countryside that appears prelapsarian; the knowledge of sin and of death is excluded. Whether we take the setting as having escaped The Fall or as having somehow recovered from it, the result is the same. The woes that afflict humanity and its corrupted world constitute little more than enlivening comic alarms in Highwater.

Among the inhabitants of the small community, only deputy sheriff Calvin Wiggs is at all tainted by post-Edenic mistrust and disillusionment. His first name, indeed, might playfully allude to the gloomy theology of his famous Protestant forebear. However that may be, his long-distance call to the State Police attempts to recruit an agency of rigid law and punishment into the hamlet in which *The Trouble with Harry* takes place. Harry himself is an intruder from outside, a representative of the less pure and sequestered human beings whom Sam (John Forsythe) refers to scornfully as "little people with hats." (The last detail of his description serves also to emphasize their separation from nature.) Calvin Wiggs may bluster, but his power does not extend beyond that required to make a fool of himself. The State Police do not come, and Harry's invasion quickly turns him into a benign corpse.

This unchallenged ascendancy of the Edenic makes *The Trouble with Harry* unique among Hitchcock's films. All his other works, whether finally dominated by romantic innocence or ironic cynicism, explicitly acknowledge the stained and vulnerable condition of humanity. In films like *Vertigo* and *Psycho*, the inevitable corruption of human life and of the world defeats all attempts to rise above it; in happier works, a spirit of redeeming grace acts through love to repel the night world, restore the protagonists to innocence, and allow them to achieve full self-realization. But such sources of conflict—whether tragic or comic—scarcely exist in *The Trouble with Harry*.

We do not expect such an absence in any movie, and the unfamiliar radical fantasy on which Hitchcock's comedy is based has led some commentators to an understanding fundamentally opposite to mine. Despite its tone and the outcome of its plot, Rohmer and Chabrol and Spoto—the latter more equivocally—pronounce it a film of singular misanthropy.[1] Nothing obvious in *The Trouble with Harry* reveals a

---

[1] Rohmer and Chabrol, *Hitchcock*, p. 137; and Spoto, *The Art of Alfred Hitchcock*, p. 260.

secret Puritan hatred for sex or obsession with death; but we cannot forget the mixture of sorrow and crime in our own lives, and so we may suspect satire in the portrayal of unalloyed innocence in *The Trouble with Harry*. But its characters are unafflicted by the circumspection that experience has engendered in its audience. The movie itself is innocent of moral double entendre. It is no more or less than it appears to be. And in being so, it could hardly be more surprising.

The primitive drawings accompanying the titles are composed of childlike, mostly natural, images. They are followed by the brilliant colors of the New England fall woods, at their most lively just before winter dormancy. Both the Steinberg sketches and the glorious dying of the forest embody dominant themes of the rest of the film, in which growth and death mix inseparably. Again and again, Harry will be buried and exhumed, die and return, be planted and harvested.

Other intimations of regeneration proliferate. Over coffee, Miss Gravely tells the Captain about the demise of her father, "caught in a threshing machine." Calvin Wiggs asks Marlowe if he might have been sketching "somewhere down by Mansfield Meadows," an appropriate place, perhaps, for the inadvertent harvesting of Miss Gravely's parent. (The name of the meadow recalls *Young and Innocent*, with its dominant images of woods and fields and its hero's aliases of "Beechtree Manningcroft" and "Beechcroft Manningtree.") The Doctor's last name is "Greenbow"; and Miss Gravely's first name, "Ivy," balances her funereal surname.

As summer ends with the blaze of fall and the abundance of harvest, so death itself in *The Trouble with Harry* brings a marvelous fecundity. Captain Wiles will be proved as wrong as drought when he urges that the corpse of Harry is "no good to anyone now." The late Harry's first posthumous matchmaking comes when Miss Gravely, stepping over his body, invites The Captain to her home. Shortly thereafter the spinster, full of new life indirectly infused by Harry's corpse, exclaims on the beauty of the day, and of Marlowe's painting and singing. The flattered artist, in his turn, supervises her haircut and make-up, the restoration of her neglected youth. Sam promises to recreate "the true Miss Gravely, sensitive, young in feeling, timeless with love and understanding." The Captain takes a similar, if less ethereal, view of his new friend: "Not too late, you know. She's a well-preserved woman . . . yes, very well-preserved. And preserves have to be opened, someday."

The Cupid-like corpse also works its wonders on the Captain. Burying Harry, he pounds the dirt with his shovel; "there's nothing like finding yourself in love! No! It adds zest to your work, zest!" Love and death in the autumnal romance of the Captain and Miss Gravely are reemphasized when the amorous spinster confesses, "I'm grateful to you for burying my body." And, she might add, for resurrecting her body also.

Harry's death yields a pair of shoes for a passing bum. Much more important, it brings Jennifer Rodgers (Shirley MacLaine) and Sam Marlowe together and sets Jennifer free to marry again. The Captain acknowledges Harry's part in the engagement of the central lovers when he apologizes to Sam, "if I grumbled too much at my share of the work in burying Harry, I'm sorry. I can see now it was well worth it." Even Harry benefits. As she's cleaning him up at her house, Jennifer remarks, "Isn't it odd? After refusing for so long, here I am finally doing Harry's laundry."

The dead rabbit maintains in its small way the same sort of post-mortem fertility as Harry. For Arnie, it produces a pet frog and two blueberry muffins. For the Captain, when he realizes that his third bullet killed the rabbit rather than Harry, it brings release from the misapprehension that he is an inadvertent murderer. "You never know," says Arnie with broader accuracy than he understands, "when a dead rabbit might come in handy." The theme of resurrection works in even so minor and sometimes dissonant a figure as Calvin Wiggs, who restores antique automobiles—brings them back, as it were, to life.

Rebirth and the fecundity of death are ordinary and natural in *The Trouble with Harry* because of the transcendence of time by love and the flexibility of time itself. Just after one of Harry's disinterments, Doctor Greenbow arrives on the scene, reading aloud from Shakespeare's 116th sonnet. The four lovers overhear fragments: "Love's not time's fool . . . Love alters not with his brief hours and weeks,/ But bears it out even to the edge of doom./ If this be error and upon me proved,/ I never writ, nor no man ever loved." We may infer the importance of these lines from the fact that they are not quoted in the novel on which the movie is based.

The themes of the redemption of time and love's triumph over death are not realized in the novel, either. They are Hitchcock's additions to what is otherwise little more than a zany but inconsequential tale of love and adultery, a sort of outdoor drawing-room farce. In accord with the Edenic environment of Highwater in Hitchcock's movie, several actions of adultery central to the novel are removed entirely from the film.

In his child-wise confusion, Arnie stumbles to an understanding of time that is, in its own way, as sophisticated as Shakespeare's. He asks Sam when tomorrow is, and Sam replies, "day after today."

ARNIE: That's yesterday. Today's tomorrow.
SAM: It was.
A: When was tomorrow yesterday, Mr. Marlowe?
S: Today.
A: Oh, sure, yesterday.

Yesterday, today, and tomorrow fuse. As the movie ends, Arnie again finds Harry, who has been restored to his first last resting place. Since tomorrow is yesterday for Arnie, he will tell his mother, and presumably deputy sheriff Wiggs, that he found Harry's body today.

Given the productivity of the dead and the fertile fluidity of time, death itself becomes neutral at worst, more often genuinely friendly to human aspirations. Jennifer tells Arnie that Harry is "in a deep sleep. A deep, *wonderful* sleep." Later she tells Sam that Harry "looked exactly the same when he was alive, except he was vertical." Dr. Greenbow trips repeatedly over Harry without noticing that he is dead. When he does finally examine the corpse, the doctor pronounces that Harry died naturally, of "a seizure"—a diagnosis so vague and exculpating that everyone, including the audience, must take satisfaction in it.

For the rejected Harry, dying turns into homecoming. "A long way from home," pronounces the Captain, but "he died around here, that's what counts now." Discussing a burial place for the body, The Captain almost envies Harry the comfort of being "cozy in winter and cool in the summer." "You're a lucky fellow, Harry Worp," he concludes. When Jennifer says that she will take the body to her house, the doctor responds with absent-minded, professional sentimentality: "going home for the last time." But the final time, in this asynchronous world, is also the first. Jennifer at last, for the first time, receives her now late husband.

Love, the paradoxical fruit of death in *The Trouble with Harry*, is similarly characterized by homey comfort. As Jennifer and Sam come together, their attraction takes a curious form. "I feel awful comfortable with you, Sam," confesses Jennifer. Sam admits to the same relaxed passion, "you know, I feel the same way too. It's a good feeling—feeling comfortable with someone who feels that way too." The Captain, after Jennifer agrees to marry Marlowe, congratulates him with the mild observation that "marriage is a comfortable way to spend the winter." His own courtship of Miss Gravely has been fueled with the peaceful domestic satisfactions of muffins, coffee, and elderberry wine.

Love and death in *The Trouble with Harry* are treated straightforwardly, without shame, terror, or prurience. Sam's response to Jennifer when he first meets her could hardly be more direct: "You're the most beautiful, wonderful thing I've ever seen. . . . I'd like to paint you nude." "Some other time, Mr. Marlowe," she replies calmly. Within minutes she is telling her visitor of her first marriage to Robert, her second to his brother Harry, the "certain enthusiasm" she worked up for her second marriage night, and the dismaying fact that Harry "never came in." At lower voltage, the Captain and Miss Gravely pursue their romance with a similar innocence.

A closet door that spontaneously swings open in Jennifer's living room suggests, in addition to Harry's tendency to pop out of his grave, simple harmlessness. The closet is conspicuously empty and the closet door "only a closet door," as Miss Gravely assures the startled Captain. Love, death, and closets are no more than themselves. They harbor no guilt, no fright, no skeletons. We should scarcely wonder that Sam's unfallen world allows him the conviction that "we're all nice. I don't see how anyone could help but like us."

"Blessed are they who expect nothing, for they shall not be disappointed." The Captain's benediction is part of a series of Christian allusions that, quite typically for Hitchcock, forms a subset of the more general pattern of death and rebirth. The opening shot of *The Trouble with Harry* frames a country church, its bells ringing tranquilly. When Arnie brings his mother to see the body he has discovered, she greets it with "Harry, thank Providence, the last of Harry!" The vaguely religious overtones continue as Sam assures the Captain that in accidentally killing Harry he became the instrument of divine will, and that he should be grateful that he was able to do his share "in accomplishing the destiny of a fellow being." The Captain himself nods again toward devoutness when he murmurs that they are burying Harry "with hasty reverence."

Religious motifs are unquestionably present in *The Trouble with Harry*, but they do not signal a central preoccupation. They rather make up one of many iterations—imagistic, aural, allusive, psychological—of the theme of death's fertility and life's indefatigable rebirth. Those who expect nothing are indeed undisappointed. Grace extends its power toward all of them, in the undiscouraged millionaire who returns to buy Sam's paintings, in the abundance of a dead rabbit and a dying season, and, most crucially, in love.

The portrayal of art within the movie repeats the comfortable directness of life in Highwater. The simplicity of the drawings that accompany the opening credits anticipates the same quality in the film and its characters. Sam, the artist within the work of art, has the same casual ingenuousness about his painting that he shows during his courtship of Jennifer Rodgers. Sketching the autumn landscape of Mansfield Meadows, he notices Harry's body only when its feet appear unexpectedly in his drawing. Once he does discover the corpse, it becomes grist for his artistic mill, just as it is for Hitchcock's. He crouches by Harry's face sketching it with a naive absorption rather like Arnie's unalarmed interest when he comes across the body.

On every occasion, Marlowe behaves unselfconsciously and naturally. His wristwatch broken, he tells time by the sun. He is too excited about his restoration of Miss Gravely to bother with the passing rich man who stops to inspect his paintings. Without rudeness, he makes it clear that he could not care less about the opinion of the art critic with whom the millionaire returns. The payment he asks for his paintings is the barter of an affectionate child. He requests what his equally innocent and modest friends want: for Jennifer, strawberries; a chemical set for Arnie; a chrome-plated cash register for Wiggie; for Miss Gravely, a hope chest "full of hope"; a Davy Crockett outfit for the tugboat captain who aspires to be a hunter. For the artist himself, in love and planning to marry, a discreetly whispered request for a double bed.

The art in and of *The Trouble with Harry* is as straightforward as its characters; it constitutes just one more ordinary fact in the harmonious relation of the human and natural world. By the standards of most of Hitchcock's movies, conspicuous cinematic virtuosity and startling twists of the plot are subdued. The camera, in particular, remains unusually transparent in its recording of the action. Its most obtrusive composition, the repeated short focal-length shot of the body of Harry with looming feet pointing skyward, has about it the same artless bluntness as Arnie's declarations or the Captain's harmless yarns.

Artistic expression elsewhere in the film retains its own simplicity. The style of Marlowe's painting is abstract, but the paintings that we see are saturated with the colors and shapes of the New England landscape in which he lives. His themes, at least as he describes them, are as extravagant and basic as his style. One of his paintings is about nothing less than "the creation of the world." Though he tells Calvin Wiggs that his imagination "is peopled with enough faces to cover the earth," Sam lives and creates in pastoral tranquillity away from the fallen city hordes. His art and his life as an artist are ultimately as ingenuous as the movie in which he appears.

"The trouble with Harry is over," reads a superfluous closing title superimposed on the last image of Harry's feet and the fading New England fall landscape. The sentence recalls in its direct clarity the end of old folk tales and stories for children. Everyone will surely live happily ever after. The closing title also recalls the primitive phase of the cinema itself, the early silent era, with its technical unsophistication and its rudimentary narratives.

The comedy of *The Trouble with Harry*, contrary to what Hitchcock and some critics have asserted, does not originate primarily in verbal wit or incongruous, deadpan humor. It rather derives from the total exclusion of destruction from the world of the film. No event or person in *The Trouble with Harry* is allowed to cause or suffer real pain. Nor do they seriously threaten to do so. The comic mode of the film finally results from its obsessive repetition of the theme of rebirth; for if time and death have no power to injure, what terrors can remain?

From another point of view, the comedy of *The Trouble with Harry* exists traditionally alongside its romance. It portrays the coming together of a group of strangely separate people whose only social bonds, at the beginning of the movie, seem to be the legal ones enforced by deputy sheriff Wiggs. By the end of the film, they are united, with the freshly engaged lovers at the center of a reinvigorated and cohesive small society.

For all its superficial eccentricity, *The Trouble with Harry* does not drift anomalously outside the mainstream of Hitchcock's films. Like Sam Marlowe's renderings of New England, it may be seen as a compression of the essential dream that nourishes Hitchcock's work as a whole. That dream envisions a life in which human beings are complete and fulfilled, justice prevails without the rigidity and inaccuracy of law, and the world and its inhabitants live in harmony retrieved from the corruptions of experience.

Because *The Trouble with Harry* assumes rather than achieves such a world, it is the strangest of Hitchcock's films at the same time that it reveals most clearly what is most typical. The unfallen good that it embodies may even remind us of the glory it lacks. In the romances, that glory springs from harrowing journeys reluctantly undertaken but leading finally to safe harbor, from confrontations with the darkest recesses of society and human nature, and from the transcendence and completion of self that is achieved in love. We may also miss in the undisturbed characters and settings of *The Trouble with Harry* the terrible beauties and artistic magnitude of more dangerous Hitchcock works, from *The Manxman* through *Shadow of a Doubt* and *Notorious*, to the ironic films of the 1950s and 1960s.

The Fall from Paradise has always been recognized as being paradoxically fortunate as well as catastrophic. If *The Trouble with Harry* avoids the misery, neither can it express the stature and complexity of men and women who struggle, albeit sometimes to defeat, against the corruption of the world and of their own natures. Hitchcock needed to make only one *The Trouble with Harry*, only one parable of an unfallen world. Virtue, as diverse thinkers have argued in various ways, has few forms; error has many. This circumstance puts Hitchcock, along with Milton, Blake, and most other artists, at least partly in sympathy with the Devil.

The gorgeous thematic richness of Hitchcock's last film, *Family Plot*, makes an illuminating contrast with the relatively monothematic *The Trouble with Harry*. In the exuberance of its postlapsarian knavery and moral fluidity, it creates a world that is at once wicked and forgiving; one in which the wish fulfillments of art, religion, and sheer fraud penetrate and energize ordinary reality. The suggestively named Adamson rises from the ashes of his murderous faked death only to be incarcerated in a subterranean prison of his own making by an equally dishonest, though benign, confidence woman. The convolution of this plot has moral and aesthetic ingenuity very different from the simplicity of *The Trouble with Harry*. This is not to say that *The Trouble with Harry* is an inferior, or less interesting, film than *Family Plot*. It is to say that the absurdities of human vanity and foolishness, the sorrows of human frailty, and the terrors of evil are for Hitchcock, as for other artists, the source of most subject matter.

Forms of death and rebirth not only occur in virtually all Hitchcock's works, but they usually occupy the thematic center of them. *The Trouble with Harry*, distant as it may appear at first viewing from other Hitchcock films, is in a crucial way entirely characteristic of its director's work. Its relaxed comedy embodies a theme that serves as mainspring to the vast majority of Hitchcock's movies. As we watch his mother's music rescue Hank near the end of the second *The Man Who Knew Too Much*, or the nick-of-time breaking of Jefferies's fall at the end of *Rear Window*, or the miracle that saves Manny in *The Wrong Man*, or Robie's escape from nighttime assassination in *To Catch a Thief*, or Judy's plunge and Scottie's anguish in the last sequence of *Vertigo* (to take examples only from films Hitchcock made around the time he made *The Trouble with Harry*), we are watching variations on the same theme, that of miraculous escape and resurrection, or of its hope and disappointment. When we watch *The Trouble with Harry*, we see a peculiarly radical, cheery rendition of the same central action. We see the filmmaker's purest realization of uncorrupted identity, innocent love, and restorative time—the quest for all of which in one way or another shaped Hitchcock's movies for more than five decades.

INDEX